# European Spatial
# Research and Planning

# European Spatial
# Research and Planning

Edited by
**Andreas Faludi**

**LINCOLN INSTITUTE**
OF LAND POLICY
CAMBRIDGE, MASSACHUSETTS

Texts and maps stemming from research projects under the ESPON programme presented in this book do not necessarily reflect the opinion of the ESPON Monitoring Committee.

*Library of Congress Cataloging-in-Publication Data*

European spatial research and planning / edited by Andreas Faludi.
     p. cm.
 Based on a seminar held at the University of Luxembourg on May 3–4, 2007.
 Includes index.
 ISBN 978-1-55844-177-4
 1.  Regional planning—European Union countries—Congresses. 2.  European Union countries—Economic policy—Congresses. 3.  Land use—European Union countries—Planning—Congresses. 4.  Intergovernmental cooperation—Europe—Congresses.  I. Faludi, Andreas. II. Lincoln Institute of Land Policy.
 HT395.E8E848 2008
 338.94—dc22      2008004017

*Designed by Janis Owens, Books By Design, Inc.*

Composed in Minion by Books By Design, Inc., in Cambridge, Massachusetts. Printed and bound by Puritan Press Incorporated in Hollis, New Hampshire. The paper is Utopia II, an acid-free sheet.

MANUFACTURED IN THE UNITED STATES OF AMERICA

# CONTENTS

# FIGURES AND TABLES

## Figures

## Tables

| | |
|---|---|
| ASTRA | Developing Policies and Adaptation Strategies to Climate Change in the Baltic Sea Region |
| BBR | Federal Office for Building and Regional Planning |
| CAP | Common Agricultural Policy |
| CDCR | Committee for the Development and Conversion of Regions |
| CEG | Centre for Geographical Studies of the University of Lisbon |
| CEMAT | Conférence Européenne des Ministres Responsables de l'Aménagement du Territoire |
| COCOF | Coordination Committee of the Funds |
| CSD | Committee on Spatial Development |
| CU | Coordination Unit |
| DG Regio | Directorate-General for Regional Policy |
| DG Relex | Directorate-General for External Relations |
| DSF | Decision Support Frame |
| ECP | European contact point |
| EIA | environmental impact assessment |
| EM-DAT | Emergency Disasters Database |
| ENP | European Neighborhood Policy |
| ENPI | European and Neighborhood Partnership Instrument |
| ESDP | *European Spatial Development Perspective* |
| ESPON | European Spatial Planning Observation Network |
| EU | European Union |
| FDI | foreign direct investment |
| FUA | functional urban area |
| GVA | gross value added |
| IA | impact assessment |
| ICT | information and communication technology |
| IGC | Intergovernmental Conference |
| ISO | International Standards Organization |
| ITPS | Swedish Institute for Growth Policy Studies |
| LFA | less favored area |
| MEGA | metropolitan European growth area |
| NIS | New Independent States of the former USSR |
| NMAC | new member states and accession countries |
| NSRF | National Strategic Reference Framework |
| OMC | open method of coordination |
| OP | operational programs |
| PSR | potential support ratio |
| RDR | Rural Development Regulation |
| SEA | strategic environmental assessment |
| SEAREG | Sea Level Change Affecting the Spatial Development of the Baltic Sea Region |

| | |
|---|---|
| SEEP | South-Eastern Europe Perspective |
| SMEs | small and medium enterprises |
| SPESP | Study Programme on European Spatial Planning |
| TA | *Territorial Agenda* |
| TCR | third cohesion report |
| TEN | Trans-European Networks |
| TEN-E | Trans-European Energy Networks |
| TEN-T | Trans-European Transport Networks |
| TEQUILA | Territorial Efficiency Quality Identity Layered Assessment multicriteria |
| TFR | total fertility rate |
| TIA | territorial impact assessment |
| TIM | Territorial Impact Model |
| TPG | transnational project group |
| TSP | *Territorial State and Perspective of the European Union* |
| UNCTAD | UN Conference on Trade and Development |
| WTO | World Trade Organization |

With the publication of *European Spatial Research and Planning*, the Lincoln Institute of Land Policy adds a third volume to its series of investigations of spatial planning, research, and policy in Europe, all under the magisterial editorship of Andreas Faludi. Each of these books examines the European experience with an expectation that it may hold lessons for land policy in the United States. This book taps into the treasure trove of research that is ESPON, the European Spatial Planning Observation Network, which has yielded a plethora of studies on the real and anticipated outcomes of European territorial policy. The ESPON corpus provides our authors with the means to examine developments at the intersection of research and policy: "evidence-informed" if not exactly "evidence-based" policy.

The three volumes chart what has turned out to be a rapidly evolving European discourse. The first volume of the series, published in 2002, *European Spatial Planning*, dealt with policies derived from the *European Spatial Development Perspective* (ESDP), which had been adopted in 1999. Then, the main idea for American planners was strategic development policy at the continental scale based on alternative spatial visions of core and periphery and a European envy of the United States with its multiple zones of integration with the global economy. By the second volume, *Territorial Cohesion and the European Model of Society* (2007), the European Union (EU) had moved on from the ESDP, picking up 10 additional member states along the way. Our book highlighted the aspiration for equity across the newly enlarged European space. At the time of the present volume, with the EU standing at 27 members, Europe is emerging from a period of reflection following rejection of the Constitution, with a new *Territorial Agenda* to guide policy, supported by the ESPON empirical base.

What is significantly new in this agenda? Viewed from the United States, there is the sense that planners are "attaching themselves to the competitiveness discourse," as Andreas puts it, with an implication that efficiency will trump equity in this round of the policy debate. But in Europe, this is a discourse that is accompanied by, at the least, a sense of urgency, and, for some, of impending crisis, involving climate change, energy insecurity, and potential demographic collapse. The ESPON research underpinning this volume reveals that policy goals like "sustainable economic growth" and "territorial cohesion" have far-reaching consequences across sectors and geography. For example, EU policies that favor higher GDP will likely increase greenhouse gas emissions, while a cohesion strategy, resulting in lower GDP, would favor meeting emissions targets. And while EU cohesion policies may have resulted in decreased inequality between countries, they have led to an increase in spatial inequality within countries, according to ex-post territorial impact assessments.

In the case of transportation policy, ex-ante scenario analysis has shed light on the relationship between infrastructure investment and regional development. The Trans-European Networks (TEN), projected out to 2020, were found to result in converging accessibility and GDP between core and periphery in relative terms, but with the gap increasing in absolute terms. Over this period, the scenarios point to an overall tendency to lower polycentricity in Europe, as transport policy advantages large urban centers, notwithstanding pricing strategies leading to more expensive transport that will tend to strengthen polycentricity. Perhaps of greatest interest to followers of the significant European investment in major infrastructure projects like high-speed rail is the finding that large increases in regional accessibility are expected to translate into only small increases in regional economic activity. This will no doubt bear further examination as American planners consider the role of transportation infrastructure within a national development framework as part of initiatives like America 2050.

Perhaps the most striking area of difference between Europe and the United States in the context of territorial policy has to do with demography. Europe is facing a population deficit by midcentury of the same order as the expected increase in U.S. population in that period. While it is true that the United States has by no means come to grips with its own immigration issues, it is perhaps still fair to observe that immigration policy will continue to contribute significantly to the tension between Europe's continental vision, and its place within a greater regional neighborhood, and the wider world.

*Armando Carbonell*
*Chairman*
*Department of Planning and Urban Form*

This is the third in a series of volumes published by the Lincoln Institute of Land Policy that I have had the honor of editing. Previous volumes are *European Spatial Planning*, published in 2002, and *Territorial Cohesion and the European Model of Society*, published in 2007. As the art of European spatial planning develops, so do the aspects relevant for an international and in particular a North American audience. The topic of this volume relates to the concerted efforts to acknowledge and disseminate evidence gathered by the European Spatial Planning Observation Network (ESPON), hence the title *European Spatial Research and Planning*.

This book would not have been possible without the constant interest in these issues and support provided by Armando Carbonell, the chairman of the Department of Planning and Urban Form at the Lincoln Institute. He is a widely traveled and well-connected observer, not only of the North American and international planning communities, but also of the European scene. He conceived of the idea of bringing European spatial planning efforts closer to a North American audience. Together with Robert D. Yaro, president of the Regional Plan Association of New York, New Jersey, and Connecticut, Armando brought master's students from the University of Pennsylvania, where both were practice professors, to Europe to work on what was initially called the American Spatial Development Perspective. Later groups from the University of Pennsylvania were joined by students and their teachers from other schools to focus on specific metropolitan areas in the United States.

The Lincoln Institute, the Regional Plan Association, and others continue to work on this initiative, now dubbed America 2050, to consider the vast implications of U.S. population and economic growth between now and 2050. This comprehensive strategy seeks to match the historic planning efforts by U.S. presidents Thomas Jefferson and Theodore Roosevelt in their respective centuries.

It is extremely gratifying to learn that European spatial planning should have such ripple effects. To the insider, the sometimes small efforts of the several dozen planners involved in the European enterprise seem less grandiose than they may seem from the outside. Also, since publication of the *European Spatial Development Perspective* in 1999, the European planning discourse has taken a new turn and is increasingly couched in terms of a policy to achieve "territorial cohesion."

What has been missing all along is a sound analytical base to this discussion. The makers of the *European Spatial Development Perspective* (ESDP) were keenly aware of this and hoped for a network of research centers to be set up—and financed—by European institutions. As always, there was much soul searching about whether this was an appropriate task for these institutions and about how existing national initiatives were to be integrated. In the end, the European Union consented to fund ESPON, originally to provide the basis for a substantial review of ESDP.

In the mid-2000s hundreds of researchers started producing volumes of research reports on many aspects of European spatial development and planning. This whetted the appetite of the key players to bring all this new evidence to bear on the evolving territorial cohesion policy of the European Union (EU) and to do so from the bottom up by means of an initiative of the member states. In 2004 the idea of an "evidence-based document" to inform the EU territorial cohesion policy was born.

The ins and outs of these efforts are discussed in the introduction to this volume and in several other chapters covering the process. The discussion extends to the intriguing issue of whether the idea of evidence-based planning was viable in the first instance. Undeniably, though, the evidence produced by ESPON, often invoking innovative approaches to research and analysis, was fascinating, and it gave rise to the idea of this volume.

As with the previous two volumes, the approach to this book began with inviting a select group of people from all over Europe to give papers on their experience with various aspects of ESPON's work. A seminar took place on 3 and 4 May 2007 at the University of Luxembourg with the generous assistance of Christian Schulz (professor of European spatial planning) and his team there.

The Grand Duchy of Luxembourg is a staunch supporter of many European initiatives, including those relating to European spatial planning and ESPON. Luxembourg now supports the effort, acting as the management authority and the paying authority and assisting with the financing of the ESPON Coordination Unit located there, an example of the synthesis between top-down and bottom-up initiatives in the EU.

Holding the seminar in Luxembourg had the added advantage of enabling Peter Mehlbye, the director of the Coordination Unit, to attend the seminar and to enlighten the participants about ongoing efforts to formulate a new ESPON program for the period 2007–2013. Clearly, in years to come there will be more to tell about European spatial planning. Meanwhile, I want to acknowledge Peter Mehlbye's generous assistance in smoothing our way to obtain permission for using material from ESPON research in this book. The permission granted excludes the right of using the ESPON map design for new maps produced by projects outside the ESPON framework.

*Andreas Faludi*
*Delft, The Netherlands*
*September 2007*

# European Spatial
# Research and Planning

# Introduction

Andreas Faludi

A t Leipzig on 25 May 2007 ministers responsible for spatial planning and development of the member states of the European Union adopted the *Territorial Agenda of the European Union: Towards a More Competitive and Sustainable Europe of Diverse Regions* (Territorial Agenda 2007). As the subtitle indicates, this document relates to the Lisbon Strategy, which aimed for the EU to become by 2010 "the most competitive and dynamic knowledge-based economy in the world, capable of sustainable economic growth with more and better jobs and greater social cohesion" (European Council 2000). Inserting sustainability on a par with competitiveness in the subtitle makes clear that the ministers wish to take sustainable development seriously, as agreed at Gothenburg (CEC 2001b).

The Lisbon Strategy may have been deemed unrealistic since it was developed, but creating growth and jobs remains the goal of EU policy (CEC 2005). The *Territorial Agenda* argues that the diversity of Europe's regions is conducive to that goal. Making use of their endogenous potential, also described as their territorial capital (OECD 2001), the regions can each contribute to attaining the goal.

This introduction is about European planners attaching themselves to the competitiveness discourse, while at the same time sustaining their commitment to a specifically European model of society, different from any American model (Judt 2005, 748; Faludi 2007). This introduction is also and in particular about how evidence, produced in a collaborative effort by a network of more than 600 researchers involved in the European Spatial Planning Observation Network (ESPON), is being brought to bear on European spatial planning. The EU can rarely operate with the same sense of purpose as the United States—a federation of more than 200 years' standing—but the European example in planning may serve as a source of inspiration. After all, ESPON could easily be the most elaborate collaborative research effort feeding into planning policy ever undertaken.

The date of the Leipzig meeting was almost to the day 10 years after the meeting of the planning ministers at Noordwijk, who gave their blessing to the first official draft of the *European Spatial Development Perspective* (ESDP). None of the ministers assembled at Leipzig were in office 10 years ago. Indeed, almost half of the countries represented were not even EU members in 1997. On 1 May 2004, the EU admitted 10 new members, most of them from central and eastern Europe, and Bulgaria and Romania joined on 1 January 2007. So the EU as presently constituted with its 27 members looks very different from when the ESDP was being prepared, and the planning challenges are different, too. As a venue, Leipzig also had symbolic significance (Böhme and Schön 2006). Adopted in 1994, the so-called Leipzig Principles had been the foundation of the ESDP.

The stakes are high. In 2008 a review of the EU budget will start, as agreed as part of the Financial Perspectives 2007–2013. That review will, among other things, critically examine the second-largest budget item, cohesion policy, the item most relevant to European planning efforts. With a view to that future, the *Territorial Agenda* is attempting to factor territorial cohesion into the equation of Europe's competitiveness. The aim is thus to make territorial cohesion policy a pillar of a revamped cohesion policy.

The *Territorial Agenda* is rooted in the ESDP (CEC 1999). A joint product of the member states—with substantial assistance from the Commission of the European Communities, better known as the European Commission, or simply the Commission—the ESDP was a major achievement of the 1990s (Faludi 2002; Faludi and Waterhout 2002). As a result of member state reluctance to grant it a role, the Commission withdrew its support and invoked the concept of territorial cohesion instead (Faludi 2006). As the Financial Perspectives 2007–2013 come into operation, and pending the resolution of the issue of an EU mandate for territorial cohesion policy, the Commission pursues a tentative territorial cohesion policy by invoking spatial or territorial criteria in evaluating "National Strategic Reference Frameworks" (NSRFs) and "Operational Programmes" (OPs) prepared in pursuance of the *Community Strategic Guidelines* (Council of the European Union 2006). Under the umbrella of the new third objective of cohesion policy, European territorial cooperation, successful ESDP follow-ups like the Community Initiative INTERREG and ESPON will continue, but now as part of mainstream cohesion policy.

In this introduction, the focus is on ESPON, a remarkable learning exercise that pursues relevant themes and, since a belated start in mid-2002, brings together researchers from across Europe. As the ESPON 2006 program has it: "The organizational structure of the ESPON . . . raises expectations for intensive networking between the research institutes for all the various study subjects which will serve the objective of supporting the establishment of a scientific community in the different fields addressed by the ESPON" (ESPON 2003, 10–11). The plethora of results—tens of thousands of pages of text with hundreds of maps, all available on the Web site (www.espon.eu)—has induced member states to resume their planning initiative and produce the evidence-based document *The Territorial State and Perspectives of the European Union: Towards a Stronger European Territorial Cohesion in the Light of the Lisbon and Gothenburg Ambitions* (2007).

The first section of this introduction gives an overview of developments since the ESDP that have led to more recent initiatives. The second section focuses on the role of evidence and experts in producing the two new documents. The introduction ends with a preview of chapters 1–10.

## European Planning Since the Turn of the Century

According to the ESDP, the three spheres of European planning are (1) polycentric development and urban-rural partnership; (2) access to infrastructure and knowledge; and (3) prudent management of the natural and cultural resources. However, at the European level, there is no more talk, as in the ESDP, of European spatial development policy, let alone of spatial planning—except for the mention of spatial planning in the title of ESPON, as a kind of relic of the past. The reason for eschewing the use of these terms is that in 2000 the Commission ended its support for the ESDP process. As a consequence, the Committee on Spatial Development, which did the groundwork for the ESDP, was disbanded. Listed in the treaty establishing a constitution for Europe as an objective and as a competence shared between the Union and the member states on a par with economic and social cohesion, the new concept of territorial cohesion would have given the EU, and the Commission, a key role in developing any relevant policies. However, French and Dutch voters who objected to the constitution rendered its ratification unrealistic. In June 2007, the European Council of Heads of State and Government decided to abandon the constitution in favor of a treaty amending the Treaty on the European Union and the Treaty establishing the European Community, a decision which was finalized at their meeting in late October, to be followed by the signing of the document in December 2007. The prospects of it coming into force—in 2009 or later, depending on the ratification process—are good. At any rate, the new treaty refers once again to "economic, social and territorial cohesion" as an objective of the Union and as a "shared competence between the Union and the Member States" (Presidency of the IGC 2007).

Meanwhile, in pursuance of the Lisbon Strategy, EU policy priorities generally have shifted from "soft" concerns, with which planning is associated, toward the pursuit of competitiveness, to be achieved through promoting innovation (Giddens 2007; see chapter 3). Territorial cohesion policy of whatever denomination must be seen to increase competitiveness.

The origin of cohesion policy lies in the mid-1970s, when the then European Community started giving financial support to member states pursuing their own regional policies. Under Jacques Delors, Commission president in 1985–1995, the rudimentary policy of the 1970s was revamped to serve the twin objectives of economic and social cohesion in the Single European Act of 1986. Within national and regional envelopes that are the outcomes of protracted intergovernmental bargaining, regional and local authorities, as well as other stakeholders, apply for funding, to be used in addition to their own resources on projects designed to pursue a set number of priorities. The approach is thus programmatic, but at the same time relies on input from below. This has led to a remarkable form of multilevel governance, giving the Commission access to regional and local stakeholders and vice versa (Hooghe and Marks 2001).

Presently, the lion's share of the funds goes to regions in central and eastern Europe, but regions with "geographical handicaps" (for instance, peripheral and even ultra-peripheral regions, mountain regions, and islands) are also eligible as a matter of course. The policy is to compensate them for disadvantages suffered in competing in the single market.

This policy came under fire in the Sapir Report (Sapir et al. 2004) on EU economic governance, which argued that cohesion policy failed to promote competitiveness and was bureaucratic, to boot. Subsequently, some net contributors to the EU budget posed the challenge of replacing cohesion policy with financial transfers to the new member states—in fact a return to the policies of the 1970s. The argument was to cut bureaucracy by removing the Commission as the key player in regional policy.

Another issue of more immediate importance in the debate over the Financial Perspectives 2007–2013 was the overall spending ceiling, calculated as a percentage of the GDP of the EU. This overshadowed the discussion on the reform of the budget. In the end, the amounts allocated were reduced to a level lower than what the Commission had deemed necessary. At the same time, cohesion policy, the Common Agricultural Policy (CAP), and the equally contentious U.K. budget rebate were allowed to continue, but with a commitment to reviewing the budget framework, including all the controversial issues, starting in 2008. The aim is to arrive at a new setup in time for the next Financial Perspectives for the period after 2013.

The Commission heard the challenge to its cohesion policy loud and clear and redirected it to support the Lisbon Strategy. In fact, cohesion policy is one of the few instruments of the Commission used for this purpose. Otherwise, the Lisbon Strategy depends on the willingness and ability of member states to work toward targets for reforming labor markets, increasing female participation, investing in R&D, and so forth. Member states are only committed to formulating National Reform Programmes and reporting on their implementation using agreed indicators. The Commission produces summary accounts of their achievements, the idea being that the worst performers will want to improve their efforts.

For cohesion policy, a similar cycle is in place. The Commission proposed new *Community Strategic Guidelines* for cohesion policy for the approval of the Council of the European Union (commonly known as the Council of Ministers). Member states formulated NSRFs followed by OPs. At the time of this writing—October 2007—the Commission was still discussing whether some of them conformed to the guidelines and to the relevant council regulation (Official Journal of the European Union 2006). There will be an important midterm review in 2010.

The *Community Strategic Guidelines* describe the territorial dimension of cohesion policy:

> One of the features of cohesion policy—in contrast to sectoral policies—lies in its capacity to adapt to the particular needs and characteristics of specific geographical challenges and opportunities. Under cohesion policy, geography matters. Accordingly, when developing their programmes and concentrating resources on key priorities, member states and regions

should pay particular attention to these specific geographical circumstances. (Council of the European Union 2006, 40)

The responsible Directorate-General for Regional Policy has issued a guidance document for the mandatory ex-ante evaluation of the NSRFs and OPs (Directorate-General 2006). Its annex 4 describes how specific needs and characteristics of territories should be taken into account, reflecting an appreciation of the particular problems and opportunities that result from their geographic situations. The annex also proposes indicators to be used in doing that, thereby referring to the work of ESPON. (For more on the territorial impact assessment and the indicators used, see chapter 2.) The guidance document even suggests that NSRFs and OPs should include sections on territorial cohesion. However, evaluating the NSRFs, Polverari et al. (2006, 78) conclude that territorial aspects have not played as strategic a role as might have been expected. Similar to a study by Bachtler, Ferry, Méndez, and McMaster (2007) of the OPs, their work shows that with the exception of France, only a few new member states (for instance, Hungary and Poland) invoke the concept of territorial cohesion. It is worth noting, however, that the Commission's guidance document came out in August 2006, when the preparation of the NSRFs was already well under way. At the Leipzig meeting, the representative of the responsible Directorate-General for Regional Policy gave a somewhat more upbeat assessment of the "urban and territorial dimension" of the documents available at the time (Directorate-General 2007).

Meanwhile, the work by researchers throughout Europe in the framework of ESPON has borne fruit in more ways than just providing indicators for evaluating programs. In 2004 the Dutch presidency of the European Union—in coordination with other member states sympathetic to the idea of territorial cohesion policy, like France and Luxembourg (Faludi and Waterhout 2005)—invited the ministers of the member states responsible for territorial cohesion to an informal meeting at Rotterdam, the first such meeting since the ESDP process had come to an end. There ministers decided to produce an evidence-based document drawing on the work that was becoming available from ESPON. The ESDP had sorely lacked a solid analytical base (Böhme and Schön 2006, 61; Faludi and Waterhout 2002, 166–172), a fact that led to the belated formation of ESPON in 2002—three years after the ESDP was completed. That is not how it is being framed, but producing an evidence-based document is a repeat, albeit in adapted form and with better data on which to base recommendations, of the ESDP process. The idea is to use available evidence to make a convincing case for taking into account the spatial or territorial dimension of various policies.

At Luxembourg six months after the Rotterdam meeting, the ministers reassembled and accepted a scoping document to prepare what would eventually become a document entitled *The Territorial State and Perspectives of the European Union*. Later on, it was decided to also produce the much shorter political document called the *Territorial Agenda*, which formed the object of the ministerial meeting at Leipzig. The experts considered the emergent *Territorial State and Perspectives* too complex to be put before the ministers. In particular, the ESDP process had shown that maps were controversial in any policy document of this kind, so the *Territorial Agenda* does not contain any. With many maps culled from the work of ESPON, the *Territorial State and Perspectives* was presented at Leipzig merely as a background document. Clearly, on the way from collecting the evidence to formulating policy, many decision points have been passed. Evidence-based planning is not a straightforward matter of drawing conclusions based on the facts.

The remainder of this section discusses the *Territorial Agenda* as a strategic document with proposals for contributing to the EU agenda of promoting jobs and growth. The document also insists that account be taken of the needs and characteristics of specific geographical challenges and opportunities. In short, its message—like that of the *Community Strategic Guidelines*—is that geography matters.

An eight-page document, the *Territorial Agenda* comes in four parts. The first part clearly states its main focus as contributing to the Lisbon and Gothenburg strategies; it defines territorial cohesion as a permanent and cooperative process involving various actors and stakeholders. The second part begins by identifying six major challenges: (1) climate change (discussed in chapter 6 of this volume); (2) rising energy prices and the accelerating integration of regions in global economic competition; (3) the impact of the enlargement of the European Union; (4) the overexploitation of ecological and cultural resources; (5) the loss of biodiversity, "particularly through increasing development sprawl while remote areas are facing depopulation"; and (6) the effects of demographic change and migration on the labor market, the supply of public services, and the housing market (discussed in chapter 4 of this volume).

With a glance at the European social model, a topic of continuing debate (Giddens, Diamond, and Liddle 2006; Giddens 2007), the second part of the agenda states that territorial cohesion is a prerequisite of sustainable economic growth and job creation. Emphasis is on making use of regionally diversified territorial potential and on the increasing territorial influence of Community policies.

After recounting the three spheres of European planning according to the ESDP mentioned previously, the third part of the *Territorial Agenda* outlines new priorities for developing the EU territory: (1) strengthening polycentric development and innovation through networking of city regions and cities; (2) developing new forms of territorial governance between rural and urban areas; (3) promoting regional clusters of competition and innovation, specifically across borders; (4) supporting and extending Trans-European Networks (TEN); (5) promoting trans-European risk management (the chief concern of the authors of chapter 6); and (6) strengthening ecological structures and cultural resources for a new approach to development.

What is new on the list of priorities is risk management, including the impacts of climate change, a topic that has come up in the wake of floods and droughts over the past years and is receiving increasing emphasis, due in part to media attention, the film *An Inconvenient Truth* having been discussed in preparatory expert meetings. It is only fair to add though that, whereas they are at the top of the list of challenges, climate change and energy figure less prominently in the list of priorities than one might expect.

However, there is much to do about competitiveness under the priorities. Coming before Lisbon, the ESDP had already related a polycentric urban system to Europe's competitiveness, culminating in the ESDP's proposal to encourage the development of more global economic integration zones outside the "pentagon" of London-Paris-Milan-Munich-Hamburg. The ESDP had invoked the example of the United States possessing such zones on the East Coast, the West Coast, in the Midwest, and in the South, thus giving it a competitive advantage. Promoting polycentric territorial development with a view to making better use of available resources in European regions is also the main plank of the *Territorial Agenda*, but without invoking the concept of global economic integration zones.

The fourth part of the *Territorial Agenda* urges European institutions to pay more regard to the territorial dimension of policies. There is also a demand for more in-depth analyses in the ESPON 2013 program of the effects of EU policies on territorial cohesion and for operational indicators. This emphasis on territorial monitoring is based on the analysis of the territorial impacts of EU policies and what could be done about managing them in chapter 3 of the *Territorial State and Perspectives*, which admits that the ministers for spatial planning and development themselves cannot do more than delivering a sound evidence base and putting the territorial dimension of EU policies on the EU agenda. For effective management of the territorial impact of EU policies they

> appear to be dependent on the commitment of the formal EU institutions, especially the European Commission, as the initiator of EU Policies. In other words, leadership in managing the territorial impact of EU policies appears only possible if the European Commission and the EU Ministers for Spatial Development cooperate closely as a driving force for other stakeholders. (Territorial State 2007, 56)

The *Territorial State and Perspectives* document refers to the white paper on European governance (CEC 2001a), which compliments the ESDP for taking steps toward more policy coherence. It then points out that the Commission "has made initial attempts to address the politically sensitive issue of a coherent approach to the territorial impact of EU policies," but that it "remains a rather premature and fragile matter on the EU agenda" (Territorial State 2007, 56). In plain English: Territorial impact assessment is controversial, since member states fear yet another procedure, like strategic environmental assessment (SEA)—considered cumbersome by some—being imposed on them. This is why an earlier proposal to introduce territorial impact assessment did not make it into the final document.

A separate set of recommendations in the *Territorial Agenda* concerns cooperation between the Commission and the member states. It talks about the need for in-depth dialogue and the opportunities that should be provided by what are called the "existing committees." Previous drafts of the *Territorial Agenda* requested that the Commission establish an internal territorial cohesion contact point; hard pressed to fulfill ever more tasks, the Commission apparently retorted at a preparatory meeting in November 2006 that it was unable to do that. The final *Territorial Agenda* as approved by the ministers contains merely the commitment by the ministers themselves to set up a network of territorial cohesion contact points. The earlier draft invited the Commission also to publish what is called a communication on territorial cohesion, an idea the Commission itself had launched at Luxembourg but shelved in the wake of the negative referenda. Apparently, a high-ranking Commission official had cold-shouldered the idea in the absence of ratification of the Constitution. However, the Leipzig *Presidency Conclusions* go at least as far as requesting the Commission to publish a report on territorial cohesion by 2008 (German Presidency 2007, 5). Searching for relevant input, the Commission has circulated a questionnaire asking member states to give their views.

The *Territorial Agenda* asks the member states themselves to integrate the priorities it sets out, as well as the territorial aspects of the *Community Strategic Guidelines*, in national, regional, and local development policies, but without attending to the general lack of capacity for doing so documented by Schout and Jordan (2007).

The longest list of follow-up actions relates to what the ministers themselves will do. Easily the most important one is the request, reiterated in the conclusions of the German presidency (2007), for the Slovene presidency of early 2008 to take the *Territorial Agenda* into account in preparing the 2008 spring European Council traditionally devoted to discussing the progress of the Lisbon Strategy. Otherwise, too, the ministers have firm ideas as to where they are going. For instance, they intend to facilitate debate on a long list of EU dossiers from a territorial point of view. The Portuguese presidency is organizing an Informal Meeting of Ministers on Territorial Cohesion and Regional Development—the designations of such meetings have the habit of changing—in late 2007 to discuss the first "Action Programme" under the *Territorial Agenda*.

After Slovenia, France will hold the EU presidency. A supporter of territorial cohesion policy, France is certain to advance its cause but still has to announce whether it will hold a ministerial meeting. In 2000, the French showed a preference for expert meetings and seminars. Be that as it may, the *Territorial Agenda* will come up for review under the Hungarian presidency in the first half of 2011.

What transpires is, first, that the ministers have come to accept that the EU—and thus the Commission—needs to have a territorial cohesion policy, irrespective of whether the constitution in its present or an amended form will be ratified. (As indicated previously, the prospects are now that the new treaty replacing the constitution, which makes reference to territorial cohesion, will hopefully be ratified. If it is ratified, the question of an official EU mandate for territorial cohesion policy will be resolved.)

Second, discussion of the *Territorial Agenda* at the European Council in the spring of 2008 would be the first occurrence of territorial issues receiving attention from that prestigious body. This is hopeful. As the only one of the new member states to adopt the common currency so far, Slovenia commands much good will, and even before becoming an EU member, Slovenia had taken planning initiatives in the framework of the Council of Europe.

Optimism needs to be qualified, though. It is the ministers responsible for spatial planning and development and their expert advisers who have come to a somewhat more positive view of EU territorial cohesion policy. There are two reasons for their conversion:

1. Experts have gone through an intensive learning experience, forming a supranational community described as a "roving band of planners" in the process (Faludi 1997). After the ESDP came a multitude of projects under the Community Initiative INTERREG. Those collaborative, hands-on exercises were cofinanced by the EU, with, according to Müller et al. (2005, 1), more than 10,000 people involved. That must have had a diffuse effect in terms of the Europeanization of state, regional, and urban planning asked for in the ESDP (CEC 1999, 45).

2. Ministers responsible for spatial planning are not in a strong position to coordinate, as is their calling, national sectors and their policies, backed as these sectors are by relevant directorates-general of the European Commission. Thus, environmental policy makers draw strength from relevant EU policies; transport planners have the Trans-European Networks to refer to; and, although with the *Territorial Agenda* planners are doing their best to relate to it, economic policy makers are closer to the EU growth and jobs agenda. So it would be attractive for planners if they, too, could draw on EU territorial cohesion policy for legitimizing their role and aspirations.

As a final comment, the story of the *Territorial Agenda*, like that of the ESDP, is one of experts engaging in bureaucratic politics and taking along their ministers to defend their case. With the possible exception of some French circles (Faludi 2006; Bovar and Peyrony 2006), there is no overwhelming political concern, nor—with the notable exceptions of the Association of European Regions, the Committee of the Regions (an official advisory committee of the EU), and the Council of Maritime and Peripheral Regions in Europe—is there a lobby for territorial cohesion. The object of the *Territorial Agenda* is to give more prominence to territorial cohesion. It should be judged by whether it succeeds in doing so.

## Producing the Evidence

As indicated previously, the catalyst for producing the *Territorial Agenda* was the new evidence provided by ESPON.

Information about ESPON, its organization, and its achievements is available from a midterm evaluation required for all such programs (MVA Consultancy 2003), a less usual update of same (MVA Consultancy 2005), and a subsequent commissioned study concerned with the lessons to be drawn from ESPON and the strategy to be followed in the future (Rambøll Management 2006). There are also a number of so-called synthesis reports, the final one under the telling title "Territory Matters for Competitiveness and Cohesion: Facets of Regional Diversity and Potentials in Europe" (ESPON 2006b), reflecting among other things on the process of producing the evidence provided by ESPON. There is also a scientific report compiled by a group of key experts (ESPON 2006a). All this has fed into the ESPON 2013 program (ESPON 2007), still under review by the European Commission at the time of this writing.

Academic papers on the organization of ESPON are slower in coming. Most of those available are by researchers who are, or have been, involved in the process. The pioneer among academic observers of European spatial planning, Richard H. Williams (1999) has drawn attention to the novel approach introduced in the Study Programme on European Spatial Planning (SPESP). He participated in that experimental forerunner of the ESPON, also discussed by Bengs (2002). Other recent papers are Van Gestel and Faludi (2005), Hague (2006), Böhme and Schön (2006), and Prezioso (2007). Bengs (2006) continues to follow the ESPON critically. The authors of chapter 1 in this volume update and synthesize all this information.

Originally, ESPON was intended to provide the analytical base for amplifying the ESDP agenda, "putting some flesh on the generic skeleton of ideas that is the ESDP" (Bengs 2002, 13). The ESDP itself did not have such a base, at least not one that was consistent across the member states. Indeed, for a long time, the makers of the ESDP were hoping for the ESPON to be set up in time for first results to feed into the final document. That was an idle hope because the Commission argued that the lack of a specific EU mandate in that area—always stressed by the member states when it came to keeping the EU and the Commission at bay—made it impossible to allocate a budget line for such a research network. The Commission did finance the experimental SPESP, however. Williams (1999, 7) surmised that the point of the exercise was to demonstrate that "networked research does not work, thus making the case for creating an institution analogous to the European Environment Agency." Conceivably, there has been a dispute over this within the Commission. Bengs (2006, 6) reports on an incident during the SPESP program when a high-ranking Commission representative disputed not only the guidance given six months earlier by his colleague, but also the whole point of networked research—the value of which was later to be confirmed by the official evaluation of the SPESP.

The choice between a network and an independent EU agency was an issue from the beginning. Böhme and Schön (2006, 67) speculate about whether, once territorial cohesion has become a shared competence, a European agency would after all be more suitable than a network. Be that as it may, presently the only fixed structure is the ESPON Coordination Unit located in Luxembourg under arrangements by which the government of the Grand Duchy foots the bill.

To return to the situation at the beginning of the decade, the positive evaluation of the SPESP left no option but to pursue the network approach, now included in the objectives of ESPON. So after more protracted discussions, ESPON got off the ground in mid-2002 under the umbrella of INTERREG. ESPON 2006, as it began to be called, covered the territory, first, of the 15 and, as of May 2004, the 25 EU member states. In addition, the territories of two new members that were to join on 1 January 2007, plus those of the nonmembers Norway and Switzerland, were included, so that the ESPON 2006 proudly spoke of the EU29. The usual rules for EU funding applied, although they had been adopted for quite different types of activities. This is a point to which we will return.

ESPON 2013, the follow-up to ESPON 2006, will operate as a European observation network for territorial development and cohesion as soon as the relevant regulations have been approved. It covers an even larger space: the current EU27; the three official candidates, Croatia, the former Yugoslav Republic of Macedonia, and Turkey; and the nonmembers of the EU and paying members of ESPON, Norway and Switzerland, augmented by Iceland as a new partner. Neighboring countries will be encouraged to join. Tiny Liechtenstein may also join. ESPON 2013 will soon be once again pursuing relevant themes, bringing together hundreds of researchers doing innovative work.

Under complicated arrangements, 85 percent of the funds for the actual research will come from the EU, and the rest will come from the participating states. The EU funds will be provided under the "territorial cooperation" objective of cohesion policy.

Like European spatial planning, ESPON is expert driven. As indicated, its origins reach back to the early days of the ESDP process when it became plain that the analytical base for a European planning document of any description was weak to nonexistent. The idea was for a European network of major research institutes to generate the necessary data, but despite persistent efforts, spearheaded by Luxembourg beginning in 1997, the financing of such a network turned out to be a thorny issue for the reason given above: The member states refused to recognize an EU competence in the matter. The way out was to label the SPESP an experimental and innovative action. Eventually, ESPON was brought under Article 53 of the INTERREG regulations and, significantly, its name changed to European Spatial Planning *Observation* Network—rather than *Observatory* Network, thus indicating that ESPON is intended not as a network of existing research institutes but rather as a more free-floating arrangement.

The stated purpose of ESPON was to lay the foundation for an ESDP II, although that was quickly forgotten as ESDP II became an unrealistic prospect; ESPON 2006, however, did research relating to the ESDP agenda, of course. The ESPON program had seven objectives:

1. Adding a European focus to national research

2. Amplifying the ESDP for transnational and national spaces

3. Developing instruments and creating institutions for the application of the ESDP

4. Exploring the spatial dimension of EU and national-sector policies

5. Improving coordination of those policies

6. Bridging the gap between policy makers, administrators, and academic analysts

7. Networking within the relevant European academic community

Projects fell into four categories. There were, first, thematic studies relating to main ESDP themes, from polycentric development to natural and cultural heritage. Second, there were impact studies of EU-sector policies, from transport (discussed in this book by Klaus Spiekermann and Michael Wegener in chapter 5) to pre-accession aid and programs to promote development in countries with no immediate prospect of joining (discussed in a global context by Pierre Beckouche and Claude Grasland in chapter 8). Of these, the study of the territorial impact of the Common Agricultural Policy—discussed among other sector policies for its impact on territorial cohesion in chapter 2—proved particularly controversial. It showed that the CAP favored the core regions, thus counteracting the attempt of cohesion policy to make up for the disadvantages suffered by the least favored regions, mostly in the periphery (Shucksmith, Thomson, and Roberts 2005). Bengs (2006, 8) suggests that there were even attempts to suppress the findings of this study. Third, there were coordinating, so-called cross-thematic studies. Defining coordination as a research task allowed more funds to be allocated to this important task than the meager overhead expenditure allowed under the relevant regulations (Van Gestel and Faludi 2005, 87; Böhme and Schön 2006, 64). Developing integrated tools for European spatial development and formulating spatial scenarios (the latter discussed by Jacques Robert and Moritz Lennert in chapter 7) also came under this category, but Hague (2006, 28) argues that the coordinative tasks assigned to the projects concerned were to the detriment of theoretical depth. Finally, studies and scientific support projects, including an innovative data navigator designed to facilitate access to information available throughout Europe, formed a mixed category.

The geographic scope was described previously as that of a putative EU29. In terms of geographic detail, the studies generally went as far as what is called the NUTS 3 level (regions), but not to the next-lower level of what are called Local Administrative Units (formerly NUTS 4). The reason was the lack of data across Europe for more fine-grained studies. This reduced the value of the results to smaller member states and their regions. There was also much concern, articulated by Bengs (2002) and others, about the appropriateness of definitions derived from the urbanized core of Europe for analyzing the situation in the thinly populated periphery. It is not uncommon for issues and definitions identified from a European perspective to give a distorted picture of situations as seen through the eyes of those directly affected. (In chapter 6, Schmidt-Thomé and Greiving show this also to be the case for the identification of some hazards.)

As indicated, ESPON 2006 was subject to restrictions under regulations pertaining to this type of program. In addition to the ceiling on overhead expenditures, the contract model spelled trouble, in particular for the lead partners of the Transnational Project Groups doing the work. In addition, the overall budget was small. Control and management were in the hands of a Managing Authority, a Paying Authority, and a Monitoring Committee. Supported by the Coordination Unit, the latter, which included representatives of the member states and the

Commission, was firmly in charge of content. In addition to this complex structure, there were European Contact Points in each of the countries participating. These were supposed to generate interest for the public tenders, assist with obtaining the necessary data, and disseminate results; with their resource endowments varying, however, they did not always work as intended.

Commissioning research involved public tenders, but the number of tenders decreased over time. Large research institutes, many from universities, mostly from northwest Europe, for whom the research was of intrinsic interest, were overrepresented. So cumbersome were the procedures that some of the Transnational Project Groups were forced to subsidize the studies they were involved in (Rambøll Management 2006, 18). Those participating complained also about interventions and additional demands from responsible authorities (Rambøll Management 2006, 15; Van Gestel and Faludi 2005, 82; Hague 2006, 26; Bengs 2006, 6). Comments in a study by Rambøll Management (2006) also suggest that the Monitoring Committee was politicized to a point that, rather than deliberating on common strategies, national representatives took partisan views. Undoubtedly, that led to distortions in the process of producing the objective evidence on which future territorial cohesion policy should be based.

The main finding of the Rambøll study was that ESPON 2006 had created more added value for the scientific community than for practitioners and policy makers. Since the study took a user and demand perspective, it is of little surprise that its recommendation was to strengthen the potential value of ESPON for these practitioners and policy makers. The study also recommended giving the program more focus and aiming for simple solutions to topical problems. This is bound to increase the ever present "structural tension between the commissioners of research and the research community" (Hague 2006, 25; see also Bengs 2006, 7; Faludi and Waterhout 2006, 10–11; ESPON 2006a, 12).

The Rambøll study is unusual. As indicated, the study came on top of the routine midterm evaluation and its less routine update, which suggests that the Commission wanted to get the next version of ESPON right. In early 2006 two successive drafts of the new *ESPON 2013 Programme: European Observation Network on Territorial Development and Cohesion* were put out for consultation.

When it is operational, ESPON 2013 will carry out activities under the following priorities:

1. Applied research on territorial development, competitiveness, and cohesion: evidence on territorial trends, perspectives, and policy impacts

2. Targeted analysis based on user demand: European perspective on development of different types of territories

3. Scientific platforms and tools: territorial indicators and data, analytical tools, and scientific support

4. Capitalization, ownership, and participation: capacity building, dialogue, and networking

5. Technical assistance, analytical support, and communication (ESPON 2007, 30–31)

This is the outcome of a SWOT analysis of ESPON 2006 performed by the Monitoring Committee in consultation with its counterpart at the European Commission. The foregone conclusion was that an efficient and modern regional policy "has to be based on necessary evidence and knowledge to ensure a solid policy implementation" (ESPON 2007, 23). ESPON 2013 accepts the recommendations of the Rambøll study to focus on the needs of practitioners and policy makers, but the "demand from policy development voiced as noted by members of the ESPON Monitoring Committee will be the key selection criteria for the thematic orientations" (ESPON 2007, 34).

Although ESPON 2013 promises more attractive research contracts, thus remedying some of the practical problems in ESPON 2006, critics worried about the interface between research and policy making will not be satisfied to hear that, if anything, the short-term, user-, and policy-driven emphasis will increase. Presumably, this will be at the expense of opportunities for long-term, fundamental, and inevitably critical pursuits.

The issue between researchers and policy makers is a long-standing one, and in ESPON, too, researchers hoping to be able to work systematically on an objective evidence base for policy were disappointed. Rather, the Commission wanted "just-in-time" results to suit its agenda (Hague 2006, 26), and the results needed to be what one Commission representative famously described as "punchy" (Van Gestel and Faludi 2005, 85). The tension is too fundamental ever to be resolved, but in ESPON arrangements veer in the direction of favoring the commissioners of research.

This relates to more fundamental issues in evidence-based policy, discussed by Faludi and Waterhout (2006). Attempts to base policy on evidence reach from Roman censuses, through Patrick Geddes's "survey before plan," to recent examples of national observatories or research institutes covered in a special issue of a journal for which their paper is the introduction. Faludi and Waterhout discuss the different institutional dynamics involved. While research normally follows a set approach from formulating hypotheses to designing research, collecting empirical evidence, and drawing conclusions, a process that has a long gestation period, policy making tends to be less predictable and more dynamic. Policy is often influenced by events of the day and, in particular, media attention to those events. It is difficult to forge a direct relationship between a research program and the delivery of a specific policy, leading Davoudi (2006) to conclude that, rather than talking about policy as evidence based, the more modest but realistic aim should be for policy to be "evidence informed." This suggests a less direct, but still positive, relation between the two.

Indeed, Faludi and Waterhout (2006, 9) conclude that there can be "no question of evidence forming a self-evident, objective basis for action. Rather, on methodological grounds, what is accepted as decisive evidence is a matter of choice, and as such is value-laden and political. The search for evidence, i.e. the formulation of research programs and proposals, is also a political choice." In chapter 5, too, the authors, based on their experience in ESPON, subtly but critically discuss this issue. Undeniably, though, the planners involved in the *Territorial Agenda* process have taken great strides toward underpinning their recommendations with European-wide evidence. In that sense, the *Territorial Agenda* is clearly evidence informed, and that is all its makers should have expected of it.

## Preview

The chapters that follow bear witness to the fact that the *Territorial Agenda* is evidence informed.

Unlike the present author, all the other authors whose work appears in this volume have been directly involved in the work of ESPON. The first chapter is about the program as such. Cliff Hague and Verena Hachmann discuss its organization, achievements, and future in more detail than the cursory discussion above could supply. In chapter 2 Kai Böhme and Thiemo Eser focus on a substantive issue, arguably one of the most important in the *Territorial Agenda*: territorial impact assessment in the context of various other assessment procedures, including the impact assessment to which EU legislation is being submitted. They also discuss results of various impact studies conducted in the framework of ESPON.

Janne Antikainen, in chapter 3, examines polycentricity, in regard to the Lisbon Strategy and to the pursuit of competitiveness in Europe. He uses Finland, which is regarded as a model of competitiveness and innovation, as a case study. He differentiates between polycentricity as it pertains to urban systems and as a strategic policy concept for promoting knowledge and innovation.

In chapter 4 Diogo de Abreu discusses the issue, accepted to be perennial in Europe, of planning for demographic decline, which is likely to condition spatial and social policies. Replenishing the diminishing labor force to meet the needs of an aging population presents itself as a possible solution. The chapter discusses the levels of immigration that this would require, as well as a variety of demographic indicators associated with different scenarios.

The next three chapters emphasize sustainability. Klaus Spiekermann and Michael Wegener focus on accessibility, competitiveness, and cohesion in chapter 5. The European territory is being transformed by the accelerated speed of movement. Accessibility at the global and European scales is seen as a core determinant of competitiveness, but it has implications for two other major EU goals: balanced development and sustainability. Increasing mobility is one of the reasons for failure to meet the Kyoto greenhouse gas emission targets, and for the growing vulnerability to energy price shocks. Philipp Schmidt-Thomé and Stefan Greiving discuss the implications for spatial development of natural hazards and climate change in chapter 6. They point out that risk patterns are site specific. The most appropriate strategy is to reduce vulnerability, and spatial planning can play an important role. In chapter 7 Jacques Robert and Moritz Lennert report on the "Spatial Scenarios" project, one of the integrative studies under ESPON 2006. The scenarios explore the spatial consequences of political choices considered fundamental in today's policy context in Europe, but the main message is that issues considered fundamental now may not have the greatest impact in the future. Climate change—also discussed by Schmidt-Thomé and Greiving—accelerating globalization, the aging population, and a new energy paradigm must urgently be taken into account.

In chapter 8 Pierre Beckouche and Claude Grasland focus on another challenge arising from Europe's position in the wider world. China, India, Japan, and the United States are considered competitors of Europe. One way of facing the competition would be to strengthen Europe's links with its neighbors. The European Neighbourhood Policy should enhance the local dimension of projects, thereby promoting decentralized cooperation, weakly developed both in Russia and in the Mediterranean countries.

Kai Böhme and Bas Waterhout focus on the Europeanization of planning in chapter 9. Europeanization is the result, not only of the ESDP and its successor, the *Territorial Agenda*, but also and in particular of other policies that, almost unintentionally, influence territorial development in Europe. Thus, research into Europeanization needs to include those policies.

The final chapter is by Thiemo Eser and Peter Schmeitz. The authors, both centrally involved in the *Territorial Agenda*, present thematic, institutional, and political-strategic perspectives and develop story lines from each of them. This approach reveals strengths and weaknesses in the *Territorial Agenda* and the *Territorial State and Perspectives* document on which it is based, as well as the hidden agenda behind them.

Between them, the ten chapters provide a comprehensive view of how the search for evidence to support the ESDP agenda—now the *Territorial Agenda of the European Union*—has proceeded, what the evidence has been in some key areas, what the implications are, and what other conclusions could have been drawn. The authors also demonstrate that a learning exercise like ESPON can contribute to shaping a political agenda, which—as mentioned at the beginning of this introduction—could perhaps serve as a source of inspiration for fellow planners across the Atlantic.

## References

Bachtler, J., M. Ferry, C. Méndez, and I. McMaster. 2007. The 2007–2013 Operational Programmes: A preliminary assessment. *IQ-NET Thematic Papers* (European Policies Research Centre, University of Strathclyde, Glasgow) 19(2).

Bengs, C., ed. 2002. *Facing ESPON* (Nordregio Report 2002:1). Stockholm: Nordregio.

———. 2006. ESPON in context. *European Journal of Spatial Development* (October). http://www.nordregio.se/EJSD/debate061023.pdf.

Böhme, K., and P. Schön. 2006. From Leipzig to Leipzig: Territorial research delivers evidence for the new Territorial Agenda of the European Union. In *Evidence-based planning*, A. Faludi, ed. Special issue, *disP* 165, 42(2): 61–70.

Bovar, O., and J. Peyrony. 2006. Le cas français de l'Observatoire des territoires: L'évidence par la prospective ou par l'observation? In *Evidence-based planning*, A. Faludi, ed. Special issue, *disP* 165, 42(2): 25–33.

CEC (Commission of the European Communities). 1999. *European Spatial Development Perspective: Towards balanced and sustainable development of the territory of the EU.* Luxembourg: Office for Official Publications of the European Communities.

———. 2001a. *European governance: A white paper.* Luxembourg: Office for Official Publications of the European Communities.

———. 2001b. *A sustainable Europe for a better world: A European Union strategy for sustainable development.* Luxembourg: Office for Official Publications of the European Communities.

———. 2005. *Working together for growth and jobs: A new start for the Lisbon Strategy.* Luxembourg: Office for Official Publications of the European Communities.

Council of the European Union. 2006. *Council decision on community strategic guidelines on cohesion.* Interinstitutional file 2006/0131, 18 August. http://register.consilium.europa.eu/pdf/en/06/st11/st11807.en06.pdf.

Davoudi, S. 2006. Evidence-based planning: Rhetoric and reality. In *Evidence-based planning*, A. Faludi, ed. Special issue, *disP* 165, 42(2): 14–24.

Directorate-General. 2006. *The new programming period, 2007–2013: Indicative guidelines on evaluation methods—Ex ante evaluation* (Working paper no. 1). Directorate-General for Regional Policy, European Commission. http://ec.europa.eu/regional_policy/sources/docoffic/2007/working/wd1_exante_en.pdf.

———. 2007. *The territorial and urban dimension in the national strategic reference frameworks and operational programmes 2007–2013: A first assessment.* Directorate-General for Regional Policy, European Commission. http://ec.europa.eu/regional_policy/themes/urban/leipzig_report.pdf.

ESPON. 2003. *The ESPON 2006 Programme: Programme on the spatial development of an enlarging European Union.* Luxembourg: ESPON Coordination Unit. http://www.espon.eu/mmp/online/website/content/programme/199/file_291/espon_pc_final.pdf.

———. 2006a. *Applied territorial research: Building a scientific platform for competitiveness and cohesion* (ESPON Scientific Report II, Autumn 2006). Luxembourg: ESPON Coordination Unit.

———. 2006b. *Territory matters for competitiveness and cohesion: Facets of regional diversity and potentials in Europe* (ESPON Synthesis Report III, Autumn 2006). Luxembourg: ESPON Coordination Unit.

———. 2007. *ESPON 2013 Programme: European observation network on territorial development and cohesion* (Operational Programme, version 3, resubmitted 16 July). Luxembourg: ESPON Coordination Unit. http://www.espon.eu/mmp/online/website/content/programme/1145/file_2261/espon_2013_op-version_3-16-7-2007-ec.pdf.

European Council. 2000. *Presidency conclusions—Lisbon European Council, 23 and 24 March.* http://ue.eu.int/ueDocs/cms_Data/docs/pressData/en/ec/00100-r1.en0.htm.

Faludi, A. 1997. A roving band of planners. In *Shaping Europe: The European Spatial Development Perspective*, A. Faludi and W. Zonneveld, eds. Special issue, *Built Environment* 23(4): 281–287.

———, ed. 2002. *European spatial planning.* Cambridge, MA: Lincoln Institute of Land Policy.

———. 2006. From European spatial development to territorial cohesion policy. *Regional Studies* 40(6): 667–678.

———, ed. 2007. *Territorial cohesion and the European model of society*, Cambridge, MA: Lincoln Institute of Land Policy.

Faludi, A., and B. Waterhout. 2002. *The making of the European Spatial Development Perspective: No masterplan.* RTPI Library Series. London: Routledge.

———. 2005. The usual suspects: The Rotterdam informal ministerial meeting on territorial cohesion. *Tijdschrift voor Economische en Sociale Geografie* 96(3): 338–342.

———. 2006. Introducing evidence-based planning. In *Evidence-based planning*, A. Faludi, ed. Special issue, *disP* 165, 42(2): 3–13.

German Presidency. 2007. *Conclusions of the German EU Council presidency on the informal ministerial meeting on urban development and territorial cohesion.* http://www.bmvbs.de/Anlage/original_1005297/Conclusions-of-the-German-EU-Council-presidency-on-the-Informal-Ministerial-Meeting-accessible.pdf.

Gestel, T. van, and A. Faludi. 2005. Towards a European territorial cohesion assessment network: A bright future for ESPON? In *Territorial cohesion: An unidentified political objective*, A. Faludi, ed. Special issue, *Town Planning Review* 76(1): 81–92.

Giddens, A. 2006. *Europe in the global age.* London: Polity Press.

Giddens, A., P. Diamond, and R. Liddle, eds. 2006. *Global Europe, social Europe.* London: Polity Press.

Hague, C. 2006. ESPON and territorial research and practice in Europe. In *European territorial research in progress: Conference proceedings of the first ESPON scientific conference*, 23–35. Luxembourg: ESPON Coordination Unit.

Hooghe, L., and G. Marks. 2001. *Multilevel governance and European integration.* New York: Rowman & Littlefield.

Judt, T. 2005. *Postwar: A history of Europe since 1945.* London: Random House.

Müller, A., with F. Dosch, W. Görmar, V. Hachmann, and N. Schäfer. 2005. *Bericht 2005 Transnationale Zusammenarbeit/TransCoop 05 Report.* Bonn: Bundesamt für Bauwesen und Raumordnung.

MVA Consultancy. 2003. *Mid-term evaluation of the ESPON 2006 programme: Final report.* http://www.espon.eu/mmp/online/website/content/programme/125/file_392/fr_mid-term_eval-full.pdf.

———. 2005. *ESPON Mid-term evaluation update: Final report.* http://www.espon.eu/mmp/online/website/content/programme/125/file_354/mte_final-report_26-9-2005.pdf.

OECD. 2001. *Territorial Outlook.* Paris: OECD.

Official Journal of the European Union. 2006. *Council Regulation (EC) No 1083/2006 of 11 July 2006 laying down general provisions on the European Regional Development Fund, the European Social Fund and the Cohesion Fund and repealing Regulation (EC) No 1260/1999.* http://eur-lex.europa.eu/LexUriServ/LexUriServ.do?uri=OJ:L:2006:210:0025:01:EN:HTML.

Polverari, L., I. McMaster, F. Gross, J. Bachtler, M. Ferry, and D. Yuill. 2006. Strategic planning for Structural Funds in 2007–2013: A review of strategies and programmes. *IQ-NET Thematic Papers* (European Policies Research Centre, University of Strathclyde, Glasgow) 18(2).

Presidency of the IGC. 2007. *Draft treaty amending the Treaty on European Union and the Treaty establishing the European Community.* http://www.consilium.europa.eu/uedocs/cmsUpload/cg00001re01en.pdf.

Prezioso, M. 2007. Why the ESPON programme is concerned more with "policy implications" than with "good science." *European Journal of Spatial Development* (March). http://www.nordregio.se/EJSD/debate070312.pdf.

Rambøll Management. 2006. *Study on "territorial cohesion, lessons learned from the ESPON programme projects and strategy for the future": Final report.* http://www.espon.eu/mmp/online/website/content/programme/1186/file_2380/final_report_espon_study.pdf.

Sapir, A., P. Aghion, G. Bertola, M. Hellwig, J. Pisany-Ferry, D. Rosita, J. Viñals, and H. Wallace, with M. Butti, M. Nava, and P. M. Smith. 2004. *An agenda for a growing Europe: The Sapir Report.* Oxford: Oxford University Press.

Schout, J. A., and A. J. Jordan. 2007. From cohesion to territorial policy integration (TPI): Exploring the governance challenges in the European Union. *European Planning Studies* 15(6): 835–851.

Shucksmith, M., K. Thomson, and K. Roberts, eds. 2005. *CAP and the regions: The territorial impact of the Common Agricultural Policy.* Wallingford, Oxfordshire, England: CABI.

Territorial Agenda. 2007. *Territorial Agenda of the European Union: Towards a more competitive and sustainable Europe of diverse regions.* http://www.bmvbs.de/Anlage/original_1005295/Territorial-Agenda-of-the-European-Union-Agreed-on-25-May-2007-barrier-free.pdf.

Territorial State. 2007. *The Territorial State and Perspectives of the European Union: Towards a stronger European territorial cohesion in the light of the Lisbon and Gothenburg ambitions.* http://www.bmvbs.de/Anlage/original_1005296/The-Territorial-State-and-Perspectives-of-the-European-Union.pdf.

Williams, R. H. 1999. Constructing the European Spatial Development Perspective: Consensus without a competence. *Regional Studies* 33:793–797.

# CHAPTER 1

# Organization, Achievements, and the Future of ESPON

Cliff Hague and Verena Hachmann

International research across Europe has always been more difficult than study of the United States as an amalgam of different states. Language is a significant barrier in Europe; researchers in the U.K., for example, have generally been more in contact with North American writings in English than with publications in tongues from the European mainland. Political divisions have also created major barriers. Until the mid-1970s Spain and Portugal were ruled by dictators tainted by associations with fascism. From 1945 until the end of the iron curtain, research contacts across Europe's east-west divide were difficult to maintain. Active collaboration to produce policy-relevant research was almost impossible. All official data from Soviet bloc countries was suspect: The totalitarian system both nurtured and fed on scientism to a degree that hindered self-understanding.

Even comparative research among countries within the European Economic Community was a problem because of differences in institutions and data. During the 1990s compendia on spatial planning systems were commissioned and published to try to increase understanding of the different systems in the then 15 member states (see, e.g., CEC 1997). There are some differences in planning cultures between different states in the United States (e.g., between Oregon and Texas), and local governments may differ in their zoning regulations, but in Europe the differentiation has been wider and deeper. There are different planning traditions within Europe, partly reflecting different legal codes (see, e.g., Newman and Thornley 1996). Furthermore, those differences are linked to diverse intellectual traditions—of geography, regional economics, environmental studies, politics, even architecture and engineering—on which different approaches to planning have been built.

## The ESDP

The background to the ESDP has been reviewed by Faludi (2002) and by Faludi and Waterhout (2002). In the early 1990s exploratory documents (CEC 1991, 1994) began to look at spatial development in the EU. While Americans are used to seeing maps of the United States showing such elements as population and employment, this was the first time that spatial planners in Europe had been confronted by a document that had the then 12-member state community, rather than their own national or regional boundaries, as its reference point. In his book *European Union Spatial Policy and Planning* (1996), Williams provides the background for this development.

Valuable as these documents were, they did not constitute an evidence base on which territorial development choices could be made transparently. Similarly, the ESDP itself was primarily a narrative asserting the key objectives of cohesion, conservation, and balanced development. To a large extent it was a case of "policy first, evidence later." The dispersed evidence base simply could not be pieced together quickly enough. The original idea had been that ESPON would be established in time to provide the data for the ESDP (Faludi and Waterhout 2002). This intent was frustrated by political wrangles over a suitable legal framework for the ESPON program. While the ESDP process could not wait for ESPON to be set up, the important point was that ESPON was conceived as a research network that would do technical work for the ESDP and the subsequent reviews of the ESDP that were anticipated. What ESPON has achieved can be criticized, and indeed has been criticized, for example by Bengs (2006) and Prezioso (2007); however, in the context of what preceded it, ESPON has been a rather heroic venture with much solid achievement.

## The Evidence Gaps

As the introduction noted, the ESDP lacked a solid analytical base. True, the main spatial development disparities in Europe were identified with supporting evidence. For example, relative differences in GDP per capita between the richest 25 regions and the poorest 25 narrowed from a factor of 2.7 in 1986 to one of 2.4 by 1996, though regional disparities within most of the member states were increasing (CEC 1999, 9). Similarly, the legitimacy of aiming for a harmonious, balanced, and sustainable development was demonstrated by reference to the Treaty of Amsterdam (CEC 1999, 13). However, a conceptual leap of faith, guided by reasoning but not evidence, was required to reach the point where the first guideline advanced was "Development of a polycentric and balanced urban system and strengthening the partnership between urban and rural areas" (CEC 1999, 19).

What exactly is a "polycentric and balanced urban system"? Are some parts of Europe closer to this ideal than others, and if so are they notably more harmonious, balanced, and sustainable? What is the nature of a "partnership" between urban and rural areas? Definitions of an urban area differ among EU countries, so the task of rooting such assertions in evidence was always going to be difficult. Nevertheless, polycentric development was politically appealing, because it promised increasing the competitive critical mass of the EU while also delivering regional balance (Hague and Kirk 2003). An evidence base might have spoiled the story line.

The second ESDP guideline called for "promotion of integrated transport and communication concepts, which support the polycentric development of the EU territory and are an important pre-condition for enabling European cities and regions to pursue their integration into the European Monetary Union (EMU)." It continued, "Parity of access to infrastructure and knowledge should be realized gradually. Regionally adapted solutions must be found for this" (CEC 1999, 20). EMU was the system that created the euro as a common currency among some of the member states. Parity of access to infrastructure and knowledge again raises questions of definition and measurement. The guideline hints at the tensions likely to follow from EMU, between the aspiration for parity and the reality of cumulative comparative advantage bestowed by the friction of existing infrastructure.

Similarly, the third guideline called for "wise management" of the natural and cultural heritage. However, the environmental narrative within the ESDP was not integrated into the discussion of polycentric development (Hague and Kirk 2003; Richardson and Jensen 2000). Bengs (2002) went so far as to say that many of the ESDP objectives were oxymorons, that speaking of "balanced competition" was like speaking of a "round triangle."

Thus, the ESDP was rooted in consensus-building language games, rather than in scientific evidence. There had to be recourse to what Waterhout (2002) called "bridging concepts," such as polycentricity. The ESDP was a political document crafted to get agreement between member states and the Commission. The politics behind the ESDP left open a range of questions that would benefit from critical academic scrutiny and reinterpretation against an evidence base. There was a need for an ESPON, but what kind of role would ESPON have?

## ESPON's Brief

ESPON's applied research projects were structured in three main categories: (1) thematic studies; (2) policy impact studies; and (3) coordinating cross-thematic studies. A fourth stream of work comprised some short exploratory studies and scientific support projects, most notably a compendium of national data sources, which was known as the Data Navigator. Table 1.1 shows the relationship between the topics for the first round of ESPON projects (tendered in the summer of 2002) and key ESDP themes.

The table shows that the initial work of ESPON was shaped strongly by the ESDP. In particular, chapter 2 of the ESDP was about the "influence of Community policies on the territory of the EU." It listed seven policy fields where successive treaties of the Union had given the EU powers whose exercise affected territorial development. Four of those policy fields (Trans-European Networks; Common Agricultural Policy; Structural Funds; and research, technology, and development) featured in the first round of ESPON projects. Another, Community competition policy, would be addressed in a later project on the territorial implications of the Lisbon-Gothenburg Agenda. It is perhaps surprising that environmental policy was addressed only in a project (Geological Survey of Finland 2006) toward the end of the ESPON 2006 program. The only ESPON omission from the ESDP's list of seven was loan activities of the European Investment Bank.

**TABLE 1.1**

# The Relation Between ESPON Projects and the ESDP

| ESPON Project Number and Title | ESDP Connection |
|---|---|
| **1.1.1** The role, specific situation, and potentials of urban areas as nodes in a polycentric development | Strong links with the ESDP objective of polycentric development in support of a balanced and harmonious European territory, with cities as key drivers in the development of territories. The project defined and mapped indicators of polycentricity. |
| **1.1.2** Urban-rural relations in Europe | Strong links to the ESDP, which saw urban-rural relations as a means of addressing problems of rural restructuring while also protecting natural and cultural heritage and reducing uncontrolled urban expansion. The project defined and featured urban-rural relations in Europe and endorsed ESDP policy recommendations. |
| **1.2.1** Transport services and networks: territorial trends and basic supply of infrastructure for territorial cohesion | This project delivered new evidence on the ESDP guideline of "parity of access to infrastructure and knowledge" as a means of promoting better territorial balance and cohesion. It showed that, at European scale, a clear core-periphery pattern exists for accessibility, in particular for road and rail access. |
| **1.2.2** Telecommunication services and networks: Territorial trends and basic supply of infrastructure for territorial cohesion | The project built on the ESDP objective of "improvement of access to and use of telecommunication facilities," especially to compensate for disadvantages caused by distance and low density in peripheral regions. The research revealed several "digital divides"—both urban and rural and linked to differing national IT cultures. |
| **2.1.1** The territorial impact of EU transport and Trans-European Network (TEN) policies | ESDP identified TEN as one of several "EU policies with spatial impact." The project showed the contradictions and conflicts in achieving the ESDP's objectives of an integrated approach for improved transport links, a polycentric development model, and efficient and sustainable transport and communication systems. |
| **2.1.2** The territorial impact of EU research and development policies | Another of the "EU policies with spatial impact" identified in ESDP. The ESDP's objective of a spatially balanced diffusion of innovation and knowledge was explored. The report provided evidence to support a more territorially focused approach to the implementation of R&D policies. It also highlighted the leading role of capital cities. |
| **2.1.3** The territorial impact of the Common Agricultural Policy and rural development policy | CAP was also one of the "EU policies with spatial impact." The project found that CAP tended to benefit regions in the core. |
| **2.2.3** Territorial effects of the Structural Funds in urban areas | Structural Funds were another of the "EU policies with spatial impact." The study also encompassed the ESDP concern for "dynamic, attractive and competitive cities and urbanised regions." However, this project encountered severe data problems. |
| **3.1** Integrated tools for European spatial development | This relates to the central ESDP aim of introducing a spatial planning approach. |

The ESDP called for territorial impact assessment (TIA) a number of times—for example, in relation to large infrastructure projects (Option 29), for water management projects (Option 52), or in trans-border situations (recommendation after paragraph 178). It saw TIA as a procedure for assessing the impacts of policies and proposed developments against spatial policy objectives. However, it gave little or no guidance on how a TIA might be done, so in setting up an array of TIA projects, ESPON was filling a methodological need arising from the ESDP.

The evaluation of ESPON 2006 for the Directorate-General for Regional Policy argued that the program lacked focus (Rambøll Management 2006). While the proliferation of small projects toward the end of the program may have given that impression, the evidence from table 1.1 is that the early stage of ESPON was very focused on the ESDP's agenda.

What table 1.1 does not reveal, but is also important, is the extent to which the Commission set the agenda, not least in respect of the Terms of Reference for each project. Early in 2002 there was some consultation among the fledgling ESPON community about what might go into the Terms of Reference—in other words, what were the research priorities and desired outputs within each project? However, the suggestions from the Commission were consistently the ones that were enacted. The Commission wanted indicators above all else, the topic discussed by Böhme and Eser in chapter 2.

## ESPON 2002–2006

ESPON was set up in 2002 with a five-year program period. The networking approach in ESPON 2006 meant not only cooperation between the consortium members directly involved in a project as a Transnational Project Group (TPG), but also cooperation between different TPGs. Every six months ESPON convened a seminar to which TPG representatives were invited to present progress reports and findings. Those events were also attended by the network of national European Contact Points (ECPs) and by some policy makers responsible for the ESPON program. Those regular meetings involved discussion between researchers on methodological challenges and potential shortcomings. They also included briefings by the Commission about developing policy and information needs, and reviews of the program by staff from the ESPON Coordination Unit (CU).

In hindsight the most crucial of those meetings was the one in Crete in May 2003. The first such meeting in the autumn of 2002 at Mondorf-les-Bains in Luxembourg had been about getting ESPON started. In Crete there was a lot of discussion, at times quite heated, about the need for the separate TPGs to see themselves as part of the program as a whole, and to respond to the requests and opportunities presented by the Commission for influencing the third cohesion report (CEC 2004). The 46-page *Crete Guidance Paper* that followed was produced by the lead partner of the initial coordinating cross-thematic project, "Integrated Tools for European Spatial Development," the Federal Office for Building and Regional Planning, better known by its German acronym as the BBR. It set the framework within which the project teams should work. Significantly, the *Crete Guidance Paper* stated, "The very general question all projects have in common would be: 'Are observed trends in line with the basic goals of European spatial development policies (like balanced and polycentric development)? Do the results of European policies support these goals?'" (Bundesamt für Bauwesen und Raumordnung 2003, 2). Thus, the research agenda was firmly pointed at the issue of whether trends were toward or away from "balanced and polycentric development"—not on an evidence-based critique of the concept itself.

## The Structure of the Program

The Luxembourg Ministry of the Interior and Spatial Development acted as the Managing Authority and Paying Authority. The CU, based in Luxembourg, coordinated and facilitated ESPON, making the links between European territorial policy and policy and research communities across the 29 countries in the program. The strategic management and monitoring were the responsibility of the Monitoring Committee (MC). Each state contributing to ESPON had a representative on the MC, which usually met four times a year, the chair rotating with the EU presidency. The Commission was also a member of the MC. Most members of the MC were civil servants, for whom ESPON was just one of several parts of their job. Their knowledge of spatial planning was variable, and representation changed as individuals moved on within their careers. Sometimes a "political card" may have been played: Norway's decision in 2003 to contribute to ESPON was quickly followed by the announcement of a project on the impacts of fisheries policies. In general, though, as far as can be discerned, there was much more discussion than voting. Faced with a disparate and enlarging set of member-state representatives, the small but full-time and very effective CU and the Commission together were in a strong position to shape agendas and outcomes.

Thereafter, the most directly involved actors within ESPON were the TPGs, consisting of smaller or larger transnational groups of researchers with backgrounds in territorial development or neighboring disciplines. ESPON projects were awarded to TPGs on the basis of competitive tendering. A TPG had to include partners from at least three European countries. Rambøll Management (2006, 14) argues that the Terms of Reference set for projects usually did not identify the requirements of the three ESPON user groups—policy makers, practitioners, and scientists.

The program was extremely successful in creating an extensive and diverse network of researchers. Over 600 researchers from 130 institutions were involved (Böhme et al. 2006, 98–103). However, there is a distinct geography to the map of project partners, especially lead partners (see figure 1.1). A cluster consisting of the Benelux countries plus France and Germany extends through Switzerland to the north of Italy. There is a Scandinavian outlier based in Stockholm and some nodes in the capitals of some of the larger states that joined in 2004.

Given previous comments about different traditions in European planning, this pattern is worth some comment. In practice, a lead partner might be only two

FIGURE 1.1

Lead Partners and Project Partners of the ESPON 2006 Program

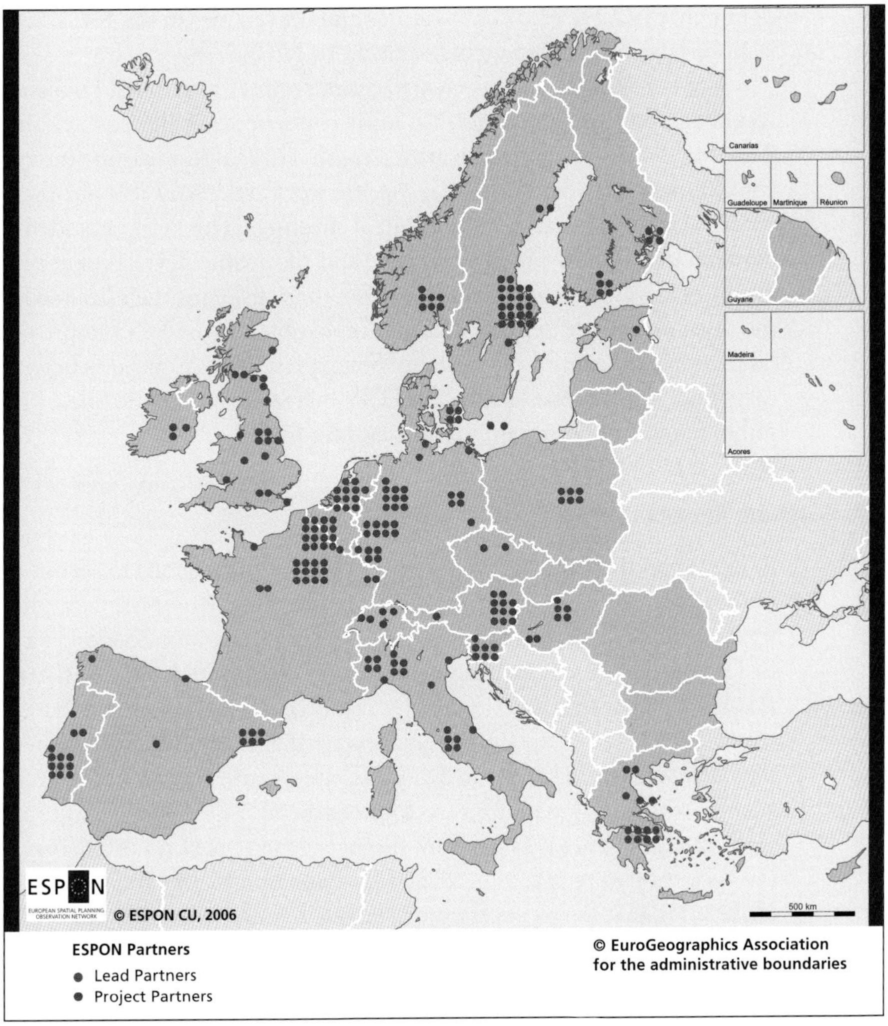

Source: ESPON 2006.

or three individual researchers who may not see themselves as "planners" in any professional sense. However, using institutionalist concepts, the map implies that the mental models and "rules of the game" embedded in the traditions of Benelux-France-Germany and Sweden have probably shaped the program's outputs more than those of any of the other traditions. There is a strong tradition of applied, policy-related research in Scandinavia, for example, and a governance culture in which consensus and respect for experts feature strongly. Furthermore, the financial arrangements within ESPON had the unintended effect of making involvement in projects unattractive to many private-sector research firms (Rambøll Management 2006, 18) and universities, such as those in the U.K., which seek full-cost recovery on research overheads. As Rambøll Management (2006, 14) noted, there was a predominance of large research institutes and universities in the TPGs. Several organizations have been partners in five or more TPGs.

A network of ECPs was created. Each country appointed its own ECP, which resulted in considerable diversity. Some countries kept the post within their ministry; others gave the job to an arm's-length national research institute; some asked consultants or academics to take on the work; relatively few put the post out to tender. A few ECPs rarely showed up at meetings. The ECPs provided an interface between the CU, the project partners, and the spatial development research communities in the member states. However, their diversity, their limited funding, and the sheer volume of reports made it impossible for the ECPs to provide a consistent, rigorous check on the evidence being presented. As projects began to produce their final reports, the task of the ECPs increasingly became one of national dissemination of the program's results and findings.

## The Research Agenda

At the outset the Data Navigator project was commissioned to set out information on key data sources within each ESPON country. However, data problems confronted many TPGs. Comparable data—in particular, time series data—were hard to find for all 29 countries. Furthermore, ECPs could not consistently provide assistance in accessing national data resources to the extent that had been anticipated. Even some of the European agencies that held relevant data needed persuasion before releasing them to ESPON teams. Eurostat, the EU's official statistical agency, with the status of a directorate-general, gave ESPON "minimal cooperation" (Bengs 2006, 8). Few, if any, projects experienced no problems collecting all the data they were asked to collect. In a couple of cases the problems proved so challenging that the projects were in effect abandoned as incomplete. For example, the team attempting to measure the impact of Structural Funds in urban areas were forced to conclude that despite "an extensive assessment of available data sources . . . the number of consistent and comparable indicators available at NUTS 3 scale is quite limited" (ECOTEC Research and Consulting et al. 2004, 51).

Ten "thematic" projects were commissioned. What did they include and exclude, and why? Projects concerned with polycentric development (1.1.1 in table 1.1), urban-rural relations (1.1.2), transport services and networks (1.2.1), and telecommunications (1.2.2) were all consistent with key ESDP concerns. Similarly, the project that looked at enlargement of the EU (1.1.3) did so in the context of polycentric development, while the ESDP concern for wise management of the natural and cultural heritage was pursued through projects 1.3.2 and 1.3.3, respectively. There was also a project on natural and technological hazards (1.3.1) and one on demography (1.1.4). The results of most of these projects are discussed elsewhere in this volume. The remaining thematic project was on the information society (1.2.3).

In spatial planning terms, the notable omissions are labor markets and property markets, though employment data were used in a number of projects. Tourism was not directly addressed in the thematic research agenda, though like the social dimension (1.4.2), it became one of the small studies (1.4.5) in the final phase of ESPON 2006.

The policy impact studies discussed in chapter 2 by Böhme and Eser went to the core of the spatial planning idea, in that they subjected a range of EU sector policies to territorial analysis and made the case for better integration with territorial development. The list of topics was wide ranging and picked up all the key EU policy fields with significant territorial implications—transport (2.1.1), research and development (2.1.2), Common Agricultural Policy (2.1.3), energy (2.1.4), fisheries (2.1.5), Structural Funds (2.2.1 and 2.2.3), and pre-accession aid (2.2.2), as well as environmental policies (2.4.1).

A study on the impacts of the ESDP (2.3.1) is discussed by Böhme and Waterhout in chapter 9. The impacts of national and regional spatial planning policies and traditions were not probed through a specific project, though the "zoom-in" project (2.4.2) did look at national priorities and conditions. The only project on governance (2.3.2) was tendered about halfway through the life of ESPON, despite the topic being a key backdrop to many other projects.

In 2000 the EU adopted the Lisbon Strategy, through which it is seeking to become the world's leading knowledge economy. Since 2001, it has also had the Gothenburg Agenda, which commits the Union to work for sustainable development. Together those two agreements form powerful drivers for the EU in an international context. Their territorial implications were the subject of project 3.3. The scenarios project (3.2) was commissioned to develop decision-support instruments for various policy options that could be used to tackle future territorial challenges. In chapter 7 Robert and Lennert report on this study.

Resources were limited, and ESPON squeezed a lot of research on a lot of topics from its relatively small budget. The flow of funds had to be managed across the 2002–2006 life of ESPON—not everything could be done at once. Doing the policy impact studies took a certain amount of courage—few bureaucratic empires welcome others setting out to measure the unintended impacts of their policies or to gather evidence to support the argument that they should conduct policy making in a manner more permeable to the priorities of agencies outside their own sector.

ESPON's research agenda was, above all, that of the directorate-general responsible for regional policy, DG Regio. The impact studies gave ammunition to confront other directorates within the Commission with the territorial consequences of their policies. The thematic studies were potentially means to provide the robust and objective data that would dilute the capacity for member states and regions to use special pleading to shape territorial policy decisions. ESPON's agenda was intended also to provide an evidential base for promoting the idea of territorial cohesion as a key area for EU legal competence, through inclusion in the constitution that was adopted by member states in 2004.

The spatial scale for analysis in the projects was NUTS 3, roughly equivalent to local authority areas and too coarse to allow for any focus on intra-urban inequalities, for example. The focus was on Europe as a whole—or rather the 29 countries in ESPON; the Balkan states are a conspicuous gray area on ESPON maps. With the exception of the project Europe in the World (3.4.1), discussed in chapter 8 by Beckouche and Grasland, ESPON was overwhelmingly focused on internal relations within the European space rather than global connections to the wider world or even to the neighboring countries around the rim of the EU.

### Key Findings from the 2002–2006 Program

The *ESPON Synthesis Report III* (Böhme et al. 2006) and the *ESPON Atlas* (Bundesamt für Bauwesen und Raumordnung 2006) provide the most convenient summary of results, though inevitably they are selective, and the commentary here must be still more selective. The final synthesis report noted important shifts from preconceived models of the structures of European territorial development. The dominant image, underpinning much of traditional European regional policy, was of a core and a periphery, a concentric model where disadvantage and poor economic performance increase with physical distance from the heartland region around the Benelux area and the Rhine delta. In the ESDP this core became the pentagon, an area bounded by London, Paris, Milan, Munich, and Hamburg.

ESPON found that the core was spreading along a number of corridors. The existence of several strong urban areas outside the core was highlighted. Those are mainly the capital cities—Madrid, Stockholm, Oslo, Athens, Dublin, Helsinki, Warsaw, and Budapest—but also include Barcelona and Gothenburg. These findings imply important issues for competitiveness and cohesion and for interscalar policy integration. The boom in the capital city regions of countries outside the core helps to narrow gaps at European scale and thus contributes to both competitiveness and cohesion. However, within a nation-state the further growth of the capital is likely to widen the gap between it and the more peripheral regions, undermining cohesion policy. The pattern is especially noticeable in some of the states that became members in 2004.

The research also showed that there are "holes within the pentagon"—places that, although central in European terms, have profiles of disadvantage commonly associated with the periphery. The legacy of deindustrialization still hangs over some of the former manufacturing and coal-mining areas, for example.

In general, ESPON confirmed the importance of urban areas (though its data did not allow intra-urban analysis, which would have revealed some startling discrepancies that disappear in the city-average statistics). The program also made the case for the importance of small and medium-sized towns, however, especially through project 1.4.1 on that theme. Depopulation of less accessible rural areas was also extensively documented, together with the emergence of a post-productive countryside.

Some of the most interesting findings concerned the territorial impacts of sector policies, which are discussed also in chapter 2. Table 1.2 gives a summary picture.

Arguably, the findings from the policy impact studies have a more critical

**TABLE 1.2**

## Territorial Impacts of EU Sector Policies

| Policy | Impact |
|---|---|
| Structural Funds | Help increase territorial cohesion across the EU, but have little impact between regions within a country; however, they can empower local authorities and stimulate regional innovation. |
| Pre-accession aid | Helps increase territorial cohesion at the EU level, but has mixed results at national scale; contributes to institutional capacity building regionally and locally. |
| R&D | Consolidates rather than changes the geographical pattern of R&D at EU and national scales. However, many less favored regions benefit disproportionately from the Framework Programmes. Important benefits to territorial potential at regional and local scales. |
| Transport | Contributes to cohesion in relative terms though absolute gaps may be widened. Pricing policy to reflect full costs of transport will disadvantage remote regions at European and national scales. Underdeveloped regions may benefit from infrastructure improvements. |
| Energy | Network development and market liberalization should improve cohesion, but regions with low self-sufficiency in mainstream energy supplies and high sensitivity to price changes are at risk. Renewables could boost regional economies at the micro scale. |
| Agriculture | Pillar 1 does not currently assist cohesion policy at European scale and nationally. Pillar 2 has some beneficial local-scale impacts, but overall could make a stronger contribution to cohesion across the EU. |
| LEADER | Has developed tangible benefits in lagging regions and vulnerable rural territories. Lessons from LEADER might be transferred to other policy instruments. |
| Fisheries | Funds may contribute to EU cohesion, but are likely to work against cohesion within a country by aiding more prosperous communities most. While the overall picture is complex, Common Fisheries Policies could potentially make a stronger contribution to aiding cohesion. |

**Source:** Böhme et al., 2006, 77.

"edge" to them than the ones from the thematic studies, which largely took a polycentric urban system as the desired end state and offered policy recommendations on how to move to greater polycentricity and balance. In several projects, the policy recommendation sections of the reports were disappointing, or as Rambøll Management (2006, 36) noted, "not always entirely clear." Sometimes they appeared to have been completed in a rush and to offer ideas rather than being built out of scrutiny of evidence and assessment of policy aims and impacts. Overall, ESPON 2002–2006 was primarily an exercise in assembling the evidence relevant to ESDP objectives and developing indicators, typologies, and maps from it. The key message, supported by the evidence, is the title of the final synthesis report, "Territory Matters for Competitiveness and Cohesion."

## Using ESPON Findings

How have the ESPON findings been used? Has ESPON produced a robust base of evidence on which to make territorial policy? To answer these questions, this section looks first at the use made by the Commission of early ESPON findings in producing the third cohesion report (CEC 2004).

### The Third Cohesion Report

In an ideal world, data would be collected, analyzed, and presented for critical interpretation by open-minded policy makers. Real life is somewhat different. The third cohesion report (TCR) was published early in 2004. Its purpose was "to set out the European Commission's vision for the future of Europe's policy to reduce disparities and to promote greater economic, social and territorial cohesion" (CEC 2004, iii). Territorial cohesion had not been identified as a concern of the EU in either of the earlier cohesion reports, which spoke of economic and social cohesion (though it was mentioned in passing in the Treaty of Amsterdam in 1999). This added particular importance to the third report. However, the timetable meant that ESPON findings had to be ready by September 2003 if they were to be used. The previous phase, of Structural Funds, was due to end in 2006, and the adoption of the Lisbon Strategy, and the impending enlargement of the Union, posed fundamental and immediate questions about policy to address territorial disparities. The third cohesion report was important to Europe's "territorial project," but it came along sooner than ESPON would have wished.

ESPON maps made a contribution to the third cohesion report, alongside those provided by much more established data agencies, notably Eurostat. Among the ESPON maps used were "Changes in Population 1996–99" and "Potential Accessibility by Road 2001," "…Rail 2001," and "…Air 2001." However, the schedule for the preparation of the third cohesion report left little or no time for the first round of ESPON projects to get their results out. Most of those projects had only commenced in the second half of 2002, and in less than a year they were being asked for results, though the projects were not planned to end until the spring of 2004.

It is difficult to point to specific aspects of the political settlement made by member states on the Structural Funds 2007–2013 that could be directly and exclusively attributed to ESPON data. Again, policy making rarely runs along such a linear path. ESPON was able to deliver evidence supporting the case that "territory matters," however, and to do so against a very demanding timetable. This more than anything else established the credibility of ESPON and laid the basis for its continuation beyond 2006. However, Bengs has argued that the political rhetoric in the cohesion report overrode academic analysis; he notes, "Rhetoric that generates doubts with regard to the scientific basis of a proposition is not very convincing" (2005, 108). Thus, the evidence base that ESPON had been able to generate in its first year of operation still did not amount to a convincing case to support the successor policies to those advocated in the ESDP.

The Fourth Report on Economic and Social Cohesion (CEC 2007) includes a statement acknowledging the role of ESPON, on an otherwise blank page before the foreword. It says, "The analysis in this report has benefited from the research on accessibility, energy, urban issues and spatial scenarios carried out under the ESPON programme over the period 2000–2006. Community's support for ESPON for 2007–2013 has been increased significantly in recognition of the contribution territorial research can make to a better understanding of territorial trends." Thus ESPON has been able to play a significant role at a critical stage, as the EU grew from 15 to 27 members, a process that involved not only extension of its territory, but also a sharp increase in disparities of living conditions among regions within the Union.

## Building the *Territorial Agenda*

Faludi's introduction provided a succinct discussion of the gestation of the *Territorial Agenda*, and the process is described more fully by Eser and Schmeitz in chapter 10. The findings from ESPON informed the "background paper," *The Territorial State and Perspectives of the European Union.* The important drafting stage of the paper was undertaken during the Luxembourg presidency by people who had been close to—or even directly involved in—ESPON. ESPON was not the only inspiration or evidence base; INTERREG experience figures prominently in the paper. However, it would not be an overstatement to say that ESPON provided an indispensable platform for the construction of the narrative. The paper regularly points up topics where further ESPON research would be valuable.

The contribution ESPON made to *The Territorial State* was not so much a specific empirical finding, a new data set or indicator, or a new map—though it did all of those. More important was the breadth of ESPON's coverage, both spatially and thematically, and the embedding of a pan-European way of viewing Europe's diversity. The result was cumulative rather than an individual "eureka" moment. ESPON underpinned the narrative about regional diversity, while allowing for some order and focus to be laid over that diversity. The political construction and management of that diversity necessarily is at the very heart of the EU project and also of the idea of cohesion. On a continent that spent the twentieth century murderously divided, why and how should very different places work together, share budgets and policies, feel a common identity? Realpolitik makes words like *convergence* and *cohesion* essential in EU discourses, but recognition of diversity as both a reality and an asset is equally essential. The opening paragraph of the ESDP warmly acknowledged Europe's diversity; the plethora of ESPON maps and typologies has helped to articulate just what that diversity means in terms of regional development and potentials.

## National and Regional Governments

How did ESPON see its results being used at spatial scales below the continental? In commenting on the results from projects completed in the first half of the program, ESPON advised, "For policy makers and practitioners, in different policy sectors and at different administrative levels looking at ESPON maps, the challenge is to extract the larger territorial context and get inspiration for including a territorial dimension in further policy development" (ESPON 2005, 14). One can discern some influences from ESPON in documents like the *Medium-Term Urban Development Programme of Budapest 2005–2013* (Budapest Fovaros Onkormanyzata n.d.) and *Development of Regions in Latvia* (State Regional Development Agency 2004). The *National Planning Framework for Scotland*, published in 2004, also reflects a process of raising Euro-awareness begun through the ESDP. The fact that ESPON was operating and beginning to produce comparative European data sustained the work, and the discourse within the *Framework* looks outward from Scotland as well as inward.

The Rambøll Management report (2006) probed the value of ESPON to different user groups and at different spatial scales. It argued that the NUTS 3 scale of ESPON maps meant that they were most useful at the pan-European level and then at the national level. There was some value to policy makers at the regional level, but for planning practitioners working at the local level, the information was simply too coarse to be helpful. There was also some differentiation between countries. For example, NUTS 3 comparisons within the country, as well as across Europe, are valuable in the "big six" countries (France, Germany, Italy, Poland, Spain, and the U.K.) but rather meaningless for the small countries—Luxembourg, Malta, and Cyprus—where there is no internal differentiation on the ESPON maps and tables. However, as the previous quote from ECOTEC Research and Consulting et al. (2004, 51) regarding the project on Structural Funds in urban areas shows, ESPON at NUTS 3 was already working at, and sometimes beyond, the limits of availability of comparable and comprehensive data.

Overall, Rambøll argued that the technical nature of the project reports and their sheer length meant that the prime beneficiaries in terms of added value were scientists, followed at some distance by policy makers, with mainstream planning practitioners getting less benefit still. Language was another important factor. The reports are all in English, so non-English readers need translations or at least summaries in their own language to access them.

The European Council of Spatial Planners (2006, 3) commented on the problems its members had with the ESDP: "Many planning practitioners found it hard to understand the impact on their daily planning activities." The council voiced similar concerns about the idea of territorial cohesion, which suggests that the gap between European-scale concepts and local planning practice is not unique to ESPON. However, part of the problem is that ESPON has largely concentrated on statistics, trends, and spatial analysis and had less to say about processes and policy analysis. The nearest ESPON came to giving how-to advice to local practitioners is perhaps in a table near the end of the final synthesis report. The table drew on findings from a number of ESPON projects, albeit only in one of them was governance the key focus (see table 1.3). It sets out the qualities of "smart public administration" that can deliver livable, sustainable, and competitive places, and the implications of ESPON findings in relation to those qualities.

Arguably, dissemination is a big task. ESPON had two phases. For the first two years, 2002–2004, no final outputs were available; it was difficult to interest policy makers and practitioners—other than DG Regio with its need for findings to use in the TCR—in an empty prospectus. Then although reports began to appear in great volume, they often were not user friendly, so again there were barriers to their use. The synthesis reports (Böhme et al. 2006) and atlas (Bundesamt für Bauwesen und Raumordnung 2006) help, but distilled and succinctly focused national summaries in national languages are probably a prerequisite to reaching any significant number of practitioners. Some countries, including Austria and the Netherlands, and the Flanders region of Belgium are producing such reports.

One problem was that ESPON was uneasy about using in-depth case studies as a research method. This reflected a justifiable concern that case studies can be time consuming, descriptive, and atypical. ESPON's priority was to deliver comprehensive data and indices quickly, but the lack of strong case studies made it more difficult to connect the findings to the level of policy and practice at which most spatial planners operate.

Much of this dissemination task has fallen on the shoulders of the ECPs. ESPON made a small amount of funds available through a competitive tendering process for use in ECP networking. As a starting point, this was very valuable, but follow-up investment by national governments, as well as through ESPON, is necessary to really build the connections. One example of such a network was ESPON Going Regional. This involved two seminars in 2005: one in Belfast, which looked at the implications of ESPON findings for rural and peripheral regions; and the other in London, which did a similar job for urban and metropolitan areas in northwest Europe. Even more innovative was the South-Eastern Europe Perspective (SEEP) seminar put on in Athens by a group led by the ECP for Greece. The seminar was able to reach out and bring planners from the non-EU Balkan states into the discourse about the implications of territorial trends and policies for that broad region of Europe. Nevertheless, a recurring theme from such attempts to bring ESPON findings to practitioners was that previously they had been unaware of ESPON's work.

## ESPON-INTERACT Thematic Studies

A key practical action to build European cooperation has been the INTERREG Community Initiative. It has developed over more than a decade and provides partial funding from the EU to allow partners, usually local authorities, to work together on focused projects that typically run for two to three years. INTERREG was an important vehicle to take forward concepts from the ESDP and put them into practice. Similarly, experience and examples from INTERREG projects figure prominently in *The Territorial State*. Despite their strengths, however, INTERREG

TABLE 1.3

## Elements of Smart Public Administration

| Quality | Europe | National | Regional/Local |
|---|---|---|---|
| Integration and synergy | Some good practices, e.g., the Solidarity Fund after the Elbe floods, attempt to integrate environment into sector polices and link cohesion policy to growth and jobs. However, better integration of a territorial dimension into other policies would be beneficial. | When national priorities coincide with those at EU scale, vertical integration and policy coherence are most likely. | Subsidiarity and a sense of ownership are important for local delivery of policies. Partnerships are important for synergy. Spatial planning practice needs to integrate heritage with a growth and jobs agenda. |
| Innovation and creativity | EU is highly attractive in terms of quality of life—economically, culturally, and environmentally. However, 2007–2013 Structural Funds downgrade cultural projects. | All countries have assets. INTERREG is stimulus for innovative projects. There are opportunities for cooperation around imaginative projects like the Sefarad route. | Culture-led regeneration can play an important role, especially in some weaker regions. There are opportunities to nurture cultural clusters. |
| Conservation of heritage and environmental quality | Natura 2000 is a valuable initiative. However, Europe's natural heritage is under pressure. New guidelines for cohesion recognize that environmental protection underpins economic growth. | There are pressures on the natural environment, especially around the Mediterranean and countries experiencing high growth rates. | Effective spatial planning systems play a key role in conserving heritage and enhancing quality of life. |
| Strategy and vision | ESDP is not championed at the EU level. A territorial strategy is needed for Lisbon/Gothenburg. | Timing and ownership are important, as shown by application of ESDP. | There is a risk of losing cultural and natural heritage assets if plans and policies are not in place. |
| Mobilization and inclusion | Cultural diversity is an important part of Europe's territorial capital. Access to services of general interest is an important territorial cohesion issue, especially in remote rural areas. | Structural Funds and INTERREG mobilize action, but their focus must be relevant to national and regional priorities. National welfare systems largely define social quality. | Participation needs to reach beyond the main public-sector players. Valorizing cultural assets can mobilize communities. |
| Implementation | Effective vertical links are developing, but territorial dimension of sector policies could enhance implementation of territorial cohesion policies. | Different countries are at different stages in move to governance. | This is the key level for partnerships and implementation. |

Source: Böhme et al., 2006, 86.

projects have often found it difficult to work as effective international networks. The INTERACT program was established to try to tackle some of the difficulties and to smooth the path for participants in INTERREG. One of its tasks is to transfer data and initiatives between ESPON and INTERREG projects.

ESPON and INTERACT formally collaborated on a number of thematic topics with the intention of helping to spread data and findings from ESPON to INTERREG projects and to promote ideas for new projects. Thus, through that work with INTERACT, ESPON sought to build links into practice. Due to diverging program agendas and time schedules between INTERREG and ESPON, however, it was not always possible to set up a systematic process of direct cooperation. Most of the spatial visions for the INTERREG program areas were set up around the year 2000, for example, before ESPON started.

The five themes on which ESPON worked with INTERACT were these:

- Transport, communication, and accessibility
- Natural resources and risk management
- Polycentric development and urban-rural relations
- Cross-border cooperation
- Spatial visions and scenarios

It is too soon to assess how much the collaboration has resulted in a transfer of ESPON evidence into policy making through INTERREG projects; such projects typically take over a year to set up and get approved. However, the selection of themes is relevant to the priorities that will steer the allocation of funds for the 2007–2013 INTERREG period. The four priority funding areas for transnational cooperation through INTERREG will be innovation, environment, accessibility, and sustainable urban development. Furthermore, the new program particularly boosts funds for cross-border cooperation projects, reflecting a situation where, since the enlargement of 2004, 59 percent of EU borders are now land borders, compared with only 18.5 percent before that (Bundesamt für Bauwesen und Raumordnung 2006, 56).

In principle, the injection of some of the analytical rigor and hard data from ESPON into INTERREG projects should be beneficial. It is no criticism of INTERREG activists to note that there are times when partnerships have been put together out of enthusiasm and a belief that the potential partners shared an agenda, only to find out that they were not as well matched as they believed. As just one example, in a project concerned with the spatial planning challenges faced by expanding towns, some of the partners are actually grappling with the problems of decline.

## ESPON 2007–2013

At the time of writing, the new ESPON program (Ministère de l'Intérieur et de l'Amenagement du Territoire Luxembourg, ESPON Coordination Unit 2007) had been submitted for the approval of the European Commission. The final version of the program is expected to have a budget of approximately 47 million euro. ESPON 2013 will be part of the new Objective 3 of the European Structural Funds ("Territorial Cooperation") and will continue its role as an observation network for European territorial development.

## The Main Changes

The new ESPON program will run from 2007 to 2013 and thus parallel to the current period of Structure Funds. In its version submitted to the European Commission on 12 January 2007, ESPON 2013 has been divided into five priorities:

1. Applied research on territorial development, competitiveness, and cohesion: evidence on territorial trends, perspectives, and policy impacts

2. Targeted analyses based on user demand: a European perspective on development of different types of territories

3. Scientific platform and tools: territorial indicators and data, analytical tools, and scientific support

4. Capitalization, ownership, and participation: capacity building, dialogue, and networking

5. Technical assistance, analytical support, and communication

In the framework of those program priorities, measures and actions implemented will include the following:

- Cross-thematic and thematic analysis of territorial potentials and challenges, including studies of territorial trends and prospective studies

- Territorial impact of EU policies

- Establishing a knowledge support system consisting of a pool of scientists from various thematic areas

- Targeted and integrated studies and thematic analysis and support to experimental and innovative actions

- Joint actions related to other Structural Funds programs, especially in the Territorial Cooperation Objective

- Spatial European database and data development, including territorial indicators and indexes and a territorial monitoring system and reports

- Synthesis reports, publications, European seminars, and workshops

- Communication strategy, including national dissemination

The management of ESPON 2013 will be very similar to that of ESPON 2006, with Luxembourg as the Managing Authority, a CU, a Monitoring Committee, and a network of ECPs. ESPON 2013 consists of 27 member states and the European Commission, with Switzerland, Norway, Liechtenstein, and Iceland. Additional countries, such as potential candidate states and direct neighboring states, could be involved in the research studies. One of the innovations is that ESPON 2013 will emphasize awareness-raising, for example, through "stakeholder events" with representatives from all administrative levels. This approach has already been used during the making of the *Territorial Agenda.*

Another change is that ESPON 2013 will establish a committee to support the Monitoring Committee in making decisions with regard to research projects. This new committee will mainly propose strategic issues and themes and will provide advice and guidance on the European political agenda. It will consist of the Managing Authority; three members of the Monitoring Committee, representing the countries of the respective current and two following EU presidencies; and a representative from the European Commission.

The scope to undertake targeted analysis based on user demand could prove to be the most important change. Much will depend on just how this will be carried out, but in principle it could lead to more in-depth regional work that could connect better with spatial planning practice. For example, there could be scope to explore the impacts and options of compact city and urban containment policies in the context of the competitiveness and cohesion agenda.

A further innovation will be a system of "task forces" and "sounding boards" which are intended to provide scientific peer-review and practitioner responses to projects. This is a sensible attempt to address weaknesses that became apparent during ESPON 2006.

## An Agenda for Evidence-Based Spatial Planning

Spatial planners should welcome the ESPON 2013 program. It holds promise to build on ESPON 2006 and do more, better, through the increased budget. We should almost certainly expect that the new program will produce innovations in the use and mapping of spatial information and consolidate knowledge and understanding of key spatial trends. It seems likely that ESPON will maintain the close relationship with the Directorate-General for Regional Policy that characterized its first phase. While the prospect of an enlarged and increasingly diverse Monitoring Committee may appear problematic, the risk is more likely to come from individual countries disaffected by some aspects of ESPON's work than through concerted political intervention from the Monitoring Committee as a whole. With the *Territorial Agenda* adopted, ESPON is likely to have an increasingly important and focused role as a source of data for monitoring territorial developments and impacts.

In this sense the success of ESPON has been an ability to respond adroitly to the political force field in which it is situated. However, as Bengs (2006) and Hague (2006) have argued, that success has perhaps come at a price, particularly in terms of rigorous academic critique of some key concepts and policy stances. The midterm evaluation of ESPON 2006 argued that ESPON's budget would allow it only to "pose new questions" but not to "provide the depth of study required" (MVA Consultancy 2003, 42). Similarly, Rambøll Management (2006) pointed to the need to be more focused and rigorous in ensuring the quality of the reports. Hopefully, some of the enlarged budget will be used to buy this extra depth.

What might be an agenda for evidence-based spatial planning in the context of ESPON 2013, the *Territorial Agenda*, the new funds for territorial cooperation, and the territorial dynamics revealed by the ESPON 2006 projects? A crucial need will be to make the idea of territorial cohesion robust and operable. The European Council of Spatial Planners (2006, 1) has commented, "If the objective of territorial cohesion must be achieved by territorial development, territorial or spatial planners should be given a clear definition of territorial cohesion, clarifying what qualities or properties make a region coherent. We strongly recommend that the notion of territorial cohesion is elaborated in such a way that planning practitioners get practical tools to achieve that goal in their daily work in advising politicians and preparing spatial planning proposals."

The *Territorial State* paper makes it clear that there is no support of a top-down territorial cohesion policy or new procedures. Instead, the priority is to raise awareness of the territorial dimension of EU policies and to increase their integration and coherence. Thus, another key requirement for ESPON is likely to be to consolidate and apply methods of territorial impact assessment, the topic discussed by Böhme and Eser in chapter 2.

The territorial aspects of the Lisbon-Gothenburg agenda fundamentally revolve around labor and housing markets. These are the issues that centrally confront many practicing planners every day—how to meet housing needs while protecting environments and trying to make sustainable transport options viable. At a time when countries are waking up to the need for international action to curb emissions that contribute to climate change, a topic of Schmidt-Thomé and Greiving in chapter 6, there is an important opportunity for European research to move beyond the descriptive statistics and really analyze the territorial development options. Such work may be driven forward through other avenues, such as the Framework Programme for Research sponsored by the EU. However, if the major, dedicated spatial planning program in Europe fails to focus on issues of spatial planning for sustainable settlements, it will leave a vacuum at its core.

## Conclusions

This chapter has acknowledged that ESPON is a groundbreaking program that has advanced the cause of spatial planning within Europe. Its maps, indicators, and data have made it possible to construct a credible narrative about the need for a territorial dimension in European policy making. However, the chapter has also shown important limitations on what ESPON has been able to achieve. ESPON has not reached out beyond the policy elite—in particular, the Directorate-General for Regional Policy—to create awareness of territorial dynamics and impacts. Policy analysis should be more central to the work, and there need to be better dissemination and clearer guidance to the wider spatial planning community and beyond that to the public. Nevertheless, the work done in ESPON helps build a sense of European identity and provide a stronger evidence base for policy in Europe, at a time when policy in some other parts of the globe seems to be increasingly based on conviction or theocracy.

## References

Bengs, C. 2002. Introduction: Facing ESPON. In *Facing ESPON* (Nordregio Report 2002:1), C. Bengs, ed., 1–18. Stockholm: Nordregio.

———. 2005. Policy relevant research in the EU: A researcher's view. In *International conference: Present and future of the European Spatial Development Perspective* (in Italian and English), P. Boscaino, ed. Florence, Italy: Alina.

———. 2006. ESPON in context. *European Journal of Spatial Development* (October). http://www.nordregio.se/EJSD/debate061023.pdf.

Böhme, K., S. Davoudi, C. Hague, P. Mehlbye, J. Robert, and P. Schön. 2006. *Territory matters for competitiveness and cohesion: Facets of regional diversity and potentials in Europe* (*ESPON Synthesis Report III*, Autumn 2006). Luxembourg: ESPON Coordination Unit.

Budapest Fovaros Onkormanyzata. N.d. *The Podmaniczky Programme 2005–2013: Medium-term urban development programme of Budapest* (in Hungarian and English). Budapest: Budapest Fovaros Onkormanyzata.

Bundesamt für Bauwesen und Raumordnung (BBR). 2003. *Crete Guidance Paper: ESPON Coordination towards August 2003*. Bonn: BBR. www.espon.eu/mmp/online/website/content/projects/161/index_EN.html.

———. 2006. *ESPON Atlas: Mapping the structure of the European Territory*. Bonn: BBR. www.espon.eu/mmp/online/website/content/publications/98/1235/index_EN.html.

CEC (Commission of the European Communities). 1991. *Europe 2000: Outlook for the development of the community's territory*. Luxembourg: Office for Official Publications of the European Communities.

———. 1994. *Europe 2000+: Co-operation for European territorial development*. Luxembourg: Office for Official Publications of the European Communities.

———. 1997. *The EU compendium on spatial planning systems and policies*. Luxembourg: Office for Official Publications of the European Communities.

———. 1999. *European Spatial Development Perspective: Towards balanced and sustainable development of the European Union*. Luxembourg: Office for Official Publications of the European Communities.

———. 2004. *A new partnership for cohesion: Convergence, competitiveness, cooperation* (third report on economic and social cohesion). Luxembourg: Office for Official Publications of the European Communities.

———. 2007. *Growing Regions, growing Europe* (fourth report on economic and social cohesion). Luxembourg: Office for Official Publications of the European Communities.

ECOTEC Research and Consulting et al. 2004. *ESPON Action 2.2.3: Territorial effects of the Structural Funds in urban areas: A final report to the ESPON Co-ordination Unit*. www.espon.eu/mmp/online/website/content/projects/243/351/index_EN.html.

ESPON. 2005. *In search of territorial potentials: Mid-term results by spring 2005*. Luxembourg: ESPON.

European Council of Spatial Planners. 2006. *ECTP comment on the first draft (28 August) of the Territorial State of the European Union document*. www.ceu-ectp.org/inc/cgi/dd/dd20061002.pdf.

Faludi, A., ed. 2002. *European spatial planning*. Cambridge, MA: Lincoln Institute of Land Policy.

Faludi, A., and B. Waterhout. 2002. *The making of the European Spatial Development Perspective: No masterplan*. RTPI Library Series. London: Routledge.

Geological Survey of Finland et al. 2006. *ESPON Project 2.4.1: Territorial trends and policy impacts in the field of EU environmental policy: Final report*. www.espon.eu/mmp/online/website/content/projects/243/383/file_2748/fr-2.4.1_Dec2006-full.pdf.

Hague, C. 2006. ESPON and territorial research and practice in Europe. In *European territorial research in progress: Conference proceedings of the first ESPON scientific conference*, 23–35. Luxembourg: ESPON.

Hague, C., and K. Kirk. 2003. *Polycentricity scoping study*. London: Office of the Deputy Prime Minister.

Ministère de l'Intérieur et de l'Amenagement du Territoire Luxembourg, ESPON Coordination Unit. 2007. *ESPON 2013 Programme. European observation network on territorial development and cohesion*. Third version resubmitted on 16 July 2007 for the approval of the European Commission. Luxembourg: ESPON. http://www.espon.eu/mmp/online/website/content/programme/1145/index_EN.html.

MVA Consultancy. 2003. *Mid-term evaluation of the ESPON 2006 programme: Final report*. http://www.espon.eu/mmp/online/website/content/programme/125/file_392/fr_mid-term_eval-full.pdf.

Newman, P., and A. Thornley. 1996. *Urban planning in Europe*. London: Routledge.

Prezioso, M. 2007. Why the ESPON programme is concerned more with "policy implications" than with "good science." *European Journal of Spatial Development* (March). http://www.nordregio.se/EJSD/debate070312.pdf.

Rambøll Management. 2006. *Study on "territorial cohesion, lessons learned from the ESPON programme projects and strategy for the future": Final report*. http://www.espon.eu/mmp/online/website/content/programme/1186/file_2380/final_report_espon_study.pdf.

Richardson, T., and O. Jensen. 2000. Discourses of mobility and polycentric development: A contested view of European spatial planning. *European Planning Studies* 8 (4): 503–520.

State Regional Development Agency. 2004. *Development of regions in Latvia*. Riga: State Regional Development Agency.

Strubelt, W., H-P. Gatzweiler, and R. Kaltenbrunner, eds. 2001. *Study programme on European spatial planning: Final report*. Bonn: Bundesamt für Bauwesen und Raumordnung.

Waterhout, B. 2002. Polycentric development: What is behind it? In *European spatial planning*, A. Faludi, ed., 83–103. Cambridge, MA: Lincoln Institute of Land Policy.

Williams, R. H. 1996. *European Union spatial policy and planning*. London: Paul Chapman.

# CHAPTER 2

# Territorial Impact Analysis of EU Policies

Kai Böhme and Thiemo W. Eser

The concept of territorial impact analysis (TIA) has been brought into the European debate as part of the cooperation around the *European Spatial Development Perspective* (ESDP). TIA has its roots in the tradition of obligatory spatial impact assessments in, for example, Austria (*Raumverträglichkeitsprüfung*) and Germany (*Raumordnungsverfahren*). Similar procedures exist under different names in Portugal, in the Walloon region of Belgium, and as part of environmental impact assessment (EIA) in Finland. In those countries TIA has a rather long national tradition and is used for assessing the impact of proposed spatial developments against the spatial policy concepts or goals for the area in question. In principle, TIA includes all aspects of spatial planning, the prospective and comprehensive shaping of a certain area by means of plans, as well as the ad hoc evaluation of projects as regards their effects on spatial structures (see Schindegger 2001). At a certain point the necessity of distinguishing between the terms *territorial impact analysis* for policies and *territorial impact assessment* for programs and projects was discussed; it appears that in a policy context, the literature, and daily practice, however, the term *territorial impact assessment* is used for both.

The ESDP opened the discussion of TIA at the European level, but it did not define what is meant by a TIA, restricting itself to suggesting that TIA might be useful in the context of large infrastructure projects and in the development of integrated strategies for the management of environmentally sensitive areas. Later on, at an informal ministerial meeting during the Finnish EU presidency in 1999, TIA became a topic of the ESDP Action Programme. In the course of implementing that program the U.K. delegation assumed responsibility for taking the question of TIA forward, and the idea gradually developed of TIA as a tool for assessing the impact of spatial developments against spatial policy objectives or prospects for an area.

From that point on, the discussion focused on TIA for policies, a tool to be developed and tested in the framework of ESPON. Indeed, the ESPON program asked for methods of TIA of EU sector policies and initiated a number of projects

The chapter expresses the personal views of the authors and not necessarily the institutions they are affiliated with.

in that field. In that context the critical task was to establish suitable assessment criteria to recognize the broad positive and negative effects of the proposed activities, as well as the implications of strategies of development plans and the interrelationships (and possible secondary effects) of supported actions. A key task was identifying what those effects might be in practice and over what distances they might occur. In this respect, TIA may be seen as a mechanism by which to appraise the positive and negative externalities of the activities being assessed. The main purpose of this exercise was to inform policy makers about the territorial effects of their policies.

At the ministerial meetings in Rotterdam in November 2004 and in Luxembourg in May 2005 the ministers decided to elaborate an evidence-based document, *The Territorial State and Perspectives of the European Union*, which should "offer EU institutions, Member States, regions and other stakeholders a better common insight into the territorial state and development perspectives of the European Union, and provide a clear and comprehensive information base and future spatial orientations to address key challenges and opportunities" (see Luxembourg EU Presidency 2005, 2). The final version of the document presented at the ministerial meeting in Leipzig in May 2007 included elements of EU policy impact assessments based on ESPON results. In the main, the political debate led to the *Territorial Agenda* for the EU endorsed in Leipzig (see the introduction and chapter 10 of this volume), not to any deepening of a formal track for TIA in the regulatory framework. However, the interest and demand on the political level are apparent, as not in the *Territorial Agenda* but in the Leipzig *Presidency Conclusions* (point 8) reference is made to the possibility of considering the effects on European legislation of existing institutions and procedures such as impact assessment.

Summing up, a distinct difference between the existing national models and the TIA as discussed at the European level is that national experiences and traditions focus on the territorial effects of projects, whereas the European debate addresses the territorial effects of policies. Therefore, efforts are being made to define and develop an understanding of TIAs of European policies. In this context a systematic approach to recognizing the territorial effects of policies and integrating them into policy processes needs to be considered.

## Lessons of ESPON Studies on Selected Policy Sectors

EU policies influence territorial development in Europe in many different ways (see Böhme 2006; Van Ravesteyn and Evers 2004). Often the effects are unintended and indirect—for example, through leverages on national policies. The more direct territorial impacts of a number of EU policies have been studied in the framework of ESPON through a series of applied research projects. As mentioned above, the type of assessment and the procedure differed widely, which is reflected in the results.

The particular EU policy fields assessed were agriculture, energy, environment, fishery, pre-accession aid, research and development, the Structural Funds, and transport. Below, selected results of some of the studies will be discussed; most

**TABLE 2.1**

# Main Features of Selected ESPON Studies

| Policy | Type of Effects Addressed | Method Applied |
|---|---|---|
| Common Agricultural Policy | Observable changes in economic, social, and environmental conditions | Ex-post assessment based on the geography and type of CAP support plus case studies |
| Structural Funds | Direct and indirect contributions of Structural Funds to different aspects of polycentricity and territorial cohesion at micro, meso, and macro scales | Ex-post assessment based on the geography of spending plus case studies |
| Trans-European Networks | The effects of transport policies on the increase in GDP per capita | Ex-ante evaluation of planned actions based on different types of modeling |

concentrated on ex-post assessment of the territorial impacts of the respective policies. Indeed, only the study on transport policies approaches an ex-ante assessment. The single studies were followed up by an exercise proposing an overall approach to ex-ante territorial impact assessment of EU policies, the so-called TEQUILA model (ULB/ESPON 3.2 2006).

Territorial impacts can take many forms and be understood in many different ways. As mentioned above, any impact assessment needs to identify the objectives against which the policy is to be assessed. In the case of ESPON studies of territorial impacts, the objectives have been defined by European territorial policies, which appear to be an ambiguous and moving target, starting with the ESDP and currently culminating in the *Territorial Agenda* (see chapter 10; Böhme and Schön 2006).

Accordingly, the biggest issues for most of the approaches have been (1) the development of a methodology that operationalizes the idea of territorial impacts and thus translates EU territorial policies into measurable objectives; and (2) the collection of necessary data from all across the EU at a sufficiently detailed geographical level.

The discussion of the selected ESPON studies addresses their results as well as the kinds of effects considered and the methodology used. It also raises the question of how territorial policies and their impacts are measured. A first overview of the main features of the three selected studies is provided in table 2.1.

## Territorial Impacts of the Common Agricultural Policy

About 45 percent of EU expenditure at present is on agriculture. The European Common Agricultural Policy (CAP) is politically important and, as usual in such cases, a challenging subject for any kind of systematic assessment. In the debate about the CAP, different voices can be heard, illustrating the wide range of perceptions of this policy in terms of its efficiency; its effectiveness; its beneficiaries; and its impact on agricultural production, the environment, rural economies, and society. Indeed, CAP features regularly on the news with regard to negotiations over EU budgets and reforms (see Shucksmith, Roberts, and Thomson 2006).

Given the diversity of viewpoints and related assessments, performing a TIA of this policy has not been easy. The CAP consists of two major fields of intervention, called pillars: Pillar 1 on market support and direct payment to producers, and Pillar 2 on agri-environmental and rural development expenditure. Because of their different aims and natures, it has been considered necessary to keep the pillars apart. In addition, there is a variety of more small-scale instruments and actions, such as Community Initiatives LEADER+, that deserve looking into.

A rough attempt to summarize the results of the ESPON project on the territorial impact of the CAP and rural development policy in three points might read as follows (University of Aberdeen/ESPON 2.1.3 2005):

1. **CAP Pillar 1 goes to richer regions in the core of Europe.** Pillar 1 provides market support and direct payment to producers. The policy instruments within Pillar 1 strongly reflect the agrocentric ethos that has dominated CAP throughout its history. Until recently, passing reference has been made to the role of agriculture in the food chain rather than to its links within territories. CAP Pillar 1 does not support territorial cohesion; higher levels of CAP expenditure per hectare of agricultural land are strongly associated with more prosperous regions. Pillar 1 appears to favor core areas more than the periphery of Europe, while at a local level CAP favors the more accessible areas. The strong tendency for Pillar 1 support to go to richer regions of the 15 EU member states at the time may be attributed to their larger farms, their location in the core of Europe, and their farm type. This is supported by economic studies showing that the basic market price instrument of Pillar 1 is regressive and tends to accrue disproportionately to intensive large-scale farms.

2. **CAP Pillar 2 does not support cohesion.** Pillar 2 comprises agri-environmental and other rural development expenditure and demonstrates that there has been some integration of policies in the agricultural and environment sectors. Often seen as a fundamental move toward a more integrated rural development policy, it might correspond better to territorial cohesion than Pillar 1 does. Although the evidence on Pillar 2 is mixed and the Rural Development Regulation (RDR) of the CAP is a cohesion measure, expenditure under the RDR does not appear to support cohesion objectives, as it favors the more economically viable and growing areas of the EU. Generally, Pillar 2 measures have the potential of accommodating regional strategies on the national level and thus of contributing to territorial cohesion, but to date that potential does not appear to have been fully utilized.

3. **Initiatives to support local processes are most effective for rural development.** The evaluations of Community Initiatives LEADER II and the midterm evaluation of LEADER+ suggest that such initiatives have a considerable impact on the development of rural regions, although their budgets are small compared to those of mainstream program instruments. The LEADER is an

instrument to stimulate processes in the local economy, thereby leading to indirect but enduring benefits, highlighting the importance of local entrepreneurship, among others.

Summing up, the territorial impacts of CAP are largely unsupportive of territorial cohesion in Europe, although there is scope in the given instruments to do more in that direction. Furthermore, analysis of the instruments and expenditures of CAP excludes the largest component of the support received by EU farmers, the higher prices paid by consumers within the EU. That support is estimated by the OECD to amount to 56 billion euro (see Shucksmith, Roberts, and Thomson 2006).

These findings of the ESPON project on the territorial impact of the CAP and rural development policy (University of Aberdeen/ESPON 2.1.3 2005) result from an approach based on expenditure and farm size figures, which are processed in correlation analysis.

## Territorial Policy Aims and Operationalization

The overall objectives of the third cohesion report—balanced competitiveness, social and economic cohesion, and sustainability at macro, meso, and micro levels—have been taken to represent the territorial policy aims against which CAP impacts have been assessed.

From an economic point of view, the discussion on competitiveness suggests that overall territorial cohesion will be attained only by accepting, and adjusting to, the diminishing role of agriculture in many areas. A spatial planning perspective must therefore identify alternative uses of land, buildings, and people (human resources) within "territories" and help to design region-specific plans, regulations, and fiscal systems that encourage the necessary adjustments.

For the statistical analysis, three cohesion indicators have been identified: the GDP per inhabitant and the unemployment rate in 1999, and population changes between 1995 and 1998.

## Measurement of CAP Effects

To start with, a number of key hypotheses were developed regarding the territorial impact of CAP and the RDR. A key issue arising from that was the importance of differentiating between types of policy instruments that constitute the CAP and RDR because (1) they have played a distinct role within CAP reform processes; and (2) they include different objectives and are expected to have given rise to territorially distinct effects. In particular, it was found necessary to separately analyze Pillar 1 and Pillar 2 of CAP, the former relating more closely to the production activities of farmers, while the latter is the rural development pillar. Within Pillar 1, it seemed important to consider separately the territorial incidences and impacts of market price supports and direct income payments, while—in addition to the analysis of total Pillar 2 support—support via the Less Favored Areas scheme and agri-environmental measures was also analyzed separately.

Based on the hypotheses mentioned, a statistical analysis has been carried out to assess the geographical distribution of incidences of CAP support and the extent to which changes in the CAP have been associated with observable changes in the economic, social, and environmental conditions in areas at the NUTS 3 level or its equivalent. This has been augmented by findings from previous studies from across the EU considering the spatial effects of the CAP and RDR. In order to study the potential model, the CAPRI model was disaggregated from the NUTS 2 to the NUTS 3 level and then analyzed, using mapping and linear regression techniques with respect to the EU's social and economic cohesion objectives (see Shucksmith, Roberts, and Thomson 2006).

In order to study the relationship between the CAPRI impact measures and the EU's social and economic cohesion objectives, the CAPRI results were apportioned from NUTS 2 to NUTS 3. Three CAPRI measures of policy impact were considered in this analysis: CAP direct (premium) payments, farm income calculated as gross value added (GVA) plus CAP premium payments, and global warming potential (expressed in terms of $CO_2$ equivalents).

## Territorial Impacts of European Regional Policies

Traditionally, European regional policies—in particular, the Structural Funds—are considered one of the most important instruments for the European Commission to influence regional, and thus also territorial, development. However, most of the programs in this policy field are socioeconomic programs. Earlier studies (e.g., Polverari and Bachtler 2005) have shown that the Structural Funds demonstrate little territorial awareness and what awareness they do demonstrate is rather by coincidence than on purpose.

Thus, assessing the degree to which European regional policy contributes to achieving the territorial aims of the EU was tricky, as it could be understood as assessing the internal coherence of European regional policies as such. However, an assessment of the degree to which the 1994–1999 Structural Funds have contributed to territorial cohesion also implies analyzing policies against a policy goal that did not exist when the programs and measures were created. Indeed, the Structural Funds tend to gradually develop more territorial awareness, and the funding period 2007–2013 has more to offer than the two periods before (see Polverari and McMaster 2006). Because of data constraints and the timing of the ESPON study, however, the ex-post assessment had to consider the period 1994–1999.

Summarizing the results of the ESPON project on the territorial effects of the Structural Funds (Nordregio/ESPON 2.2.1 2006) in three points might go as follows:

1. **Correlation exists between Structural Funds and regional cross-border cohesion.** In general terms poor regions received more funding than rich regions. However, there is no clear correlation between funding and economic performance. At the same time, the correlation between Structural Funds spending and increasing regional cross-border economic cohesion seems to be

fairly strong. The largest per capita spending occurred along regional borders where relative economic growth was positive on both sides of the border.

2. **Urban areas outside the core of Europe benefit most from Structural Funds**. Funding is mainly targeted toward urbanized areas. Focusing on urban areas that are of importance at the macro level, it becomes obvious that those beyond the core received substantially more assistance than those inside. Indeed, about 30 percent of funding went to areas that strengthen the European polycentric pattern.

3. **Structural Funds have leverage effects on national and regional policies and local governance practices**. The indirect and qualitative impact is likely to be more interesting than the impact on economic performance. The typology of the interrelation between national and regional policy shows a clear core-periphery picture, with policies separated from each other in the core of Europe and more related policies in the peripheral parts. The countries where European and national regional policies show a high degree of similarity are also the countries where the share of Structural Funds with respect to the regions' GDP is highest. It can be argued that the amount of Structural Funds allocated to a country matters as regards the leverage effect on national and regional policies. However, leverage effects on governance and learning can also be seen in other areas. Furthermore, institutional capacity is important.

Summing up, the main objectives of the EU Structural Funds 1994–1999 were to reduce disparities in GDP and unemployment between regions. In doing that, the Structural Funds contributed to territorial cohesion by stimulating regional and local innovation and development. However, they did so less consistently than might have been anticipated. Data for the 1994–1999 period (the last period for which comprehensive figures could be collected) revealed a complex picture in which money went to less favored parts of the EU overall, but differences between regions within a country were left largely unaffected or even accentuated (ESPON 2006b).

Furthermore, there is evidence that the funds have boosted competitiveness through leverage effects on national policies and by empowering local and regional levels of governance, resulting in innovation, strategic planning, and new partnerships.

These findings of the ESPON project on the territorial effects of the Structural Funds (Nordregio/ESPON 2.2.1 2006) result from the analysis of expenditure figures against territorial development features at three different geographical levels: the European (macro), the transnational or national (meso), and the regional (micro).

## Territorial Policy Aims and Operationalization

The key territorial policy aims against which the EU Structural Funds have been assessed are territorial cohesion and polycentric development. Territorial cohesion has been understood as an umbrella concept and as an integral part of the cohesion process, covering the territorial aspects of cohesion and the EU objectives of balanced and sustainable development and addressing the potential, the position, and the relative situation of a geographical entity. The concept of polycentricity has been operationalized by addressing (1) the morphology in the form of settlement patterns; (2) the transportation links and accessibility; (3) the functional socioeconomic specialization; and (4) the cooperation between actors in different geographical entities.

The project has put a lot of emphasis on the three-level approach, acknowledging that territorial aims should be operationalized differently at the European, the transnational or national, and the regional levels. As this differentiation also relates to the assessment of impacts, the policy concepts have been operationalized in further detail for each of the three levels (see Nordregio/ESPON 2.2.1 2006, 28–30).

## Measurement of the Effects of Structural Funds

Territorial effects have been understood by the project as the effects a specific policy intervention has on the position and development of a specific territory. These take the form of either direct effects, discernible among those directly targeted by the intervention or investment in question, or indirect effects, discernible among those who have not been directly targeted by the intervention or investment in question.

In order to assess those effects, the territorial dimension of Structural Funds spending between 1994 and 1999 has been assessed. In addition, case studies on specific regions have been conducted.

The most time-consuming task was to collect and partly calculate the data on spending under the Structural Funds between 1994 and 1999 at regional levels (NUTS 2 and NUTS 3). The analysis of the data as such already suggested first conclusions as regards the funding per capita, the total funding in euros, and the funding as a share of the GDP.

To see the degree to which the geography of spending supports territorial cohesion at the macro, meso, and micro levels, the spending data have been assessed against other ESPON data sets, namely, GDP, accessibility, the rural-urban typology, and the urban system. This simple approach allowed for easily comprehensible insights into whether the spending supports areas with the potential to contribute to a more balanced and polycentric development at European, transnational or national, and regional levels.

Data on the economic development of regions, in terms of changes of GDP, have been used to provide a simple overview of the coincidences between the development of GDP during the funding period and the amount of funding.

In particular, the assessment against the data sets on the European urban system has been interesting in determining whether major urban agglomerations outside the core have been supported more per capita than those in the center. In a similar way, the support given to balanced development at the national level has been studied by assessing the share of spending going to secondary metropolitan areas in a country.

## Territorial Impacts of European Transport Policies

Transport infrastructure is widely considered an important instrument for promoting regional development. Many regional development discussions focus on infrastructure and the access to motorways and high-speed rail networks, as well as secondary transport networks. At a European scale the level of accessibility is considered to play a significant role in determining the potential for more polycentric territorial development. In polycentric urban systems at national and regional scales, a functional division of labor exists between cities, between higher-level centers and lower-level centers in individual regions, and between cities at the same levels in the urban hierarchy. This implies that the channels of interaction—and therefore the connections—between cities of equal size and rank should be good.

Independently from the spatial approach to accessibility, the European transport policy has its own aims and logic, mainly addressing the effectiveness and efficiency of transportation throughout Europe. The white paper "European Transport Policy for 2020: Time to Decide" (CEC 2001) sets out the foundations of the European policy on Trans-European Networks (TEN), raising also the issues of real transportation costs (including the costs of accidents, environmental damage, noise, congestion, etc.).

A TIA of European transport policies needs to bring together the "territorial logic" of transport networks as a means for regional development with the "sector logic" of efficient and effective transportation and its real costs. The ESPON project on the territorial impact of EU transport and TEN policies (Christian-Albrechts-Universität zu Kiel/ESPON 2.1.1 2005) has done that for an ex-ante assessment of the European TEN and Transport Infrastructure Needs Assessment (TINA) policies. ESPON developed scenarios based on different assumptions about the implementation of all projects envisaged and the introduction of transport pricing. The following attempts to present the main findings in three points (for more on this issue see chapter 5):

1. **European transport investments contribute to cohesion in relative, not absolute, terms**. All scenarios contribute to convergence in relative terms in both accessibility and GDP per capita, except pricing scenarios that make transport more expensive. However, in absolute terms the opposite holds true: In all scenarios the gap in accessibility and GDP between the rich regions in the European core and the poorer regions at the European periphery increases.

2. **European polycentricity will increase in the east.** The polycentricity of the European urban system has increased in the past and is likely to increase in the future as large cities in the member states that joined in 2004 and 2007 catch up with cities in western Europe. Polycentricity of the European urban system will mainly grow in the new member states; it will decline in western Europe because of the continued growth of the largest cities. Polycentricity of national urban systems in Europe has declined in the past and is likely to continue to do so. Transport infrastructure policies accelerate the decline in polycentricity of national urban systems because they tend to be directed at well-connected large

urban centers. Pricing scenarios that make transport generally more expensive strengthen the polycentricity of national urban systems.

3. **Road transport is increasing in the east and rural areas**. The European core area holds a share of 39 percent of kilometers traveled in the ESPON space; in 2020 that share will decline to around 35 percent. Urban regions experience a heavier traffic load, but the load in rural areas is increasing. Accession countries have the highest relative gain in road transport. Regions near railway corridors that transport a large volume show disproportional lower relative transport flow increases than other regions.

This is a very limited reflection on an extremely rich study that presents a series of different scenarios on what the territorial impacts of the planned European transport policy measures could be. In general, the study shows that overall EU transport investments do contribute to cohesion in relative terms, although they may actually widen the absolute economic gap between regions. The TEN transport infrastructure projects planned for the period up to 2020 have a decentralizing effect and so favor peripheral regions. However, even large increases in regional accessibility produce only small benefits in terms of regional economic activity. Quite simply, transport is only one of many factors that influence the socioeconomic development of a region (ESPON 2006b).

As mentioned above, these findings on the territorial impact of EU transport and TEN policies (Christian-Albrechts-Universität zu Kiel/ESPON 2.1.1 2005) result from an approach based on a series of scenarios. For each of the scenarios specific assumptions about the implementation of TEN and TINA projects and the introduction of transport pricing have been made. Based on those assumptions, the changes in accessibility, as well as the impact on economic development (i.e., income change in GDP per capita), have been calculated.

Improved accessibility stimulates economic growth only modestly. Large increases in regional accessibility translate into only very small increases in regional economic activity. Infrastructure policies have larger effects than pricing policies, and the magnitude of the effect is related to the number and size of projects. Generally, the overall effects of transport infrastructure investments and other transport policies are small compared to those of socioeconomic and technical macro trends, such as globalization, increasing competition between cities and regions, the aging of the population, shifting labor force participation, and increases in labor productivity.

## Territorial Policy Aims and Operationalization

Territorial cohesion has been taken as the policy aim against which the impacts of transport policies have been assessed. That aim has been translated in terms of spatial income distribution. Thus, the territorial cohesion of GDP per capita is the main aspect looked into to assess the territorial impacts of European transport policy. This has again been a matter of equal distribution that has been analyzed for five different alternatives:

- Coefficient of variation (percent)
- Gini coefficient (percent)
- Geometric/arithmetic mean
- Correlation relative change versus level
- Correlation absolute change versus level

## Measurement of Transport Policy Effects

The project looked at three specific effects of infrastructure—in particular, the high-level infrastructure of the Trans-European Networks. The quality of the infrastructure at the level of the region, especially at the NUTS 3 level, depends as much on access to the network as on the quality of the network.

With regard to the development of the network by means of European transport policies, the project has developed 13 scenarios indicating different stages of development of European rail and road infrastructure and the introduction of transport pricing. For each of those scenarios, the effect of transport policy interventions on development of GDP per capita has been calculated; the project applied three models to forecast the regional economic impacts and cohesion effects of transport and telecommunication policies (ESPON 2006a):

1. The SASI model is a multiregional recursive-dynamic model of the socioeconomic development of NUTS 3 regions based on production functions.

2. The CG-Europe model is a multiregional, territorial, computable, general equilibrium model of regional economic development at the NUTS 3 level, in which transport costs appear as expenditures for transport and business travel.

3. In addition, the STIMA model assesses the impact of information and communication technologies on regional economic growth and distribution at the NUTS 2 level, based on regional production functions.

## Paving the Way for a General TIA Methodology

Starting more or less from zero, ESPON has made considerable progress in developing TIAs of EU sector policies. Among the overall achievements of ESPON in addition to the individual studies are discussions of (1) the minimum requirements for TIA generally; and (2) possible overall models for future TIAs.

Based on the experimental TIAs performed in the framework of ESPON and on additional experiences gained from national-level impact assessment procedures and the strategic environmental assessment (SEA), ESPON Project 3.1 (BBR/ESPON 3.1 2005) has developed a set of minimum requirements for TIAs (see table 2.2), which will certainly prove useful for future discussions.

The ESPON project on spatial scenarios (ULB/ESPON 3.2 2006) went one step further and developed a TIA model, called TEQUILA. This is a multicriteria model synthesizing multiple impact assessment results from other ESPON projects. The proposed econometric model results in a Territorial Impact Model (TIM) assessing the impact of the policy considered on single regions. As shown in table 2.3, the potential impact per region and criterion (given by specific studies or calculated according to "policy intensity" in each region) is multiplied by two terms expressing the specificity of the single regions and their sensitivity to a specific impact: a vulnerability term, determined mainly by geographical conditions, and a desirability term, expressed by a socioeconomic utility function. Given the present data availability, TIM can be applied at the NUTS 3 level, and the results can be easily mapped.

These two initiatives take the experience from single TIA studies carried out by ESPON to a higher level by transforming them into general approaches to TIA. However, none of them can overcome one of the major challenges many TIA exercises will continue to face: the availability of regionalized information on policy measures, inputs, and actions.

Overall the TIA studies carried out by ESPON demonstrate that they can deliver interesting insights and provide food for thought regarding the effects of EU policies. Taken together they also provoke thoughts about the interplay between and the supplementing, reinforcing, and contradictory effects of different EU policies. Indeed, every European territory (region, city, etc.) is subject to a specific combination of EU policy measures, which have diverse effects and also interact with territorial preconditions and how they affect the development of regions in Europe. Little is known about the interaction between policies and the way that interaction corresponds to territorial preconditions. So the ESPON TIAs have opened up important issues for policy making and contributed to the discussion on the costs of noncoordination between policy sectors.

The EU *Territorial Agenda* bases a considerable amount of its background information work on findings derived from ESPON projects (see chapter 10, as well as Böhme and Schön 2006). Indeed, evidence of the effects of recent policies can help policy makers to formulate informed decisions about future policies. Smart policy making means not only maximizing benefits within single sectors, but also achieving suitable policy mixes and helpful spin-offs for other EU priorities. Of particular interest in this context are the ex-ante assessments of policies.

Certainly, the work carried out under ESPON is only a first step toward delivering the necessary information on territorial impacts of policies. The above discussion has also shown that considerable efforts are still needed to develop both the overall approaches to territorial impacts of EU policies and tailor-made elements within those approaches targeting specific policy sectors.

However, the key question remains how to best position a TIA in the policy process. Keeping in mind that ESPON should contribute to policy making, answering that question should give appropriate guidance as to the further development of TIA methodology, a development that goes beyond the pure academic interest of improving the methodology.

**TABLE 2.2**

# TIA Minimum Requirements

Scoping

(a)    **What is causing the impacts?**
Definition of the policy intervention(s) concerned: registered input dimension,
e.g., EIB grants for rail network element development, R&D support grant, direct income payment for farmers, ERDF expenditures cofinancing government aids or public investments
⊃ *Min: designation of policy intervention(s) actually recorded (assignable to EU budget lines)*

(b)    **What is changed by the intervention(s)?**
Subject(s) effected, basis: hypothesis concerning cause-effect relations (with, of course, varying empirical proof),
e.g., economic growth caused by improved accessibility, increased innovation capacity by new R&D jobs, lower unemployment by subsidizing farms, increasing GDP per capita by ERDF expenditures
⊃ *Min: designation of hypothesis concerning cause-effect relations*

(c)    **Which territorial level of observation?**
Geographic reference: territories concerned (intervention/effect), territorial level(s) of observation, covering all, or selection (by what criteria),
e.g., NUTS 5, 4, 3, 2 regions, types of regions
⊃ *Min: at least NUTS 2 regions.*

(d)    **What has happened, what may happen in future?**
Temporal reference (trends, scenarios) of gathered causes and effects,
e.g., the reference to changes, trends, and developments that actually happened in recent years is of crucial importance for the political perception of the results
⊃ *Min: reference to past and future periods*

Analyzing

(e)    **What output is registered, measured, appraised?**
Topic of calculation,
e.g., relationship development investment amount—accessibility changes, R&D expenditures—employment growth, indirect payments—changes of average farm income, ERDF expenditures—increasing GDP per capita
⊃ *Min: designation of the topic of calculation*

(f)    **What is the topic described by which indicators?**
Type of indicators selected,
e.g., statistical variables, survey data, qualitative appraisals
⊃ *Min: qualitative appraisals*

(g)    **Which political goals and orientations are referred to?**
Criteria for examination (objectives, goals, concepts, derived from official documents, in particular the ESDP and the second cohesion report),
e.g., balanced territorial development (supporting concentration of activities or a decentralization at macro, meso, and/or micro level), polycentric development (at macro, meso, and/or micro level), connectedness and accessibility (supporting a core-periphery pattern or a more polycentric structure), clearance of overloaded corridors, overcoming socioeconomic disparities, improving or hampering natural and cultural assets
⊃ *Min: designation of the goals facing (if so: derived from . . .)*

*(continued)*

**TABLE 2.2**  (continued)

---

(h)    **How is the analysis performed?**
Technique of analysis,
e.g., correlation analysis, simulation model, case studies to test hypotheses, classifying regions
⊃ *Min: designation of the technique of analysis*

**Concluding**

(i)    **What is defined as "territorial"?**
Used definition of "territorial,"
e.g., convergence—divergence of regions, reference to cohesion, competitiveness, according to which spatial model, effected type(s) of regions, territorial features
⊃ *Min: designation of (assumed) meaning of "territorial" (if so: derived from . . .)*

(j)    **What do the results look like?**
General format of outcome: statements (figures, significant results),
e.g., covering the whole territory (all regions), typology of regions, mapped results (based on quantitative and/or qualitative categories)
⊃ *Min: one outcome for each region (whole territory), mapped results*

---

**Source:** ESPON 2006b.

**TABLE 2.3**

## The Territorial Impact Model

---

$TIMr = \Sigma c\ 0c\ .\ Sr,c\ .\ (PIMc\ .\ PIr\ ).\ PAr$
TIM = territorial impact (for each dimension: efficiency, quality, identity)
c = criterion of the multicriteria method
r = region
$0c$ = weight of the c criterion                    $0 \leq 0c \leq 1 : \Sigma c\ 0c = 1$
$Sr,c$ = sensitivity of region r to criterion c      $0 \leq Sr,c \leq 1$
PIM = potential impact of policy (abstract)          $-5 \leq PIMc \leq +5$ (in quality analyses)
PI = policy intensity (in region r)
PA = policy applicability (a 0/1 variable)

The rationale for the previous equation is the following: As in risk assessment, where risk = hazard (potential risk) × vulnerability, here the territorial impact is the product of a potential impact (PIM) times a sensitivity indicator (S). In its turn, Sr,c is a set (vector) of regional characteristics defining two main elements: vulnerability/receptivity to impact (mainly geographic indicators) and desirability of the dimension/criterion (technically a utility function, mainly socioeconomic indicators) for region r:
$Sr,c = Vr,c\ .\ Dr,c$

---

**Source:** ESPON 2006b.

## TIA and Policy:
## Learning from Other Evaluation and Assessment Procedures

The major challenge of any evaluation—and thus any TIA—is its integration into decision-making procedures. Only when information is provided at the right moment might it actually inform decision making and thus prove useful. Examples are mainly taken from EU policy and complemented by an approach used in the private sector: quality management. Key to the following selection of assessment procedures is a focus on the ex-ante assessment dimension.

### Evaluating EU Cohesion Policy

EU cohesion policy can already look back to a history that introduced a structured approach to programming, monitoring, and evaluation (Bachtler & Wren 2006). EU cohesion policy is an object of special attention at the highest political levels, as it spends the second-largest share of the EU budget, after the CAP, and—in comparison to the CAP—is led by more political objectives. Therefore, with regard to the objectives set in the regional context, monitoring and evaluation are much more evident. The cohesion policy approach mainly focuses on accountability and legitimacy, improving the quality and performance of the programs, and improving planning (Batterbury 2006) and is embedded in a policy cycle from ex-ante, midterm, and ex-post evaluations. The policy program is required to define overall policy objectives and strategic policy objectives, including a catalogue of input-output, result, and impact indicators. Evaluations, in particular ex-ante and midterm evaluations, investigate in principle the following questions:

- Are the program objectives derived from a systematic analysis of the reality, which in fact means establishing the evidence base for the program objectives (mostly in technical terms, based on a SWOT analysis of the program area)?

- Is the program internally and externally consistent, and does it formulate an explicit and consistent hierarchy of objectives?

- Is an appropriate indicator system in place and implemented, based on input-output, result, and impact indicators (CEC 1999)?

- Does the management and implementation system promise an efficient and effective implementation of the program, including its consistency with other EU policies?

Evaluation practice demonstrates a strong learning component in cohesion policy evaluation (Eser and Nussmüller 2006) apart from the ex-post evaluations that are more model based. Turning to the question of TIA, it is obvious that the territorial component is not considered in itself. The program objectives are set with regard to the analysis and objectives foreseen in the Structural Funds regulation. If the Structural Funds were to demand a territorial assessment of the policy programs, it would be rather easy (not taking into account the inherent problem of measuring territorial effects in themselves) to include this question of TIA in the methodology, as the development of an appropriate assessment methodology is the responsibility of the evaluation team and the program management.

In fact, the evaluation framework provides some handles for TIA, but TIA would imply an independent package within the evaluation. Methodology is rather free to choose—an approach also necessary for the TIA—whereas the evaluation framework sets the structure of what the evaluation needs to report on and requires the use of indicators.

## The Strategic Environmental Assessment

Since July 2004, Directive 2001/42/EC on the assessment of the environmental effects of certain plans and programs (the SEA) has had to be applied throughout the EU, representing an important instrument of the EU strategy for sustainable development endorsed by the Gothenburg Council in 2001 for acquiring information. According to the preamble and Article 1 of the directive, its purpose is to ensure that an environmental assessment is carried out for plans and programs likely to have significant effects on the environment, and that the effects of implementing such plans and programs are taken into account during preparation and before adoption.

The SEA follows an approach similar to that of the TIA discussed above. It is an ex-ante evaluation that measures the effects of plans and programs against environmental objectives without taking note of the objectives set out in the respective documents. The approach includes two steps. The first step consists of screening for the likely significance of environmental effects. Assumption of a likely significance requires the second step, preparation of an environmental report covering a range of factors (Annex I of Directive 2001/42/EC), including, in addition to information about the plan or program, the likely significant effects on the environment. The report must also include relevant environmental protection objectives; envisioned measures to reduce the effects; reasons for selecting the chosen alternatives; and a description of monitoring measures. Furthermore, it is expected to include all possible effects, be they secondary; cumulative; synergetic; short, medium, or long term; permanent or temporary; positive or negative. The environmental report is subject to a public consultation process and, along with the results of that process, must be taken into account during preparation of the plan or program and before adoption or submission to the legislature (Article 8). Information on how the report has been considered and on the intended monitoring must be published (Articles 9 and 10).

Guidance exists on how the SEA is supposed to be implemented, as the directive leaves some margin for interpretation of the exact procedures (see Greening Regional Development Programmes 2006; CEC 2003; Imperial College Consultants 2005). It is also evident that the directive takes a very broad approach, which has to be narrowed in accordance with the focus of the particular plan or program.

There are positive elements to be learned from the SEA: As an ex-ante assessment, it can still influence the plan or program, even though no direct sanctions are imposed and formal intervention is not possible; the plan or program is required merely to consider the assessment. At the very least, however, that means granting transparency and promoting public awareness. An individually drafted assessment has the advantage of being adapted specifically to each plan or program. However, that individual adaptation leaves more latitude for interpretation of the assessment exercise and for disagreement between the assessed and the assessor.

A negative aspect of the SEA is that environmental effects usually become clear only when projects are implemented; an ex-ante assessment merely indicates what might happen. Nevertheless, a demanding procedure (including consultation and feedback) is in place, and the scope of plans and programs subject to the SEA is considerable. The success of the SEA will depend on whether a level of practice can be found that neither overstrains the system, in particular where smaller programs are concerned, nor becomes arbitrary.

The environmental assessment also includes territorial elements; concepts such as the ecological footprint relate environmental effects to the territory concerned. This leads to the issue of whether and to what extent there could be serious overlaps between the SEA and a TIA. The advantage of the SEA as compared to the TIA is that the SEA directive stipulates that the approach is to elaborate for each program or plan an individual methodology, as environment is a fuzzy concept—though maybe less fuzzy than that of territorial cohesion.

## The European Commission's Approach to Impact Assessment

The European Commission is in the process of introducing a new integrated method for impact assessment (IA; CEC 2006), as agreed at the Gothenburg and Laeken European Councils. The IA is part of the Better Regulation Action Plan and the European Strategy for Sustainable Development. The idea is to contribute to an effective and efficient regulatory environment and—with regard to the economic, social, and environmental dimensions of sustainable development—to more coherent EU decision making.

In practice, IA is aimed at structuring and supporting the development of policies. It identifies and assesses the problem and the objectives to be pursued. It identifies the main options for achieving the objectives and analyzes the likely impacts of those options in the economic, environmental, and social realms. Advantages and disadvantages of each option should be outlined and possible synergies and trade-offs examined. The IA is a support tool for making political decisions by informing decision makers of the likely impacts of their proposals. As of 2005, all items included in the Commission's Legislative and Work Programme are subject to an IA, which can partly replace the ex-ante evaluation (CEC 2006, 7).

The following six constitutive elements form the backbone of IA:

1. Defining the problem subject to Commission action (defining problem, confirming the right of the EU to act, and elaborating a no-policy-change scenario—what would happen without action)

2. Evaluating objectives according to the SMART criteria (specificity, measurability,

acceptance, realism, time-dependency), distinction of general and specific operational objectives, consistency with other EU policies

3. Identifying policy options and alternatives; screening of policy options; assessing effectiveness, efficiency, consistency

4. Identifying likely economic, social, and environmental impacts—why they are occurring, who is affected—and identifying the most important impacts (cause and effect, likelihood, intensity)

5. Comparing policy options, balancing administrative costs against other regulatory costs, setting evaluation criteria

6. Organizing future monitoring and evaluation criteria and indicators

Key to IA is not only the structure but also the procedure, which involves the Commission services, along with other stakeholders. The procedure is first defined in a road map for the annual policy strategy of the Commission before the assessment is started. Findings of the assessment are presented, although an initiative might be cancelled. The consultation procedure starts within the Commission services and then opens up to the stakeholders, ultimately identifying the objective of the consultation, the elements of the IA for which consultation is necessary, the target groups, the appropriate consultation tool, and the appropriate time for consultation. Finally, the findings are presented in the IA report, summarizing the work undertaken and stating any assumptions or uncertainties in simple and non-technical language to allow for an easy understanding of the results.

The review of reports so far reveals the rather pragmatic approach of IAs, which are presented as an annex to each of the Commission's actions. As a rule, although the analysis can be rather elaborate, the reports are within 20–40 pages. IA is clearly an ex-ante assessment tool that—according to the goals identified—offers a systematic approach with the potential to function as an eye opener.

The territorial dimension is not but could be one element of the IA approach. However, that is not necessarily a disadvantage, as it would help to calibrate the goals regarding territorial effects compared to other effects such as economic and environmental effects.

The IA approach also highlights the necessity to be clear about goals in relation to a certain policy action. In cases where both SEA and IA procedures are being applied, overlaps do not seem to be totally under control.

## Quality Management of Policies

It is interesting to have a quick look at where monitoring, controlling, and improving the output of a company are important in the private sector (Eser 2001). Approved standards and certified norms are, in fact, common: The most prominent approaches are, first, total quality management organized in parallel with the development of products and the functions undertaken within a company according to a certified norm (Feigenbaum 1991; James 1996; Pfitzinger 1998). Second are the International Standards Organization (ISO) norms: ISO 9003 concentrates on products, 9002 on the production process, and 9001 on the approval of quality management. The latest norm, 9004, evaluates the existence and function of quality management systems. Third, despite some questions regarding whether the ISO norms are sufficient to respond to the demands of a comprehensive quality management system, they provided the ground for the United States' Malcolm Baldrige National Quality Award and the European Foundation for Quality Management's European Quality Award. The latter is based on the so-called RADAR steps, which must be completed by companies or organizations seeking the award. RADAR stands for *results* (anticipation of targets), *approaches* (procedures that support the targets), *deployment* (systematic implementation of the approaches), and *assessment and review* (evaluation based on monitoring and analysis of results and learning). There is surely much more to be said about the details of these systems (Pfitzinger 1998).

Any kind of TIA has to be anchored in a process to make sure that an impact is recognized by the organization that implements the activity; otherwise, the effect of the TIA is more or less random. Also, the objective of having a (limited) territorial impact should be considered in setting the target. Considering the narrow scope of other evaluation approaches, a permanent system of feedback and adjustments is recommended.

## TIA in the Policy Cycle

Discussing examples of EU policy TIAs and their challenges, as well as the challenges of other policy evaluation approaches, poses the question as to the degree and the way in which TIA can be useful in inserting territorial objectives in sector policies. If the assessment of the territorial dimension should be part of the policy, it must be defined in the policy objectives and subsequently assessed on a regular basis together with the other main objectives of a policy. Only systematic communication of information on the territorial impacts of policies, accompanied by active discussions with the makers of territorial policies, will lead to the permanent inclusion of the territorial dimension in sector policies.

The question is where in the policy process best to integrate that dimension and whether we need TIA as an additional evaluation regime or as an integral part of existing evaluation schemes. If so, what would its added value be and which methodology should be proposed? Considering that for the moment none of the TIAs of EU policies has had considerable effect on policy making, it might be a little early to offer final answers to those questions. However, to stimulate discussion, some tentative conclusions can be drawn, based on experiences presented in this chapter. Following the elements of the programming cycle, these conclusions can be summarized as follows:

- **Monitoring**
  Collecting information on the territorial incidences of policies (spending of

money, etc.) at the regional level can be recommended, as that is one of the pre-conditions of performing a TIA.

■ **Evaluation**
If there is regionalized information on the incidences of policies (see inputs in figure 2.1), an evaluation can easily relate that information to spatial policy aims such as polycentric development and territorial cohesion. The degree to which a TIA might be a separate evaluation or integrated into already obligatory monitoring processes depends on the importance territorial cohesion will gain in the political debate.

■ **Formulation of aims and objectives**
As long as there is no political initiative to target territorial cohesion through various EU policies or to operationalize that policy aim, territorial awareness in other programs will be difficult to achieve. This regards in particular the level of program aims and objectives.

■ **Definition of inputs and activities**
Within most EU policies overall objectives are further developed in priorities and measures that finally shape the actions taken. Here again, a certain territorial awareness can help to make sure that sector policies do not result in mutually contradictory actions on the ground. Furthermore, at this level the above mentioned monitoring of activities and their territorial incidences comes into the picture.

■ **Implementation**
It is here that territorial effects are fully developed and territorial awareness is expressed in policy development and management, as well as territorialized monitoring structures playing out in reality.

The above points can be illustrated in a simple graphic where EU sector policies and territorial policies are put next to each other. For both the process starts with the development of aims and objectives, which are further specified as inputs and activities. Regardless of the type of policies and the approach to TIA, a territorialized investigation of where which activities have been carried out will be a key issue. Once the activities have been carried out, they will show various kinds of outputs, results, and outcomes.

In most sector policies these steps are controlled in the form of a quality management system that takes into account why the policy has been set up (the need) and monitors possible changes in the requirements (see the circle on quality management in figure 2.1). In addition, the outputs, results, and outcomes are compared to the aims and objectives of the policies in a standard evaluation (see the circle on EU program evaluations in figure 2.1). Here the object of the assessment is to establish whether the policy has achieved its aims and, if so, whether that means the need no longer exists. In such evaluations the effectiveness and efficiency of the programs are often key aspects.

In addition to such an evaluation, the outputs, results, and outcomes of a pol-

**FIGURE 2.1**

Territorial Impact Assessment and the Policy (Evaluation) Cycle

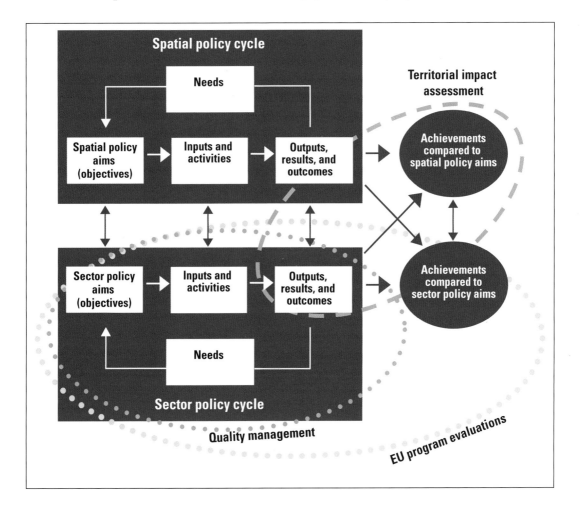

icy can be assessed with regard to the aims of territorial policies (see the circle on territorial impact assessment in figure 2.1). Such an assessment then needs also to consider all the aspects of the operationalization of policy aims, assessments, and approaches discussed earlier. The formal status of such an assessment can take different forms. Generally, we would like to point out that the proposal of a TIA directive comparable to the SEA needs to be critically discussed, as the territorial objectives are (at the moment) not nearly as operational as the environmental objectives. Drawing on experiences from the fields discussed above, some general considerations for TIAs can be developed.

## Conclusions: Linking TIA to the Policy Process

All this leaves us with the conclusion that, although difficult, TIA is possible and potentially very useful for increasing the territorial awareness and coordination of policies; the close link of TIA and policy development is a key issue. However, the demands on TIA have to be taken from the policy process. Where and how should TIA be accommodated?

The TIA policy cycle outlined in figure 2.1 gives us some indications. In principle it seems best to allow for TIA in different contexts at different levels. At first it appears to be interesting to accommodate a slimmed-down version of TIA in an existing process such as the IA of the Commission, as discussed in the German *Presidency Conclusions* (see also above). This provides an opportunity to briefly indicate the territorial issue a policy raises—and to signal a possible problem. It is obvious that territorial effects cannot be the guiding issue for all sector policies, but signaling unintended side effects could raise awareness and at least lead to a readjustment of sector policy measures. With regard to the system explained above, TIA would help to formulate policy aims and a reference framework such as territorial cohesion. In fact, such a reference framework will always be a moving target, so why not make a virtue of that? In other words, allow the definition of territorial impact to be determined by each TIA, which would allow a continual update of discussion about the concept, acknowledging that territory is indeed a concept that is reinvented in the present zeitgeist (much more, for example, than environment).

However, we are also aware that any TIA requires a sound analytical base for evaluation and that the precondition is the development of monitoring systems. The basic structure of those systems might better be predefined than developed on a case-by-case basis, as foreseen in SEA regarding environmental impacts. Also, some sound territorial databases and analytical tools should be made available—ready to use—by an organization such as the ESPON Program (www.espon.eu) in order to keep the efforts modest when TIA input is required for a procedure such as an IA. Indeed, there are indications that, for example, SEA is too heavy an instrument; it has been criticized on this point even by environmentalists.

The positioning of TIA of the CAP in the policy process showed that TIA has not been directly embedded in the concrete policy cycle. However, the approach followed by the project is suitable for a midterm or ex-post assessment enriching the evaluation of the policy. Thus, this type of TIA could play a role in the policy cycle and in quality management. The same is true for the TIA of regional policy. The transport TIA elaborated in the ESPON context, as described above, would be suitable for an ex-ante assessment in an early stage of policy development. Indeed, this is the first example of an ex-ante assessment of the territorial impacts of EU policies carried out by ESPON.

The general methodology of the TEQUILA model could give guidance in two directions: One direction is, of course, a very elaborate model, ideally of a quantified nature. However, it would be interesting to see how such a model could be reduced to an easy-to-manage, slim form of assessment that would help to signal a territorial problem as described above with regard to the Commission's IA.

As for the future, the ESPON work has shown that the operationalization of policy aims, the methodology applied in TIA, and the integration in the policy process are crucial elements defining the outcome and the usefulness of a TIA.

Any assessment of policies needs to clearly state the goals against which the policy in question is to be assessed. This applies also to TIA. A targeted and successful TIA needs to clearly define what kind of territorial objectives are to be considered. If that is not done, the exercise will soon be derailed and risk not delivering any useful results.

In the context of ESPON, mostly the concepts of territorial cohesion and polycentric development have been used as policy aims against which the effects of selected EU policies have been assessed. Both concepts have proven rather challenging with regard to their operationalization, and different projects have developed rather different approaches and solutions.

This, together with similar experiences in other ESPON projects (e.g., the discussion about constructing a territorial cohesion index), shows that a close dialogue is needed between the scientific community working on TIA and the policy community that is supposed to benefit from the exercises. It is only through such a dialogue that the policy aims can be operationalized in such a way that the TIA results appeal to the policy maker and thus can attract the broader professional sector as well as general public interest in the way they are affecting the territory.

## References

Bachtler, J., and C. Wren. 2006. Evaluation of European Union cohesion policy: Research questions and policy challenges. *Regional Studies* 40(2): 143–154.

Batterbury, S. 2006. Principles and purposes of the European Union cohesion policy evaluation. *Regional Studies* 40(2): 179–188.

BBR/ESPON 3.1. 2005. *Integrated tools for European spatial development: Final report of ESPON Project 3.1.* http://www.espon.eu/mmp/online/website/content/projects/260/714/index_EN .html

Böhme, K. 2006. Visst påverkar EU fysisk planering i Sverige. In *Planering med nya förutsättningar*, G. Blücher and G. Graninger, eds., 39–56. Linköping, Sweden: Linköping University Interdisciplinary Studies.

Böhme, K., and P. Schön. 2006. From Leipzig to Leipzig: Territorial research delivers evidence for the new Territorial Agenda of the European Union. In *Evidence-based planning*, A. Faludi, ed. Special issue, *disP* 165, 42(2): 61–70.

CEC (Commission of the European Communities). 1999. *Evaluating socio-economic programmes: MEANS Collection, vols. 1–6.* Luxembourg: Office for Official Publications of the European Communities.

———. 2001. *European transport policy for 2020: Time to decide.* Luxembourg: Office for Official Publications of the European Communities.

———. 2003. *Commission's guidance on the implementation of Directive 2001/42/EC on the assessment of the effects of certain plans and programmes on the environment.* Luxembourg: Office for Official Publications of the European Communities.

————. 2006. *Impact assessment guidelines* (SEC [2005] 791). Brussels: European Commission. http://ec.europa.eu/governance/impact/docs_en.htm.

Christian-Albrechts-Universität zu Kiel/ESPON 2.1.1. 2005. *Territorial impact of EU transport and TEN policies: Final report of ESPON Project 2.1.1.* http://www.espon.eu/mmp/online/ website/content/projects/243/239/index_EN.html.

Eser, T. W. 2001. Evaluation und Qualitätsmanagement: Anforderungen und Konsequenzen für die EU Strukturpolitik. *Informationen zur Raumentwicklung* 6/7: 327–340.

Eser, T. W., and E. Nussmüller. 2006. Mid-term evaluations of community initiatives under European Union Structural Funds: A process between accounting and common learning. *Regional Studies* 40(2): 249–258.

ESPON. 2006a. *Applied territorial research: Building a scientific platform for competitiveness and cohesion* (ESPON Scientific Report II, Autumn 2006). Luxembourg: ESPON.

————. 2006b. *Territory matters for competitiveness and cohesion: Facets of regional diversity and potentials in Europe.* Luxembourg: ESPON.

Feigenbaum, A. V. 1991. *Total quality management.* New York: McGraw-Hill.

Greening Regional Development Programmes. 2006. *Handbook on SEA for cohesion policy 2007–2013.* http://www.environment-agency.gov.uk/commondata/acrobat/grdp_sea_handbook _1394193.pdf?referrer=/grdp/.

Imperial College Consultants. 2005. *The relationship between the EIA and SEA directives: Final report to the European Commission.* London: Imperial College Consultants.

James, P. 1996. *Total quality management: An introductory text.* Hemel Hempstead, England: Prentice-Hall.

Luxembourg EU Presidency. 2005. *EU informal ministerial meeting on territorial cohesion 20/21.05.2005: Presidency conclusions.* Luxembourg: Luxembourg EU Presidency.

Nordregio/ESPON 2.2.1. 2006. *Territorial effects of Structural Funds: Final report of ESPON Project 2.2.1.* http://www.espon.eu/mmp/online/website/content/projects/243/330/index_EN .html.

Pfitzinger, E. 1998. *Der Weg von DIN EN 9000ff zu Total Quality Management.* Berlin: Beuth.

Polverari, L., and J. Bachtler. 2005. The contribution of European Structural Funds to territorial cohesion. *Town Planning Review* 76(1): 29–42.

Polverari, L., and I. McMaster. 2006. Territorial cohesion and new cohesion policy: Challenges for old and new member states. In *European territorial research in progress,* ESPON, ed., 83–98. Luxembourg: ESPON.

Schindegger, F. 2001. *Prospects for further work on TIA.* Paper presented at ECTP Seminar on Territorial Impact Assessment, Louvain-la-Neuve, 26 October 2001.

Shucksmith, M., D. Roberts, and K. Thomson. 2006. The territorial impacts of the Common Agricultural Policy. In *European territorial research in progress,* ESPON, ed., 69–82. Luxembourg: ESPON.

ULB/ESPON 3.2. 2006. *Spatial scenarios in relation to the ESDP and EU cohesion policy: Draft final report of ESPON Project 3.2.* http://www.espon.eu/mmp/online/website/content/ projects/260/716/index_EN.html.

University of Aberdeen/ESPON 2.1.3. 2005. *Territorial impact of CAP and rural development policy: Final report of ESPON Project 2.1.3.* http://www.espon.eu/mmp/online/website/ content/projects/243/277/index_EN.html.

Van Ravesteyn, N., and D. Evers. 2004. *Unseen Europe: A survey of EU politics and its impacts on spatial development in the Netherlands.* The Hague, Netherlands: Institute for Spatial Planning.

# CHAPTER 3

# Polycentricity Under the Looking Glass

Janne Antikainen

Globalization contributes to reinforcing both competition and cooperation among cities, and, paradoxically, competition goes hand in hand with collaboration. Globalization is increasing the economic competition between cities and making cities more vulnerable to external shocks and economic restructuring. Cities, regions, and nations are more than the locus of firms in competition; for example, they compete for workers, public resources, and investments. Competition per se may fail to achieve optimal economic development, however, and needs to be complemented by various forms of institutionalized cooperation, notably in the areas of knowledge and competence (OECD 2005).

The concept of polycentricity of settlement structures originated as an empirical concept in the 1930s. Central place theory (formulated by Walter Christaller in 1933) explained hierarchical decentralization of cities by the fact that different goods and services command service areas of different sizes (ESPON 2005).

A modern breakthrough of this idea on a European scale has been achieved in the ESPD (1999) and in the third cohesion report (European Commission 2004), where the aim is a "balanced polycentric urban system." Urban regions thus play a fundamental role in knowledge- and competence-based regional development and in the implementation of the European-wide Lisbon Strategy.

The definition of *morphological polycentrism* applied in the ESPON project studying polycentricity was that a region consists of more than two cities that are historically and politically independent (no hierarchy), are in proximity to each other, and have a functional relation and are complementary to each other. This definition departed from that of polycentricity as an ambiguous, multiscalar, and ill-defined normative concept and stressed two structural elements of particular relevance to polycentricity: morphological elements, laying out the size and territorial distribution of urban areas in a given territory; and relational elements, based on the networks of flows and cooperation between urban areas at different scales (Meijers 2007).

Polycentricity also can be understood as a concept that tackles the challenge of coordination and differentiation of various sector policies. The idea of this kind of crossing of polycentricity is simplified in figure 3.1. Various sectors have an impact on regional development, even though there is no explicit territorial dimension to their policy (step 1 in figure 3.1). However, the territorial dimension (step 2) can be that level where the total effects of various policies can be analyzed, although there is no active coordination between sectors. In step 3 there is active coordination between policies—in other words, the impacts of various policies on territory are analyzed, before or after the policies are implemented. The territorial dimension adds value to sector policies by seeking synergies between them. Polycentricity is introduced in step 4, where policies are differentiated according to different territorial types. Polycentricity is an active tool for differentiation, taking into account different territorial contexts and in that way making policies more targeted and more effective.

Polycentricity is built on functional links between various players; regional development is a result of actions by multiactor networks. Such networks are formed within one functional region, but more and more between regions and internationally. Networks of businesses and universities are internationalizing their actions day by day. The critical question is how quickly public-sector actors, being the third part of the triple helix of university-industry-government relations (for more on this concept, see Etzkowitz 2006), are internationalizing their actions.

As the European Commission (2005) states, Europe is characterized by a unique polycentric structure of large, medium, and small cities. To become effective, the network of metropolitan regions has to be linked with small and medium-size urban areas. Both elements, the large metropolitan regions with European and global importance and the smaller cities and urban areas that play an important role in their national contexts, together form the backbone of a polycentric European urban system. Europe needs diverse urban regions. Diversity is needed also at the urban system and urban network levels. By European standards urban regions in, for example, northeastern Europe (Finland, Sweden, Estonia, Latvia, and Lithuania) are small, with long distances separating them. However, small and specialized urban regions also possess the prerequisites for success. Through the urban network everyone's expertise and strengths are efficiently brought into play. Cooperation between cities allows them to better identify their comparative advantages, their needs for specialized goods and services, and their complementarities (OECD 2005). Networking and increasing division of labor among urban regions can counteract geographical concentration. Through their special expertise in their regions businesses are genuine operators in global networks.

## The *Territorial Agenda* and Polycentricity

The *Territorial Agenda* (2007) of the EU focuses on the economic aspects of the ESDP. The *Territorial Agenda* has no binding character. It delivers policy recommendations for public administrations and institutions at EU and national levels. Its evidence base is provided by *The Territorial State and Perspectives of the European Union*. Regarding the polycentric structure of Europe, the report notes the following:

Outside the dominant European core area there are more sparsely but quite evenly distributed networks of individual metropolitan regions and other urban regions to counterweight the predominance of the core area towards a more polycentric structure at EU scale. . . . Generally these areas are important as engines of development which contribute to the dispersing European core-periphery pattern. Some of these areas are even outperforming the metropolitan areas in the core of Europe, with regard to specific economically significant factors. . . . Urban areas outside metropolitan areas are often important motors for their region and some of them are leading locations when it comes to research and development or highly specialized services and products. . . . Some small and medium-sized cities host functions of higher importance than larger cities and even show better economic growth figures than large agglomeration

**FIGURE 3.1**

## Territorial Dimension and Polycentricity at Work

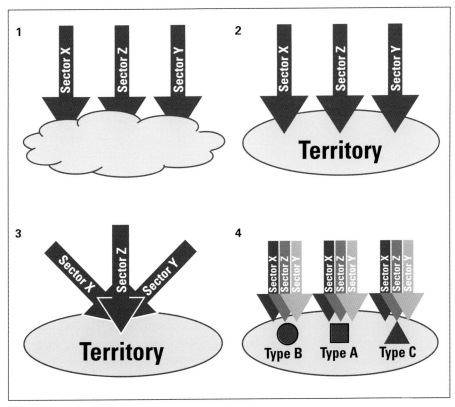

The territorial dimension seeks synergies between various sector policies (steps 1–3), while polycentricity is a tool for differentiating between territorial types (step 4).

areas. These functions are closely related to the territorial potential and endogenous capital of an area. Additionally, small and medium-sized cities are of importance both for their wider geographical context, especially in regions outside the core of Europe without large metropolitan areas, and with regard to certain functions even internationally. (Territorial State 2007, par. 106–109)

On the policy, the report continues:

Strengthening territorial cohesion requires a strong focus on the role of Europe's cities as motors for growth and development. . . . Effective policy intervention at the level of the EU [is] necessary but difficult. It implies a further shift from purely sectoral and top-down policy approaches towards integrated and multilevel approaches for each specific territorial setting. In particular, the creation of a strong European network of metropolitan regions, enabling Europe to play a fully competitive role in the global economy, requires a supreme effort. . . . [There is] a two fold challenge for territorial cohesion: first, to find an effective mix of complementarity and competition within and between the urban clusters in each metropolitan region and, second, to achieve a more balanced European pattern of metropolitan regions. EU policies can stimulate cooperation and development and facilitate a sustainable and competitive environment. . . . The challenge is to avoid achieving growth and innovation of metropolitan regions at the expense of smaller and medium-sized cities. On the contrary, strengthening metropolitan and urban networks should go together and be mutually reinforcing. (Territorial State 2007, par. 158–160)

A new understanding of territorial governance, development, and planning in Europe's regions and cities is necessary. On one hand, EU policies should consider more explicitly the development perspectives of the regional and local "basis." On the other hand, regional and local development policies should focus more explicitly on European needs. The different regional diversities are strengthened through supporting regional specialization by each region and city. Regions and cities in Europe are part of an increasingly polycentric territorial pattern. In order to strengthen the process of "polycentralization" it is more than ever necessary to diversify tasks and to realize a division of functions. This calls for an innovative and modern mix of branches in agglomerations, cities, and urban areas. Metropolitan regions and regional centers are to be strengthened through appropriate policies in their function as engines of economic development.

On building clusters, *The Territorial State and Perspectives of the European Union* notes:

As a result of globalization, increasing competition between regions and the need to use resources in a sustainable way, there is a growing necessity to stimulate clusters across borders. Moreover, a paradigm shift is necessary from securing fair play within the system to coaching clusters to become globally competitive. National actors have a major role in facilitating networks. In addition, it seems to be indispensable to shift from subsidizing the poor to investing in the potential of different territories. . . . Cities and regions are localizing and anchoring the Lisbon Strategy. Strong partnerships are required. The key challenge for the EU in this respect is to facilitate such bottom-up processes more effectively. Genuine European clusters are needed, but cluster and innovation policies still tend to be national in nature. Innovation policies would become more effective if they would be connected more strongly and directly with regional development policies. (Territorial State 2007, par. 164–165)

National territorial development schemes and reports should take territorial priorities for economic growth and job creation into account and consider them against the background of European development perspectives. Territorial priorities and territorial cohesion aspects, being agreed upon at both the EU and the national levels, should be integrated in national as well as EU sector policies. Each EU member state should ensure, according to its national institutional framework conditions, that the needs of local and regional stakeholders are taken into consideration when designing spatially relevant policies. The civil society should be integrated in the political debate on territorial priorities. Structural Funds programs should take territorial and urban development–related issues reflecting the aims of the *Territorial Agenda* more explicitly on board. Finally, European regions and cities should cooperate with each other more intensively in order to strengthen their diversities and to better use the opportunities of cross-border and transnational cooperation based on common territorial priorities.

## Building Polycentricity Through Networks

Each and every urban region has a long tradition—a genotype—of its development. Urban regions have been born, have grown, and have added layer after layer during various phases of the growth of trade, industry, public-, and finally private-sector services. One cannot influence tradition, but one can set conditions for future development. In addition to endogenous factors, key features of urban regions now are the ability to be part of networks and their regenerative capacity. Banking on one-sided structures has turned out to be destructive. Networks now provide a possibility for further specialization and the division of labor between urban regions. Structural changes will inevitably come—the challenge is to prepare actors in urban regions to be able to adapt to the changes and to find their locus in globalization (i.e., international competition), not to maintain current fixed structures.

The role of national players has changed during the past years: They are now more and more part of the bottom in the bottom-up development process—

instead of being mere top-down dictators or part of the up in the bottom-up process. In other words, instead of the hollowing out of the nation-state (as the situation was characterized in the 1990s; see, e.g., Jessop 1994), one can generalize that national players have major strategic roles by facilitating networks.

This reemergence of the nation-state is stemming from new challenges to the regions of Europe. In some countries internal competition between regions, or a policy favoring regions that are lagging behind, is being replaced by a focus on the more serious challenge: on one hand, how regions considered competitive in Europe actually fare in comparison with Asian or American regions, and, on the other hand, what the possibilities are for regions in the process of, or in danger of, experiencing structural change to make their functions more knowledge and competence oriented.

Since the 1990s, the nature of regional policy has been changing, with an increasing focus on urban, competence-oriented, and innovation-oriented initiatives. In previous decades, national regional policy in European countries has predominantly been aid based and geographically targeted, directed mainly at supporting investment in regions lagging behind. More recently, regional policy has broadened its scope, becoming in most countries primarily program based, a policy that operates in selected regions and aims to enhance the contribution of regions to knowledge- and growth-based development—in other words, increasing competitiveness. In that context, urban regions are increasingly seen as relevant focal areas for regional policy, helping to promote economic development in the regions while providing a basis for ensuring that surrounding areas are more effectively connected to growth processes (Yuill and Vironen 2006).

Polycentricity is based on networking policies. Building networks and clusters has two territorial dimensions: one taking place within functional urban areas and regions, and the other taking place between them. Integrating regional activities while maintaining sufficient European and national cooperation presents one of the greatest challenges of innovation-driven networking and cluster policy. Building networks and links between cities and regions challenges the traditional understanding that geographical proximity is a critical condition in forming a cluster. In promoting competitiveness and innovativeness, physical geography matters either very much or not at all. Building clusters is no longer only about local development or linking areas within a daily urban system. When building networks and clusters, we are looking for similarities in terms of economic and competence orientation and then complementarities and division of labor within a particular cluster.

Links between urban areas and regions have been built primarily within national contexts since the early 1990s. Now it is time to build networks and clusters internationally. Transnational links are built with cross-border neighboring areas and development zones, but more and more also within meso-regions—that is, regions covering several countries, like the Baltic Sea region, within Europe and globally. Hot spots of competitiveness and innovation also exist outside Europe. Rather than turn inward, the Nordic countries and Europe must build active links, especially with North America and Asia.

Major urban areas, especially metropolitan areas, are the main hot spots in competence- and innovation-driven development, especially in creating new innovations (see, e.g., Florida 2005). Cool—creative, attractive, and interesting—spots are actually hot spots. Brains go where they are stimulated. Business goes where brains go. But there is no size determination in building clusters: Small and medium-size cities and rural areas are important, especially in applying knowledge but also in creating innovation. Smaller regions are often more efficient and regenerative. Through networking, the "critical mass" of regions is increased, economies of scale and scope generated, and synergies created. All cities and regions must have the opportunity to be part of a network. The aim is to promote the strengths and specializations of smaller centers, as well as cooperation between them, so as to reinforce the networks covering all the regions.

Top-level competence based on R&D and efficient financing for companies of all sizes require a wider regional basis (innovative milieus), which is built on high-quality education and continuous training, dynamic local labor markets, attractive living conditions, and tolerance for diversity. Tacit knowledge, social capital, and trust between triple-helix actors are fuel for development on the regional level. In general, the networks of actors that influence the development of the region should be strengthened through European and national policies.

In the process of regionalizing innovation policy and building transnational networks and clusters, the core sectors are business and industry, innovation and technology, research, science, and education. In addition to core competitiveness, the emphasis is on the vitality of urban regions. This reflects a softer attitude in cluster policy. Sociocultural elements have a more direct impact on the location decisions of people and businesses. When cluster policy is understood in a broader sense—as building innovative milieus—relevant sectors are infrastructure (transport, communication, housing, and environment), but also sectors like labor and social services and health.

## The Case of Finland

The Nordic countries and Finland have been held up as successful models of combining innovativeness and competitiveness with welfare and social safety nets (see, e.g., Castells and Himanen 2001; Sapir 2004; Giddens 2006). This section gives a short history of Finnish urbanization and its emphasis on competitiveness.

The structure of the Finnish urban system is a result of various historical layers and phases of urbanization. In the industrialization period from the late nineteenth century to the 1960s, the main location factors were related to natural resources and, in particular, the logistics of the forest sector (cf. Kortelainen 2002). This resource-based development partly declined in the "great move" from rural to urban areas between the 1960s and early 1970s (Oksa 1985). The Finnish urban system that has emerged since the mid-1970s is characterized by the growth of cities of different sizes and the suburbanization of urban regions. This phenomenon has, in terms of the Finnish discussion, been labeled regionalization

(Antikainen and Vartiainen 2002a). The strongest areas in this evolving system were the rather extensive urbanized triangle around Helsinki, Tampere, and Turku in the south and some isolated regional centers such as Oulu, Jyväskylä, Vaasa, Kuopio, and Joensuu, all capitals of more peripheral regions but with relatively strong universities (figure 3.2).

Christallerian thinking influenced the Finnish tradition of urban and regional planning in the 1960s, and hierarchical models were eagerly drawn up until the 1980s. This led to paradoxical development features in which more attention was paid to the mechanical service structure than to the genuine functional economic basis of urban regions (Ministry of the Interior 2006b). The relatively balanced nature of regional development was based predominantly on the foundation of a strong national welfare state. The evolving welfare state institutions supported the growth of regional and local centers in the less-favored regions. Smaller centers were strengthened by welfare reforms such as those in the municipal elementary school and health care systems, whereas medium-size regional centers were strengthened by establishing new universities and by building a modern regional administrative system. Moreover, a new regional industrial policy supported investments in less-favored regions.

Following the deep recession and subsequent recovery in the beginning of the 1990s (see Sengenberger 2002), the new growth in the mid-1990s was based mainly on the success of the information and communication technologies (ICT) sector (especially Nokia) and its subcontractors. The new growth concentrated in five large urban regions (Helsinki, Tampere, Oulu, Jyväskylä, and Turku) and in one Nokia-driven industrial location (Salo, near Turku). The poorest development in urban areas was identified, first, in small, industrialized, urban regions with a single industrial base (e.g., paper or steel), and, second, in regional centers based on public-sector services, which suffered particularly from serious cutbacks in the 1990s (see, e.g., Association of Finnish Local and Regional Authorities 1999; Huovari, Kangasharju, and Alanen 2001; Antikainen and Vartiainen 2002b). In the latter half of the 1990s and the early years of the 2000s, domestic migration flows climbed to the level of the early 1970s. During the 1990s social and spatial issues in Finland became increasingly characterized by urban problems and challenges, but also by stressing the role of cities in generating growth.

The issue of unbalanced regional development has traditionally been considered from the perspective of rural and peripheral areas. Consequently, there is strong ideological and political support for balanced development among regions in Finland, and, therefore, urban policy is still deeply related to both the notion of a balanced urban system and the role of regional centers in reinforcing the development of the surrounding rural areas.

In the mid-1990s, Finland started a new regional development strategy in which the maintenance of a polycentric urban structure was elaborated as the backbone for balanced territorial development. As the Regional Development Act states, "The aim . . . is to further the strengths and specializations of regional centers and cooperation between them so as to reinforce the network covering all the regions" (Ministry of the Interior 2002, section 15). In the new Finnish urban pol-

FIGURE 3.2
The Finnish Urban Network

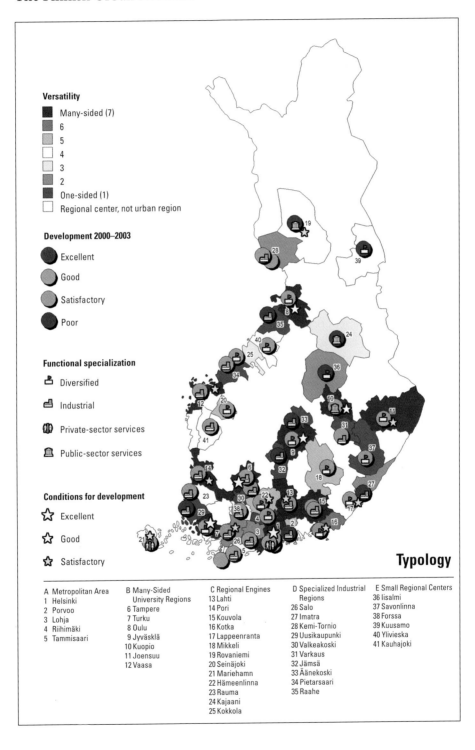

**Versatility**
- Many-sided (7)
- 6
- 5
- 4
- 3
- 2
- One-sided (1)
- Regional center, not urban region

**Development 2000–2003**
- Excellent
- Good
- Satisfactory
- Poor

**Functional specialization**
- Diversified
- Industrial
- Private-sector services
- Public-sector services

**Conditions for development**
- Excellent
- Good
- Satisfactory

**Typology**

| A Metropolitan Area | B Many-Sided | C Regional Engines | D Specialized Industrial | E Small Regional Centers |
|---|---|---|---|---|
| 1 Helsinki | University Regions | 13 Lahti | Regions | 36 Iisalmi |
| 2 Porvoo | 6 Tampere | 14 Pori | 26 Salo | 37 Savonlinna |
| 3 Lohja | 7 Turku | 15 Kouvola | 27 Imatra | 38 Forssa |
| 4 Riihimäki | 8 Oulu | 16 Kotka | 28 Kemi-Tornio | 39 Kuusamo |
| 5 Tammisaari | 9 Jyväsklä | 17 Lappeenranta | 29 Uusikaupunki | 40 Ylivieska |
| | 10 Kuopio | 18 Mikkeli | 30 Valkeakoski | 41 Kauhajoki |
| | 11 Joensuu | 19 Rovaniemi | 31 Varkaus | |
| | 12 Vaasa | 20 Seinäjoki | 32 Jämsä | |
| | | 21 Mariehamn | 33 Äänekoski | |
| | | 22 Hämeenlinna | 34 Pietarsaari | |
| | | 23 Rauma | 35 Raahe | |
| | | 24 Kajaani | | |
| | | 25 Kokkola | | |

icy doctrine, cities act as nodal points for the creation of new jobs, economic growth, and welfare. In this way, urban policy is one form of a wider, R&D-driven economic policy. Knowledge and innovation are the engines that generate new business enterprises and maintain the success of existing companies. Instead of a classical welfare (or, in EU terms, cohesion) policy, characterized by redistribution, the recent polycentric urban policy is strongly opportunity oriented, with an emphasis on growth through exploiting existing strengths and possibilities.

The core of Finnish urban policy is to promote local economic competitiveness, and supporting the specialization of urban regions is a key issue. An aim is to strengthen the competence base of urban regions, integrate them into the national innovation system, and link them to global information hubs. Key actors in this respect are the information-intensive institutions, universities, and other research and development units and higher education institutions. Their role has become very explicit: For example, universities and polytechnics must have strategies for their roles as actors in regional development (Antikainen and Vartiainen 2005).

While the concept of polycentricity was originally merely a structural concept describing the Finnish urban system, it is now evolving to become a strategic policy concept (Antikainen and Vartiainen 2005). In this way, recent Finnish urban policy is characterized by the "growth center" approach—an approach that was already being heavily discussed in Finland in the 1970s. At that time it was officially rejected, because the espoused target of regional policy then was to have a uniform territorial structure along the urban-rural axis instead of an explicitly differentiated policy for centers of different sizes.

## A Programmatic Approach to Urban Issues

In general, polycentric policies in Finland have taken the form of three main urban programs: the Centre of Expertise Programme (1994), the Urban Programme (1997), and the Regional Centre Programme (2001). The flagship of regional innovation policy is the Centre of Expertise Programme. In an indirect way, it is an urban-centered program, as it reflects the idea that the core of any regional innovation system is the functional urban region. The program was launched by the Ministry of the Interior in 1994 and extended in 1998 and 2002. It started in the eight largest urban regions but by 2006 was functioning in 18 regions and four networks of cities. It concentrates on utilizing the expertise of 45 selected, internationally competitive fields and on developing business activities. The selection of the fields of expertise, which vary from nanotechnology to culture, was based first on local initiatives and finally on a national competition, so that a certain division of functions between regions would emerge. Thus, the institutional mechanism is shared, but local needs are taken into account in policy making (Antikainen and Vartiainen 2005). According to the final evaluation of the Centre of Expertise Programme, the operations have shifted from regional networking toward more focused operations, aiming at promoting the development of selected enterprise networks and groups of operators in various fields of expertise, which has led to a more direct impact on enterprises and often, also, to the geographical expansion of the Centre of Expertise impact from regional operations toward national-level operations (Ministry of the Interior 2007).

Furthermore, the Centre of Expertise Programme has succeeded in profiling regional innovation policy, promoting specialization among regions, and channeling development resources extensively to the development of regional spearhead fields. Centre of Expertise operations have acted as a development project catalyst in spearhead fields and gathered fragmented development investments under broader entities.

In 1997 the Ministry of the Interior launched the Urban Programme, which gave urban policy in general a boost. The program clearly had a catalytic effect on strategic thinking in the urban regions concerned (Karppi 2000). The emphasis was on the vitality of urban regions. In addition to competitiveness, other strands of thought on urban development remained important, and issues such as housing and social exclusion were addressed. This reflected a softer attitude in urban policy (Antikainen and Vartiainen 2005).

In 2001, the government launched a new program, the Regional Centre Programme, to be coordinated by the Ministry of the Interior. The program replaced the Urban Programme, and the concept of urban policy evolved into a regional center policy. The new program emphasized the polycentric character of the national urban system and the need to strengthen it. Again, this national regional policy bases its objectives and actions on the distinctive qualities of the regions and recognition of their individual strengths. The aim is to develop cities of different sizes into strong regional and local centers. The Regional Centre Programme also stresses the effects of its measures on the surrounding regions. The general objectives of its policy are (1) boosting the competitiveness of the regions; (2) strengthening the network of actors affecting the development of the urban region (fostering the triple helix); (3) tightening cooperation in regional centers and surrounding regions; (4) strengthening cooperation between regional centers; and thus (5) balancing the regional and national structure. In the period 2001–2006 the Regional Centre Programme was implemented in 34 regions. The focus of the program is on medium-size and small urban centers. In 2004 three urban regions adjacent to Helsinki were included (Antikainen and Vartiainen 2005). According to the final evaluation of the Regional Centre Programme, the program represents a new type of regional policy instrument whose key features are a strengthened multicentered, network-based, regional structure; a functional and efficient regional structure as a factor in Finland's international competitiveness; the support of regional specialization and promotion of extensive interregional cooperation; systematic development work; regional orientation in regional development strategies and implementation of measures; and central government direction through creating conditions via networking and support for other cooperative activities in place of financial incentives and restrictions (Ministry of the Interior 2006a). According to the evaluation results, the objectives regarding regional cooperation strategies, decision-making structures, and cooperation networks have been realized relatively successfully.

Responsibility for the coordination of urban policy in Finland lies with the

Ministry of the Interior. Other essential ministries are also involved, so the programs are mostly based on partnership and cooperation between various ministries, government bodies responsible for regional administration, regional councils, and municipalities. Basic funding by the government currently amounts to approximately 10 million euro per year per program, in both the Centre of Expertise and the Regional Centre programmes. Funding is seed money by nature: The government's seed funding of about 56 million euro in 1999–2006 generated a total funding of 580 million euro (Ministry of the Interior 2007; Lemola 2006).

The main criticism of the Regional Centre Programme concerns the effectiveness of decision-making and cooperation procedures between administrative sectors attempting to support an integrated, overall view of regional development. In particular, various development projects of various administrative sectors implemented at the level of urban regions need to be coordinated at an appropriately high political and civil servant level (Antikainen and Vartiainen 2005). The Centre of Expertise Programme has been criticized for a loss of focus—that is, an exaggerated number of selected fields of expertise and regions.

Both the Centre of Expertise and the Regional Centre Programmes were renewed in 2007. The new version of the Centre of Expertise programme is based on areas of expertise in 13 selected national clusters. In 2007–2013 the program is to focus on (1) internationality in R&D and business activities; (2) boosting the growth of knowledge-intensive companies; and (3) linking the program more closely with national innovation policies. As a result, the number of developed fields of expertise has actually risen from 45 to 63. At least two urban regions must share the same interest; thus, networking between urban regions is a definitive criterion. The role of the Regional Centre Programme is to build a wider basis for knowledge- and competence-based development, to raise the attractiveness of urban regions, and to strengthen the organizing capacity in urban regions. Also, this program will have a strong national networking function. The Regional Centre Programme is currently being implemented in 35 urban regions outside the Uusimaa region (where the capital, Helsinki, is located), and urban programs are run by three urban regions in the Uusimaa region.

## The Urban Network Study

In Finland, a tool called urban network study has been employed for evidence-based planning and development. For an effective polycentric policy, it was considered essential that the characteristics of urban regions were explicitly analyzed and their special requirements mapped out. The national urban system of Finland was framed in the Urban Network Study 1998, initiated by the first permanent national Committee for Urban Policy (Vartiainen and Antikainen 1998) and updated in 2001 (Antikainen 2001a, 2001b) and in 2006 (Ministry of the Interior 2006b). The main goal of the study was to identify regions that have a wider significance in the national urban system. This was accomplished by grading an urban region's significance at the national level by using statistical criteria and by studying its versatility and functional specialization. The greater the variety of urban functions in an urban region, the more versatile it is. Diverse functional specialization means no dominant employment sector. The preconditions for development were also analyzed and compared with the characteristics of the actual regional development. The 1998 study resulted in a description of urban development in Finland in the middle of the 1990s. In the 2001 study the main emphasis was on the changes that had occurred in the urban network and the functional urban regions in the 1990s, thus describing the urban network in 1999. The 2006 study updated the picture to 2003. The method has remained the same, although moderate updates have been made to the analysis in order to incorporate the changes in Finnish society. The urban network studies are used first to categorize urban regions and, also, in the differentiation of urban policy.

The studies resulted in three guidelines for developing urban policy and, in particular, the Regional Centre Programme. First, development policies should primarily be implemented at the territorial level of functional urban regions, which have also been identified as daily urban systems or travel-to-work areas. Using functional urban regions both as the level of analysis and as a target of regional policy enables internal development dynamics to be distinguished more explicitly from the features of external development. Internal dynamics refers to development conditions and features within the functional urban region, while external development relates to the interregional, national, and international levels. Second, policy attention should be paid not only to the major urban regions (those of over 100,000 inhabitants), but also to the medium and small urban regions (25,000–100,000 inhabitants), as they play a significant role in the Finnish context. The third guideline is that development measures should be differentiated according to the characteristics of each functional urban region, thus relating to a region's profile and the division of labor between the nodes in the national urban system (Antikainen and Vartiainen 2005).

## Which Direction for Polycentricity in Finland?

Even though, at this moment, Finland has a relatively well-balanced urban system, changes that have occurred since the mid-1990s can be considered alarming in terms of achieving the aim of a nationally balanced and countrywide settlement structure. Urban regions are becoming more globalized, which means that the national buffer between global economic fluctuations and regional development will become thinner. The ability of regional development policies to solve the employment problems of industrialized and public sector–oriented regions, as well as serious structural unemployment in many growth regions, is therefore much more limited than it was in the 1970s and 1980s (Antikainen and Vartiainen 2005).

There is growing agreement among Finnish policy makers regarding the role of urban regions as the locomotives of socioeconomic development, but less certainty exists as to the right strategies to address that role. Dilemmas include the question of whether the focus should be on further competitive development of the major urban regions or on the less competitive smaller urban regions. The purpose of Finnish regional development policy is to find an optimal combination between regional competitiveness and balanced development among regions. National cohesion policies favoring regions that are lagging behind are progressively turning into regional development policies that increasingly focus on economic competitiveness (Antikainen and Vartiainen 2005).

Throughout history, the success of Finnish regions has been linked strongly to a certain growth industry and to a certain corporation or corporations in the same economic field. Until the 1970s the industries were forestry, paper, and steel, and in the 1970s, 1980s, and 1990s the industry was ICT. While the problems of one-sided industrial regions are familiar all over Europe, Finland also needs to address the problems of cities that are dependent on a wide and redundant public service sector. Those problems are relatively new, and insufficient attention has so far been paid to them.

However, it is expected that not even all the existing growth centers will automatically prosper in the future. Dependency on a one-sided regional economy based on ICT is dangerous, too. It is evident that knowledge and competence have now become the most relevant factors of production across all industries. The criteria for future success seem to be multidimensional, and sociocultural factors will become more directly connected to conditions for the locational decision-making processes undertaken by the general population and by business. Finland's future assets are, among others, the innovation systems that have developed. Also, it is often argued that the strength of Finnish information society is based on the equality of basic social structures—and in that way on a relatively balanced urban system (cf. Castells and Himanen 2001; Antikainen and Vartiainen 2005).

In the search for new "winners," Finnish regional policy has been focused on small and medium-size urban regions, particularly those with a strong competence base—for example, regions with a university and internationally competitive industrial clusters. During the first years of the twenty-first century, there have been some signs of success in some medium-size urban regions that have regained an important role in the national urban system and where traditional fields of expertise have been combined with technologies (e.g., chemistry, food products). The success of medium-size urban regions depends also on how well the idea of having a polycentric urban system will be integrated in other main regional policy programs and the regional strategies of various sector ministries.

Up to this day, the notion of balanced development of urban regions refers, in Finland, to a polycentric urban system that also covers the more remote areas. Some more critical voices are asking, however, whether that ambitious goal of having as many as 20–35 regional centers is at all realistic. It has even been proposed that 38 regions should "remain on the map" (35 regional centers and three urban regions in Uusimaa). At the other extreme, a selection of just the four largest urban regions has been mentioned. In between those extremes, there is the choice of the major urban regions (approximately 10) or one developing urban region in each county (20). Obviously, in the worst case, the whole idea of balanced development would collapse due to a dispersal of the limited regional policy resources (Antikainen and Vartiainen 2005).

Finland is entering a new phase of facilitating networks by renewing its urban policy tools. In 2007 urban regions are applying for the new Centre of Expertise and Regional Centre programmes. Already during the application period, we have seen new networking activity taking place. Actual results will become clear in the future. The next phase is to actively network urban regions internationally. Thus, in knowledge-, innovation-, and competence-based regional development, the focus should be on growth-oriented European and national urban policies, but not at the expense of social and environmental aspects.

## The Urban Network of Europe

The key tool for evidence-based planning—the urban network study method—was applied also in the European context in ESPON (ESPON 2005; for an alternative view see ESPON 2006). The identification of functional urban areas of Europe (FUAs) was based on an analysis of certain features and functions of FUAs, namely, population (mass function), transport function, tourism function, industrial function, knowledge functions, business decision-making functions, and administrative functions. These functions provide an initial indication of an urban region's role in Europe: For both private- and public-sector investments the demographic weight naturally constitutes the most favored indicator for choosing the location of certain services and facilities. The connectivity of the FUAs constitutes one of the central factors of polycentrism. Tourism is an indicator for attractiveness. Manufacturing industries remain the backbone of the economy in many countries. Knowledge functions are indicators of new and potential growth. The distribution of the headquarters of top European firms is an indicator of economic attractiveness, but strong hierarchies within urban systems are often due to the development of administrative functions in the public sector.

There were three conditions, at least one of which had to be fulfilled, for an urban area to be considered functionally significant: (1) a population of over 50,000 inhabitants and an urban core (agglomeration) of more than 15,000 (excluding artificially large "urban" areas with only a minor urban core); (2) a population of more than 0.5 percent of the national population and an urban core of more than 15,000 inhabitants (in less populated countries smaller FUAs were taken into account); and (3) local importance in transport, knowledge, or decision-making functions or regional importance in administrative, tourism, or industrial functions. The total number of FUAs was 1,595 in 2004.

The typology of urban areas is based on the average importance of the seven functions mentioned above. In the final stage, tourism and administration were disregarded, however, so the final analysis was based on the average of five functions. Functional areas were further classified into three groups according to their significance: 76 are metropolitan European growth areas (MEGAs), 261 are transnational/national, and 1,258 are regional/local (figure 3.3).

The results of the polycentricity study did not satisfy all commentators in Europe, and an alternative ESPON study called Study on Urban Functions was

**FIGURE 3.3**

## Typology of Functional Urban Areas in Europe

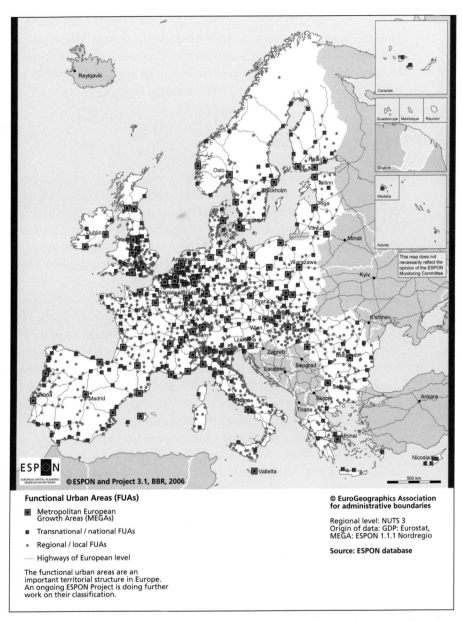

**Functional Urban Areas (FUAs)**

■ Metropolitan European
  Growth Areas (MEGAs)

▪ Transnational / national FUAs

• Regional / local FUAs

— Highways of European level

The functional urban areas are an
important territorial structure in Europe.
An ongoing ESPON Project is doing further
work on their classification.

© EuroGeographics Association
for administrative boundaries

Regional level: NUTS 3
Origin of data: GDP: Eurostat,
MEGA: ESPON 1.1.1 Nordregio

**Source: ESPON database**

© ESPON and Project 3.1, BBR, 2006

launched. It tackled polycentricity as a morphological issue, however, focusing
solely on the size distribution of FUAs (Meijers 2007). Different approaches and
methods resulted in different results (for more details see ESPON 2005; ESPON
2006; Meijers 2007).

The Urban Network Study was only a minor (morphological) step on the way
to analyzing functional links between cities, chiefly because its criteria were
applied differently at national and European levels. Furthermore, functional (sys-

tems of FUAs consisting of different specialized and complementary urban functions), economic (systems of FUAs highly integrated into the labor market, industrial clusters, and trade), and political (systems of FUAs working together on joint strategies) forms of polycentrism all have their own definitions, which also have regional, national, and European-level counterparts. Indeed, a major challenge of the ESPON polycentricity project was the European-wide statistical examination and mapping of economic and functional polycentric regions.

## Making Europe More Polycentric

The "Europeanization" of spatial planning (see chapter 9), concrete milestones such as the ESDP (1999), and the establishment of the European Spatial Planning Observation Network (ESPON) to strengthen development of a common European planning discourse (see the introduction and chapter 1) have had a significant impact on how countries and regions can be positioned within the spatial structure of Europe (Eskelinen and Hirvonen 2006). They have also had a strong impact on the formulation of the goals of the Lisbon Agenda. The next milestone is the *Territorial Agenda* (discussed in the introduction and in chapter 2), which has been intellectually fed by European and also Finnish spatial planners involved in ESPON.

Support for polycentricity is a widely accepted starting point for development policies throughout Europe. Polycentricity has two goals: competitiveness and territorial cohesion. On one hand, it promotes regional competitiveness by the concentration and agglomeration of activities and by the division of labor; on the other hand, it promotes territorial balance by spreading growth centers geographically evenly and to areas lagging behind. Of all 29 countries studied in ESPON, 18 are explicitly promoting polycentricity, and only three fail to mention or consider polycentricity in any aspect in their development policies. Polycentricity is supported by a range of various other policies, although it is still rather sector oriented. Competitiveness is a policy goal—but always explicitly in terms of polycentricity—in 19 countries and cohesion in 13 countries. In total, 11 countries have both competitiveness and cohesion as policy goals (Zonneveld, Meijers, and Waterhout 2005; ESPON 2005).

Both in European and national discourses, polycentricity is a widely accepted principle, but it is based on national sector policies. In most of the European countries—for example, in Belgium, Germany, Portugal, Spain, and Sweden—urban policy is focused on challenges faced by large urban regions (cf. Yuill 2005; Kuokkanen 2005). Growth-oriented urban policies are still marginal in European countries. Finland, the Netherlands, and Norway could be mentioned as countries carrying out such policies, and in Sweden the VINNVÄXT Programme has been close to the model in the Netherlands. In Finland, France, Norway, and the Netherlands, the role of small and medium-size urban regions has been emphasized.

In Finland innovation policies have been connected more strongly and directly with regional development than in many other European countries. The

Centre of Expertise Programme was a national social innovation of the early 1990s, without any prior connection to EU policies. So it was natural for Finnish authorities to actively promote polycentricity in the ESDP process of the late 1990s. In the Regional Centre Programme polycentricity is an explicit aim and can be interpreted as it is understood in the ESDP, although the program is run by the Ministry of the Interior instead of the Ministry of the Environment, where spatial planning questions are dealt with.

On the fringe of Europe, in the Nordic countries, for example, urban policy is different from core-continental urban policy, among others, due to differences in community structures. In countries with relatively small urban agglomerations and long distances between them, polycentricity is primarily a strategic concept between urban regions, whereas in the heavily urbanized areas of Europe the approach is more physical with relevance for physical planning within urban regions.

Up to this time, the notion of balanced development among urban regions refers, in Finland, to a polycentric urban system, which also covers the more remote areas. On the basis of international comparisons it can be claimed that a functioning information economy requires a certain functional concentration (Ottaviano and Pinelli 2004), although the spatial form and degree of that concentration, as well as the minimum size and number of competitive regions within a given urban system, remains an open-ended concept.

The growing challenge is to institutionalize networks, which relates to the challenge of coordinating and providing a framework for joint development work at international (European), national, and regional levels. The main criticism concerns the effectiveness of decision-making and cooperation procedures between administrative sectors attempting to support an integrated, overall view of regional development. In particular, the various development projects of different administrative sectors, implemented at the level of urban regions, need to be coordinated at an adequately high political and civil servant level, which is a precondition for successful spatial development and planning as advocated in the ESDP and for achieving policy goals set out in the *Territorial Agenda*. Key to the successful implementation of the various development projects are development and networking strategies, reform of modes of operation, and management of cooperation and networks, which calls for good governance and organizational capacity. Overall, urban regions are good platforms for development measures.

Cities and regions are localizing and anchoring the Lisbon Strategy to places. A stronger partnership between local, regional, national, and transnational bodies is required. Bottom-up processes should be facilitated by state and transnational players. There is a need for local and regional innovation strategies. Genuine European clusters are needed, but any cluster and innovation policy is still very national by nature. Innovation policies should be connected more strongly and directly with regional development policies, which recognize the vital role of cities.

# References

Antikainen, J. 2001a. Functional regions of the future: The Finnish Urban Network Study 2001. *Journal of Nordregio* 3:20–23.

———. 2001b. Kaupunkiverkkotutkimus 2001 [Urban Network Study 2001]. Aluekeskusja kaupunkipolitiikan yhteistyöryhmän julkaisu 1/01. Helsinki: Ministry of the Interior.

———. 2002a. Finnish districts and regional differentiation. *Fennia* 180 (1–2): 183–190.

———. 2002b. Socio-economic development in Finnish urban regions. In *Labour flexibility: A factor of the economic and social performance of Finland in the 1990s*, P. Koistinen and W. Sengenberger, eds., 63–84. Tampere, Finland: Tampere University Press.

Antikainen, J., and P. Vartiainen. 2005. Polycentricity in Finland: From structure to strategy. *Built Environment* 31 (2): 143–152.

Association of Finnish Local and Regional Authorities. 1999. *Menestys kasaantuu: Alueet erilaistuvat. Selvitys aluekehityksen suunnasta 1990–luvulla.* Helsinki: Association of Finnish Local and Regional Authorities.

Castells, M., and P. Himanen. 2001. *The Finnish model of the information society.* Sitra Reports series 17, Helsinki.

Christaller, W. 1933. *Die zentralen Orte in Süddeutschland.* Repr., Darmstadt: Wissenschaftliche Buchgesellschaft, 1968.

ESDP. 1999. *European Spatial Development Perspective: Towards a balanced and sustainable development of the territory of the EU.* Luxembourg: Office for Official Publications of the European Communities.

Eskelinen, H., and T. Hirvonen, eds. 2006. *Positioning Finland in a European space.* Helsinki: Ministry of the Environment and Ministry of the Interior.

ESPON. 2005. *ESPON 111: Potentials for polycentric development in Europe* (revised final report). Luxembourg: ESPON.

———. 2006. *ESPON 143: Study on Urban Functions* (draft final report). Luxembourg: ESPON.

Etzkowitz, H. 2006. Transforming universities as triple helix catalysts: Towards European innovation areas. In *Cities making competitive and liveable Europe.* Helsinki: Ministry of the Interior.

European Commission. 2004. *A new partnership for cohesion: Convergence, competitiveness, co-operation.* Third report on economic and social cohesion COM (2004/107 final). Luxembourg: Office for Official Publications of the European Communities.

———. 2005. *Cohesion policy and cities: The urban contribution to growth and jobs in the regions.* Commission staff working paper (23 November). Brussels: Office for Official Publications of the European Communities.

Florida, R. 2005. *Cities and the creative class.* London: Routledge.

Giddens, A. 2006. *Europe in the global age.* London: Polity Press.

Huovari, J., A. Kangasharju, and A. Alanen. 2001. *Alueiden kilpailukyky.* Pellervon taloudellisen tutkimuslaitoksen raportteja [Pellervo Economic Research Institute reports] no. 176. Helsinki: Pellervo Economic Research Institute.

Jessop, B. 1994. Post-Fordism and the state. In *Post-Fordism: A reader*, A. Amin, ed., 57–84. London: Blackwell.

Karppi, I., ed. 2000. *Kaupunkiohjelmat kaupunkipolitiikan toteuttajina. Kaupunkiohjelmamenettelyn arviointi 1999.* Sisäasiainministeriön Aluekehitysosaston julkaisuja 5/2000. Helsinki: Ministry of the Interior.

Kortelainen, J. 2002. Forest industry on the map of Finland. *Fennia* 180 (1–2): 227–235.

Kuokkanen, K. 2005. *Kaupunkipolitiikan peruslukeljut ja käytännön toimet viidessä länsieurooppalaisessa maassa.* Acta no. 172. Helsinki: Kuntaliitto.

Lemola, T. 2006. *Alueellisen innovaatiopolitiikan suunta.* Kauppa- ja teollisuusministeriön julka-isuja 10/2006. Helsinki: Ministry of the Trade and Industry.

Meijers, E. 2007. *Measuring polycentricity and its promises.* Working paper, Delft University of Technology. Available from E.J.Meijers@tudelft.nl.

Ministry of the Interior. 2002. *Regional Development Act* (602/2002). Unofficial translation, http://www.finlex.fi/pdf/saadkaan/E0020602.pdf.

———. 2006a. *Aluekeskusohjelman tulokset ja vaikutukset-arviointi 2001–2006* (final evaluation report of the Regional Centre Programme). Sisäasiainministeriön julkaisu 48/2006. Helsinki: Ministry of the Interior.

———. 2006b. *Kaupunkiverkko ja kaupunkiseudut 2006.* Sisäasiainministeriön julkaisusarja 10/2006. Helsinki: Ministry of the Interior.

———. 2007. *Final evaluation report of the Centre of Expertise Programme.* Helsinki: Ministry of the Interior.

OECD. 2005. *Territorial review of Finland.* Paris: Ministry of the Interior.

Oksa, J., ed. 1985. *Papers on social change in North Karelia.* Working paper 12. Joensuu, Finland: Karelian Institute, University of Joensuu.

Ottaviano, G. I. P., and D. Pinelli. 2004. *The challenge of globalization for Finland and its regions: The new economic geography perspective* (publication 24/2004). Helsinki: Prime Minister's Office.

Sapir, A., P. Aghion, G. Bertola, M. Hellwig, J. Pisany-Ferry, D. Rosita, J. Viñals, and H. Wallace, with M. Butti, M. Nava, and P. M. Smith. 2004. *An agenda for a growing Europe: The Sapir Report.* Oxford: Oxford University Press.

Sengenberger, W. 2002. Employment, development and economic performance of Finland. In *Labour flexibility: A factor of the economic and social performance of Finland in the 1990s,* P. Koistinen and W. Sengenberger, eds., 15–45. Tampere, Finland: Tampere University Press.

Territorial Agenda. 2007. *Territorial Agenda of the European Union: Towards a more competitive and sustainable Europe of diverse regions.* http://www.bmvbs.de/Anlage/original_1005295 /Territorial-Agenda-of-the-European-Union-Agreed-on-25-May-2007-accessible.pdf.

Territorial State. 2007. *The Territorial State and Perspectives of the European Union: Towards a stronger European territorial cohesion in the light of the Lisbon and Gothenburg ambitions.* http://www.bmvbs.de/Anlage/original_1005296/The-Territorial-State-and-Perspectives-of -the-European-Union.pdf.

Vartiainen, P., and J. Antikainen. 1998. *Kaupunkiverkkotutkimus 1998.* Kaupunkipolitiikan yhteistyöryhmän julkaisu 2/98. Helsinki: Ministry of the Interior.

Yuill, D. 2005. *Preparing for the next policy phase: A comparative overview of recent regional policy developments.* EoRPA paper 05/1, 41. Glasgow: University of Strathclyde, European Policies Research Centre.

Yuill, D., and H. Vironen. 2006. Regional policy, urban areas and innovation: A policy review. In *Cities making competitive and liveable Europe.* Helsinki: Ministry of the Interior.

Zonneveld, W., E. Meijers, and B. Waterhout. 2005. Polycentric development policies in Europe: Overview and debate. *Built Environment* 31 (2): 163–173.

# CHAPTER 4

# Planning for Decline: The Demographic Imperative

Diogo de Abreu

Over the last few decades, Europe has undergone a series of profound economic, political, and social transformations. These changes have taken place under varying demographic conditions: first, in the postwar years, in a context of economic euphoria and strong demographic dynamism; then, during the 1960s and 1970s, against the backdrop of a slowdown in the economy (including the first oil crisis) and a change in the procreative behavior of Europeans caused by the diffusion of efficient contraceptive methods; finally, in more recent times, alongside a dramatic change in the population structure, with generalized aging, depopulation in many areas and population congestion in others, and intense migration, both internally from rural areas and areas undergoing industrial decline and externally from less developed countries.

At the same time, Europe has experienced in succession postwar reconstruction; a strong industrialization process; generalized tertiarization and development of a leisure and tourist society; and, later on, the challenges posed by globalization and the corresponding reorganization of production and consumption spaces.

The discussion of the demographic issue, though always present, has most often and for most people been based on ideological arguments and standpoints (cf. the pro- and anti-Malthusian debate), rather than, and more appropriately, as a mix of restrictions and opportunities that must be understood and drawn upon according to the needs of territorial and social development. Neither the layperson nor the average politician commands a clear understanding of population concepts, realities, and facts; both commit various errors and misunderstandings within a strongly ideological package.

What Europeans are now facing is indeed the shaping of a new map of Europe before their eyes. The main changes taking place obviously include the following:

- Aging population
- Lack of working-age population
- Intense internal migratory movements and significant immigration from abroad
- Depopulation in many regions
- Rapid population growth in other areas

The trends toward aging and its correlated phenomena are now well known in Europe. However, even among those scholars and academics who do not work directly with demographic issues, the sheer magnitude that aging and the aforementioned related processes will assume in the future is not yet fully realized. Moreover, as a consequence of their ideological significance, those processes are understood even less by the vast majority of policy makers. That is why the implications of the aging process, as well as possible solutions, are yet to be acknowledged and accepted by most policy makers—and by the general public. Hence, an accurate characterization of the demographic processes under way and the collection and production of reliable information on the possible future trajectory of demographic parameters is of the utmost importance.

This chapter contributes to a better understanding of the demographic processes that are affecting, and will continue to affect, the European population. Most of the ideas, models used, and main conclusions presented here are a result of research undertaken within the ambit of the first ESPON program, where the author of this chapter led a team of researchers at the Centre for Geographical Studies of the University of Lisbon (CEG) as partners within the framework of the ESPON 1.1.4 Project, "The Spatial Effects of Demographic Trends and Migration," coordinated by the Swedish Institute for Growth Policy Studies (ITPS) of Stockholm.

The future population evolution in Europe can be analyzed from two main perspectives. The first is to assess the magnitude of the various aspects of these phenomena by quantifying the processes at stake to the best of our ability and insofar as the available data allow it. In this chapter, this will be done for the continent as a whole and for several selected groups of countries. The second perspective considers that even the most stable trends that characterize the European demography exhibit intense spatial differentiation—that is, different characteristics and trajectories, depending on the areas under consideration. That is why, in our research, we have opted simultaneously for global analyses (of the former European Union configuration, EU15; plus the 10 accession countries, EU15+10; and the group made up of Romania, Bulgaria, Norway, and Switzerland) and for analyses at the national and regional levels (by countries and by regions at the NUTS 2 level, one of the levels of the statistical nomenclature adopted in the EU), both of which will be briefly presented and discussed. The criteria used for selecting the groups of countries and the regional units had to do with data availability, as well as with enabling a better understanding of the relevant variables, since each variable we considered is best understood at a certain geographical level. For example, in the case of the potential support ratio (PSR, a ratio between the population of working age and the elderly), the forecast analyses, which are closely associated with redistribution processes, are best carried out at the country level, whereas analyses of the aging and depopulation processes, as well as those of certain economic and demographic performance indicators, are most interesting at the regional level, mainly because NUTS 2 provides the basis for the Objective 1 regions classification—Objective 1 regions being those that receive most of the support under the Structural Funds.

Demographic processes are characterized by long, even very long, time lags, not only as regards the components of "natural" behavior, but also between policy measures and their respective effects. In many instances, lags are as long as several decades, as exemplified by the lag between the moment of birth and the entry into the labor market, or that between the beginning of an economically active life and the moment of retirement. That is why the root causes of the current aging of the European population lie in the demographic trajectory of the last few decades; it is also why any policy actions taken now will have significant effects on the demographic characteristics of the population only some decades into the future.

In Europe, aging of the population is, and will continue to be, an undisputed fact. The two main reasons behind it are, first, the increase in life expectancy of the population due to medical progress and improved social support and care for the elderly; and, second and most important, the sharp overall decline in fertility that Europe, like several other developed regions in the world, has experienced since the 1960s. The combination of those two factors has sped up the pace and increased the intensity of population aging, and, even though minor changes are to be expected, it is unlikely that the future behavior of the population will change dramatically with respect to either of those aspects. At the regional level, it is likely that the aging process in certain areas will be followed by severe depopulation, as the elderly die without being replaced.

## Population Growth

Over the last half century, population growth in Europe has undergone a radical change. An average annual rate of about 8.3 per thousand between 1950 and 1975 fell to 2.9 per thousand between 1975 and 2000. In the late 1990s, a number of regions began to experience population decline. In the 29 countries under analysis taken together—that is, the 27 current member states of the EU plus Switzerland and Norway—total population grew by less than 1 percent.

The overall figures conceal considerable regional diversity. For instance, in the second half of the 1990s, total population declined in 531 out of the 1,326 NUTS 3 areas. It is also possible to identify a clear center-periphery differentiation, both in Europe as a whole and at the national level, where the largest population increases now occur in Europe's economic centers, the major metropolitan areas in each country and the areas of tourist activity. Sharp differences can also be found between the countries with a good economic performance and those undergoing crises. The sharpest depopulation processes have been taking place in the more remote and isolated areas, such as Europe's extreme north and the interior parts of Portugal and Spain (see figure 4.1).

The general situation in Europe is already quite worrying, as some very large areas have been experiencing negative population growth. Moreover, we find that many of the areas undergoing depopulation have also been experiencing other demography-related problems, such as aging and labor shortages—as shown in figures 4.2A and 4.2B, in which the percent of people 65 or older in the population and the value of the PSR are represented.

FIGURE 4.1
## Population Growth in Europe, 1990–2000

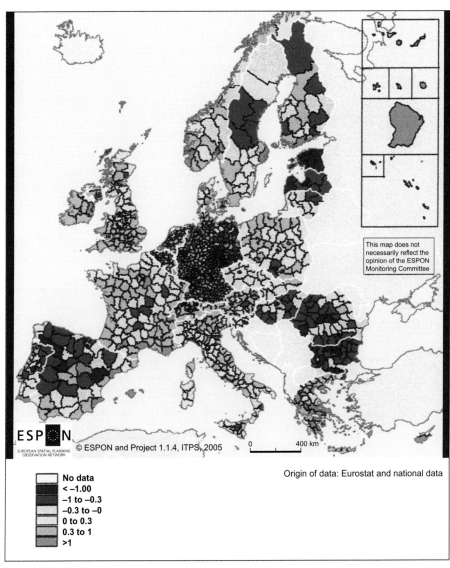

Source: ESPON 2005, 64.

**FIGURE 4.2A**

## Percent of People over 65 in the Population

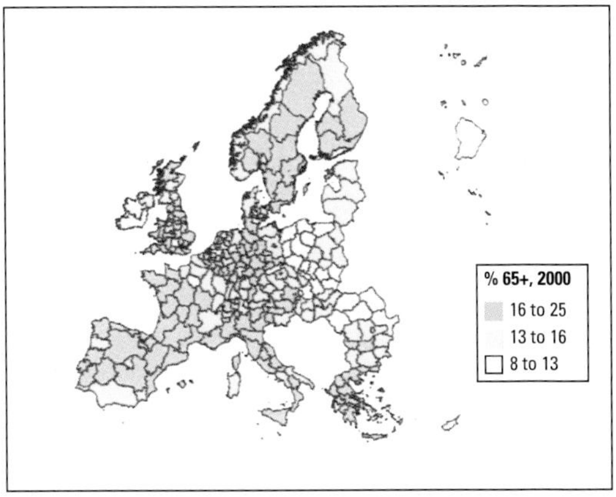

**FIGURE 4.2B**

## Potential Support Ratio

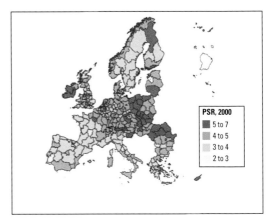

**Sources:** Eurostat and national data. © ESPON and Project 1.1.4, ITPS, 2005.

The demographic trajectories of various regions are closely associated with their economic and social performances. Depopulation and aging strongly affect social and economic conditions through a reduction in the volume and the aging of the labor force; at the same time, changes in regional economies give rise to migration flows that alter the demographic characteristics of those regions.

The variation in the European population, both overall and at the regional level, is a consequence of both natural and migration balances—and the latter is largely a function of regional economic performance.

## The Demographic Transition

Mortality and fertility are the two components of the natural variation of the population, and their trajectories in the recent past are what lies beneath the demographic problem that Europe now faces. The so-called modern demography regime is characterized by a decline in mortality followed by a decline in fertility. Because the two processes do not occur simultaneously, as life expectancy at birth increases, there is a period in which the characteristics of the population change significantly. This is usually called the transition period (ESPON 2006b, 54), and it corresponds to the adjustment of a population from one experiencing high death and fertility rates to one with much lower fertility rates and greater life expectancy.

The "demographic transition model" provides us with the central tool for analyzing the way rural societies (especially European ones) evolved to industrial societies and to their current status as postindustrial. The driving force in this model is the idea of a change in the net worth of children. In rural societies, children are mostly a benefit, as they add to the family labor force. In postindustrial societies, however, they mostly represent a cost, because parents have to bear the costs of their education (from kindergarten to university, often away from the family home) and of rearing them at home.

## Convergence of Mortality and Fertility Rates

As might be expected, mortality has been consistently decreasing in Europe, mostly due to the drop in the number of deaths due to infectious diseases, even though that drop has been partly offset by the increase in other causes of death such as cancer and diseases of the circulatory system. However, crude death rates have remained relatively stable in recent times, as the decline in age-specific mortality rates has been offset by the aging of the population. The crude death rate in Portugal, for example, barely changed over the last half century, from 10.6 per thousand in 1960 to 10.4 in 1990; the respective figures for the EU27 were 10.2 in 1960, 10.1 in 2002, and 9.8 in 2005 (figure 4.3).

In contrast, crude birth rates have decreased sharply, and their extremely low values in recent times are the main trend responsible for the current stage of the demographic transition process. The number of births in a given region is a function of the total fertility rate (TFR) and of the age and gender structure of its population. In developed countries, a TFR between 2.10 and 2.15 is generally assumed to be the minimum for ensuring intergenerational replacement. This TFR is strongly affected by the social and cultural characteristics of a society and its members, particularly the role of women, the influence of religion, and the local power of the churches. Fertility is also dependent on economic features such as income (usually measured in term of GDP per capita), employment, unemployment, female labor force participation, social benefits, availability of child care facilities, and costs of child rearing. Finally, different family policies[1] in various countries, as well as in the same country at various times, also influence the fertility behavior of populations.

Throughout Europe, the aforementioned transition period has occurred at different times, and it has taken different shapes. Generally speaking, the process began in the countries of northern and western Europe and spread east and south. Over the long run (1960–2000), fertility has shown a sharply decreasing trend, dropping below the intergenerational replacement level. However, significant regional divergence occurred between 1960 and 1980—a time when the TFR decreased in some countries but remained relatively constant in others—followed by convergence in the 1980–1990 period. Throughout the 1960–2000 period, there were thus significant regional differences, as well as short-term and long-term temporal fluctuations (figures 4.4A–D).

Figures 4.4A–D, which show the evolution of the TFR in a variety of European countries, indeed show that (1) there was significant convergence during that

---

[1] According to OECD, family policies are generally policies that increase fertility, mainly reducing barriers to having children and increasing resources of households with dependent children.

**FIGURE 4.3**

## Crude Death Rate in the EU27, 1960–2005

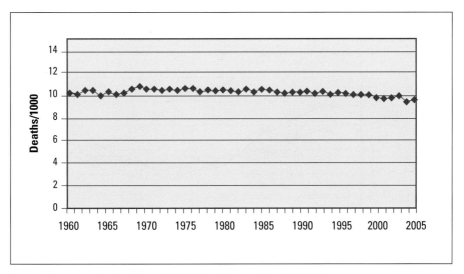

**Sources:** Eurostat and national data. © ESPON and Project 1.1.4, ITPS, 2005.

period, from an average TFR of 2.7 in 1960 to an average of 1.5 in 2000; (2) by the year 2000, the TFR was below the intergenerational replacement level in all the countries; (3) the countries that experienced a decrease later during that period were also the ones where that decrease was most sudden and intense; and (4) TFR recuperations are rare and always limited in intensity and duration.

The spatial distribution of the total fertility rate in Europe at the NUTS 2 level in 1999, the year for which Eurostat prepared a complete database, shows that few of the NUTS 2 regions (certain rural areas of northern Norway and Finland, where the aging and depopulation process has already come to an end) were above the replacement level, and that Germany and eastern and southern Europe exhibited the lowest fertility rates of all. (See figure 4.5.)

Future fertility increases therefore seem very unlikely, save for some major social and cultural changes. Still, the relatively small influence of changes in the fertility rates upon the total resident population in the next few decades will be shown later on in this text.

## Inevitable Aging

As a consequence of the increase in life expectancy and the drop in fertility, Europe's population is generally getting older. By the year 2000, people over the age of 65 accounted for 16.3 percent of the population in the EU15, 15.7 percent in the EU25, and 15.6 percent in the EU29—again, with considerable spatial differentiation (figure 4.2A). Italy exhibited the highest value (18.0 percent), followed by Greece and Sweden (both 17.3 percent) and Spain and Belgium (16.8 percent).

FIGURE 4.4A

## Total Fertility Rate (TFR) in Northern Europe, 1960–2000

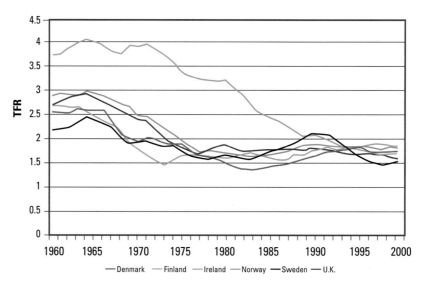

**Source:** ESPON 2005, 78. © ESPON and Project 1.1.4, ITPS, 2005.

FIGURE 4.4B

## TFR in Western Europe, 1960–2000

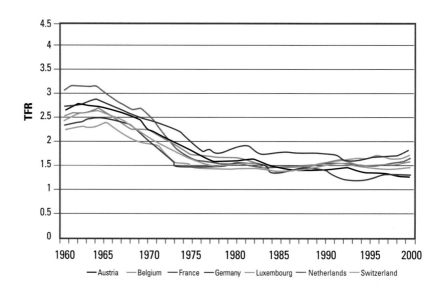

**Source:** ESPON 2005, 78. © ESPON and Project 1.1.4, ITPS, 2005.

FIGURE 4.4C

## TFR in Southern Europe, 1960–2000

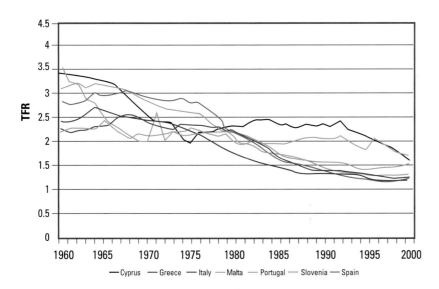

Source: ESPON 2005, 79. © ESPON and Project 1.1.4, ITPS, 2005.

FIGURE 4.4D

## TFR in Eastern Europe, 1960–2000

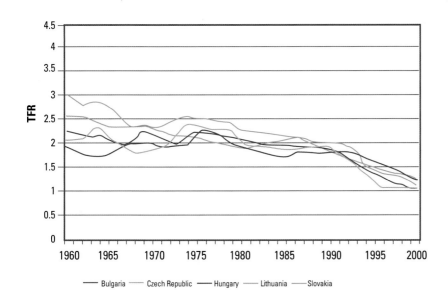

Source: ESPON 2005, 79. © ESPON and Project 1.1.4, ITPS, 2005.

FIGURE 4.5
# TFR in 1999 (NUTS 2)

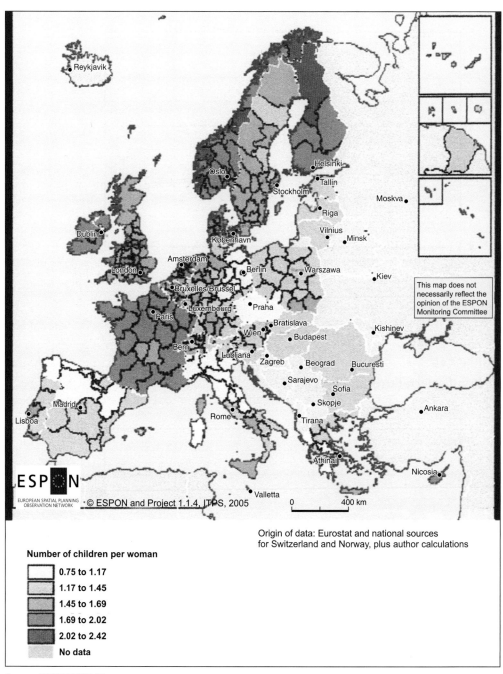

Origin of data: Eurostat and national sources
for Switzerland and Norway, plus author calculations

**Number of children per woman**

|  |  |
|---|---|
| | 0.75 to 1.17 |
| | 1.17 to 1.45 |
| | 1.45 to 1.69 |
| | 1.69 to 2.02 |
| | 2.02 to 2.42 |
| | No data |

**Source:** ESPON 2005, 84.

The countries with the least relative weight of elderly people were Ireland (11.2 percent), Slovakia (11.4 percent), and Cyprus (11.6 percent).

Due to the decreasing weight of youngsters in the European demography, the trend toward an increase in the share of people of retirement age is irreversible. Aging of the population is a phenomenon that is with us to stay, and that must be taken into account when making decisions at both political and individual levels.

## Labor Shortage

The relation between an aging population and labor supply is a well-known topic of discussion. In the past, in the context of population growth, an aging population was largely a consequence of increases in life expectancy, but now it is also a direct consequence of low birth rates. As is becoming increasingly apparent, several years with a small and decreasing number of births have produced some very small age cohorts. This is a problem of multiplicative properties that extend into the future, as those cohorts give birth to fewer children upon arriving at the reproductive age (even under constant age-specific fertility rates), simply because there are fewer of them.

After a period of constant and severe aging, the oldest and largest cohorts reach a point at which survival rates are very low—and the trend toward depopulation then takes hold in many regions. Whether that natural trend gives rise to depopulation is, of course, also dependent on a region's economic performance.

At the end of the transition cycle, the demographic structure is characterized by greater stability, although perfect "natural" stability is possible only after a (long) period of birth cohorts of a similar size.

In many regions, one of the implications of an aging population is a shortage of labor resulting from two different sources. First, the production system cannot draw on local manpower, which no longer exists in significant numbers, nor can it draw on migrant labor, because the lack of regional economic competitiveness makes it impossible to pay wages that can compensate for the costs of residential change. Second, the number of elderly people creates an added demand for health and social care.

Some regions will specialize as "retirement paradises," attracting retired people who want to move to places where climate, environmental quality, and other amenities are better than in the place they used to live. A lower cost of living may also be an important factor. Such regions are economically dynamic places, where the presence of the elderly is a driving force for development, creating a demand for goods and specialized services that cater to their age-specific needs.

## Migratory Flows

Mortality and fertility explain the natural variation of a population, but the migratory balance represents the necessary adjustment between the existing population in a region and the regional demand for labor. Migration flows, whether internal or from abroad, are currently responsible for most of Europe's remaining demographic dynamism.

Internal migrations are more intense than the flows between countries, which implies that there still exist international barriers to population mobility. Even though intra-European international mobility is increasing, and becoming increasingly easier due to policies pursued by the EU, the fact is that significant cultural and social barriers to labor mobility remain within the European space.

The migration patterns inside Europe in the past five decades can be summarized as follows:

- The mass migration flows from the poor, peripheral European countries to the central rich areas, which were quite significant up until the 1970s, have ceased. East-west migration, quite significant during the first half of the 1990s, has also decreased rapidly since that time.

- The attractiveness of metropolitan areas has tended to decline, despite some temporary revival in the 1990s, and is instead being replaced by intense peri-urbanization processes.

- Certain rural areas affected by a large-scale exodus during the course of the 1960s, particularly in the peripheries, have experienced some demographic revival, especially in northwestern Europe.

- In the early industrial areas, migratory balances, already negative during the full-employment days of the 1960s, have further deteriorated with the industrial decline that ensued, causing the level of unemployment to rise in those regions.

- Some leisure areas, many by the seaside (the Mediterranean coast of Italy, France, Greece, and Spain, as well as the southern coast of Portugal and England, and even certain parts of Finland, Sweden, and Norway), have become increasingly attractive.

Over the past decade, the main features of Europe's migration patterns have been an increase in flows from rich to poor regions; massive immigration to western Europe (particularly to metropolitan areas); significant intra-national flows, especially by young workers and students (from east to west in Germany, but also in the U.K. and from south to north in Italy); and, as a consequence of some of the intra-national flows, persistence and even reinforcement of the suburbanization processes under way in peripheral areas of the main metropoli. At the same time, the rural exodus phenomenon has waned in many peripheral regions of Europe and a trend toward counter-urbanization has developed in northern and western Europe. Finally, all over Europe, persistence of the internal macro-regional contrasts is also visible (figure 4.6).

In many regions throughout the world, immigration thus appears, for experts, policy makers, and authorities, as the only possible answer to the dual problem of an aging population and labor force decline. Many experts have not fully acknowledged that reality, however.

The question is how to identify which solutions could lead in a timely fashion to the outcomes that Europe needs. In order to curb the accelerating aging of the population, a younger and more economically active population is necessary.

FIGURE 4.6

## Migratory Balance, 1996–1999

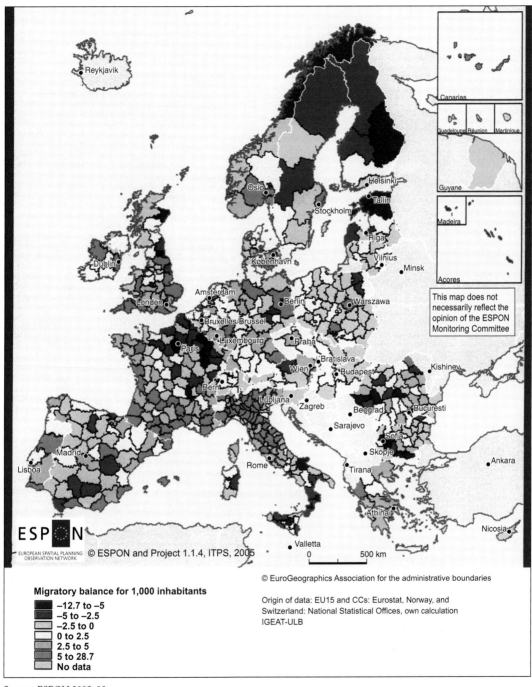

This map does not necessarily reflect the opinion of the ESPON Monitoring Committee

© ESPON and Project 1.1.4, ITPS, 2005

0          500 km

© EuroGeographics Association for the administrative boundaries

**Migratory balance for 1,000 inhabitants**
- −12.7 to −5
- −5 to −2.5
- −2.5 to 0
- 0 to 2.5
- 2.5 to 5
- 5 to 28.7
- No data

Origin of data: EU15 and CCs: Eurostat, Norway, and Switzerland: National Statistical Offices, own calculation IGEAT-ULB

**Source:** ESPON 2005, 98.

Several proposals have been put forth, and they may be summarized as advocating either an increase in the number of births or better use of the population's working potential, which can be achieved only through greater labor force participation, earlier average entry into the labor force, retirement at a higher average age, or including more women in the formal labor market.

Whatever our a priori judgments may be with respect to solving the problem via those solutions, it is easy to calculate their overall effects. Because each year of anticipation (or delay), when it comes to entering (or leaving) the labor force, adds (or subtracts) at most one-fortieth to the labor force, we can weigh the impact of those measures in addressing the problem once we know the required population and working force.

The first option, increasing the number of births, is subject to severe limitations. Later on in this chapter, we present the results of a sensitivity analysis carried out with respect to changes in fertility, which shows that only relatively minor and slow-acting effects are to be expected. That implies that even very high specific birth rates, although a possible solution, would have only a small effect that would take time to be significant. At least during the first two decades of implementing such an option, the *total* dependency rate would increase due to the added number of children, placing an even greater burden on the working population.

Despite all these efforts to better use the present population's working potential, its relatively small volume leads us to conclude that the only possible solution to the problem of labor shortages in the short run is immigration. Consequently, it is possible to forecast that Europe not only is, but will increasingly be, a major destination for international migrants and a continent subject to strong migratory pressure as a result of the sequential processes of aging, labor shortage, and depopulation.

## Projected Demographic Developments

To ensure that European citizens benefit from the level and rate of development they have grown used to expecting, both the EU Council and Commission and the various national governments have been pursuing the goals set in the Lisbon Strategy in order to turn Europe into a more globally competitive economy.

As we have seen, those efforts must take into account both the current demographic reality and, especially, the likely future developments in that sphere. For the first time in recent history, Europe is faced with multiple challenges: how to develop economically and socially in an increasingly global economy with a rapidly aging population.

The future characteristics of the European population have, in the main, already been determined by virtue of its present volume and composition. It suffices to draw on available data, along with a number of acceptable scenarios, to project the trends, interactions, and time lags that will determine the characteristics of the population.

## Description of the Models

This is what we have sought to do by developing a set of demographic models, which have also been used within the ambit of the 1.1.4 ESPON working group (ESPON 2004, 113, 185). The goal was for these models to be efficient, rigorous, and trustworthy; allow for age and regional desegregation; be easy to integrate with basic economic information; and be flexible to use. The base is a simulation model based on simple cohort survival techniques with certain restrictions—thus, they are not actual projection models. Instead, they are meant to assess the existing tensions, that assessment being provided by the number of migrants required under certain scenarios.

The data that were used are much better than the previously existing data, because we have drawn exhaustively not only on the Eurostat and United Nations databases, but also on a wealth of information provided directly by several national statistics offices, thanks to an enormous cooperation effort within the ESPON network.

Out of many other possibilities, nine scenarios were selected. The first five take into account only demographic assumptions. The first one, referred to as model A, does not allow for any migratory flows. The other four, designated as model B, either assume the current migration rates (B0) or estimate the level of migration required to maintain a constant total population (B1), a constant population inside the working age (B2), or a constant PSR (B3). The remaining four scenarios (models C1 to C4) consider changes in labor productivity 0.5 percent and 1 percent above and below the rate of economic growth, respectively.

The historical trend is between models C2 and C4 (productivity 1 percent and 0.5 percent below economic growth), but in a possible context of greater opposition to immigration, model C1 or C3 (productivity 1 percent and 0.5 percent above economic growth) may become a more likely prospect.

Each model highlights a different aspect of the future demographic and migratory trends in Europe.

## Global Results

Generally speaking, the results of these projections are not surprising; their magnitude and significance are impressive, however. That the European population will tend to decrease after an intense aging process is clearly visible. In model A (zero migration), the total population will drop from its current (2000–2001) level of 494 million to 383 million (−23 percent), and even under the current volume of immigration (model B0) it will drop to 398 million (around −19 percent). In order to maintain the PSR at its current level (model B3), the population in 2050 would have to reach an astonishing 1,015 million (more than twice its current level), which shows the difficulties the "welfare state" system will face in the future. The results for all nine models are shown in figure 4.7A.

In figure 4.7B, where only the eight central models are represented, it is easier to see the differences between them. The two scenarios based on recent demographic

**FIGURE 4.7A**

**Population Forecasts**
**(all nine models)**

**FIGURE 4.7B**

**Population Forecasts**
**(the eight central models)**

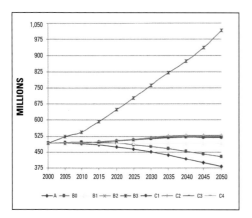

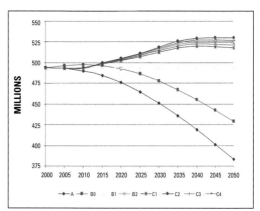

**Sources:** Eurostat, national data, and the author's estimates from the model. © ESPON and Project 1.1.4, ITPS, 2005.

trends (models A and B0) lead to a strong population decrease, even assuming current migration levels, which are considered by many to be high. The results of the projections under those two scenarios also show (figure 4.7B) that the decrease accelerates after 2025, following the death of the last "baby boomers."

## Natural Trends

If we consider only the "natural" demographic dynamics, that is, without migration—an impossible scenario, but one that illustrates the demographic tensions in Europe—the total population of the EU29 would decrease by 111 million people by 2050, returning to the level of the 1960s. At the country level, only Ireland would experience an absolute increase (+14 percent); all other countries would undergo population decline, intensely in some cases—for example, Latvia (–42 percent) and Belgium (–39 percent). If we examine instead the overall pattern by NUTS 2 regions (figure 4.8), surprisingly, the best situations would be found in Europe's extreme north (following an intense aging and depopulation process) and in Catholic Ireland; the worst situations would be found in East Germany, the Baltic States, and Southern Europe in general (especially northern and central Italy).

At the same time, the age structure will change dramatically. The magnitude of the aging phenomenon in Europe is already significant, and all projections show that it will continue to increase substantially and irreversibly.

The relative share of the elderly (people over the age of 65) will increase from 16 percent in 2000 to 27 percent in 2050 (figure 4.9), with significant country variations at the NUTS 2 level. Cyprus, Slovakia, Slovenia, Czech Republic, and Poland are only now entering the aging process, and their aging figures for 2050 are relatively low; two groups of countries are rapidly aging, however. The first is made up

FIGURE 4.8

## Population Variation (%), 2000–2050 (Model A)

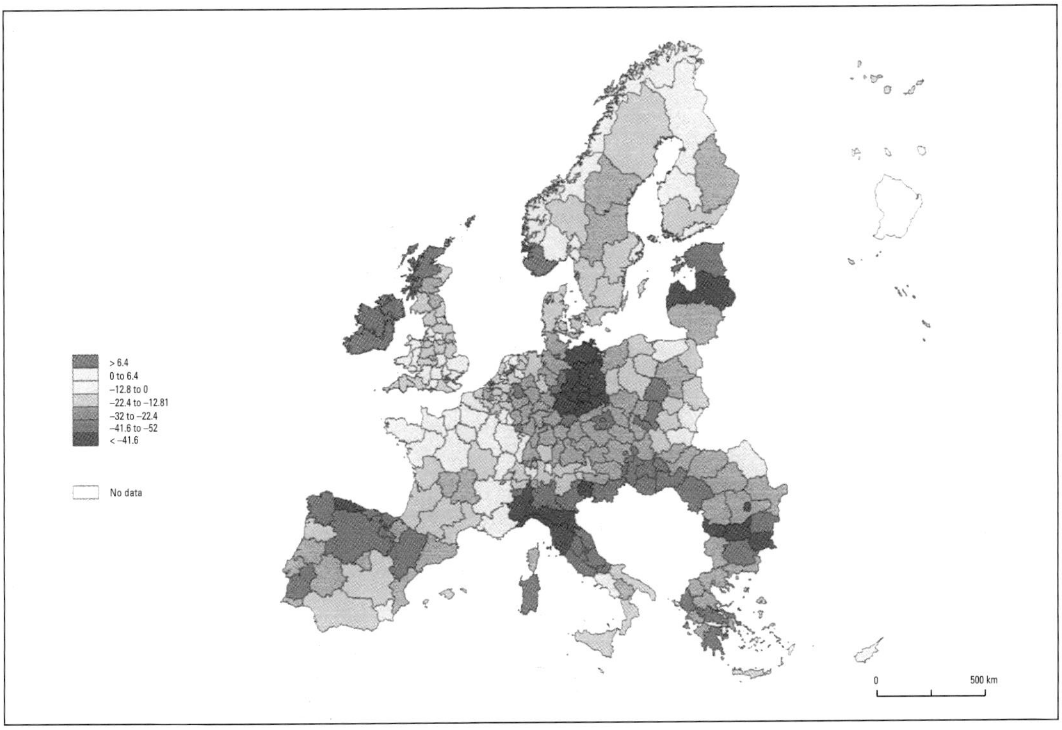

> 6.4
0 to 6.4
−12.8 to 0
−22.4 to −12.81
−32 to −22.4
−41.6 to −52
< −41.6

No data

0     500 km

**Sources:** Eurostat, national data, and the author's estimates from the model. © ESPON and Project 1.1.4, ITPS, 2005.

of countries at the ends of their aging cycles, such as Hungary and Belgium; the other is made up of countries at the beginning of a second cycle, such as the U.K. and some of the Nordic countries.

Also rather surprisingly, even if we take current levels of immigration into account, the situation improves only slightly: The European population would still decrease by about 65 million, and the countries experiencing positive growth rates would be Luxembourg, Ireland, Malta, Cyprus, Norway, Denmark, the U.K., Portugal, and the Netherlands (figure 4.10).

The relative share of people aged 65+ in Europe in 2050 would then be 25.2 percent, which means that the contribution of sustained labor migration inflows, at current levels, over the next 50 years would only cause the decrease of that share from 25.2 to 23.4 percent.

Simultaneously, over the next 50 years, the PSR (potential support ratio), an indicator of the regional capacity to support the social security retirement schemes, as it is the number of individuals of working age (15–64) relative to those of retirement age (65+), will strongly decline all over Europe, with even greater intensity than depopulation and aging. From a ratio of 4.3 workers for each retired person in 2000, the PSR will drop by 2050 to 2.2 under zero net migration and 2.4 under current immigration levels.

## FIGURE 4.9

# Trends of Aging by NUTS 2

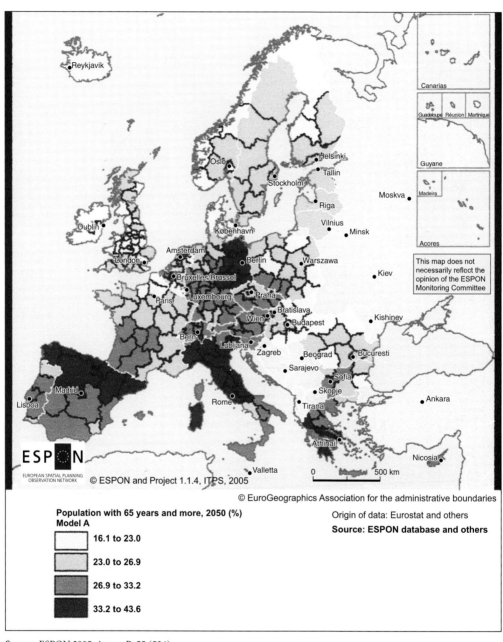

Population with 65 years and more, 2050 (%)
Model A

- 16.1 to 23.0
- 23.0 to 26.9
- 26.9 to 33.2
- 33.2 to 43.6

Origin of data: Eurostat and others
**Source: ESPON database and others**

© ESPON and Project 1.1.4, ITPS, 2005

© EuroGeographics Association for the administrative boundaries

**Source:** ESPON 2005, Annex B, 55 (524).

**FIGURE 4.10**

## Population Variation, 2000–2050 (Model B0)

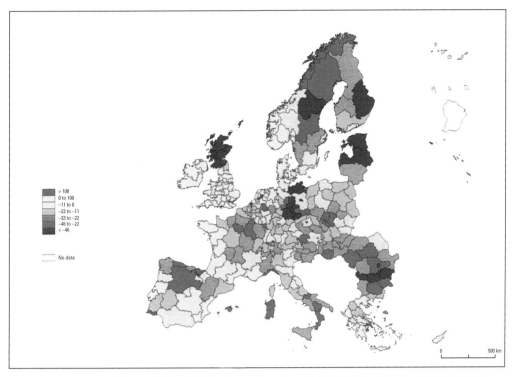

> 100
0 to 100
−11 to 0
−22 to −11
−33 to −22
−46 to −22
< −46

No data

**Sources:** Eurostat, national data, and the author's estimates from the model. © ESPON and Project 1.1.4, ITPS, 2005.

Despite variable geographical and temporal patterns, and even though it is highly dependent on the characteristics of each country and region, the most critical period for the ratio of elderly to working-age people in most scenarios will be somewhere between 2015 and 2030, followed shortly after by a more stable trajectory (figures 4.11A and 4.11B).

That stability will be due to the system itself providing solutions, in formal or informal ways, to two important aspects of the problem: the intensity of the main current demographic trends; and the time lag between a person's birth and entrance into the labor force and the reproductive stage of life, which usually takes place some 25 or more years later. This means that, when it comes to demographic issues, solutions are not immediate and may not take effect until more than 30 years from the emergence of a problem.

The remaining models were designed to estimate the rate of immigration required to keep certain demographic and economic variables at their current levels. Under the current immigration rate, the average number of migrants entering the EU29 in the period between now and 2050 would be around 750,000 per year. To keep the total population at its current level (model B1), however, will require

**FIGURE 4.11**

## PSR Variation for EU15, EU25, and EU29, 2000–2050

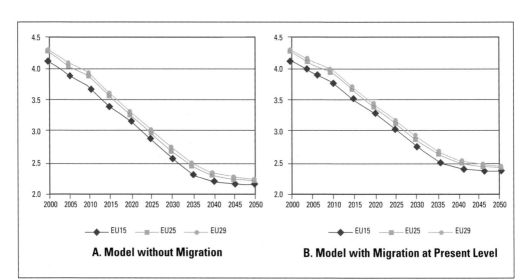

**Sources:** Eurostat, national data, and the author's estimates from the model. © ESPON and Project 1.1.4, ITPS, 2005.

some 700,000 migrants per year in the beginning of the period, almost three times as much (around 2 million per year) in the middle of the period, and around 3 million by the year 2050.

To hold the labor force constant (model B2), more immigrants will be necessary in the first 25 years (2.9 million per year), with less immigration required toward the end of the period (2.7 million). This is a consequence of the effect of newly arrived immigrants on the demographic characteristics of the population in general.

The models based on economic assumptions (model Cs) show the relation between productivity levels and required migration flows. For the EU29, a 1 percent positive or negative change in productivity will imply a decrease of 126,000 or an increase of 125,000 in the required number of immigrants by 2025 and a decrease of 110,000 or an increase of 107,000 by 2050, respectively.

However, the B3 model, which shows the level of immigration required to maintain the PSR at its current level, seems most startling, as it indicates that Europe must somehow integrate an *annual* 11.3 million newcomers in the first half of the period and 16.1 million people at the end of the period (figures 4.12 and 4.13).

These figures also show quite clearly that the volume of projected migration expected or required differs substantially in the various models, depending on their respective assumptions.

If the volume of immigration is high in relation to the total population (as in the B3 and C scenarios), the demographic model clearly shows that the effects of

**FIGURE 4.12**

Migration Flows in Europe Under the Assumptions of the Various Models (volume by 5-year periods)

**FIGURE 4.13**

Cumulative Migration Flows in Europe Under the Assumptions of the Various Models

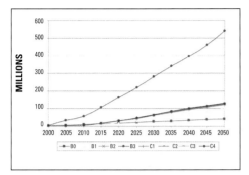

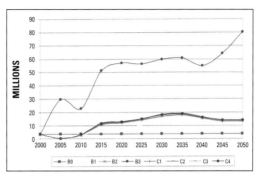

**Sources:** Eurostat, national data, and the author's estimates from the model. © ESPON and Project 1.1.4, ITPS, 2005.

the migration flows tend to exhibit a wavelike, cyclical behavior. The results show a strong cyclical trend with a variation range between 5 and 10 per 1,000 (wave amplitude) and a wave period of about five years.

## Fertility

In all the scenarios, constant specific birth rates have been assumed. Therefore, in 2050 significant differences emerge between the scenarios as a consequence of the differences in initial age structure and evolution.

In 2000 the overall crude fertility rate across Europe was 10.5 per thousand. By 2050 forecasts under the different scenarios vary between 9.45 (in the impossible scenario that requires holding the PSR constant and doubling the total population); 9.05–9.07 in the economic models; 8.8 under the current rate of immigration; and 8.6 in the zero migration scenario. These results also illustrate the limited impact of present migration flows on the relative increase in the number of births. The model therefore serves as an indicator of trends that are already present in the population in different ways, depending on region and scenario.

## Mortality

As in the case of fertility, although all the models assume constant specific regional mortality rates, some differences emerge among the results, because of differences in initial age structures and evolutions. Those differences are of special significance insofar as they indicate the existence of larger trends that affect the regional demography.

Model A shows what the future will be like in most European regions under zero net migration: a sharp aging process, immediately followed by a rapid depopulation process due to a strong increase in mortality, as the larger cohorts of old and very old people die in large numbers in a short period of time. The other models show that the inflow of immigrants makes it possible for the end of the baby boom generation to have a much less sudden impact.

The overall crude mortality rate in EU29 in 2000 was 10.1, but in 2050 the projections vary between 10.4 (scenario B3, in which, even holding the PSR constant, the mortality rate increases slightly), around 14.4–14.6 in the economic scenarios, 16.8 under the current rate of immigration, and 18.1 under zero net migration.

## Labor Shortage

It is much more difficult to deal with and estimate the level of labor shortages, because it is a consequence of the number of workers in each region and the demand for labor, which depends on a series of regional economic factors—with regard to which, medium- and long-term forecasts are particularly unreliable.

Bearing in mind that labor shortages can be either absolute or specialized, the models and scenarios can tell us something about the problems that may be expected. Except in the B3 scenario, the relative weight of the population of working age (15–64) in the total population will decrease from 67.2 percent in 2000 to somewhere between 59.6 percent (zero migration) and 63.4 percent (economic performance similar to the present), respectively, in 2050.

A general conclusion might then be that, in all the possible future scenarios, the relative weight of the labor force in the population will decline and, in many regions, the availability of workers will be not enough to meet the demand.

Even in the short term, many European regions will no longer be able to replace their own labor force, because in many places the ratio between the 10-year cohorts entering and leaving the labor force in the next 10 years is lower than one (see figure 4.14, where the current values are represented at the NUTS 2 level).

## Aging and Depopulation

If we compare the relative weight of the elderly in 2000 with the results obtained with model A for 2050 in the 29 countries and 276 regions of Europe, we find that the latter (2050) figures are always larger (1.74 and 1.68 times as large for countries and regions, respectively). This difference amounts to as much as 10 percent in terms of that ratio (9.4 and 10.5 for the countries and NUTS 2, respectively, to be more precise).

Generally speaking, depopulation comes immediately after the aging process, as the very old die without being replaced. These two processes are therefore related, although not in a perfect way: The correlation between aging and depopulation ($r = 0.75$ for the 276 NUTS 2 regions) is in fact higher for the regions than for the countries, yielding a typology of European regions (figure 4.15).

This typology shows the various European regions classified according to the characteristics of their aging and depopulation processes—ranging from those in green, with a young population structure and experiencing rapid population growth, to those with an older population and undergoing intense population

**FIGURE 4.14**

## Labor Force Replacement Ratio in 2000

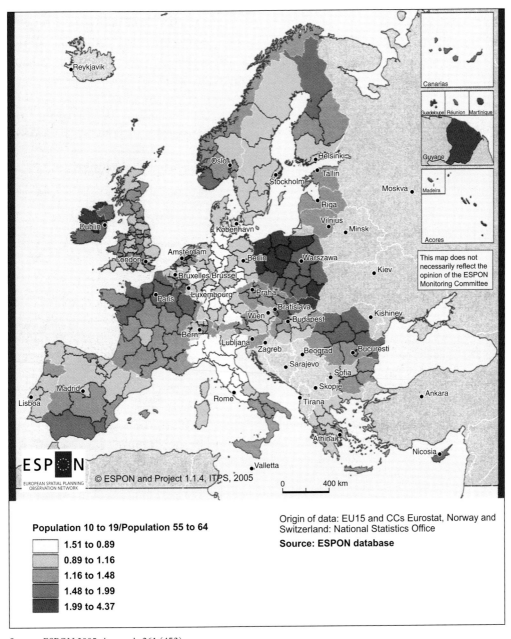

Population 10 to 19/Population 55 to 64

- 1.51 to 0.89
- 0.89 to 1.16
- 1.16 to 1.48
- 1.48 to 1.99
- 1.99 to 4.37

Origin of data: EU15 and CCs Eurostat, Norway and Switzerland: National Statistics Office

**Source: ESPON database**

**Source**: ESPON 2005, Annex A, 261 (453).

decline. The outliers in this sequence (shown on the left in figure 4.15) consist of an insignificant group of two regions in dark yellow at the bottom of that table and those regions—shown in dark red in the upper part of the table—in which there are simultaneous tendencies toward even more intense depopulation and aging.

In geographical terms, this main sequence begins in the consolidated urban areas of central France and the U.K., as well as certain peripheral areas of Norway, Finland, and Ireland. These are all regions with a good economic performance and a young population, whether due to their capacity to draw in migrants or to their relatively high birth rates—sometimes due to their having already reached the ends of their aging cycles. The other end of the sequence corresponds to the Alentejo region (in Portugal) and some parts of Romania, Hungary, and the Baltic states—all of which are regions with low income, strong depopulation, and a relatively old age structure.

## The Development Challenge

Taking all these demographic aspects into account, a key question arises in the present debate in Europe, based on the Lisbon-Gothenburg Strategy. Launched in Lisbon in March 2000, the EU Growth and Employment Strategy set as its main goal to turn the EU into the most competitive economy in the world by 2010, with full employment and diminishing social exclusion, through innovation and the generalized use of information and communication technologies (ICTs). In June 2001, at the meeting of the European Council in Gothenburg, some new ideas were added to the Growth and Employment Strategy, focusing on the environment and the economically sustainable use of natural resources. Like other economic, social, and environmental policies at the European level, these desiderata, which seem quite impossible to achieve within the scheduled time horizon, will now have to be pursued and achieved against the background of the aforementioned demographic decline.

Demographic decline therefore appears as a new and important factor that will strongly affect all development policies, programs, and projects in the decades to come, and that must be taken into account by politicians and civil servants, as well as by entrepreneurs, stockholders, stakeholders, and the European population in general.

Consequently, planning for decline is the most important challenge facing all the agents and actors with a stake in decision making in the immediate future, especially because is the first time that development will occur under such circumstances.

Population aging and the depopulation of many European regions make economic and social development much more difficult, mostly because the available human resources may not be enough to allow for development of the type prevalent in the past. The added difficulties will make themselves manifest in a variety of complex ways: The lack of people of working age and the inflow of low-skilled

FIGURE 4.15

## European Regional Typology Based on Aging and Depopulation Trends as Shown by Model A Results

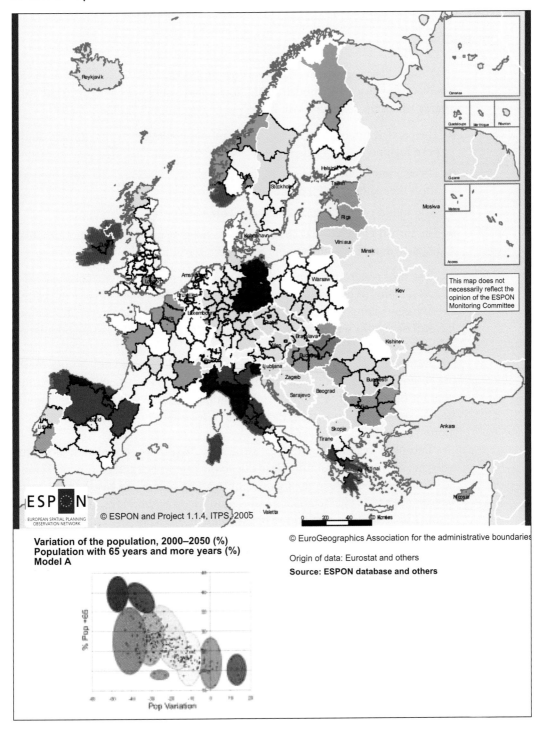

© ESPON and Project 1.1.4, ITPS, 2005

**Variation of the population, 2000–2050 (%)**
**Population with 65 years and more years (%)**
**Model A**

© EuroGeographics Association for the administrative boundaries

Origin of data: Eurostat and others

**Source: ESPON database and others**

replacement migrants will take place alongside, and in relation to, an intensified delocalization of many activities and a longer average working life by increasingly educated people, due to the expansion in life expectancy.

## Conclusions

If we look at the regional and local realities and at the various possible future scenarios as shown by the models, some important issues are brought to the fore, among which the following stand out:

- The current importance of the aging and depopulation trends in many European regions
- The economic and social consequences of those trends and the ways they will affect the regional and local development processes
- The volume of the migratory flows involved
- The formal and informal policy mechanisms that may be most appropriate to regulate those flows and the intercommunity relations they will give rise to

The final results of the models also allow for some meaningful conclusions:

As mentioned previously, the magnitude of the aging phenomenon in Europe, already significant, will continue to increase substantially and irreversibly. Only a handful of regions will be free from the pressures posed by the strong population aging processes.

Europe will experience a strong population decline in the near future. Without migration, EU29 will lose 111 million inhabitants by 2050. Even assuming migrant flows similar to those of the recent past, Europe will experience population decline (though not as sharp as in the "zero migration" model)—in the EU29 around 65 million.

European regions' abilities to attract or drive away population flows are unequal. This result is not fully clear, due to the nonexplicit integration of regional economic performance in the models. Still, as seen before and based on their current demographic characteristics and a number of assumptions, it is possible to identify those areas that exhibit strong depopulation trends.

To keep some of the demographic, economic, and social features regarded as "normal" in present-day Europe, extremely impressive migration flows are required. The inflow of immigrants required in order to reach some of those targets (e.g., holding the PSR at its current level—B3 model) is so high that it can be considered impossible; indeed, even less ambitious goals will be difficult to accomplish.

Europe's current and future demographic trajectory will pose a significant challenge and present some very serious problems to European scientists, policy makers, and the general public.

The increasing aging of the population, the lack of workers, and the reality of depopulation will emerge as central issues in many regions and for many people. If, in some cases, those problems are already serious, there is no doubt that they will be much more serious in the future and that they will remain with us for at least several decades.

As a consequence, policies aimed at increasing the number of births will certainly be necessary, as will policies aimed at expanding the universe of the economically active, which will involve including more youngsters and elderly people in the labor force, as well as increasing the levels of female labor force participation. Increases in labor productivity will also have to be part of the solution. But even if all these steps are taken, they will not be enough.

Only migration—at a huge and unprecedented scale—will make it possible for Europe's features to remain relatively similar to what they are today. And managing migration flows of such magnitude will require not only an accurate understanding of current demographic trends, but also a careful assessment and management of the cultural difficulties and challenges associated with the current immigration phenomenon.

Finally, three questions arise:

- Will Europe have to change its current dominant perspective, according to which it is necessary to change a lot so that everything remains as before, to a new paradigm in which it is necessary to change everything in order for our world not to become completely different from what it used to be?

- Will Europeans know how to carry out such a change—and will they be willing to do it?

- If so, where will all those immigrants come from?

## References

Abreu, D. 2005. Uma nova geografia para a Europa: I—Notas metodológicas sobre a quantificação da evolução das relações demográfica, social e económica nos próximos 50 anos no espaço europeu. Paper presented at X Colóquio Ibérico de Geografia, Évora, 22–24 Setembro.

ESPON. 2004. ESPON Project 1.1.4, *The spatial effects of demographic trends and migration: Third interim report.* Stockholm: Swedish Institute for Growth Policy Studies (ITPS).

———. 2005. ESPON Project 1.1.4, *The spatial effects of demographic trends and migration: Final report.* Luxembourg: ESPON. www.espon.eu/mmp/online/website/content/projects/259 /651/file_1198/fr-1.1.4-full.pdf.

———. 2006a. Action 1.1.4 (2003), *The spatial effects of demographic trends and migration: Third interim report.* Luxembourg: ESPON. www.espon.eu/mmp/online/website/content/projects/ 259/651/file_1200/3.ir_1.1.4-full.pdf.

———. 2006b. Action 3.1 (2003), *Integrated tools for European spatial development: Third interim report.* Luxembourg: ESPON.

Marques da Costa, N. 2005. Uma nova geografia para a Europa: II—A evolução demográfica na Europa: Uma visão dos próximos 50 anos. Paper presented at X Colóquio Ibérico de Geografia, Évora, 22–24 Setembro.

Rauhut, D. 2004. *Replacement migration to Sweden* (ITPS report A2004:016). Östersund, Sweden: ITPS.

United Nations. 1998. *Concise report on world population monitoring, 1999: Population growth, structure and distribution.* New York: United Nations Economic and Social Council.

————. 2000. *Replacement migration: Is it a solution to declining and aging populations?* New York: Department of Economic and Social Affairs, United Nations Secretariat.

————. 2001a. *World population aging, 1950–2050.* New York: Department of Economic and Social Affairs, United Nations Secretariat.

————. 2001b. *World population prospects: The 2000 revision.* New York: United Nations Population Division.

————. 2003. *World population prospects: The 2002 revision.* New York: United Nations Population Division.

# CHAPTER 5

# The Shrinking Continent: Accessibility, Competitiveness, and Cohesion

Klaus Spiekermann and Michael Wegener

At the beginning of the era of the railways, Heinrich Heine wrote in Paris, "The railway kills space, so we are left with time. If we only had enough money to kill time, too! It is now possible to go to Orléans in four and a half hours or in as many hours to Rouen. Wait until the lines to Belgium and Germany are built and connected with the railways there! It is as if the mountains and forests of all countries moved towards Paris. I can smell the scent of German linden trees, and the North Sea is roaring in front of my door" (Heine 1854/1964, 65). The quote circumscribes the topic of this paper, the relationship between speed and space or, in other words, the relationship between space and time.

Increasing mobility is one of the constituting features of modernity: "The history of modern societies can be read as a history of their acceleration" (Steiner 1991, 24). Modern society is a society of centaurs, creatures with a human front and an automobile abdomen (Sloterdijk 1992). Today Europe is facing a new thrust of acceleration: ever-tighter networks of motorways, high-speed railways, and air connections are pervading every corner of the continent, linking formerly isolated regions to the European core. Figure 5.1 depicts the effect of acceleration in time-space maps, in which distances are proportional to travel times (CEC 1994, 66; Spiekermann and Wegener 1994, 672; ESPON 1.2.1 2004, 259). The map at the left shows Europe based on rail travel times in the 1990s; the map at the right shows how Europe will look in 2020 if the present TEN-T outline plans are implemented. The full "space-eating" effect of high-speed rail becomes visible: In 2020 the continent will have dramatically shrunk in time-space.

The vision of a "network society," in which locations become secondary and flows of information, innovation, products, capital, and people are what really matter, is fascinating but also misleading. While it is true that in quantitative terms the volume of flows between locations has exploded, people still need places to settle down, work, rest, feel at home, and meet other people. That space matters is also behind the metaphor of the ecological footprint, which suggests that the earth has a finite carrying capacity in terms of spatial units.

European policy—not only spatial policy—has to find its way through the maze of often conflicting demands and impacts of spaces and flows. Economic policy has to deal with international flows of capital and goods in globalized markets, but also has to help local economies survive in the face of competition. Social

FIGURE 5.1

## Time-Space Maps of Rail Travel Times, 1993–2020

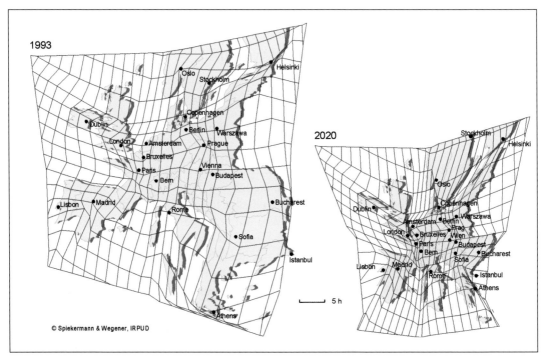

**Source:** ESPON 1.2.1 2004, 259. Reprinted from Spiekermann and Wegener 1994, 672.

policy has to find a balance between open borders and the capacity of societies to accommodate immigrants. Transport policy has to find a trade-off between the benefits of unconstrained mobility and the need to prepare for imminent energy shortages. Environmental policy has to reconcile economic interests and the imperatives of protecting sensitive landscapes and reducing greenhouse gases.

All these are, or should be, elements of European spatial policy and are closely linked to its objectives of competitiveness, cohesion, and environmental sustainability. Nowhere are the conflicts between the three goals so clearly manifest as in the dichotomy of flows and places. The "space of flows" gets even higher prominence in the face of global competition of cities and regions. Accessibility at the global and European scales becomes a core element of competitiveness under the Lisbon Agenda. Already the *European Spatial Development Perspective* (ESDP) states, "Good accessibility of regions enhances the competitiveness of European regions but also the competitiveness of Europe at large" (CEC 1999, 69).

However, connectivity also has implications for two other major EU goals: cohesion and sustainability. Promoting international trade and transport flows may bring economic benefit to some regions and disadvantage to others and endanger the environment of all. Access to high-speed information and communication technology concentrated in corridors between the largest cities may enhance their position in the global market but also reduce the prospects of smaller cities and so run counter to the polycentricity objective. The growing mobility of people and goods over ever-longer distances, mostly by road or air, is one of the major reasons many countries fail to meet the Kyoto greenhouse gas emission targets. It also makes them vulnerable to future energy price shocks.

## Transport

Transport flows provide the most apparent evidence of the inherently spatial nature of most social and economic activities. Globalization and European integration have vastly increased the importance of movements of people and goods within and between regions in Europe. In recent years, transport has received special attention in the political agenda of the European Commission. In 2001 its white paper on transport stated, "Transport is crucial for our economic competitiveness and commercial, economic and cultural exchanges. This sector of the economy accounts for some 1,000 billion, or over 10% of the EU's gross domestic product, and employs 10 million people. Transport also helps to bring Europe's citizens closer together" (CEC 2001, 3).

The white paper also addressed the inherent goal conflicts of transport:

> However, there is a permanent contradiction between society, which demands ever more mobility, and public opinion, which is becoming increasingly intolerant of chronic delays and the poor quality of some transport services. As demand for transport keeps increasing, the Community's answer cannot be just to build new infrastructure and open up markets. The transport system needs to be optimised to meet the demands of enlargement and sustainable development, as set out in the conclusions of the Gothenburg European Council. A modern transport system must be sustainable from an economic and social as well as an environmental viewpoint. (CEC 2001, 11)

The contribution of the transport sector to energy consumption and greenhouse gas emissions is significant. The Commission's green paper on energy states the following:

> It is indeed fortunate that industry has stabilised its consumption, thanks to modernisation investments. Transport, on the other hand, is without doubt the leader in energy demand. All the forecasts predict an explosion in the activity of this largest consumer of oil. . . . Transport accounts for 67% of the final demand for oil, on which it is totally dependent (98%). Energy intensity increased by 10% between 1985 and 1998. Growth forecasts from now to 2010 are phenomenal: +16% for cars, +90% for aircraft, and 50% more road traffic. (CEC 2002, 10–11)

Transport is also highly relevant for the debate about social and territorial cohesion. The quality of transport infrastructure in terms of such factors as capacity, connectivity, and travel speed determines the quality of locations relative to other locations—that is, the competitive advantage of regions. Investment in transport infrastructure leads to changing location qualities and may induce changes in spatial development patterns. If the growth objective of the Lisbon Strategy is interpreted as a call to improve the already high connectivity of the most advanced metropolitan areas, the increasing imbalances in transport provision are likely to further deepen the economic disparities between regions in Europe.

ESPON 1.2.1 (Transport Services and Networks: Territorial Trends and Basic Supply of Infrastructure for Territorial Cohesion) examined the present situation and the trends in transport in Europe with a view to how transport networks might contribute to more balanced, more polycentric, more sustainable spatial development and develop accessibility to increase the cohesion between regions (ESPON 1.2.1 2004). ESPON 1.2.1 developed three types of indicators: transport infrastructure indicators, traffic indicators, and accessibility indicators. Transport infrastructure indicators include information on supply, capacity, services, and vulnerability of transport networks to anthropogenic and natural hazards (see chapter 6). Traffic indicators include information on traffic volume on network links and flows between origins and destinations. Accessibility indicators describe the location of an area (region, city, or corridor) with respect to opportunities, activities, and assets in other areas (Wegener et al. 2001). In addition, ESPON 1.2.1 presented innovative methods of visualizing and mapping transport supply and traffic volumes.

The overwhelming message from these indicators is that the European transport system is highly unbalanced for geophysical and historical reasons. The geophysical reason is the articulation of the European continent by peninsulas and mountain ranges. The historical reason is that the European transport system was essentially shaped by the distribution of cities, with large differences of patterns in monocentric (e.g., France) and polycentric (e.g., Germany) countries.

The consequence is that there is an enormous gap in accessibility between the central and peripheral regions. Certainly, in large part that gap is due to geographical location: A central region will always remain central and a peripheral region peripheral. However, as the central regions tend to be more densely populated and more affluent, their demand for transport is higher and their transport infrastructure is more intensively used and therefore more profitable. That has historically led to earlier and more extensive infrastructure provision and that in turn to more demand, so unless counteracting policies are implemented, the gap in accessibility is likely to grow. One example of measuring accessibility is potential accessibility. Potential accessibility accumulates all potential destinations that can be reached from a location weighted by a negative function of distance or travel time or cost. Figure 5.2 shows potential accessibility by road in 2006 from a recent update of the accessibility calculations for ESPON (ESPON 2007). The concentration of high accessibility in western Germany, northern France, and the Benelux countries is obvious. Similar maps show accessibility by rail with the main nodes of the high-speed rail network standing out. Accessibility by air, however, is concentrated around airports and so is more evenly spread across the continent.

The imbalances in the European transport system are repeated with little variation if other indicators, such as access to the nearest cities, access to transport networks, network hierarchy, and transport flows, are considered. Needless to say, the negative impacts of transport, such as congestion, greenhouse gas emissions, and air pollution, are also unevenly distributed.

The policy recommendations of ESPON 1.2.1 include rigorous speed limits on roads and motorways to reduce fuel consumption, emissions, and traffic accidents; shifting goods transport to inland waterways and short-sea shipping; the creation of dedicated high-speed freight rail lines; internalizing external costs of road transport through road pricing; the reduction of network vulnerability by more modal and intermodal redundancy; and restrictions on movements of heavy vehicles in densely populated neighborhoods.

The project concluded (1) that the goal should be not to provide the same level of accessibility everywhere but to appreciate and preserve the heterogeneity and diversity of regions; and (2) that drastic measures are necessary to respect the environment and reduce congestion but at the same time avoid the relocation of firms by a polycentric spatial organization of settlements and a better organization of production systems.

## Telecommunications

Information flows are the essence of the knowledge society. The rise of the information society is the result of technological progress. The Internet has brought many-to-many access, not only to large corporations but to virtually everybody. The implication for spatial analysis is that space loses part of its importance. Activities that needed to be close together can now be conducted at distant places. Why, then, are there still large cities? Why do people continue to travel to business meetings, conferences, and opera performances? Why is there still a rush hour every morning?

It seems that there are additional dimensions to face-to-face interaction that cannot (yet) be transported via technical networks. That is why it is important to disentangle the myths around telecommunications and to test hypotheses about the spatial impacts of telecommunications in the context of globalization, further European integration, urban-rural relationships, and the core-periphery dichotomy.

ESPON 1.2.2 (Telecommunication Services and Networks: Territorial Trends and Basic Supply of Infrastructure for Territorial Cohesion) analyzed the supply of and the demand for telecommunications, exploring both "mature" and "leading-edge" technologies in what is probably the most comprehensive and detailed analysis of the spatial dimension of telecommunications infrastructure and services undertaken in Europe.

The project started from the highly dynamic telecommunications environment

FIGURE 5.2

## Potential Accessibility by Road, 2006

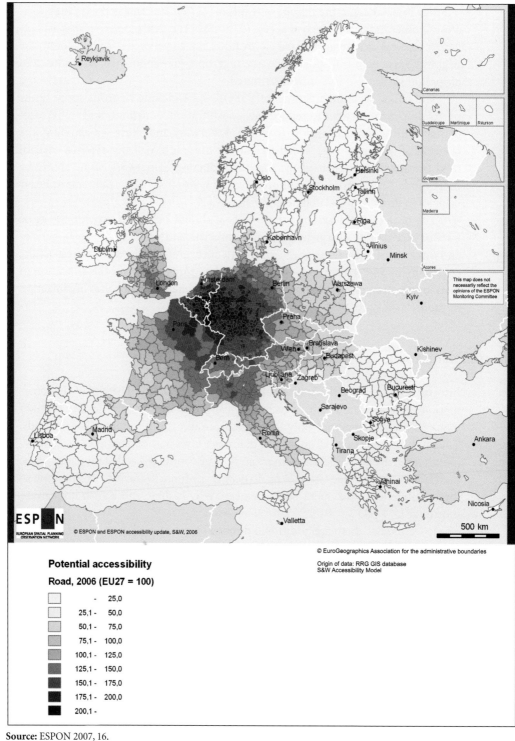

**Potential accessibility**

**Road, 2006 (EU27 = 100)**

|  |  |
|---|---|
| ☐ | -  25,0 |
| ☐ | 25,1 -  50,0 |
| ☐ | 50,1 -  75,0 |
| ☐ | 75,1 -  100,0 |
| ☐ | 100,1 -  125,0 |
| ☐ | 125,1 -  150,0 |
| ☐ | 150,1 -  175,0 |
| ☐ | 175,1 -  200,0 |
| ■ | 200,1 - |

© EuroGeographics Association for the administrative boundaries

Origin of data: RRG GIS database
S&W Accessibility Model

**Source:** ESPON 2007, 16.

created by the liberalization of telecommunications markets and the development and application of new technologies in the 1980s and 1990s and identified trends, which partly point toward a more even spread of technology and partly to continuing disparities. The overall message emerging from the project is that—notwithstanding the attempts to create a single market for telecommunications, a common regulatory framework, and a common basis for developing the information society—the situation of supply and demand for telecommunications in Europe is highly complex due to the wide range of socioeconomic circumstances in the EU member states, historical differences in patterns and trends in telecommunications development, different technologies exhibiting different geographical patterns, and particular national attitudes to intervention in the market. Despite those differences, however, some general patterns emerge:

- There is a north-south divide across the EU member states because of the strength of the Nordic countries, which lead the way in the uptake of almost all technologies.
- The European core-periphery dichotomy does not hold for telecommunications due to the strength of the Nordic periphery, but also because in mobile telephony and broadband technology the Mediterranean periphery outpaces the core.
- There is a west-east divide between the old and new EU member states across all technologies, though there is evidence of rapid progress in the new member states.
- There are differences in telecommunications diffusion in the new member states, with the most recent new member states, Bulgaria and Romania, lagging behind.

Based on the differences between countries in the adoption of telecommunications, the project identified distinctive "national telecommunications cultures," such as high communication, high computing cultures (Sweden and Finland); high voice communication cultures (Greece, Italy, and the Czech Republic); high computing cultures (Netherlands and Denmark); and low telecommunications cultures with respect to both voice and the Internet (Germany and France). If different telecommunications technologies are examined, the following computing cultures emerge:

- High uptake of PCs and the Internet is generally associated with economic development and high GDP per capita.
- Adoption of broadband technologies is usually associated with high levels of GDP per capita, population density, and geographical position close to the European core.
- Diffusion of mobile telephones is highest in peripheral regions, reflecting the north-south dichotomy noted above.

The report of ESPON 1.2.2 (2005) concludes by discussing how telecommunications policies can be used to enable all citizens to participate fully in the information society and knowledge economy and to overcome existing disparities in the supply of and demand for telecommunications networks and services within and between the EU member states. Three areas of intervention are discussed: liberalization of telecommunications markets, stimulation of demand by training and education, and stimulation of supply by supporting the provision of telecommunications infrastructure. The authors argue that, in particular, broadband technology deserves to be a focus of policies, but they emphasize that for interventions to succeed, a greater symmetry of information between public authorities and private-sector telecommunications providers needs to be established. Finally, they make a plea for an improved and harmonized data collection system covering the ESPON space, which is needed because, as they point out, only through improved databases can truly evidence-based policy making occur.

## Transport and Telecommunications and Spatial Development

The important role of transport infrastructure for regional development is one of the fundamental principles of regional economics. In its most simplified form this principle implies that regions with better access to the locations of input materials and markets will, ceteris paribus, be more productive, more competitive, and hence more successful than more remote regions.

However, today the relationship between transport infrastructure and economic development has become more complex than ever. There are successful regions in the European core confirming the theoretical expectation that location matters, but there are also centrally located regions suffering from industrial decline and high unemployment. On the other side of the spectrum, the poorest regions, as theory would predict, are at the periphery, but there are also prosperous peripheral regions such as the Nordic countries. To make things even more difficult, some of the economically fastest-growing regions are among the most peripheral ones. Figure 5.3 (ESPON 1.2.1 2004, 22) illustrates this complexity by showing the regions that perform better or worse than their geographical position would suggest.

The EU hopes to contribute to reducing the socioeconomic disparities between its regions by developing the Trans-European Transport Networks (TEN-T) in the old member states and the Transport Infrastructure Needs Assessment (TINA) networks in the new member states. However, although they are two of the most ambitious initiatives of the European Community, the value of the TEN-T and TINA programs is not undisputed.

Critics argue that many of the new connections fail to link peripheral countries to the core and instead strengthen the ties between central regions, reinforcing their accessibility advantage. Some argue that regional development policies based on the creation of infrastructure in lagging regions have not succeeded in reducing regional disparities in Europe, whereas others point out that it has yet to be ascertained that the reduction of barriers between regions has disadvantaged

**FIGURE 5.3**

## Accessibility versus Economic Performance, 2001

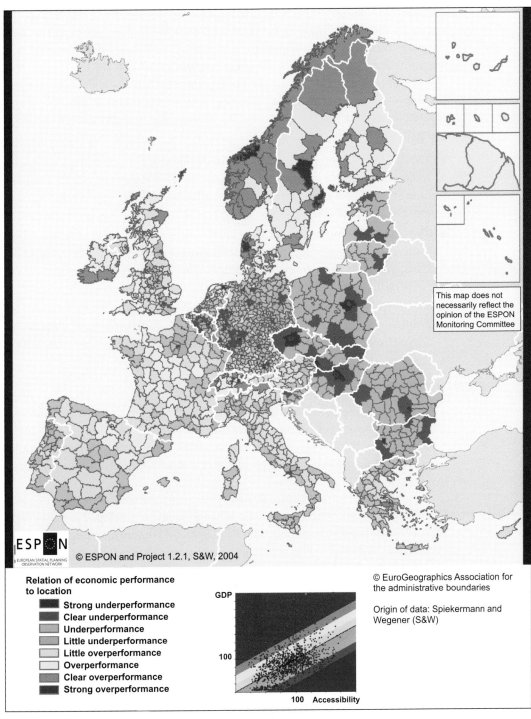

© ESPON and Project 1.2.1, S&W, 2004

This map does not necessarily reflect the opinion of the ESPON Monitoring Committee

© EuroGeographics Association for the administrative boundaries

Origin of data: Spiekermann and Wegener (S&W)

**Relation of economic performance to location**

- Strong underperformance
- Clear underperformance
- Underperformance
- Little underperformance
- Little overperformance
- Overperformance
- Clear overperformance
- Strong overperformance

GDP

100

100   Accessibility

**Source:** ESPON 1.2.1 2004, 22.

peripheral regions. From a theoretical point of view, both equalizing and polarizing can occur. A new motorway or high-speed rail connection between a peripheral and a central region, for instance, makes it easier for producers in the peripheral region to market their products in large cities; however, it may also expose the region to the competition of more advanced products from the center and so endanger formerly secure regional monopolies. These issues have received new attention through the enlargement of the European Union in 2004.

ESPON 2.1.1 (Territorial Impacts of EU Transport and TEN Policies) assessed the impacts of EU and national transport and telecommunications policies on regional economic development and cohesion in the enlarged European Union using three forecasting models:

- The SASI model is a multiregional recursive-dynamic model of regional socio-economic development (population, migration, economy) of NUTS 3 regions based on regional production functions with accessibility as a production factor (ESPON 2.1.1 2003, 52–70).

- The CGEurope model is a multiregional, spatial, computable, general equilibrium model of regional economic development at the NUTS 3 level, in which transport costs appear as expenditures for transport and business travel (ESPON 2.1.1 2003, 70–95).

- The STIMA model assesses the impact of information and communications technologies (ICT) on regional economic growth and distribution at the NUTS 2 level, based on regional production functions (ESPON 2.1.1 2003, 96–124).

## Economic Development

These models were applied to transport and ICT policy scenarios up to the year 2021. The transport policy scenarios included different priorities of TEN-T infrastructure investments (e.g., all priority projects, all projects, only cross-border projects, or only projects in lagging regions), different options of transport pricing, and combinations of both.

The transport infrastructure scenarios were implemented using the GIS-based European road, rail, waterway, and air network database developed at the University of Dortmund and maintained by RRG Spatial Planning and Geoinformation (RRG 2007). The ICT policy scenarios included one in which financial resources are allocated indiscriminately among regions, one in which they are allocated to more advanced regions, and one in which they are targeted to less developed regions.

The main general result from the scenario simulations is that the overall effects of transport infrastructure investments and other transport policies are small compared with those of socioeconomic and technical macro trends such as globalization, increasing competition between cities and regions, aging populations, and increasing labor force participation and labor productivity. The second main result is that even large increases in regional accessibility translate into only very small increases in regional economic activity. However, that statement needs to be qualified, as the magnitude of the effect seems to depend strongly on the already existing level of accessibility:

- For regions in the European core with all the benefits of a central geographical location *plus* an already highly developed transport and telecommunications infrastructure, additional gains in accessibility bring few additional incentives for economic growth.

- For regions at the European periphery, however, which suffer from a remote geographical location *plus* an underdeveloped transport infrastructure, a gain in accessibility brings significant progress in economic development. But the opposite may happen if the new connection opens a formerly isolated region to external competition. Significant positive economic effects for the new EU member states can be expected only if the TINA projects linking those countries to the major centers of economic activity in western Europe are implemented.

- Infrastructure policies have larger effects than pricing policies, and the magnitude of the effect is related to the number and size of projects. The effect of pricing scenarios depends on their direction: Scenarios that make transport less expensive have a positive, scenarios that make transport more expensive, a negative, economic effect. Negative effects of pricing policies can be mitigated by their combination with network scenarios with positive economic effects, although the net effect depends on the magnitude of the two components.

ICT investments have analogous effects. As expected, promoting ICT in the most advanced regions is economically more efficient but increases the disparities in ICT adoption between regions, whereas its promotion in lagging regions reduces disparities.

Similar scenarios were calculated in ESPON 1.1.3 (Enlargement of the European Union and the Wider European Perspective as Regards its Polycentric Spatial Structure) for the new EU member states. There the scenarios examined the effects of enlargement as such and the associated reductions in border waiting times and different strategies of transport infrastructure investments in the new member states (ESPON 1.1.3 2006, part 2, 197–218). The results were in general agreement with those achieved in ESPON 2.1.1, indicating that transport infrastructure investments in the new member states could make a significant contribution to help those countries' economies catch up with those of the old member states. Figure 5.4 demonstrates this by showing the impact on GDP per capita in a scenario in which massive infrastructure improvements in the new member states are assumed in addition to the TEN and TINA implementation plans. However, the comparison between the two maps shows that, though in relative terms economic growth is faster in the new member states than in the old member states, the old member states gain much more in absolute terms.

ESPON 3.2 (Spatial Scenarios and Orientations in Relation to the ESDP and Cohesion Policy) developed and applied the regional economic model MASST (ESPON 3.2 2006, vol. 4, 11–53; see also chapter 7). The MASST model differs

**FIGURE 5.4**

## Relative (left) and Absolute (right) GDP Effects, Scenario B5, 2031

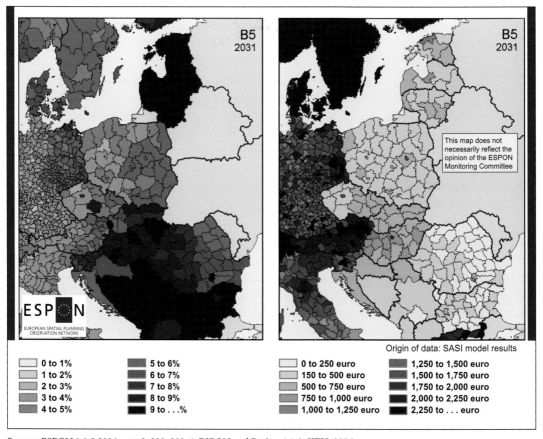

Source: ESPON 1.1.3 2006, part 2, 208–209. © ESPON and Project 1.1.3, KTH, 2006.

from the three regional economic models used in ESPON 2.1.1 by its two-level construction, in which a national model taking account of macroeconomic factors, such as private consumption, investments, public expenditure, and imports and exports, drives the lower-level regional economic model of economic development, population, and migration. The regional economic model is based on regional production functions in which transport is represented by transport infrastructure endowment provided by the KTEN travel and freight transport model (ESPON 3.2 2006, vol. 4, 54–98). The scenarios examined in ESPON 3.2 assume different transport infrastructure programs, but the programs are packaged with many other assumptions so that their contribution to the changes in regional socioeconomic impacts cannot be identified.

The KTEN model also calculated accessibility indicators, which, together with the GDP forecasts of the SASI model and other variables, were used in an experimental application of the TEQUILA (Territorial Efficiency Quality Identity Layered Assessment) multicriteria evaluation model to a scenario assuming implementation of the priority projects of the TEN-T program (ESPON 3.2 2006, vol. 5, 87–97). The evaluation confirmed the results of ESPON 2.1.1, showing that the strongest economic effects can be expected in the western regions of the new member states and the Iberian peninsula, but that the environmental balance is likely to be negative all over Europe, particularly in already heavily congested metropolitan areas, with the exception of new rail corridors in which a modal shift to rail occurs.

## Cohesion

The analysis of cohesion effects showed that different cohesion indicators give different results, and that the distinction between relative and absolute convergence or divergence is especially important. In particular, the most frequently applied indicators of cohesion (e.g., the coefficient of variation and the Gini coefficient) tend to signal convergence in many cases where in fact divergence occurs (ESPON 1.1.3, part 2, 211–214):

- If the whole European Union is considered, most scenarios contribute to convergence in relative terms in both accessibility and GDP per capita, except pricing scenarios that make transport more expensive. However, in absolute terms all scenarios increase the gap in accessibility and GDP per capita between the rich central regions and the poorer peripheral regions, again except pricing scenarios that make transport more expensive.

- If only the new member states are considered, only those infrastructure scenarios that strengthen the corridors between eastern and western Europe improve the accessibility of those countries. Other projects widen the gap between the capital cities and rural regions of the new member states. For GDP per capita, the general pattern is relative convergence and absolute divergence, except for the pricing scenarios that make transport more expensive. Scenarios that reduce the economic disparities between old and new member states may do so at the expense of larger disparities within the new member states.

The conclusions and policy recommendations of ESPON 2.1.1 (2003, 268–273) focus on the trade-offs between efficiency ("competitiveness") and spatial equity ("territorial cohesion"). The findings that all infrastructure scenarios reduce disparities in accessibility and GDP per capita might lead to the conclusion that a reorientation of European infrastructure policy is necessary. However, the caveat is that those findings are true only if conventional relative cohesion indicators are applied—that is, if convergence is measured in percentage terms. The optimistic picture disappears if absolute gains and losses are considered: A high gain in percentage terms in a poor region may be much less in absolute terms than a low percentage gain in a rich region.

The conclusions to be drawn from these results depend on one's economic beliefs. If one follows the current neoliberal economic paradigm, the conflict between efficiency and equity should not be solved by revising the TEN and TINA plans to the disadvantage of the centers. Instead, the poorer countries should receive compensation transfers so that they can develop their secondary networks and allow their peripheries to gain from the spread effects of more rapid growth in their centers. If one fears that that will lead to even greater economic disparities, however, a policy to improve the accessibility of disadvantaged peripheral regions at the expense of central regions is more appropriate. Similar considerations apply to ICT policy.

Another trade-off between equity and sustainability arises in the case of pricing policies. There is a broad consensus that transport pricing is the right way to internalize environmental externalities. The conflict with the goal of balanced spatial development appears because that cost increase is most unfavorable for lagging, rural, and peripheral regions, which are in general less affluent than the centers. The political conclusion is that pricing scenarios should not be abandoned in favor of spatial equality objectives. Rather, policies deepening regional income disparities should be accompanied by transfers in favor of loser regions. Such an instrument mix of pricing and compensation is the right way to both protect the environment and avoid undesired spatial imbalances.

## Polycentricity

The promotion of balanced polycentric urban systems is one of the major objectives of the ESDP (CEC 1999; see also chapter 3) and has been restated as a goal in the *Territorial Agenda of the European Union* (Territorial Agenda 2007, 4). Cities as nodes in networks and centers of regions are therefore important objects of investigation in ESPON.

However, until today the concept of polycentricity has remained largely at the level of rhetoric without a precise operational definition (which puts it in a class with similarly vague concepts such as "city networks" and "industrial clusters"). There exists neither a method to identify or measure polycentricity at different spatial scales nor a method to assess the impacts of polycentricity (or the lack of it) with respect to policy goals such as efficiency, equity, and sustainability. It is therefore not possible to determine an optimal degree of polycentricity between centralization and decentralization or, in other words, between the extremes of monocentricity and dispersal. That makes it difficult to formulate well-founded policy recommendations as to which cities should receive priority treatment.

That is why in ESPON 1.1.1 (Potentials for Polycentric Development in Europe) an index of polycentricity combining the three dimensions of size, location, and connectivity was proposed (ESPON 1.1.1 2004, 60–84):

- The *size* indicator measures the distribution of population and GDP and is based on the notion that a flat rank-size distribution is more polycentric than an urban system dominated by one large city.

- The *location* indicator measures the spatial distribution of cities and assumes that a uniform distribution of cities across a territory is better for a polycentric urban system than one in which all cities are clustered in one part of the territory.

- The *connectivity* indicator measures the distribution of accessibility across cities and assumes that an urban system with good connections between lower-level cities is more polycentric than one in which all connections are concentrated on the largest city.

Through the accessibility variable in the connectivity indicator the concept of polycentricity is connected with transport. As was pointed out in the introduction to this chapter, the European transport network is largely determined by the distribution of cities, but the transport system also determines the size and location of cities: Acceleration of transport creates new, larger hierarchies of cities superimposed over the small-scale urban network created at the time of the stage coach.

In ESPON 1.1.1 the index of polycentricity was calculated for the whole of Europe, all EU countries, and a case study region (ESPON 1.1.1 2004, 61–79). With respect to the connectivity indicator, Austria, Germany, and the Netherlands score highest, and the Baltic states Lithuania and Estonia score lowest. By correlating the index of polycentricity with GDP per capita, regional disparities, and energy consumption, it could be shown that countries with more polycentric urban systems are, in general, more economically efficient, and sustainable (ESPON 1.1.1 2004, 80–84).

In ESPON 1.1.3 the index of polycentricity of ESPON 1.1.1 was applied to the urban systems of the new member states in connection with the forecasts of the SASI model described above (ESPON 1.1.3 2006, part 2, 158–173, 214–217). A methodological difficulty here is that the SASI model is based on NUTS 3 regions as spatial units and not cities. With respect to the connectivity index, therefore, the assumption was made that the accessibility of an urban center changes in accord with changes in the accessibility level of the NUTS 3 region where it is located.

Figure 5.5 shows the effects of the scenarios examined in ESPON 1.1.3 on polycentricity of national urban systems in the old member states (EU15) and the new member states and accession countries (NMAC)—ESPON 1.1.3 was completed in 2006 and thus before the accession of Bulgaria and Romania. Figure 5.6 shows the effects of the same scenarios on polycentricity measured at the level of metropolitan European growth areas (MEGA) defined in ESPON 1.1.1 for the whole of the present European Union (EU27). The heavy black lines in both figures represent the development of polycentricity between 1981 and 2031 in reference scenario 00. The thinner blue and red lines indicate how the enlargement scenario A1 and the five transport infrastructure scenarios B1 to B5 deviate from the reference scenario between 2001 and 2031 (B5 is the scenario presented in figure 5.4).

Figure 5.5 shows that the urban systems of the new member states are today on average more polycentric than those of the old member states. They were even more polycentric in the past, probably because of their history as planned economies in which there was no market-driven spatial development. However, after the opening of the iron curtain in the early 1990s, their capital cities and major agglomerations attracted formerly suppressed rural-to-urban migration, with the effect that those cities grew at the expense of smaller urban centers. Polycentricity in the new member states is likely to further decline due to market forces

FIGURE 5.5

Development of Polycentricity in the Old Member States (EU15)
and New Member States and Accession Countries (NMAC),
1981–2031

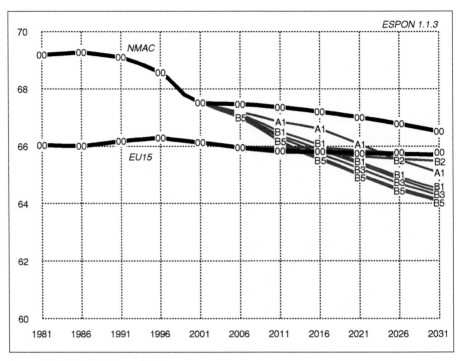

**Source:** ESPON 1.1.3 2006, part 2, 215.

and even become lower than that of the old member states. Polycentricity declines
in the old member states, too, but much more slowly than in the new member
states because of their longer experience with market-driven spatial development.
This is possibly the reason the transport infrastructure improvements in scenarios
B1 to B5 have only little effect on polycentricity in the old member states—their
transport networks are already highly developed and can be improved only marginally. Because there is still a great demand for transport infrastructure in the new
member states, infrastructure improvements have much greater effects; also, they
tend to be oriented toward the largest cities, with the effect that polycentricity
declines in proportion to the volume of infrastructure improvements in the
scenarios.

Figure 5.6, however, shows that at the highest level of the urban hierarchy in
Europe polycentricity has increased in the past and is likely to increase in the
medium-term future. This is mainly due to the fast economic growth of capital
cities and other large cities in the new member states. Already the opening of the
iron curtain in the 1990s and the integration effects of the EU enlargement in 2004

FIGURE 5.6

## Development of Polycentricity of Metropolitan European Growth Areas (MEGA) in Europe, 1981–2031

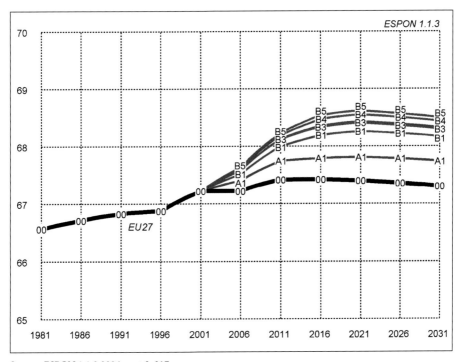

Source: ESPON 1.1.3 2006, part 2, 217.

(scenario A1) have moved those cities up in the urban hierarchy. The transport infrastructure scenarios B1 to B5 add momentum to that process.

The comparison of the two figures shows that the goal of a balanced polycentric urban system at one spatial level tends to be in conflict with the same goal at other spatial levels. Table 5.1 illustrates the relevant policy options and their associated goal conflicts. For instance, strengthening major urban centers outside the "European core" would increase spatial disparities between the already too dominant capital cities and other large cities in countries such as the Baltic states, Hungary, and the Czech Republic. However, if the promotion of balanced urban systems in those countries is a common goal, more Structural Funds and transport infrastructure have to go to medium-size cities of the new member states, at the expense of their capital cities. It is the responsibility of the future spatial policy of the EU to find a rational solution to this goal conflict. The solution cannot be the pursuit of one goal at the expense of the other. Rather, the task is to develop a balanced strategy that is differentiated in both space and time and takes account of the specific needs of different types of regions.

Such a strategy starts from a *phase model* of spatial development, according to which the promotion of growth poles is appropriate in early stages of a country's economic development, whereas a polycentric spatial structure should be developed in later stages. This allows different priorities to be set in old and new member states: Whereas in the old member states decentralized, polycentric spatial structures are promoted, in the new member states, for a limited transition period, the capital cities and other major cities may be strengthened until balanced polycentric spatial structures can be developed in these countries, too.

The rationale behind this is that scientific and technical innovations are not restricted to large agglomerations but can also be achieved, conceivably with even better results, in well-connected cities of medium size, as demonstrated by the fact that the economically most successful countries in Europe are those with the most polycentric urban systems (ESPON 1.1.1 2004, 80–84). Such a strategy is not in conflict with the competitiveness objectives of the Lisbon Strategy, but achieves them in a more sophisticated way than the one-sided promotion of the largest agglomerations.

The goal conflicts described are equally relevant for European transport and telecommunications infrastructure policy. If the competitiveness goal of the Lisbon Strategy has the highest priority, the already fast, high-capacity transport corridors between the largest agglomerations have to be upgraded even further. If, however, cohesion has the highest priority, then mainly the connections to and

**TABLE 5.1**

## Goal Conflicts of Polycentricity Policies

| Goal | Policy | Goal Conflicts |
|------|--------|----------------|
| Competitiveness at global scale (Lisbon) | Strengthen highest-level global cities in the European core | Polarization between the global cities in the European core and the cities in the rest of Europe will increase. The European urban system will be less balanced and polycentric. |
| Territorial cohesion at European scale | Strengthen major cities outside of the European core | The competitiveness of the global cities in Europe may decrease. The urban systems of individual countries will be less balanced and polycentric. |
| Territorial cohesion at national scale | Strengthen medium-level cities in the new member states and accession countries | Competitiveness of major cities in the new member states and accession countries may decrease. |
| Sustainability (Gothenburg) | Strengthen lower-level cities in the new member states and accession countries | Competitiveness of major cities in the new member states and accession countries may decrease. |

**Source:** ESPON 1.1.3 2006, part 1, 16.

between the capitals of the new member states should be improved—at the expense of regional connections within those countries. Both strategies have the negative side effect of further growth in traffic—in particular, the transport of goods. To concentrate transport investment, however, on peripheral regions may lead to unacceptable congestion bottlenecks in the agglomerations both within and outside the European core.

A transport policy following the phase model differentiates between old and new member states: In the already highly developed and urbanized old member states, existing or emerging polycentric structures are strengthened mainly by improving the accessibility of medium-level central places and compensating for the accessibility deficits of rural and peripheral regions. In the still urbanizing new member states, however, a phased strategy is appropriate. For a transition period of 10 to 15 years it is justified to enhance the growth dynamics of those countries by fast and efficient transport connections between their capital cities and major agglomerations and the economic centers in western Europe. Thereafter, however, the risk of overdominance of those cities will have to be reduced by shifting investments, first to medium-size cities and later, as in the old member states, to rural and peripheral regions.

Both strategies have to be combined with Europe-wide coordinated measures to control the expected further rise of person travel and goods transport on roads. Those measures internalize the external costs of road transport and promote the use of environment-friendly transport modes and regional economic circuits, thus contributing to the sustainability goal of the EU and preparing Europe for future fuel scarcity and higher fuel prices.

Similarly differentiated principles apply to European telecommunications policy. Here, too, different priorities for old and new member states are appropriate. In the old member states telecommunications infrastructure of the highest standard is now almost universally available. European telecommunications policy can help to overcome deficits only in very low-density peripheral regions. In the new member states, however, the telecommunications infrastructure has to be developed from scratch. Just as in transport policy, it is justified to first help the new member states to provide high-level telecommunications services in their capital cites and major agglomerations and later to improve services in medium-size cities and rural areas.

## From Research to Policy

The challenge of all applied research in planning is to proceed "from knowledge to action," to quote from the title of a seminal book by John Friedmann (1987). That challenge is also central to ESPON. How does the research on transport and telecommunications live up to the challenge? Have its results found their way into the public domain of policy making?

If one counts publications, to a certain degree the answer is positive. A few examples of publications of ESPON results on transport and telecommunications follow:

- Accessibility maps of ESPON 1.2.1 were published in the third cohesion report (CEC 2004b, 77–79)—although their updates (ESPON 2007), especially prepared for the fourth cohesion report (CEC 2007), were not used.
- Transport network and accessibility maps of ESPON 1.2.1 were published in the *Interim Territorial Cohesion Report* (CEC 2004a, 52–53, 57–58, 60, 65–66).
- The results of ESPON 1.2.2 on telecommunications were published in the *Interim Territorial Cohesion Report* (CEC 2004a, 73–76).
- Results of the transport and telecommunications infrastructure scenarios of ESPON 2.1.1 were published in the *Interim Territorial Cohesion Report* (CEC 2004a, 67–70, 72, 77–81).
- A summary of the ESPON accessibility update (ESPON 2007) was included in the background document for the *Territorial Agenda* (Territorial State 2007, 29–33).

But beyond these publications, have the ESPON recommendations on transport and telecommunications influenced actual policy making? One way to find out is to look at official EU policy documents. However, the historical precedent under which a small group of researchers at the German Federal Office for Building and Regional Planning (BBR), under the previous German Council presidency, succeeded in injecting the paradigm of decentralized concentration of German *Raumordnung* in the form of balanced polycentric development into the ESDP (CEC 1999) is not likely to be repeated.

The *Territorial Agenda* remains vague about transport and telecommunications, stating merely that "mobility and accessibility are key prerequisites for economic development in all regions of the EU" and that it is therefore important "to secure integrated and sustainable development of multimodal transport systems" and "unhampered and socially fair access to information and communication technologies" (Territorial Agenda 2007, 6). However, the *Agenda* fails to set priorities for future transport and telecommunications investments in the light of the inherent goal conflicts between competitiveness, territorial cohesion, and sustainability. The background document to the *Territorial Agenda* (Territorial State 2007, 66–67) adds more detail but is in no way more concrete.

Maybe the ESPON results on transport and telecommunications influenced the awareness and problem perception of policy makers? To answer that question is difficult. To see one's ideas show up in two lines of a Commissioner's speech does not mean much. More important are the opportunities to interact with politicians and Commission experts at ESPON seminars, national ESPON workshops, and other conferences or disseminate research results through publications in books or scientific journals. However, the Commission experts working on spatial policies are exposed to many influences from the European parliament, the Council of Ministers and the Committee of the Regions, member states and regions, and lobbyists and interest groups, and they have to survive in the competition between different directorates and units of the Commission (see Jensen and Richardson 2004). On this contested playing field, one should not overestimate the influence of rational evidence—but one must try to make it as large as possible.

The interaction between researchers and Commission experts is of a dialectic nature. Researchers doing no more than echoing the concepts of the Commission will soon be found boring, but research results that always contradict the ideas of the Commission are not helpful, either. To maximize the impact of research on policy making, a narrow path between opportunism and obstruction has to be found. And there are value issues. In a fast-changing policy framework determined by the challenges of technological development, globalization, climate change, energy scarcity, and aging societies, researchers cannot leave values to their clients; they must take a position between the partisans of efficiency, equity, and sustainability in the different directorates of the Commission. This requires a degree of independence and self-respect, but sometimes also a dose of diplomacy.

The discourse between researchers and Commission experts has also a language dimension. Self-respect requires not slavishly adopting every fashion in Euro-Frenglish (e.g., "territorial" for "spatial") or obediently using monster terms such as "equitable and sustainable growth," but insisting on precise language. While researchers must recognize the need of politicians for a terminology vague enough to bridge the gap between contradictory concepts, they themselves are committed to using language that exposes rather than hides conflicts between goals and problem perceptions. Again, this requires prudence to avoid a purist, orthodox attitude. However, the possibility of influencing, in a subversive manner, the terminology in which policies are discussed should not be underestimated.

Another point is the need for mutual respect between researchers and policy experts. Too often policy makers evaluate research results only by whether they can serve as supporting evidence for policy decisions and do not care much about how they are achieved. This is reflected in the traditional organization of ESPON reports in which the "Scientific Summary" is appended to the "Executive Summary," as if it were an unavoidable nuisance. Too often in the past researchers were advised not to be "too scientific." On the other hand, researchers need to understand the situation of the political experts. Of course, the researchers always wish to have more freedom for solid analysis and try to squeeze it out of a project wherever possible, but they, too, have to recognize the legitimate expectation of the political experts to receive timely and problem-relevant results.

Finally, how about the theme of this volume—evidence? Is the recent buzzword of the European planning discourse (Faludi and Waterhout 2006; Davoudi 2006) just another short-lived fashion, or does it indicate a true "return of rationality" (Faludi 1985)? And what does it mean for ESPON? The statement "ESPON is all about data" (ESPON 3.2 2006, vol. 1, 44) reflects a gross misunderstanding. Data are only information—they need to be converted into knowledge by selection, transformation, and interpretation (Andersson 1985). The indicators and maps developed in ESPON are a necessary intermediate step in the right direction, but they are not sufficient: They indicate problems but do not provide solutions. The real focus of ESPON should therefore be on future-oriented decision support tools in the form of exploratory models, policy impact models, and policy assessment models.

A review of analytical and forecasting models in ESPON (ESPON 2006, 28–37) has shown that in a relatively short time enormous progress can be made in capturing the complexity of the large European territory in spatial models with high spatial resolution and great sophistication. The models applied have produced policy-relevant information in response to a variety of current policy issues. There is nothing comparable on other continents, not even in North America. A particularly advanced feature of the application of models in ESPON is that in some projects several models were applied to the same policy questions using the same data. The comparison between the results of different models contributed vastly to improving their reliability and credibility.

The review has also shown that in the field of transport and telecommunications the use of models is more advanced than in other research fields of ESPON. ESPON 1.1.1, 1.1.3, 1.2.1, 2.1.1, and 3.2 applied large state-of-the-art computer models, which more often than not were developed over many years in other project environments before their application in ESPON—examples are the SASI, CGEurope, and KTEN models. Only in a few cases were complex simulation models, such as the STIMA and MASST models, specifically developed in an ESPON project.

This underlines the point that complex research tools like these require an incubation and maturation period beyond the duration of an individual ESPON project. This has consequences for the relationships between subsequent projects. Reinventing the wheel in each project, as has been the practice in ESPON 2006, is extremely wasteful. That is not to say that duplication of effort is always bad. In particular in the early stages of model development fair competition between alternative approaches stimulates creativeness and innovation. In the long run, however, the best methods and models should be identified by rigorous cross-validation of their results. At the same time, to demand that all models used in an ESPON project be made available after the project for use in other projects would ignore their experimental character at the cutting edge, as well as the fact that they represent an important intellectual property of their authors.

The issue here is how to establish continuity and incremental learning from one project to the next. The project organization of ESPON, conditioned by its funding under the INTERREG program, is not ideally suited for that. The challenges to models in the public domain are enormous. They must be transparent and interactive and help the user to understand the behavior of the system under study. Together with their data they must be continually updated and improved and meet strict quality standards. It is likely that for all that a permanent institutional framework will be required.

## Conclusions

Transport and telecommunications stand out among other fields of EU policy making by a number of unique characteristics: They are determined by rapid technological advances. They are intimately associated with economic development and hence the European goal of competitiveness. They have significant implications for two other major European goals, cohesion and sustainability, which tend to be in conflict with competitiveness. And last, but not least, they are policy fields in which the EU, through cofinancing under the Structural and Cohesion Funds, has above average competence and influence.

In this situation, scientific evidence, in the broadest sense of future-oriented decision support, can make a significant contribution to rational policy making serving multiple objectives. Fortunately, transport and telecommunications are also among the most advanced fields in spatial science in which sophisticated methods and models for forecasting and assessing the impacts of policy options exist. This speaks in favor of strengthening the role of models in ESPON 2013. However, that would require new ways of establishing continuity and incremental progress from one project to the other, which presently do not exist.

### References

Andersson, A. E. 1985. Creativity and regional development. *Papers of the Regional Science Association* 56:5–20.

CEC (Commission of the European Communities). 1994. *Europe 2000+: Co-operation for European territorial development.* Luxembourg: Office for Official Publications of the European Communities.

———. 1999. *European Spatial Development Perspective: Towards balanced and sustainable development of the territory of the European Union.* Luxembourg: Office for Official Publications of the European Communities. http://ec.europa.eu/regional_policy/sources/docoffic/official/reports/pdf/sum_en.pdf.

———. 2001. *White paper—European transport policy for 2010: Time to decide.* Luxembourg: Office for Official Publications of the European Communities. http://ec.europa.eu/transport/white_paper/index_en.htm.

———. 2002. *Energy: Let us overcome our dependence.* Luxembourg: Office for Official Publications of the European Communities. http://ec.europa.eu/energy/efficiency/doc/2005_06_green_paper_book_en.pdf.

———. 2004a. *Interim territorial cohesion report (Preliminary results of ESPON and EU Commission studies).* Luxembourg: Office for Official Publications of the European Communities. http://ec.europa.eu/regional_policy/sources/docoffic/official/reports/coheter/coheter_en.pdf.

———. 2004b. *A new partnership for cohesion: Convergence, competitiveness, cooperation.* Third Report on Economic and Social Cohesion. Luxembourg: Office for Official Publications of the European Communities. http://ec.europa.eu/regional_policy/sources/docoffic/official/reports/cohesion3/cohesion3_en.htm.

———. 2007. *Growing regions, growing Europe.* Fourth Report on Economic and Social Cohesion. Luxembourg: Office for Official Publications of the European Communities. http://ec.europa.eu/regional_policy/sources/docoffic/official/reports/cohesion4/pdf/4cr_en.pdf.

Davoudi, S. 2006. Evidence-based planning: Rhetoric and reality. In *Evidence-based planning*, A. Faludi, ed. Special issue, *disP* 165, 42(2): 14–24.

ESPON. 2006. *Applied territorial research: Building a scientific platform for competitiveness and cohesion* (ESPON Scientific Report II, Autumn 2006). Luxembourg: ESPON Coordination Unit. http://www.espon.eu/mmp/online/website/content/publications/98/1232/index_EN.html.

———. 2007. *Update of selected potential accessibility indicators* (Final report). Dortmund: Spiekermann & Wegener. http://www.espon.eu/mmp/online/website/content/projects/947/1297/index_EN.html.

ESPON 1.1.1. 2004. *Potentials for polycentric development in Europe* (Final report). Stockholm: Nordic Centre for Spatial Development. http://www.espon.eu/mmp/online/website/content/projects/259/648/file_1174/fr-1.1.1_revised-full.pdf.

ESPON 1.1.3. 2006. *Enlargement of the European Union and the wider European perspective as regards its polycentric spatial structure* (Final report). Stockholm: Royal Institute of Technology. http://www.espon.eu/mmp/online/website/content/projects/259/650/file_1190/full_revised_version_113.pdf .

ESPON 1.2.1. 2004. *Transport services and networks: Territorial trends and basic supply of infrastructure for territorial cohesion* (Final report). Tours, France: University of Tours. http://www.espon.eu/mmp/online/website/content/projects/259/652/file_2202/fr-1.2.1-full.pdf.

ESPON 1.2.2. 2005. *Telecommunication services and networks: Territorial trends and basic supply of infrastructure for territorial cohesion* (Final report). Newcastle, England: Centre for Urban and Regional Development Studies. http://www.espon.eu/mmp/online/website/content/projects/259/653/file_1214/fr-1.2.2-full.pdf.

ESPON 2.1.1. 2003. *Territorial impacts of EU transport and TEN policies* (Third interim report). Kiel: Institute of Regional Research, Christian Albrecht University of Kiel. http://www.espon.eu/mmp/online/website/content/projects/243/239/file_376/3.ir_2.1.1.pdf.

———. 2005. *Territorial impacts of EU transport and TEN policies* (Final report). Kiel: Institute of Regional Research, Christian Albrecht University of Kiel. http://www.espon.eu/mmp/online/website/content/projects/243/239/file_374/fr-2.1.1_revised.pdf.

ESPON 3.2. 2006. *Spatial scenarios and orientations in relation to the ESDP and cohesion policy* (Third interim report). Brussels: IGEAT, Free University of Brussels. http://www.espon.eu/mmp/online/website/content/projects/260/716/file_1256/3.ir_3.2-full.pdf.

Faludi, A. 1985. The return of rationality. In *Rationality in planning: Critical essays on the role of rationality in urban and regional planning*, M. Breheny and A. Hooper, eds., 27–47. London: Pion.

Faludi, A., and B. Waterhout. 2006. Introducing evidence-based planning. In *Evidence-based planning*, A. Faludi, ed. Special issue, *disP* 165, 42(2): 3–13.

Friedmann, J. 1987. *Planning in the public domain: From knowledge to action*. Princeton, NJ: Princeton University Press.

Heine, H. 1854. Lutetia II: Berichte über Politik, Kunst und Volksleben. In *Sämtliche Werke*, H. Kaufmann, ed., vol. 12, 5–160. Repr., Munich: Kindler, 1964.

Jensen, O. B., and T. Richardson. 2004. *Making European space: Mobility, power and territorial identity*. London: Routledge.

RRG (Büro für Raumforschung, Raumplanung und Geoinformation). 2007. *RRG GIS database: Transport networks*. Oldenburg i.H.: RRG. http://www.brrg.de/database.php?language=en&cId=1&dId=37.

Spiekermann, K., and M. Wegener. 1994. The shrinking continent: New time-space maps of Europe. *Environment and Planning* B21:653–673.

Sloterdijk, P. 1992. Die Gesellschaft der Kentauren: Philosophische Bemerkungen zur Automobilität. *FAZ Magazin* 24:28–38.

Steiner, J. 1991. Raumgewinn und Raumverlust: Der Januskopf der Geschwindigkeit. *Raum* 3: 24–27.

Territorial Agenda. 2007. *Territorial Agenda of the European Union: Towards a more competitive and sustainable Europe of diverse regions* (Agreed on the occasion of the Informal Ministerial Meeting on Urban Development and Territorial Cohesion in Leipzig on 24/25 May 2007). http://www.bmvbs.de/Anlage/original_1005295/Territorial-Agenda-of-the-European-Union-Agreed-on-25-May-2007-accessible.pdf.

Territorial State. 2007. *The Territorial State and Perspectives of the European Union: Towards a stronger European territorial cohesion in the light of the Lisbon and Gothenburg ambitions* (A background document for the *Territorial Agenda of the European Union*). http://www.bmvbs.de/Anlage/original_1005296/The-Territorial-State-and-Perspectives-of-the-European-Union.pdf.

Wegener, M., H. Eskelinen, F. Fürst, C. Schürmann, and K. Spiekermann. 2001. *Criteria for the spatial differentiation of the EU territory: Geographical position.* Study Programme on European Spatial Planning, Forschungen 102.2. Bonn: Federal Office for Building and Regional Planning (BBR).

# CHAPTER 6

# Response to Natural Hazards and Climate Change in Europe

Philipp Schmidt-Thomé and Stefan Greiving

A wide range of natural hazards affects the European territory (Schmidt-Thomé and Kallio 2006). Even though the damages and losses they cause are not as catastrophic as in other regions of the world (Emergency Disasters Database 2006), natural hazards do affect the potential for regional development in Europe. Damages can lead to substantial financial losses due to the high density of population, built-up areas, and infrastructure in the European Union.

The potential effects of climate change on hydrometeorological hazards suggest that certain regions may experience an increase in natural hazards in the next 100 years (Bärring and Persson 2006). Reactions to that possibility can be seen not only in the growing importance of natural hazards and related risks in some national European planning systems (e.g., Fleischhauer, Greiving, and Wanczura 2006), but also in the approach of the European Commission, which has suggested that such risks should receive more attention in the next round of applications for the European Regional Development Fund (Commission of the European Communities 2006). The overview of the extent and effects of natural hazards in Europe discussed here is mainly based on the findings of the ESPON project 1.3.1 (Schmidt-Thomé and Kallio 2006). That project, also referred to as the ESPON Hazards Project, has made the first integrated approach to mapping all spatially relevant hazards, covering almost the entire European continent. Since the project is the first one to map all hazards at the same scale, using comparable data sets with the same geographic coverage, the results are still preliminary. In analyzing the data, it must be kept in mind that they show the distribution and intensity of hazards from a European perspective. Thus, there is some inexactness due to the scale of analysis. The background of the project was the need for information on natural hazards that affect regional development in Europe. Since no European research project on natural hazards had so far delivered results covering the entire territory, there was the need for an overview that led to this partly synthetic approach.

In order to determine the importance of natural hazards across Europe, the ESPON Hazards Project carried out a weighting process using the Delphi method (Schmidt-Thomé and Kallio 2006; Olfert, Greiving, and Batista 2006). This was principally used to elaborate aggregated disaster and risk maps for Europe, but it is also useful for analyzing the importance of hazards and risks from a wide range of continental to local perspectives. Also, because of the lack of intercomparability of hazard classes on a common scale, the weighting system was used in the hazard aggregation process. According to the Delphi method, the most important natural hazards in Europe as a whole are floods, followed by forest fires and earthquakes. Zooming in on the local level yields imprecise information and is thus not recommended. By way of example, Schmidt-Thomé et al. (2006) analyzed the results obtained from the ESPON Hazards Project on a Finnish national scale, and, indeed, the weights attached to hazards departed greatly from outcomes as seen from the European perspective. According to the ESPON Hazards Project, Finland is not exposed to considerable hazards and appears to totally lack floods. The reality is quite different, however, as floods are important in Finland and have found their way into spatial planning practices (e.g., Jarva and Virkki 2006). The reasons they do not figure on the ESPON hazard maps are that (1) no large floods occurred during the observation period and (2) Finnish floods often have lower magnitudes (causing fewer fatalities) than those in other European regions. One could argue that from a global perspective, the European continent as a whole is blessed with relatively few natural hazards, as major catastrophes seldom occur there. But the regional and local importance of hazards always has to be analyzed on an appropriate scale in order to determine the impact, for example, on the local economy (e.g., Schmidt-Thomé 2006a).

Risk governance should be enhanced, on both local and European scales, because the increasing costs of natural hazards, including the impact of climate change, call for better management of risks at all policy levels. Some examples of local decision making are provided by projects cofunded under INTERREG IIIB in the Baltic Sea region. Those projects facilitated stakeholder involvement and allowed future land use decisions to be based on the potential impacts of climate change on sea level rise, floods, and other natural hazards.

## Natural Hazards Affecting the European Territory

Not all parts of the European territory are equally threatened by natural hazards, as its natural, meteorological, and geological diversity leads to characteristic regionalized hazard patterns. Seismic hazards, including volcanoes, as well as droughts and forest fires, are mainly concentrated around the Mediterranean, along some active fault lines, and in the EU's overseas territories. There is a high potential of droughts and forest fires in central, south, and southeast Europe. Storms and storm surges, on the other hand, are mainly restricted to coastal zones and hinterland areas and are climatically more threatening along the North Sea and Baltic Sea coasts than elsewhere in Europe. Floods occur along almost all large rivers but are mainly concentrated in central and eastern Europe. Flash floods and landslides occur mainly in mountain areas and avalanches in snowy alpine-type mountain areas as shown by figure 6.1 below. Local hazards can also play a role outside of the regions mentioned, however (Schmidt-Thomé and Kallio 2006).

In discussions of natural hazard mitigation strategies, a paradigm shift has occurred from purely technological solutions, such as dams for flood protection,

**FIGURE 6.1**

## Aggregated Natural Hazards in Europe

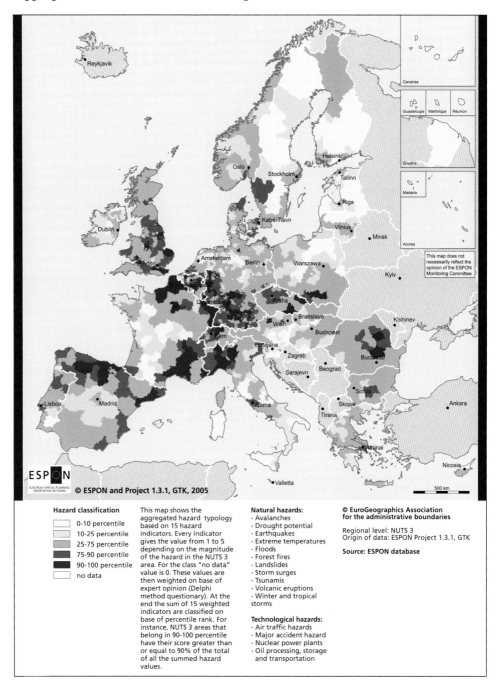

**Hazard classification**

- [ ] 0-10 percentile
- [ ] 10-25 percentile
- [ ] 25-75 percentile
- [ ] 75-90 percentile
- [ ] 90-100 percentile
- [ ] no data

This map shows the aggregated hazard typology based on 15 hazard indicators. Every indicator gives the value from 1 to 5 depending on the magnitude of the hazard in the NUTS 3 area. For the class "no data" value is 0. These values are then weighted on base of expert opinion (Delphi method questionary). At the end the sum of 15 weighted indicators are classified on base of percentile rank. For instance, NUTS 3 areas that belong in 90-100 percentile have their score greater than or equal to 90% of the total of all the summed hazard values.

**Natural hazards:**
- Avalanches
- Drought potential
- Earthquakes
- Extreme temperatures
- Floods
- Forest fires
- Landslides
- Storm surges
- Tsunamis
- Volcanic eruptions
- Winter and tropical storms

**Technological hazards:**
- Air traffic hazards
- Major accident hazard
- Nuclear power plants
- Oil processing, storage and transportation

© EuroGeographics Association for the administrative boundaries

Regional level: NUTS 3
Origin of data: ESPON Project 1.3.1, GTK

Source: ESPON database

© ESPON and Project 1.3.1, GTK, 2005

toward adaptation (e.g., Schmidt-Thomé 2006a). Since natural hazards cannot be fully prevented, the aim of mitigation includes adjusting land use forms to create space for hazards. But not all natural hazards have "spatial relevance" and can be mitigated by means of spatial planning policies. Fleischhauer (2006), therefore, uses risk schemes developed by the German Advisory Council (German Advisory Council on Global Change 1999) to develop a spatial filter, which enables the identification of spatially relevant natural hazards. The following paragraphs discuss some of the economically most important natural hazards that occur in Europe; examples of the effects of some other natural hazards are summarized in table 6.1. For a more detailed analysis see Schmidt-Thomé and Kallio (2006). The ESPON Hazards Project's results are discussed in detail in its final report (Schmidt-Thomé 2005) and in a collection of articles published by the Geological Survey of Finland (Schmidt-Thomé 2006b).

## Floods

River floods emerged as an increasing challenge to the built environment once human beings began to change, straighten, and even relocate riverbeds—natural flood-prone areas—at the same time settling in low-lying areas close to rivers. Increased soil sealing also leads to flooding, as it causes rainwater to run off directly into streams and the water mass inflow into rivers is no longer delayed by natural soil retention. The greatest number of large flood events in Europe between 1987 and 2002 occurred in northwestern Romania, southeastern France, central and southern Germany, and eastern England (Schmidt-Thomé and Kallio 2006). The making of the map shown in figure 6.1 led to several debates, as there were strong demands to also measure the magnitude of floods and not only their reoccurrence. It turned out that the debate was driven by political interests—for example, the relatively high amount of flooding represented on the map in eastern Europe was not welcome. Obviously, the intention was only to demonstrate the high flood risk in central and western countries. Similar experiences occurred with other maps during the ESPON Hazards Project.

## Droughts

The 2003 drought in Europe accounted for almost a third of Europe's economic losses due to natural hazards (Munich Reinsurance Company 2004). Droughts naturally strike mostly around the Mediterranean, due to the hot and dry summers, but the manmade causes of drought are considerable. There are numerous examples of water resource mismanagement, such as overexploiting aquifers, sealing surfaces, increasing surface runoff and restricting groundwater recharge, overusing water in dry areas, and intensive agriculture practices. Eastern European countries, apart from experiencing a high number of floods over the last 15 years, have also experienced great problems with droughts over the last 100 years (Schmidt-Thomé and Kallio 2006).

## Fires

Forest fires (wildfires) can cause considerable damage in environmental and economic terms. In general, forest fires are natural phenomena important for the regeneration of a forest because they act as a cleansing process. The highest poten-

TABLE 6.1

## Reported Effects of Selected Larger Natural Hazards on European Countries (1970–2005)

| Hazards | Number of Hazards | Deaths | Estimated Damage Costs (in 1,000€) |
|---|---|---|---|
| Floods | 274 | 3,270 | 53,577,458 |
| Storms | 215 | 1,546 | 34,403,573 |
| Earthquakes | 123 | 19,644 | 43,936,462 |
| Extreme temperatures | 69 | 47,466 | 1,889,329 |
| Forest fires | 63 | 248 | 2,471,668 |
| Landslides | 46 | 1,314 | 1,023,464 |
| Droughts | 26 | 0 | 12,989,281 |
| Volcanic eruptions | 7 | 9 | 36,769 |
| **Total** | **823** | **73,497** | **150,328,003** |

**Source**: Emergency Disasters Database (EM-DAT) 2006.

**Note**: Only disasters with the following minimum criteria are entered in the EM-DAT: 10 or more people reported killed; 100 or more people reported affected; declaration of state of emergency; and request for international assistance.

tial for fires exists in Mediterranean regions and partly in Romania and Bulgaria. The high risk of forest fires in central-northern Portugal and northwestern Spain stems from local "slash and burn" practices, which are particularly dangerous where there is already a high potential for forest fires.

## Risk and Vulnerability

Generally speaking, natural hazards pose a risk to human beings and their properties; nature and its ecosystems have always adapted to natural hazards (e.g., Schmidt-Thomé 2006a). Natural hazards can be strengthened by human activities, however, and can then pose a threat to ecosystems, at least from a human perspective. Risk is a function of a hazard (or hazards) and vulnerability. In other words, risk depends on the intensity of a hazard and the potential extent of damage, as seen from the human perspective. The key challenge is thus to control or influence the main driving forces behind risk. Economic growth and concentration of population in threatened areas lead to increasing vulnerability, even if hazards occur no more often than before. This combination of natural and manmade factors is the main cause behind the rapidly increasing losses caused by natural disasters in Europe.

The pressure of a growing population and growing GDP, along with the related demand for space, also challenges the sustainability of coastal zones, maritime and river basins, and mountain areas. For example, coastal zones are facing an extreme rate of soil sealing due to urban sprawl, especially but not exclusively around the Mediterranean. River basins experience urban sprawl and soil sealing, as well as fragmentation. Ecosystems in mountain areas suffer not only from urban sprawl but also from increasing recreational activities.

## Climate Change Affecting Natural Hazards

Climate change is expected to lead to changes in weather variables such as average and extreme temperatures, precipitation (including snow and ice cover), and wind. Because of increasingly longer dry spells, the southernmost areas of Europe face the greatest rise in natural hazards as an effect of climate change. A change of wind patterns or an increase in extreme events may lead to more severe winter storms (e.g., Bärring and Persson 2006). Examples of extreme events are the winter storms Gudrun in the Baltic Sea region in 2005 and Kyrill in northern Europe in 2007; the extremely dry summers and heat waves in 2003 and 2006; the extreme floods in central and eastern Europe in 2002 and 2005; and the forest fires on the Iberian Peninsula since the beginning of this century. Furthermore, the effects of increased precipitation on landslides and avalanches will be felt mostly at the local level, since such events are normally relatively small-scale.

Climate change has only recently been incorporated into spatial planning in Europe, and its importance is growing—for example, its inclusion in the *Territorial Agenda of the European Union* (2007). In the United Kingdom the term *sustainable* was integrated into planning during the 1990s (Bulkeley 2006); climate change is mainly integrated into planning in the form of mitigation strategies, by focusing on greenhouse gas emission reduction, for example, and, specifically, the role of traffic (Robinson 2006; Levet 2006). In the Netherlands the focus is starting to shift from mitigation to adaptation strategies (Vries 2006). Several countries have developed national strategies and have called for integrating climate change into planning; cities and regions, too, are starting to take initiatives (e.g., Marttila et al. 2005; Her Majesty's Government 2006). From a Finnish perspective, Peltonen, Haanpää, and Lehtonen (2005) give a series of recommendations to integrate climate change adaptation into urban planning. In fact, Finland has already moved beyond a national climate change adaptation strategy to a comprehensive national climate change program, integrating mitigation as well as adaptation elements for the years 2006–2010 (http://www.mmm.fi/—currently only in Finnish). In 2005 Germany created the National Climate Change Program. As with other states, besides mitigation actions, more attention has been paid to adaptation; however, spatial planning did not receive a special mention.

Mapping of natural hazards on a European scale can be used, for example, for allocating the European Regional Development Funds (Schmidt-Thomé and Schmidt-Thomé 2007). But the limitations of the scale, the resolution, and the underlying data sets have to be kept in mind. Consequently, disaster mitigation and adaptation strategies always require local assessments (e.g., Schmidt-Thomé 2006a, b).

The following section summarizes relevant national European approaches, which potentially could be applied at the European scale. These approaches would certainly require modifications and further research before they could be applied on the European level, and many of them are not yet fully applied at a national scale. But the current trends of increasing costs incurred by natural disasters have shown that such initiatives are of growing importance. Later on, some examples of practical applications of natural disaster and climate change information related to planning are presented, on both European and local levels.

## Strategies for European Risk Policy and Governance

Risk management should be an integral and explicit part of EU cohesion policy, since analyses have shown how omnipresent natural hazards are in the territory of the EU. This calls for better coordination at all spatial scales. Stressing vulnerability reduction is a key strategy. It has to be recognized that vulnerability concerns both the human and the socioeconomic side of risks, including their spatial patterns.

The aim should be a form of polycentric development, a key element in the *European Spatial Development Perspective* (ESDP 1999), to balance patterns of vulnerability in Europe. All aspects of vulnerability (economic, social, and ecological), as considered in integrated vulnerability analyses, must be taken into account, and both substantive goals and procedural rules related to vulnerability reduction and risk management must be included.

The involved stakeholders need to invoke adaptation strategies. The triangle "resistance-resilience-retreat" has to be taken into consideration when discussing policy measures (Greiving 2006b):

- Resistance—protection against (all) hazards by means of structural measures
- Resilience—minimization of the risk to life and property when a disaster occurs
- Retreat—abandonment of risky areas

The three main elements of the retreat-oriented risk management strategy, for example, are the following:

- Keeping threatened areas free from all further vulnerable land uses by means of suitable designations carried out by responsible authorities (e.g., water management, spatial planning)
- Reallocation of existing land uses away from threatened areas—designations plus a funding program or compensation for landowners
- A combination of the first two elements with extension of the retention area (backward reallocation of dikes, retention ponds) in case of flooding, or other

comparable measures like planting protective forests where an avalanche risk exists

All alternatives call for a well-prepared risk assessment in view of the necessary intervention in private property rights. That assessment will depend not only on the disaster intensity (a function of return period and magnitude), but also on the vulnerability of the land use and the coping capacity of the community affected. Reallocation might be the only appropriate alternative for those land uses, like industrial sites and public infrastructure, that are particularly vulnerable. All three elements (resistance, resilience, and retreat/reallocation) might be combined in the same area for different land uses. It can also be appropriate to concentrate on different elements for the same land use category in different areas in view of a given risk. The choice of a suitable response strategy for coping with flood risks depends not only on the level of risk a society is willing to tolerate, but also on the nature of different land uses, and is therefore a normative question. Moreover, a normative decision is needed for the kind of mitigation action required. That calls for an assessment of risk that carefully considers the vulnerability of the affected system, but also considers the concerns of the affected people (risk governance has to be seen as an integrated part of governance conceived as an overall strategy for policy making in the twenty-first century; see the section "Risk Governance" for a more detailed discussion). In this context, a return period, like the 100-year flood for the whole of Europe, or even for one catchment area, cannot be the common basis for such decisions. Moreover, in view of climate change, the return period of a certain event might change in the future.

## Promoting Trans-European Technological and Natural Risk Management

Natural hazards are risks for human beings and socioeconomic systems where settlements or infrastructures are located in natural disaster–prone areas. In Europe that is often the situation. Since natural hazards cannot be fully mitigated, the most appropriate strategy is to reduce vulnerability. That process has started in some regions, but a European approach, or a general adaptation process, including the effects of climate change on natural hazards, is still missing. The European territory as such is not so much threatened by natural hazards, but its natural, meteorological, and geological diversity leads to regionalized, characteristic disaster patterns (see figure 6.1 above). Those specific disaster patterns lead to site-specific risk patterns that are best met by regional mitigation and, more appropriately, by adaptation processes.

Since hazards and risks are unevenly distributed, we recommend setting priorities for spatial risk assessment. Priorities should focus on the spatial development impact of all potential, regionally relevant hazards. Since some hazards, even though they do not appear obvious in a European perspective, can be locally important, priorities should leave room for site-specific local assessments.

In other words, the risk a region is ready to take plays a major role in the vulnerability discussion. Settlements cannot be removed from natural hazard–prone areas, and industrial production cannot simply stop because of potential accident threats. Those affected by the risk must be incorporated in defining the acceptable risk. Account should be taken of the fact that *acceptable risk* might be defined differently in different European regions, even in view of comparable threats, as sociocultural aspects and adaptability to hazards influence the perception of risk. Presently, disaster research communities are insular, rarely interacting across individual sectors, disciplines, regions, or cultures. In consequence, different hazard and risk assessment methods exist for different hazard types. It would be more appropriate to make decisions in a multihazard setting, particularly when talking about the territorial dimension of risk. Therefore, a more homogenized and interdisciplinary perspective is needed for the assessment and management of hazards and risks (e.g., Schmidt-Thomé 2006a, b; Greiving 2006a; International Risk Governance Council 2005).

## Risk Governance

When talking about risk governance, an agreement concerning what is meant by risk has to be reached. Issues of interpretation aside, risk has two distinct dimensions:

- The "factual" dimension comprises physically measurable outcomes (e.g., a combination of potential consequences and the probability of a potentially harmful event). This dimension is represented by the assessment of risks and can be understood mainly as an analytic task, managed by experts from public administration, supported in many cases by expert reports or statements.
- The "sociocultural" dimension includes how a particular risk is viewed (e.g., whether a risk is judged acceptable, tolerable, or intolerable by society is partly influenced by the way it is perceived to intrude upon the value system of society). This sociocultural part has to be differentiated into an individual component, of how risk is perceived and estimated by different human beings, and a collective component influenced by cultural settings and, last but not least, the modern media (German Advisory Council on Global Change 1999). The pervasiveness of media attention to natural phenomena as well as to technology destroys trust, because most of what the media report is trust-destroying news.

Both findings—that risk communities are prone to be insular and the existence of the two distinct risk dimensions—set the challenge for any governance approach to risk, a challenge that in the end calls for an integrated way of dealing with risks in order to create resilient communities. Integrative approaches aim at synergies between scientific advice, public participation and communication, and risk governance. Tools are necessary to improve the robustness of policy making when faced with high uncertainty and ambiguity.

Uncertainty and ambiguity form the main challenges in dealing with risks in society (Klinke and Renn 2002):

- *Uncertainty* reduces confidence in an estimated cause-and-effect chain. It may be related to the incidence as well as the magnitude of a disastrous effect. An appropriate objective to deal with uncertainty is resilience to avoid irreversibilities and vulnerabilities.

- *Ambiguity* indicates the variability of legitimate interpretations based on identical observations or data assessments. Ambiguity exists due to differences in the criteria or norms for interpreting or judging a given situation. In consequence, a socially widely accepted developmental path should be pursued to resolve value conflicts and ensure fair treatment of concerns and visions by means of consensus-seeking discourse.

This line of argument makes clear why the management of risks has become increasingly politicized. Often, statistically measured and perceived risks do not coincide with each other. Some imminent risks receive less attention than statistically rather irrelevant risks. This means that any risk management process has to be familiar with the social construction of risk—that is, with the perception of risk by various stakeholders. Consequently, those who manage and communicate risk to the public need to start with an understanding of the emotional responses by the affected people. Risk governance principles should receive commitment at the highest level, as well as practical implementation at all levels. Developing a governance process means consulting and involving stakeholders in the assessment and management of risk. Confidence in decision-making processes is fundamental not only for the public's ability to interpret risk and perceive "real" hazards and risk, but also for a successful implementation of decisions to mitigate risk.

Definitions of risk affect policy; moreover, defining risk is an expression of power. Slovic (1999), therefore, argues that whoever controls the definition of risk controls technology policy. In consequence, the understanding of risk results in a normative concept and has a juridical, legal component (Greiving 2002).

Currently, risk governance research and practice are fragmented according to subject and the budget-holding organizations involved. The last decades have shown that risk to our social fabric transgresses boundaries between nation-states, businesses, governments, and rich and poor communities—the examples include large river floods, winter storms, and forest fires. The complex interdependence of types of risk requires a systemic approach to governance in order to ensure the resilience and sustainability of our economic fabric in Europe and beyond. Building a bridge between different approaches to risk developed by risk communities with a tendency to insularity has to be seen as a special challenge. Up to now risk governance has rarely been used in formulating hazard management strategies, and risk resilience is poorly integrated into approaches for dealing with natural hazards. This was evident in the poor performance of U.S. emergency response agencies in the aftermath of Hurricane Katrina.

The material goal of "resilience" (another term used, e.g., in climate change research, is *adaptive capacity*) can be seen as a widely accepted strategy within the natural hazard community. In contrast, a more procedural approach to "risk governance" has been created and adapted first in the area of emerging, mostly manmade risks. The use of both terms in the same context has to be seen as an innovative approach combining an appropriate path (risk governance—including identification, assessment, management, and communication of risk) with the material goal of creating resilient communities that are able to deal with the whole range of risks, natural or manmade.

Such strong stakeholder-oriented elements have been integrated into disaster management strategies (International Strategy for Disaster Reduction 2005). In addition, misfits in the interplay between institutions and stakeholders have been identified as important reasons for institutional vulnerability (Greiving 2005).

## The Role of Spatial Planning

There is no comprehensive responsibility for managing the risks emanating from natural hazards in Europe or its member states. Normally, different authorities are in charge of the assessment and management of risk, one for each disaster type. However, risk management is also a task of spatial planning. Spatial planning plays an important role in mitigation, which aims at reducing damage to people, property, and resources by taking measures before a disaster occurs (e.g., Schmidt-Thomé 2006a).

The concept of *spatial planning* is in use in several member states. Some use the English term "land use planning" (e.g., Ireland), "land planning" (Italy), or "spatial planning" (Germany: *Raumplanung*); others use "spatial development" (Poland: *Zagospodarowanie przestrzenne*) or "regional development planning" (France: *aménagement du territoire*). So the use as well as the understanding of the term is wide open. Clear definitions, however, are important to avoid mistakes. Table 6.2 offers an overview of the several forms of planning.

Disaster assessment is naturally a task for sector authorities, like water boards and geological surveys. Spatial planning plays a minor role. Nevertheless, spatial planning is one important end-user of disaster-related information provided by sector authorities. To meet the requirements of spatial planning, minimum standards for disaster mapping are indispensable. However, little attention has been paid to vulnerability. Disaster-related information, including intensity and magnitude of potentially harmful events, must be provided by sector authorities; but vulnerability-related information is, in most cases, available to spatial planners because data like distribution of population, location of settlement areas, and technical infrastructure are basic information required for any kind of planning activity (see Fleischhauer, Greiving, and Wanczura 2006).

*Risk management* is defined as lowering the potential for loss from extreme events. That definition shows that risk management is influenced by the decisions of stakeholders. Decision making is a normative, politically influenced strategy for tolerating or altering risks. The authority in charge has to decide on the main planning goals to deal with hazards. The outcome is the result of weighing various aspects against one another. The following questions are of concern:

**TABLE 6.2**

## Overview of the European Planning System

| Spatial Level | Spatially Relevant Planning | | Spatially Nonrelevant Planning |
|---|---|---|---|
| | Comprehensive | Sectoral (transport, water, geology, emergency response, etc.) | Forms of nonspatial management on different spatial levels |
| Europe | European spatial development (no binding character) | Environmental policies, TEN, CAP | E.g., budget planning |
| Member state | Spatial development planning | E.g., national transport network plan | E.g., defense planning, education |
| Submember state level (federal state, region, or other spatial unit) | Provincial planning (partly land use related) | E.g., river basin authorities in charge of management plans, partly land use planning and management related | E.g., cultural development, education planning |
| Municipality (all planning on this level can be subsumed together under the term "Urban Planning and Management") | Local land use planning | E.g., waste, sewage planning, public transport planning; municipalities are in charge of (land use management) | E.g., primary education, municipal budget planning |

*SPATIAL PLANNING* spans the Comprehensive column; *SECTORAL AUTHORITIES* spans the Sectoral column.

**Source:** Greiving 2006b.

- What is the level of risk that society (or any stakeholder) is willing to accept?
- What are the protection goals for the objects that are threatened by specific hazards? Or what are the foreseeable environmental effects from an intended investment in case a disaster occurs?

Spatial planning plays only one of many roles within the disaster cycle, which consists of mitigation, preparedness, response, and recovery. Moreover, assessment of the given risk is a duty of specialized agencies as listed in table 6.3.

The agencies displayed in table 6.3 are considered to be key players in the area of hazard mitigation. Disaster mitigation includes actions that have a long-term impact (e.g., nonstructural mitigation activities, but also structural mitigation activities.

Table 6.4 differentiates between regional planning, land use planning, and sec-

**TABLE 6.3**

## Hazards Addressed by Spatial Planning in Europe

| Country | Types of Hazard | Authority in Charge of Risk Assessment | Existence of Hazard Maps | Existence of Risk Maps | Vulnerability Indicators | Multirisk Aspect Considered? | Authority in Charge of Risk Management | Attention to Public Awareness |
|---------|-----------------|----------------------------------------|--------------------------|------------------------|--------------------------|------------------------------|----------------------------------------|-------------------------------|
| Finland | FL, LS, FF, EQ, EE | SA | o | – | PD | – | SA, SP | o |
| France | LS, FL, FF, EQ | SA | + | o | PD | + | SA, SP | + |
| Germany | FL, LS, EE, LS | SA | + | o | DP | – | SA, SP | o |
| Greece | FL, FF, VO, EQ | SA | o | o | No data | – | SA, SP | o |
| Italy | FL, LS, VO, FF | SA | o | o | No data | o | SA, SP | No data |
| Poland | LS, FL, FF, EQ | SA | o | o | DP, PD, OI | – | SA, SP | + |
| Spain | FL, LS, FF, VO, EQ | SA | + | o | PD, OI | – | SA, SP | No data |
| U.K. | LS, FL | SA | o | o | No data | – | SA, SP | + |

LS = Landslides
FL = Floods
FF = Forest Fires
VO = Volcanic hazards
EQ = Earthquakes
EE = Extreme meteorological events

SA = Sector authority
SP = Spatial planning
DP = Economic damage potential
PD = Population density
OI = Other indicators

+ High importance/Yes
o Medium importance/Partly
– Low/No importance/No

**Source:** Fleischhauer, Greiving, and Wanczura 2006.

**TABLE 6.4**

## Contribution of Spatial-Oriented Planning and Supporting Instruments to Risk Management Strategies

| Risk Management Strategy | Regional Planning | Local Land Use Planning | Sector Authorities | Supporting Instruments |
|---|---|---|---|---|
| **Prevention-oriented mitigation** | E.g., planning, settlement, and transport structures that cause fewer greenhouse gas emissions | Supporting the use of regenerative energies | Strategies for reducing greenhouse gas emissions (e.g., transport structures) | Kyoto Protocol; strategies for reducing greenhouse gas emissions; tax system |
| **Nonstructural mitigation (a): reducing hazard impacts** | Maintenance of protective features of the natural environment that absorb or reduce hazard impacts (retention areas, sand dunes) | Local rainwater infiltration | Flood protection plans; coastal protection plans; reforestation; adapted land cultivation | Interregional cooperation; economic instruments; information management |
| **Nonstructural mitigation (b): reducing damage potential** | Designations in regional plans like flood hazard areas | Zoning instruments | Adequate allocation of threatened infrastructure | |
| **Structural mitigation** | Securing the availability of space for protective infrastructure | Prevention measures as part of building permissions | Engineering design, protective infrastructure (shoreline dams) | |
| **Reaction: preparedness, response, recovery** | — | Rebuilding planning | Emergency plans, e.g., SEVESO II safety report | Information and training to support public awareness and emergency management |

**Source**: Greiving and Fleischhauer 2006.

tor authorities. Supporting instruments are also mentioned. The role of regional planning, as well as land use planning, is discussed below.

The role of spatial planning in mitigation includes the following actions, to be taken at different planning levels (e.g., provincial, local):

■ *Regional planning.* This provides a relatively general framework for local as well as sectoral plans and programs—even in Germany and other countries where regulatory planning instruments exist at the regional level. In consequence, it is sufficient to identify potentially threatened areas to avoid, for example, further settlement activities.

■ *Land use planning.* On the local level, more detailed disaster assessment is needed. Land use planning has to be understood in most countries as a binding basis for building permissions, based on concrete designations, which relate to particular plots of land. In order to adopt restrictive and protective land use designations because of disaster potential on one hand and the vulnerability of the possible land and building uses on the other, precise disaster-related information is crucial, even for preparatory land use plans.

The following strategies have to be seen as the main elements of a disaster response by spatial planning:

- *Keeping areas free of development.* The following characteristics should keep land free from development:
  - It is prone to hazards (e.g., flood-prone areas, avalanche-prone areas).
  - It is needed to lower the effects of a disastrous event (e.g., water retention areas).
  - It is needed to guarantee the effectiveness of response activities (e.g., escape lanes and gathering points).
- *Differentiated decisions on land use.* Apart from keeping certain areas free from development, spatial planning may also decide on acceptable land use types according to the intensity and frequency of the existing disaster (e.g., agricultural use of a flood-prone area might be allowed but residential use forbidden).
- *Recommendations in legally binding land use or zoning plans.* Although recommendations about certain construction requirements belong to the area of building permissions, some recommendations may be made at the level of land use or zoning plans (e.g., minimum elevation of buildings above floor, prohibition of basements, prohibition of oil heating, and type of roofs).
- *Influence of disaster intensity and frequency (i.e., disaster potential).* Spatial planning can also contribute to a reduction of the disaster potential (e.g., protection or extent of river flood retention areas, protective forest).

In order to carry out their role in disaster mitigation, spatial planners depend on reliable information to make decisions about which areas should be kept free, which land uses should be allowed, which building restrictions should be prescribed, and where planning can contribute to minimizing disaster potential. For each decision, planning level, and disaster, spatial planning requires certain disaster-related information.

In this context, current practice is far removed from the state of the art, as described below (see Fleischhauer, Greiving, and Wanczura 2006). The central question is how sectoral information (especially the extent and intensity of hazards) is translated into spatial terms at different spatial levels. Information on the extent and intensity of a hazard is important for the production of hazard maps: Identifying and delineating hazard zones at an appropriate scale can show the extent of a hazard; the intensity of a hazard can be shown by differentiating hazard-prone areas accordingly.

A multihazard map is in the first instance the sum of relevant single-hazard maps. Possible interactions and cumulative effects have to be considered, and restrictions are made according to the greatest hazard existing in a specific area (no matter what it is).

Hazard-related information provided by sector authorities needs to be translated into the language of spatial planning. The binding character of hazard zoning becomes part of the binding character of the whole spatial plan. That means that spatial planning has to take into account the hazard information provided within, and as part of, the decision-making process, coming to different decisions depending on the type of development and the hazard intensity of the zone the development will be in.

Different risk classes call for appropriate responses that consider resistance, resilience, and retreat, according to the level of risk and its acceptability. Here, a practicable scientific basis is needed for making normative decisions. This takes into account different risk characteristics of natural hazards. The risk curves in figure 6.2 have a peak at the point where the annualized average damage is at a maximum. A maximum risk can be the result of either a moderate average damage in combination with a high frequency, or a high damage related with a low frequency. On the basis of the identified maximum risk, risk classes can be defined from which risk management measures could be derived (Greiving 2006b).

Because this methodology is practicable and can be generally understood, it may serve as a basis for making acceptable decisions. Reasonably, a higher maximum risk may justify more serious mitigation measures, like reallocation of existing settlements, than a lower one. In the end, some less vulnerable land uses (temporary outdoor activities, extensive agricultural uses) may be tolerated even in risky areas. A proposed transformation of existing land uses calls for a new risk assessment showing how the intended transformation is going to modify the following:

- existing hazards levels
- existing exposure levels
- existing physical vulnerability levels
- existing coping capacity levels

In other areas, the lower level of risk might call for less serious measures (resilience or resistance).

However, the possible influence of climate change may influence the given risk and call for a new response. The impact of climate change on risk, and consequently on the reasonableness of certain management measures, can also be expressed in terms of the changing efficiency of those measures, as expressed by the diagram in figure 6.3.

Presently, it might be most efficient to carry on as before, without taking any measures. In case of an event, the society just resists the damages (resistance). Over time, however, and, for example, with a rising sea level, it may become more efficient to protect areas with certain measures, as illustrated by figure 6.4. At a turning point, the share between marginal costs and marginal benefits becomes lower and efficiency decreases (resilience). Eventually, further protection measures are no longer efficient (retreat). Certain scenarios could justify a change of "efficiency curves." For example, the different emission scenarios used by the IPCC will influence efficiency to a different extent, but the message remains the same: The turn-

**FIGURE 6.2**

## From Risk Assessment to Risk Management

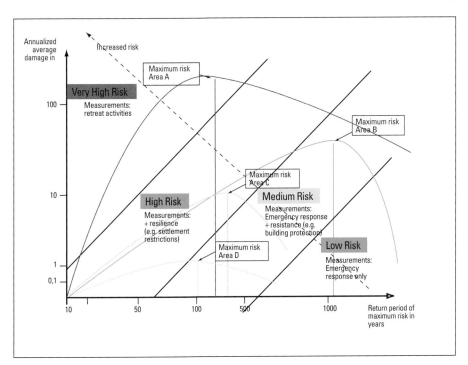

**Source:** Greiving 2006b.

ing point moves to the left; resilience and retreat become more efficient—even before a disaster strikes.

This implies the following changes from present practices in spatial planning:

- *Phase of resistance:* Low risk. Plan A (unnecessary to consider hazards and vulnerability except emergency response).

- *Phase of resilience:* Medium to high risk. Improve Plan A to consider hazards and vulnerability due to climate change impacts; improve protection for highly vulnerable areas depending on the given risk (see figure 6.4). In parallel planning start to think about new spatial structures for when further protection measures are no longer efficient (Plan B); relocate highly vulnerable land uses and adapt protections (e.g., improve structures for those land uses that are still beneficial in threatened areas). (In this way, society would be better prepared for recovery after a disaster, understood as a window of opportunity: A complete new settlement structure would already be available to replace destroyed facilities.)

- *Phase of retreat:* Very high risk due to ongoing climate change impacts. Leave the area completely once additional measures (resilience) are no longer efficient (Plan C).

FIGURE 6.3

## Efficiency of Measures Depending on Timing

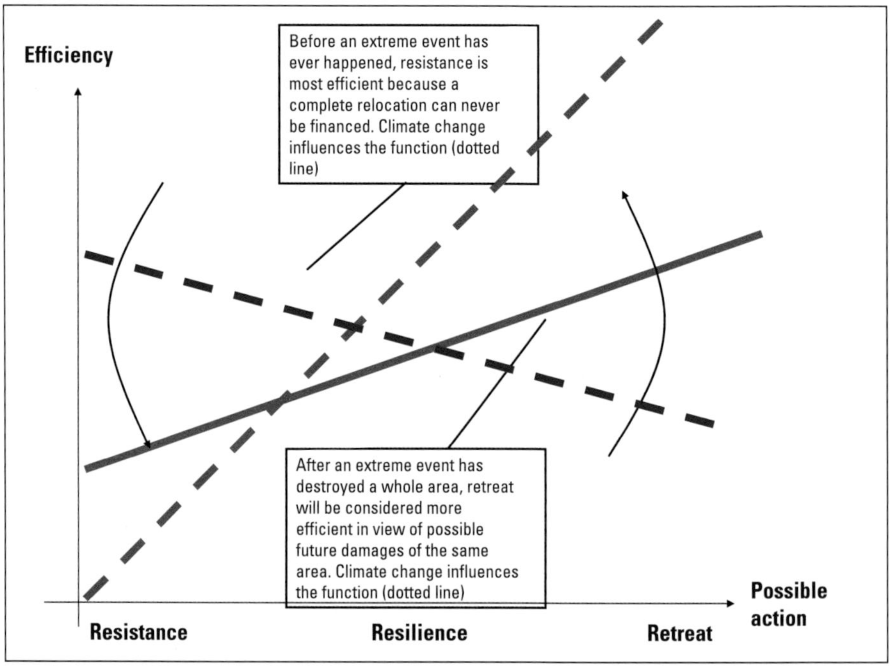

Source: Greiving 2006b.

The different phases shown in figure 6.4 express the changing appropriateness of resilient measures by the example of coastal areas affected by sea level rise.

## Practical Applications

The first part of this chapter outlined the distribution of hazards, as well as potential climate change impacts, in the European territory. Risk management and governance were pointed out as important factors in the categorization and understanding of risks for society. Spatial planning was identified as the tool with probably the most potential to manage hazards and risks in territorial development. But where to go from here in a European perspective? What follows are examples of applications of the ESPON Hazards Project. These are only first steps, but they can be integrated into a European approach to better manage environmental risks for the benefit of sustainable territorial development.

### Applying ESPON Hazards Project Results

The results of the ESPON Hazards Project (Schmidt-Thomé 2005) have been used

**FIGURE 6.4**

## Change in Efficiency of Adaptation Measures over Time (e.g., due to rising sea level)

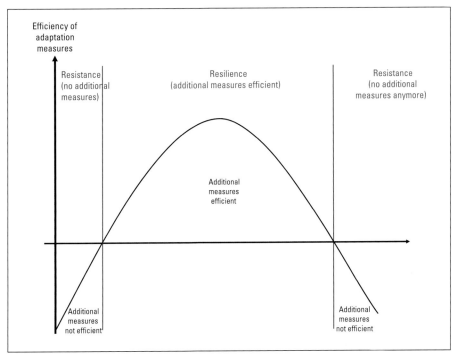

**Source:** Greiving 2006b.

to outline the disaster- and risk-related topics discussed in the *Territorial Agenda of the European Union* (2007) and its background document, *The Territorial State and Perspectives of the European Union* (2007). The *Territorial Agenda* aims at setting a strategic and action-oriented framework for supporting territorial development. One of the envisaged strategic goals of the European Union is territorial cohesion (along with economic and social cohesion), as many structural problems of the EU are rooted in economic territorial disparities. The *Territorial Agenda* therefore supports the aims of the Lisbon (European competitiveness) and Gothenburg (sustainable development) strategies. The European Commission (2006) has highlighted the importance for regional development of considering environmental risks and climate change, and information on those issues has been integrated into the *Territorial Agenda.* That development came rather quickly, as natural hazards and climate change were not perceived as relevant for regional development in the INTERREG III Programme (2000–2007). Project proposals dealing with those topics faced difficulties and were often labeled "out of scope." It was mainly the increase in cost caused by disasters and the broader media coverage of such issues that led to a different perception (Schmidt-Thomé 2006a). The main results of the ESPON Hazards Project—an overview of the geographical distribution of natural hazards and the effects on them of expected climate change—were thus integrated into the *Territorial Agenda*. As it is supported by the European ministers responsible for territorial development, the *Agenda* has the potential to influence future territorial development strategies (and related funding) in the EU and its member states.

The results of the ESPON Hazards Project have also been used in a study for the European Commission that analyzed disaster patterns in Europe and disaster-related projects conducted under the European Regional Development Funds (INTERREG Initiative). Once the European Commission (2006) had identified environmental risks and climate change as relevant challenges for regional development, it needed information, not only on the areas affected, but also on the current state of knowledge about hazards from a regional development perspective. The ESPON-INTERACT Hazards Study developed a database that categorized projects according to the hazards studied and the INTERREG strands they were allocated to (Schmidt-Thomé, Klein, and Schmidt-Thomé 2006). It was clear that the preliminary ESPON-INTERACT Hazards Study could help only to identify areas with obvious disaster patterns that had so far not been studied by regional development projects. The study concluded, for example, that floods, droughts, and extreme temperatures were covered pretty extensively in regional development projects, but forest fires were covered rarely or, interestingly, not at all in some of the most fire-prone areas around the Mediterranean (Schmidt-Thomé and Schmidt-Thomé 2007; see figure 6.5). The results of this applied study were not meant to criticize any region for current use of European Regional Development Funds, but rather to give indications of where future funds could be applied.

Another important outcome was an outline for a handbook on risk assessment and management (Schmidt-Thomé 2005). This was in response to a demand by the Commission and might be developed further.

## Local Examples of Planning Support

The challenging impacts of a rising sea level and changing flood-prone areas in the Baltic Sea region led to an INTERREG project that focused on stakeholder communication (Schmidt-Thomé 2006c). To facilitate the discussion, a Decision Support Frame (DSF) was developed (Schmidt-Thomé and Peltonen 2006). The DSF includes guidelines for communication between different stakeholders and provides information and case studies to demonstrate the interactions between the changing global climate and local planning, showing the eventual necessity of mitigation strategies.

The DSF is structured as a four-pillar matrix representing the main tasks and tools needed to communicate the sea level scenario and its analysis on an interdisciplinary basis, in cooperation with spatial planners as well as local and regional authorities and other stakeholders (see figure 6.6). The first pillar contains modeling and GIS applications, but the key factor for addressing the socioeconomic system of an area and mitigating the negative impacts of climate change is the Vulner-

**FIGURE 6.5**

## Forest Fire Hazard and INTERREG IIIB Projects Related to Forest Fires in European Regions

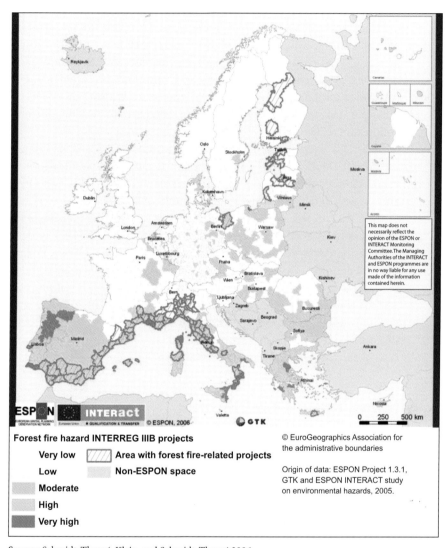

**Source:** Schmidt-Thomé, Klein, and Schmidt-Thomé 2006.

ability Assessment (second pillar). Third, the Knowledge Base pillar includes available background information for legal and planning aspects; it also gives precise, short overviews of the current state of climate change studies and serves as a platform to find examples of other study areas and best practices in climate change impact mitigation strategies. The fourth pillar, the Discussion Platform, is the tool that supports cooperation by providing examples and methods of the roles and interests of the actors and networks involved (Schmidt-Thomé and Peltonen 2006).

The DSF serves as a structuring and facilitating tool within risk governance. It handles requirements such as the integration of scientific, economic, social, and cultural aspects and the effective engagement of stakeholders. It presents a "user interface" between research and practice, providing easy-to-access information for planners and decision makers on different spatial levels and for other interested parties. The strength of the DSF is its transparency and flexibility. Its input is not restricted to any normative data sets with minimum requirements; a DSF can be performed with only a few data. A DSF can be started with an expert opinion and the input data set enhanced when more data become available (Schmidt-Thomé and Peltonen 2006).

The DSF was successfully applied in the SEAREG (Sea Level Change Affecting the Spatial Development of the Baltic Sea Region) case studies—for example, in Pärnu (Klein and Staudt 2006), Itä Uusimaa (Virkki, Kallio, and Orenius 2006), and Gdansk (Staudt, Kordalski, and Zmuda 2006). Pärnu has used the results of the SEAREG project and its follow-up project, Developing Policies and Adaptation Strategies to Climate Change in the Baltic Sea Region (ASTRA), in decisions concerning the construction of sea walls (Schmidt-Thomé 2006a). Poland is one of the first nations in the Baltic Sea region to adopt climate change and subsequent sea level–rise scenarios in its long-term coastal strategy (communication at an ASTRA conference by the Maritime Office, Gdynia, Poland). The DSF approach is currently applied and further developed under the BSR INTERREG IIIB ASTRA project (see www.astra-project.org). It is being further developed and applied in coastal areas in Finland, Latvia, Estonia, Lithuania, Germany, and Poland.

## Lessons Learned from the Research So Far

The approaches to risk assessment and management outlined above are examples of national initiatives of some European countries and of the impact of the European Community represented by the Commission. They show the current state of knowledge and practices on how the topic of hazards (and partly also climate change) can be taken up by planners and other stakeholders in order to deal with risks. Nevertheless, an integrated approach that considers all natural hazards that can potentially affect an area is still missing. Currently, most initiatives and guidelines focus only on the most prominent (or most recent) natural hazards, as evidenced by the forthcoming European directive on flood risk management. In most countries where natural hazards are respected in spatial planning, the focus is predominantly on floods, due to the public attention to recent events. Integrated multidisaster approaches, as well as proper attention to governance principles, are rare; the most comprehensive example of an intentionally integrated multidisaster assessment is probably to be found in Massachusetts (Schmidt-Thomé 2006a; Fleischhauer, Greiving, and Wanczura 2006). Recent extreme events that have led to hazards, as well as disaster interactions, have shown, though, that an integrated

**FIGURE 6.6**

SEAREG Decision Support Frame

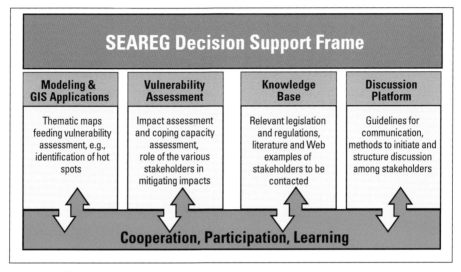

**Source:** Schmidt-Thomé and Peltonen 2006.

approach that takes all potential hazards into account would be more appropriate (Schmidt-Thomé 2006a). Therefore, the ESPON Hazards Project first identified all spatially relevant hazards that can affect the European territory and then gathered relevant data to represent those hazards in map form (Schmidt-Thomé 2006b).

Despite the shortcomings of such a spearhead approach, the value of the results lies in the methodology of first analyzing the potential sources of hazards, then developing single-hazard maps, and finally integrating those maps into aggregated hazard and risk maps. The next step is to discuss how the resulting risk can be analyzed. It is also necessary to clearly define natural hazards and to distinguish between them and other natural processes (Schmidt-Thomé 2006a). As mentioned above, the aggregation process of hazards is complicated because hazards have different spatial impacts, durations, and recurrences. The different dimensions of vulnerability are hardly harmonious due to the fact that some dimensions of vulnerability are disaster dependent and others are not. In particular, the question of which parameters (e.g., frequency, magnitude, population density, damage potential) should serve as the basis for risk zones, and consequently for delineating areas for restricted land use, only shows the normative character of risk assessment and management. The actions to be taken depend on the level of risk a society is willing to accept.

The weighting method chosen by the ESPON Hazards Project to aggregate the hazards according to their importance from a European perspective has worked well and is scientifically accepted. However, it also led to unsatisfactory results in some cases. Italy, for example, appears to be less prone to natural hazards than other countries, according to the aggregated map. One of the reasons is that hazards that are important in Italy (e.g., volcanoes, tsunamis) are less important in most other countries in Europe and have therefore been weighted as less important generally. It must be emphasized that each time the scope or scale of an aggregation is changed, the weighting has to be started all over again.

When discussing the potential impacts of climate change on natural hazards, it is important to distinguish between hazards that are affected by climate change and those that are not. Often those differences, however, as well as potential interactions between hazards in a changing climate, are not yet well known and are currently subject to further research (Schmidt-Thomé 2006a; see also, e.g., www.astra -project.org).

## Conclusions

In conclusion it can be said that large hazard mapping projects that cover an entire continent make sense in order to obtain an overview. During the implementation and development phase of the single- and aggregated hazard maps it became clear to the project team how little knowledge was available regarding the extent and magnitude of hazards from a European perspective. Many researchers, and the European Commission, had excellent local knowledge of hazards, but few people had an overall European picture; and those who did were mostly looking at single, not multiple, hazards. Moreover, a lot more research is needed to better understand the different dimensions of vulnerability (e.g., those that are not determined by physical structures, such as the vulnerability of institutional settings or social groups). Such studies can support sensitization to the topic, which can lead to more integrated approaches and a European response strategy toward natural hazards that is adapted to the hazard profiles of different regions. Ideally, single and multiple hazards will become more respected in spatial planning approaches. Any initiative, whether on the national, regional, or local level, that aims to improve disaster resilience seems to receive stronger support from the European Commission via the European Regional Development Fund. Moreover, the new Seventh Research Framework Programme of the EU has recently paid special attention to this field of research.

This chapter has outlined only the first initiatives and current approaches of the role that spatial planning can play in making the living environment a safer place for human beings. It is important to further evaluate, develop, and politically support the potentials of spatial planning in hazard and risk mitigation, especially in the light of climate change and the resulting challenges for territorial development.

## References

Bärring, L., and G. Persson. 2006. Influence of climate change on natural hazards in Europe. In *Natural and technological hazards and risks affecting the spatial development of European regions*, P. Schmidt-Thomé, ed., 93–107. Espoo: Geological Survey of Finland.
Bulkeley, H. 2006. A changing climate for planning. In *Planning Theory and Practice* 7(2):

203–213.

Commission of the European Communities. 2006. Proposal for a Council decision on Community strategic guidelines on cohesion (SEC [2006], 929). Brussels: CEC. http://ec.europa.eu/regional_policy/sources/docoffic/2007/osc/com_2006_0386_en.pdf.

Emergency Disasters Database (EM-DAT). 2006. Trends and relationships for the period 1900–2005. http://www.em-dat.net/disasters/trends.htm.

ESDP. 1999. *European Spatial Development Perspective: Towards a balanced and sustainable development of the Union territory.* Adopted in May 1999 at the Potsdam informal Council of ministers responsible for spatial planning. http://europa.eu/scadplus/leg/en/lvb/g24401.htm.

Fleischhauer, M. 2006. Spatial relevance of natural and technological hazards. In *Natural and technological hazards and risks affecting the spatial development of European regions*, P. Schmidt-Thomé, ed., 7–15. Espoo: Geological Survey of Finland.

Fleischhauer, M., S. Greiving, and S. Wanczura, eds. 2006. *Natural hazards and spatial planning in Europe.* Dortmund: Dortmunder Vertrieb für Bau- und Planungsliteratur.

German Advisory Council on Global Change. 1999. *World in transition: Strategies for managing global environmental risks.* Berlin: Springer Press.

Greiving, S. 2002. *Räumliche Planung und Risiko.* Munich: Gerling Academy Press.

———. 2005. Concepts and indicators for measuring institutional vulnerability. In *Proceedings of the second meeting of the UN Expert Group on Vulnerability.* Bonn: UN-EHS.

———. 2006a. Integrated risk assessment of multihazards: A new methodology. In *Natural and technological hazards and risks affecting the spatial development of European regions*, P. Schmidt-Thomé, ed., 75–81. Espoo: Geological Survey of Finland.

———. 2006b. Retreat: Options and hindrances for a flood risk mitigation by means of spatial planning. *Proceedings of the Communities Living with Flood Risk in a Changing Climate Conference of the INTERREG Floodscape.* Cambridge, U.K., 27 June 2006.

Greiving, S., and M. Fleischhauer. 2006. Spatial planning response towards natural and technological hazards. In *Natural and technological hazards and risks affecting the spatial development of European regions*, P. Schmidt-Thomé, ed. Espoo: Geological Survey of Finland.

Her Majesty's Government. 2006. *Climate Change: The UK Programme 2006* (CM6764 SE/2006/43). London: Secretary of State for the Environment, Food and Rural Affairs. http://www.defra.gov.uk/environment/climatechange/uk/ukccp/pdf/ukccp06-all.pdf.

International Risk Governance Council. 2005. Basic concepts of risk characterisation and risk governance. Geneva: International Risk Governance Council.

International Strategy for Disaster Reduction, ed. 2005. *Hyogo Framework of Action, 2005–2015: Building the resilience of nations and communities to hazards* (Extract from the final report of the World Conference on Disaster Reduction). Geneva: International Strategy for Disaster Reduction.

Jarva, J., and H. Virkki. 2006. Dealing with hazards: Practice in the Finnish spatial planning system. In *Natural hazards and spatial planning in Europe*, M. Fleischhauer, S. Greiving, and S. Wanczura, eds., 19–36. Dortmund: Dortmunder Vertrieb für Bau und Planungsliteratur.

Klein, J., and M. Staudt. 2006. Evaluation of future sea level rise impacts in Pärnu / Estonia. In *Sea level changes affecting the spatial development of the Baltic Sea region*, P. Schmidt-Thome, ed., 71–81. Espoo: Geological Survey of Finland.

Klinke, R., and O. Renn. 2002. A new approach to risk evaluation and management: Risk-based, precaution-based and discourse-based strategies. *Risk Analysis* 22:1071–1094.

Levet, R. 2006. Planning for climate change: Reality time. In *Planning Theory and Practice* 7(2): 214–217.

Marttila, V., H. Granholm, J. Laanikari, T. Yrjölä, A. Aalto, P. Heikinheimo, J. Honkatuki, H. Järvinen, J. Liski, R. Merivirta, and M. Paunio, eds. 2005. *Finland's national strategy for adap-*

*tation to climate change.* Helsinki: Ministry of Agriculture and Forestry. http://www.mmm.fi/sopeutumisstrategia/.

Munich Reinsurance Company. 2004. Great natural catastrophes. *Topics Geo 1/2004: Annual Review of Natural Catastrophes 2003.*

National Climate Change Program. 2005. http://www.bmu.de/files/pdfs/allgemein/application/pdf/klimapaket_aug2007_en.pdf.

Olfert, A., S. Greiving, and M. J. Batista. 2006. Regional multirisk review, disaster weighting and spatial planning response to risk: Results from European case studies. In *Natural and technological hazards and risks affecting the spatial development of European regions*, P. Schmidt-Thomé, ed., 125–151. Espoo: Geological Survey of Finland.

Peltonen, L., S. Haanpää, and S. Lehtonen. 2005. *The challenge of climate change adaptation in urban planning* (FINADAPT working paper 13). Helsinki: Finnish Environment Institute Mimeographs 343.

Robinson, P. 2006. Canadian municipal response to climate change: Measurable progress and persistent challenges for planners. *Planning Theory and Practice* 7(2): 218–222.

Schmidt-Thomé, P., ed. 2005. *The spatial effects and management of natural and technological hazards in Europe: Final report of the European Spatial Planning and Observation Network (ESPON) project 1.3.1.* Espoo: Geological Survey of Finland.

———. 2006a. *Integration of natural hazards, risk and climate change into spatial planning practices.* Academic dissertation no. 193 of the University of Helsinki. Geological Survey of Finland.

———, ed. 2006b. *Natural and technological hazards and risks affecting the spatial development of European regions.* Espoo: Geological Survey of Finland.

———, ed. 2006c. *Sea level changes affecting the spatial development of the Baltic Sea region.* Espoo: Geological Survey of Finland.

Schmidt-Thomé, P., J. Jarva, S. Haanpää, S. Lehtonen, and L. Peltonen. 2006. A country without hazards? In *Positioning Finland in a European space*, H. Eskelinen and T. Hirvonen, eds, 121–135. Helsinki: Ministry of the Environment, Ministry of the Interior.

Schmidt-Thomé, P., and H. Kallio. 2006. Natural and technological disaster maps of Europe. In *Natural and technological hazards and risks affecting the spatial development of European regions*, P. Schmidt-Thomé, ed., 17–63. Espoo: Geological Survey of Finland.

Schmidt-Thomé, P., J. Klein, and K. Schmidt-Thomé. 2006. *Environmental hazards and risk management: Thematic study of INTERREG and ESPON activities* (ESPON-INTERACT report). www.interact-eu.net; www.gtk.fi/projects/espon.

Schmidt-Thomé, P., and L. Peltonen. 2006. Sea level change assessment in the Baltic Sea region and spatial planning responses. In *Sea level changes affecting the spatial development of the Baltic Sea region*, P. Schmidt-Thomé, ed., 7–17. Espoo: Geological Survey of Finland.

Schmidt-Thomé, P., and K. Schmidt-Thomé. 2007. Natural hazards and climate change: Stakeholder communication and decision-making processes. An analysis of the outcomes of the 2006 Davos conference on disaster reduction. *Management of Environmental Quality* 18(3): 329–339.

Slovic, P. 1999. Trust, emotion, sex, politics, and science: Surveying the risk-assessment battlefield. *Risk Analysis* 19(4).

Staudt, M., Z. Kordalski, and J. Zmuda. 2006. Assessment of modelled sea level rise impacts in the Gdańsk region, Poland. In *Sea level changes affecting the spatial development of the Baltic Sea region*, P. Schmidt-Thomé, ed., 121–130. Espoo: Geological Survey of Finland.

*Territorial Agenda of the European Union.* 2007. Draft to be presented by ministers responsible for territorial development on the occasion of the informal ministerial meeting on territorial cohesion to be held in Leipzig, 25 May 2007. www.territorial-agenda.eu.

*The Territorial State and Perspectives of the European Union.* 2007. Draft. A background document for the *Territorial Agenda of the European Union.* www.territorial-agenda.eu.

Virkki, H., H. Kallio, and O. Orenius. 2006. Sea level rise and flood risk assessment in Itä-Uusimaa. In *Sea level changes affecting the spatial development of the Baltic Sea region*, P. Schmidt-Thomé, ed., 95–106. Espoo: Geological Survey of Finland.

Vries, J. de. 2006. Climate change and spatial planning below sea-level: Water, water and more water. *Planning Theory and Practice* 7(2): 223–226.

# CHAPTER 7

# Figuring Out the Shape of Europe: Spatial Scenarios

Jacques Robert and Moritz Lennert

As mentioned in Andreas Faludi's introduction to this collection, the *Territorial Agenda of the European Union* marks a new turn in the ongoing effort to develop a coherent European view of the main challenges and tasks, and also the functions, of spatial planning and regional development policies. It presents itself as "a strategic and action oriented framework for the territorial development of Europe" (Territorial Agenda 2007). As such it is obviously forward looking, defining the priorities for *future* policies in order to accommodate and shape *future* developments.

Before long-term policies can be defined or improved, however, it is essential that decision makers become aware of the driving forces that will shape territorial developments in the decades to come. It is also of primary importance to anticipate the real power and the limitations of public policies in guiding territorial development. That was the main objective of the scenarios elaborated within the ESPON 3.2 Spatial Scenarios project, which investigated the possible territorial impacts of existing as well as emergent challenges and considered various possible policy responses. The main result of the project is a trend scenario that highlights the impacts of the most relevant driving forces in a practically unchanged policy context. On the basis of the trend scenario, two policy scenarios were elaborated, based, on one hand, on an orientation toward more economic, social, and territorial cohesion and, on the other, on higher competitiveness in the global context. By comparing and confronting the outcomes and their strengths and weaknesses, the main features of a final, more desirable scenario could be identified, as well as the combination of policies to make it possible.

## The Trend Perspective

By its very nature, a baseline (or "trend") scenario is based on the continuation of trends and on the principle that no major changes occur in ongoing policies. It is

The authors would like to acknowledge the collective work of the entire research team of ESPON 3.2 (2006), on which this chapter is based. The research was cofinanced by the European Regional Development Fund in the context of the ESPON INTERREG Initiative.

important, however, to consider that in certain fields, such as demography, past trends will continue, while in other fields, such as energy, recent developments seem much more relevant for the future than long-term trends. In addition, a baseline scenario has also to consider a number of policy measures adopted recently (such as the Kyoto agreement), even if the impacts of such measures are not yet well understood. In other words, a baseline scenario is not identical to the extrapolation into the future of long-term trends of the past.

## Europe's External Context

After the enlargements of May 2004 and January 2007, and considering the intensification of cooperation between the EU and Norway and Switzerland, the integration of Europe is now being pursued on an almost continental scale. The enlargements have fundamentally changed the scale of regional disparities in Europe. At the same time, the widening of this integrated area initially suggests that Europe has become more autonomous and less subject to external influences. The reality is somewhat different, however, as numerous factors relating to the external geopolitical context (also discussed in chapter 8) are gaining in importance, factors that will have a substantial impact on the European territory.

At world scale, Europe's relative demographic potential is decreasing, especially with regard to the growing Asian, but also American, demographic poles. As economic disparities at the world scale remain significant, despite the rapid catching up of a number of emerging economies, external migration pressure will continue to increase. The primary sources are the countries of the southern and eastern Mediterranean basin and of Africa, which have considerably higher population growth rates and much younger population structures than Europe. Migration flows to Europe increasingly come from countries farther afield and from a broader spectrum of cultural, economic, and social backgrounds. Although the more central and developed parts of Europe (the so-called pentagon of London, Paris, Milan, Munich, and Hamburg) remain the preferred destinations, certain regions in southern Europe are also significantly affected as, increasingly, are central and eastern Europe. The pressure will continue to increase. The volume and structure of immigration will, however, remain highly dependent on the policy mix adopted and its implementation. In a trend perspective and in a context where the EU's competence in immigration matters remains limited, the evolution will be characterized by continuing, though rather contained, illegal immigration.

Accelerating globalization is certainly the most important external factor with significant territorial impacts. Globalization has numerous facets, however, the impacts of which are not unidirectional. In terms of foreign trade, and despite the concerns generated by rising import levels, Europe still displays a modest level of economic openness with a ratio between total external trade and GDP at market prices during the period 1996–2000 of only 14 percent. This headline figure is comparable to those of the United States (13.5 percent) and Japan (17.5 percent). This then raises the question of the real intensity of globalization through trade.

The EU's most important external trade partners are generally located some distance away (United States, East Asia, Gulf States). Among the neighboring regions, significant trade flows exist with the Russian Federation and countries of the southern and eastern Mediterranean. In the context of progressive globalization, trade flows with Latin America and emerging Asian countries can be expected to intensify, while trade with Africa is not expected to grow significantly. Europe has a strong position in the exports of technological, industrial, and agricultural products and, increasingly, of services. In the context of the World Trade Organization (WTO), numerous trade barriers for manufactured products have been removed, and further trade liberalization is expected in services and agriculture.

Globalization has a strong and accelerating influence on the job market and thus on the territorial distribution of employment opportunities. That is why this aspect of globalization looms large in the mind of the general public. The relocation of businesses outside Europe is the most sensitive aspect. Increasingly, not only manufacturing but also services such as software production and programming, telephone marketing, law and tax consultancy, accounting, and financial information analysis are being affected.

There are important additional dimensions to globalization, however, such as a growing intercontinental interpenetration in the ownership of businesses, indicated by the increasing number of mergers and acquisitions involving partners from various continents. Although numerous European companies expand on other continents through foreign direct investment (FDI), the risk is also growing that more and more European companies will be taken over by non-European groups, as fiscal and social regulations restrain capital accumulation in Europe more than in a number of emerging economies. In addition, the European economy, as far as its business structure is concerned, is more fragmented than that of its major competitors. Companies controlled by European decision makers are generally more inclined to maintain and develop jobs of strategic significance (management, R&D, design, etc.) in Europe than companies run by non-Europeans. This aspect of globalization is likely to gain in importance.

With regard to territorial impacts, the regions benefiting most in employment and income are the first- and second-level metropolitan areas, including those of central and eastern Europe. Other, mainly centrally located, regions benefit only if a number of conditions are fulfilled: economies strongly supported by R&D; medium-size cities with strong cultural, scientific, or tourist potential; good environmental conditions. By contrast, a number of regions with low or intermediate technologies (heavy industries, textiles, clothing, basic manufacturing activities, etc.) have been, and continue to be, negatively affected. Globalization also endangers the "Marshallian" districts based on small and medium enterprises (SMEs) with low R&D input. Looking at future trends, it is likely that more and more urbanized and also more rural regions will be negatively affected, while the benefits will largely remain concentrated in a limited number of regions with advanced metropolitan functions and a select few others with specific characteristics. Globalization is therefore likely to sharpen territorial imbalances within Europe.

Europe's external context will continue to be characterized by growing external energy dependency, especially fossil energy (oil, gas, coal), but also nuclear energy (uranium). The progressive depletion of the North Sea resources and the increase of oil and gas prices, with the possibility of oil peaking, will make the issue of Europe's energy security a central pillar of its foreign and security policy.

With regard to the EU itself, future enlargements will contribute to determining the characteristics of the external context. After the enlargements of 2004 and 2007 and considering the general political situation in Europe, the baseline perspective assumes that further enlargements will not take place for some time to come, with the countries of the western Balkans perhaps joining by 2020 and Turkey not before 2030. This means that the EU neighborhood policy will have to play an important role in helping to maintain stability along the EU's external borders.

## Demography and Integration Issues

Europe remains out of sync with global population trends, as discussed in chapter 4 by Diogo de Abreu. The natural population evolution continues to either decline or remain level at zero in the majority of European states. One structural trend that is likely to continue is the increasing proportion of people of pensionable age. The countries with the oldest populations are Italy, Greece, Sweden, Belgium, Spain, Portugal, Germany, Bulgaria, and France, while those with the youngest populations are Cyprus, Slovakia, and Ireland. As the "baby boomers" retire, the indigenous labor force will inevitably shrink. There will not be enough entrants to replace those leaving the labor market, although a decrease in unemployment will partially compensate for that. This will make sustained economic expansion and the preservation of welfare levels difficult. To meet the challenges of an aging society, the EU and the member states individually all attempt in various ways to facilitate entry into the labor market by creating policies to further promote female employment in all age brackets, particularly in the older age categories, and to fully utilize the female potential among immigrants. This obviously implies the need for job creation. The challenge here is also to close the gender pay gap and to facilitate the reconciliation of work and family life. Recently, a debate over replacement immigration has begun in various countries and at the EU level. Aging is not a spatially uniform process. In addition to the differences between countries noted above, differences between regions are even more significant. While parts of the territory—mainly the metropolitan regions—are and will remain congested, many more rural regions are experiencing depopulation. Large cities with an obsolete economic base are also losing population, however, while some competitive rural areas are increasingly able to attract retirees and the self-employed, thereby developing their new "residential" economies.

Immigration from outside Europe—both legal and illegal—is far from negligible and, for a number of countries, is the sole means of maintaining population levels. The respective shares of population originating from immigration and the annual levels of immigration vary widely, however, although the destinations of immigrants are now more evenly spread, helped no doubt by the EU's policy toward asylum seekers under the Dublin Convention. With regard to the destinations of immigrants, the urban-rural divide is significant. Most cities, notably most capital cities, have a much higher proportion of foreign nationals, foreign-born and second- and third-generation immigrants, than smaller towns or rural areas. The attraction of cities can be explained by factors such as the extended supply of services and access to housing, the possibility of remaining close to family and kin, and, in the case of illegal immigrants, the greater ability to remain anonymous.

The levels of immigration inevitably raise the issue of economic and sociocultural integration. Access to employment is of key significance. At least as far as official figures are concerned, immigrants from less developed countries suffer from substantially lower activity rates and higher unemployment rates than either the EU or the national averages. It should also be noted that a significant proportion of illegal immigrants is also illegally employed at extremely low wages and without social security. That segment of the labor market has been growing. Immigrants from nonindustrialized countries more often suffer from poverty and social exclusion than the native population. That, together with the growing size and emancipation of previously marginalized ethnic minorities, increases the risks of sociocultural conflict. The debate around multiculturalism and whether assimilation is preferable to maintaining separate ethnic and religious identities has become increasingly intense, with much of the focus on education and its potential as an effective integration tool. That is only likely to gain in importance.

Intra-European migration flows are another important factor in territorial development. Their nature is very diverse. They comprise retirees from northern Europe moving to the Mediterranean, as well as East Europeans moving to western Europe in search of jobs. In the context of European integration and the development of corporate enterprises, intra-European mobility in the service sector is also growing. The same is true for students. East-west migration related to the recent EU enlargements has largely been underestimated, causing some scarcity of qualified manpower in the countries of origin. The intensification of intra-European migration in the decades to come is highly probable in a context where national borders will become weaker while regional disparities remain significant and the number of retirees increases.

Lifestyles are progressively changing, in part influenced by population aging. Clear indications exist of increasing mobility and changing consumption patterns in older population segments. In light of economic globalization and the intensification of information flows, international experience is becoming increasingly common, affecting European lifestyles, consumption patterns, and values. At the same time, the perception of decreasing security, especially in cities, has led to progressively less solidarity. Mobility patterns are also affected by changing values and attitudes. Long holidays have largely been replaced by more frequent "mini-breaks." Nonwork-related mobility (leisure, culture, consumption, education) has increased, while home working has increased and will continue to do so. Cheaper airfares have encouraged long-distance leisure mobility, although rises in energy prices could significantly affect that sector in the future.

## Innovation Capabilities and New Key Technologies

Although the need for more innovation is acknowledged (Lisbon Strategy), the gap between Europe and other advanced economies (United States, Japan) remains. Based on current trends and despite Europe "catching up," it would take more than 50 years for Europe to reach the U.S. level. Only a small group of European countries show above-average performance (Switzerland, Finland, Sweden, Denmark, and Germany). As far as the promotion of innovation is concerned, there are strong territorial imbalances, with a number of high-performing regions located in the new member states.

Europe's technological landscape will nevertheless be shaped by the breakthrough of a number of key new technologies, possibly with significant territorial impacts. The progress of the knowledge economy is inescapable and is strongly related to biotechnology, nanotechnology, material technologies, and ICT. In theory, further developments in ICT and related applications should benefit SMEs, which nevertheless continue to show a below-average rate of adoption. The expansion of biotechnologies is expected to fundamentally change livestock breeding and the production of plants ("green biotechnologies"). The debate concerning genetically modified species will intensify. New developments in "red biotechnologies" will be significant for medical care (new drugs and vaccines). The application of "gray biotechnologies," for instance in industrial production processes and environmental engineering, aims at reducing energy consumption and waste and promoting the use of less harmful substances. As noted previously, the energy sector is, and will remain, subject to numerous technological innovations. Some are quite ambitious, with breakthroughs likely only in the medium to long term (decarbonization of fossil fuels, nuclear fusion, etc.). Numerous transport innovations (car engines, electronic systems, materials, security systems, propulsion systems for ships, etc.) are under development. They will contribute to energy savings, higher security, higher speed, emission reduction, and more efficient use of the transport infrastructure.

The territorial impacts of technological innovations tend to be highly diversified, and thus a distinction has to be made between impacts related to technology production and those related to its applications and use. Production will largely remain concentrated in metropolitan areas. Applications, however, will show a more even pattern, with some favoring the more central and urbanized regions and others the more rural areas. But the diffusion of new technologies is not immediate, and the less developed and more remote regions are generally late in adopting innovative solutions. In a trend perspective, that lag will remain significant, as territorial disparities within Europe are strong and the center-periphery gradient is high. Public policy can accelerate diffusion, however.

## Toward a New Energy Paradigm

Europe is relatively poor in conventional energy reserves. The EU25 imports around 80 percent of its oil, with that figure perhaps rising to 90 percent by 2020. The EU25 currently imports 40 percent of its natural gas, which is projected to reach almost 70 percent by 2020. The enlarged EU still has substantial reserves of coal, but imported coal is far cheaper, so coal production continues to decline, especially in central and eastern Europe. Europe also has little uranium. Conventional renewable energy sources (hydropower) cover a modest part of Europe's energy demand (less than 5 percent) and are already almost fully exploited. Increasing external dependence, as noted previously, means that energy security will be crucial and thus that the vicissitudes of global geopolitics will continue to significantly affect Europe's future. The increase in oil and gas prices in recent years reveals structural imbalances at the world scale, with global demand rapidly increasing (new emerging economies) and supply being constrained by depletion, insufficient investment, political troubles, and cartel policies. Military conflicts in the Middle East (Iraq) and the risks of their further expansion add to the need to move toward a new energy paradigm, departing once and for all from the so-called carbon economy.

While only modest energy savings followed the oil crisis of the 1970s, Europe is now on its way to a substantial change in its energy supply system, reflecting a new awareness of the limited availability of fossil fuel resources and the inescapable environmental impact of growth in energy demand. This new paradigm has numerous facets. Improving the efficiency of consumption through the introduction of energy-saving techniques both in buildings (houses, offices) and in economic activities (manufacturing, agriculture) is essential. High energy prices are also speeding up the structural transformation of the economy toward a more technological and service-based model. The exploitation of renewable sources (solar, wind, biomass, tide and wave hydropower) is accelerating, leading to numerous new technologies and substantial investments. While new technologies are also emerging in the transport sector (biofuels, hybrid engines, fuel cell engines), more structural energy issues around transport and mobility are being reconsidered (modal shift, potential mobility reduction, substitution of mobility through wider use of telecommunications). The impacts of climate change on the energy sector are also being taken into account, for both demand and supply. Technological development is not limited to renewables, however, but also concerns the modernization of more conventional energy supply techniques (coal gasification and liquefaction, new generations of nuclear power plants), as well as the emergence of new technology clusters (hydrogen technologies). The energy challenge will be one of the most important for Europe's future, likely to generate both external (ensuring the security of energy imports) and internal (revival of nuclear electricity production) tensions.

The assumptions for the trend perspective have to integrate the move toward this new energy paradigm, as it is inescapable, while a significant number of territorial impacts at very different scales are likely to result from it. Energy-intensive manufacturing in Europe with low added value will be increasingly abandoned. This may affect central and eastern more strongly than western Europe. On the other hand, Europe is likely to become a world leader in technologies relating to renewable energy sources and to new energy systems, an evolution favoring the technologically advanced regions of the "pentagon." Rural areas will be significantly affected by the new energy paradigm, in both positive and negative terms. While the rapid development of biomass production (biofuels, etc.) will generate new income, compensating for the decline of EU support to agriculture, it may also cause serious environmental problems relating to intensive agriculture and forestry and, increasingly, conflicts between food and energy production, leading to higher food prices. Further negative aspects include the impacts of higher energy prices on the competitiveness of agriculture and on the accessibility of remote rural areas. At the same time, land set-asides can be taken into use for the production of energy crops where appropriate. In that respect, southern regions are less favored because of the likelihood of more droughts.

In the long term, increasing energy and, thus, transport prices will have a significant impact on settlement patterns. One can already observe a trend, albeit still weak, toward more compact cities and the concentration of new settlements around public transport hubs. That is more or less offset, however, by price increases of land and housing in large cities, which cause further suburbanization. Tensions between those competing factors will remain high. In a trend perspective, mobility will be reduced by increasing home working and the wider use of telecommunications for all kinds of service-related activities. The urban environment will benefit from breakthroughs in car engines (hybrid cars, fuel-cell engines) that are much less damaging to the environment. Further environmental concerns may result from the development of new nuclear power plants, however, and from the proliferation of wind energy facilities in attractive landscapes and tourist areas.

## Transport and Accessibility

Europe's transport situation, also discussed in chapter 5, is characterized by high levels of congestion in urban areas and on major interurban transport corridors; a strong imbalance between transport modes in favor of road and air transport; missing links in transport infrastructure, especially in the new member countries; and a lack of interoperability within specific transport modes. Transport systems have not kept pace with European integration and still largely reflect national patterns and characteristics. While congestion mainly affects the more central regions and the obsolete networks of central and eastern Europe, the European peripheries are generally poorly accessible.

Various factors will contribute to future change. As far as flows are concerned, ongoing European integration and the recent EU enlargements, in particular, generate increasing transit flows across a number of countries, requiring a rapid recalibration of the transport infrastructure. Structural changes in the European economy favor the transport of light products with high added value, while transport of raw materials and heavy industrial products is declining. The development of high-speed train networks strengthens the relative accessibility of the regions serviced, in particular the most central ones. The emergence of low-cost airlines not only makes air traffic more competitive, even against rail over relatively short distances, but also boosts the development of regional airports. In many respects, that has been beneficial for the accessibility of more peripheral and landlocked regions.

Transport policies are not free of contradictions. While the EU adopted a policy aiming at sustainable transport with a smaller environmental footprint and a more balanced modal split in the early 1990s, the priorities in central and eastern Europe—but not only there, because similar programs have been implemented in western Europe—in recent years were on motorway development. Such policies are being justified by growing motorization and the obsolescence of existing road networks. Developments in the energy sector should favor more energy-efficient transport modes, particularly in the rail and maritime sectors. However, that is as yet uncertain. Though oil price increases may have an impact, it is likely that prices will have to rise to a truly phenomenal level to have a significant impact, as the desire for the "freedom" that car ownership potentially brings is basically inelastic in economic terms.

However, increasing oil prices will undoubtedly have an impact on various segments of the transport sector. Technological developments are advancing, as already noted, and new attitudes and practices are emerging, such as car sharing and the increased use of public transport where possible. Public policies at the local and regional levels generally take the new energy situation into consideration and favor the development of public transport. It is to be expected that the new energy paradigm will become ever more fully integrated into transport policy at the EU and national levels.

## Challenges for Sustainability and the Impacts of Climate Change

The environmental situation in Europe has generally improved, thanks to political intervention that has led to a tighter regulatory regime being imposed on polluters and, ultimately, to fundamental changes in the structure of the economy. Nevertheless, a number of challenges persist, many of which have a particularly significant territorial dimension. As far as water quality is concerned, the main source of diffuse pollution is agriculture, particularly the release of nitrates as a result of fertilizer and manure use. Groundwater is therefore expected to become even more polluted, since nitrates and pesticides enter groundwater slowly. While rivers are now recovering from *severe* pollution as a result of a sharp reduction in point source pollution, *diffuse* pollution will continue to pose a threat to the quality of drinking water in numerous areas, in both eastern and western Europe. Areas likely to be particularly affected are the Paris Basin, the Benelux regions, northern Italy, and northern Germany. Moreover, the intensive production of energy crops is likely only to increase the problem.

Water shortage will become an increasingly serious problem in southern Europe due to the alarming increase in droughts, calling for new strategies (desalinization of seawater, water transfer between river basins, limitation of irrigation and of the expansion of tourist resorts, changes in agricultural production, etc.).

As with groundwater, a tighter regulatory framework has also contributed to a significant improvement in air quality (lower ozone concentrations; a reduction in the emission of fine particulates and sulfur dioxide, nitrogen oxides, and greenhouse gases). The continued growth, despite higher energy prices, of road traffic driven by economic development and infrastructure investment, is likely to endanger air quality recovery, however, even if new generations of less polluting car engines emerge. Growing motorization in central and eastern Europe may offset improvements that result from closing down obsolete industrial plants. Forthcoming EU regulations and the further implementation of existing ones, as well as other international agreements (the follow-up to the Kyoto Protocol), will substantially influence Europe's environment.

The development of natural areas and biodiversity is subject to a number of contradictory developments. The implementation of the Natura 2000 program of the EU has provided sufficient protection for the most valuable natural areas, covering a large part of the European territory. However, connectivity between those areas through ecological corridors has not been fully achieved, and a multitude of other factors, such as the pressure of infrastructure development, tourism, holiday homes, and the abandonment of farms, continue to threaten biodiversity. In the open fields in the polders and deltas, where agriculture is becoming increasingly industrialized, natural landscape elements will continue to disappear. Many natural areas in the new member states will be converted into farmland. Significant environmental damage is also to be expected in attractive coastal and mountain areas, such that, in a trend perspective, biodiversity will not significantly progress and will even regress in a number of areas.

Public awareness of the importance of climate change for territorial development and environmental protection has already reached a significant level in the early 2000s. Significant damage has occurred over the past decade, with floods, droughts, heat waves, and forest fires all becoming more frequent, developments that are discussed in chapter 6. Moreover, it is assumed that the frequency of such events will increase. Some impacts have a more structural character, which can be more readily counteracted, than others. Progressive drought is a structural factor in southern Europe and will significantly affect agricultural productivity and tourist development. The abandonment of large areas of dryland agriculture is likely to result in the return of wilderness areas, but also in more forest fires. Drought also has severe impacts on the production of hydropower and increases the need to import energy. Winter sports activities are likely to decline in the southern half of Europe, including the Alps. A number of regions may benefit from progressive climate change—for example, rural areas in northern Europe, where new potential arises for agriculture, and the mountain areas there, where demand for winter tourism will increase. Policies related to climate change will remain rather heterogeneous. The need for more prevention is far from being recognized globally, and significant differences between European countries remain, with some investing in flood prevention while others limit their interventions to postevent cleanup and repair.

### Europe in 2030: The Final Image of the Trend Perspective

Figure 7.1 illustrates the *attraction and polarization potential of metropolitan areas in 2030*. In that figure, we can see a remarkable concentration of strong metropolitan areas in the pentagon, but also in less central regions (mainly capital cities and other European engines). The pentagon of the early 2000s, grouping the *areas of concentration of flows and activities*, has expanded, mainly along the main transport corridors in the direction of metropolitan regions like Barcelona and Madrid, Rome, Glasgow, Copenhagen, Stockholm and Oslo, Berlin and Warsaw, Prague, Vienna, and Budapest. The basic characteristics of settlement systems in terms of *polycentricity* have not changed fundamentally. Various types of areas have run significant risks of economic decline in relation to progressive globalization and European integration. The trend toward the *marginalization of rural areas*, already observed in the early 2000s, has continued, but with regional variations. In some areas, the number of available jobs has declined significantly. In others, population aging and even depopulation have reached critical levels. Accelerating globalization has affected a significant number of industrial regions with low or intermediate technologies, exposing the *risk of declining industrial activity*. The most severely affected areas lie in central and eastern Europe. *External immigration* (legal and illegal) has continued, with immigrants settling mainly in metropolitan areas, including central and eastern European cities. The areas with a *high potential for tourism and retirement* are the coastal, lake, and mountain regions, while other *aging areas* are mainly found in remote rural regions lacking attractiveness. Various regions are subject to the *impacts of natural hazards*, many of which are linked to climate change. The least affected regions lie in northern Europe.

## The *Territorial Agenda:* A Response to the Trends?

The result of an intergovernmental process, the *Territorial Agenda* (2007) is characterized by all the vagueness necessary to build consensus. In addition, in terms of actions it focuses more on modes of governance than on actual policies. Contents are touched upon only in the form of policy priorities, which do not differ significantly from those in the *European Spatial Development Perspective* (ESDP). The only "innovation" is the inclusion of the list of challenges in paragraph 7, which reflects the trends identified above. Within the policy priorities those challenges are mentioned only marginally, however, and it remains to be seen to what extent the foreseen policy process can deliver concrete answers to them.

In order to evaluate the extent to which this current policy process responds to the challenges identified in the trend scenario, one has to turn to the background document, *The Territorial State and Perspectives of the European Union* (Territorial State 2007).

It is immediately obvious that the decision to embed territorial policy in the Lisbon Agenda limits the scope for reflection. "The key political challenge for the Union at this moment is to become economically more competitive and dynamic"

**FIGURE 7.1**

Trend Scenario: Final Image, 2030

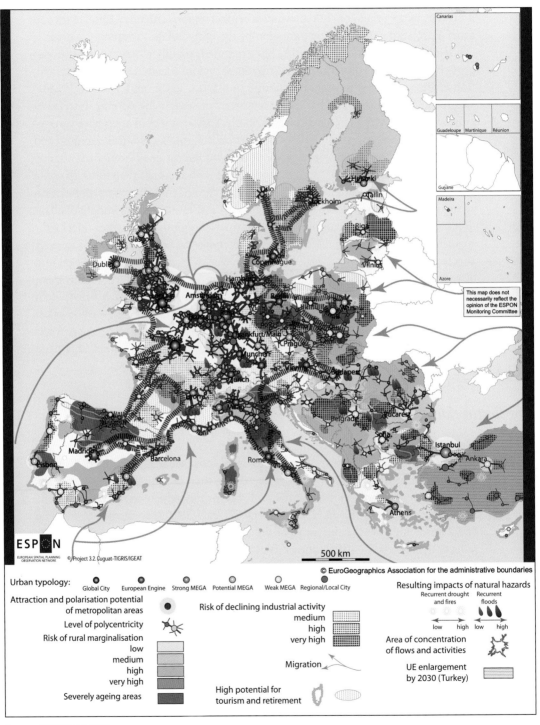

**Source:** ESPON 3.2. 2006.

(Territorial State 2007, 8). Thus, the priorities are based on policy objectives and not on the evidence of challenges ahead.

This leads to reducing regions to areas of attraction for economic activities, with success depending on the exploitation of their territorial capital, in a process that transforms these (vaguely defined) "regions" into individual, responsible actors, thereby ignoring the fact that they are part of a greater whole, which often determines their fate more decisively than they themselves can (see ESPON 3.4.2 2006, chapter 1.3.2).

The document aims at defining the perspectives for European territorial development. Those perspectives are political visions, however, not trend perspectives. The resulting six policy priorities at the beginning of part C stick to the vision of the ESDP and thus appear backward looking and not based on the analysis of future trends.

Finally, concerning the types of policies, the document claims, "If territorial cohesion is the policy objective, territorial development policies are the policy tools" (Territorial State 2007, 52). This is obviously a positioning of the makers of territorial policy on the European scene. However, this overestimates the influence of territorial, as compared to nonterritorial, policies, even though the document quite rightly pushes for making territory an inherent aspect of all policy making. As the following policy scenarios show, territorial policies are only to a very small part the driving forces that shape our territories.

## Preparing the Debate of 2008: Competitiveness or Cohesion

On the basis of a choice made in collaboration with the ESPON Monitoring Committee, the political body overseeing the ESPON program, the two prospective policy scenarios developed in the ESPON project juxtapose two fundamental elements of European (and probably any) policy: competitiveness and cohesion. As Andreas Faludi elaborates on these two concepts in his introduction, we will not do so here, except to note that these two terms continue to dominate the European debate, as can be seen in the words of the EU Commissioner for regional policy, Danuta Hübner, who urges a "paradigm shift" in the definition of cohesion policy, calling for "a dynamic process of empowerment helping overall European economic growth and competitiveness," and thus distancing herself from the traditional, equity-oriented approach to cohesion policy (Hübner 2007). Research is needed to evaluate the impacts of such a paradigm shift, and the ESPON scenarios are an attempt at such evaluation. It is important to understand, however, that what follows are roll-forward policy scenarios: Rather than exploring what a perfectly cohesive or a perfectly competitive Europe would look like, they explore what impact a choice made today in favor of one or the other as a policy priority might have on different territories in Europe and on the spatial structure of the continent as a whole. This also allows us to investigate ways in which these two concepts are complementary or contradictory in their respective impacts.

### The Policy System of the Cohesion-Oriented Territorial Scenario

In this scenario, the main EU policy priorities are economic, social, and territorial cohesion and not global competitiveness. This does not mean that improvements in competitiveness are excluded, but rather that in case of incompatibilities between cohesion and competitiveness, priority will be given to cohesion. This is, for instance, the case where more competitiveness is likely to increase territorial disparities. It is important to indicate that measures related to competitiveness in the context of structural policies are fully integrated into the scenario, however, even if they are likely to generate intraregional disparities within less developed regions. Up to 2030, the deepening of EU policies is preferred to further enlargement.

The cornerstone of the cohesion-oriented scenario is a set of policies favoring such elements as families (aiming at increasing fertility rates), education, employment, immigration, and integration. A number of policies are made more flexible—for instance, concerning child care arrangements and retirement. Confronting institutional forms of ageism and removing compulsory retirement ages are part of this process, although the latter is less popular among occupational groups engaged in physically demanding work. Flexibility is also extended to other aspects of life, such as education, making family commitments more manageable. Allowances paid to grandparents and other older and retired relatives, instead of, or as well as, to parents are also becoming a means of integrating third and fourth generations into community life and maintaining healthy life expectancy rates. Migration policies within the EU are better coordinated and adapted to the goal of "replacement." They are strictly controlled as regards country of origin, area and region of destination, and occupational group. Specific controls are also introduced with sociocultural integration in mind. Even though illegal migration continues, the figures are declining following the introduction of EU ID cards. Lifelong learning is also becoming increasingly popular, opening up a wide variety of services and new forms of employment. The "democratization" of remote forms of mass communication (ICT, etc.) is policy led and plays a part in reestablishing the viability of rural, semirural, and some remote areas. In order to achieve greater cohesion by means of social and cultural integration, serious efforts are made to address challenges of religious and racial diversity, which have been the source of much conflict in previous periods. The largely media-driven obsession with individual identity is tackled through shared cultural events and activities designed to cultivate shared regional and European identities. Citizenship and language classes become a residency requirement, and restrictions on religious schools are complemented by policies to circumvent the segregation of minority groups with, for example, quotas for the children of ethnic and religious minorities and the facilitation of intercultural interaction from an early age through such practices as educational exchanges. While assimilation is not forced, such "soft" measures encourage more peaceable coexistence and sow the seeds for the long-term integration of disparate communities.

Another major difference from the trend scenario is to be found in public policies addressing balanced regional development and territorial cohesion. Maintaining and even strengthening EU cohesion policy is the result both of EU enlargements and of a reaction to the territorial imbalances generated by accelerating globalization in the early 2000s. Enhancing the vitality of less favored regions appears as a fundamental long-term objective, because in the long run the economic and social costs of having regions deteriorate are extremely high. The new cohesion policies include numerous measures aimed at increasing the competitiveness of the less favored regions and avoiding their marginalization. As a renewed and strengthened cohesion policy is also more expensive, EU budgets have to be correspondingly adapted and various resources diverted. The Common Agricultural Policy (CAP), transport policies, and research and development policies are adapted to give priority to less favored regions. In terms of ICT infrastructure, there is progress in dispersing broadband into less densely populated regions. Further liberalization of public services is not envisaged, because that would harm less developed areas where such services are not profitable. Closing down such services is also deemed damaging for the demographic and economic development of those areas. Considerable spending is undertaken for cohesion purposes. Furthermore, the deepening of European integration generates many new EU regulations—for example, in terms of environmental and consumer protection—which lead to rising costs, both for the public purse as well as for businesses.

Transport policies are more oriented toward cohesion and sustainable development than in the trend scenario, and market demand is less absolute as a criterion. Significant financial resources from the Regional and Cohesion Funds are allocated to transport infrastructure in the cohesion countries and in the less developed regions. One of the main priorities here is the development of an efficient transport infrastructure along major corridors in, as well as between, the new member states and with the EU15. A significant difference compared with the trend scenario is that, in addition to major corridors, support is also given to a number of strategic regional transport axes in the context of rural development, the purpose being to connect as many medium-size and small towns as possible to the trunk networks. The cohesion-oriented scenario also pays greater attention to a better balance of transport modes and promotes efficient railway and waterway systems. In central and eastern Europe, obsolete railway systems are modernized in order to limit the growth of road transport, a policy that also addresses constraints imposed by oil price and supply.

In the scenario, structural policies pay much attention to energy issues and allocate more resources in eligible regions to support energy saving and the diversification of supplies. The Trans-European Energy Networks (TEN-E) are further developed, but mainly to the benefit of less developed countries and regions (central and eastern Europe, European peripheries). The rural development policy also allocates substantial resources to the production of energy in rural areas. Energy systems are modernized in less developed regions, which benefit more from structural support than richer regions. In this respect, the "catching up" of the new member states in the energy supply and energy transport sectors is significant. Obsolete energy systems are rapidly replaced by modern ones, including renewable energy sources. Decentralized systems of energy production and distribution are developed, encompassing rural areas together with their small and medium-size towns.

The environment is viewed as one of the main pillars of European solidarity. Environmental targets are set at a higher level than in the trend scenario, and significant resources from the Structural Funds and rural development policy are allocated to environmental improvement and protection in less favored areas. There is more attention to environmentally friendly transport modes and related investments, especially in the railway sector. Kyoto implementation is also taken seriously, which translates into more rigorous controls at the source for industry and transport and the promotion and subsidization of environmentally friendly practices. There is more attention for the protection and enhancement of the natural and cultural heritage than in the trend scenario. In less favored areas, significant resources from the Structural Funds go to the protection and enhancement of natural areas and the implementation of Natura 2000. Important efforts are made in southern Europe to prevent forest fires through better forest management. Stronger rural development in European peripheral regions favors the maintenance of cultural and natural landscapes as a resource for rural tourism.

## A Territorial View of the Impacts of a Cohesion-Oriented Policy

By 2030 Europe has a more regionally balanced population structure and population growth, even in a number of areas previously threatened by depopulation. Economic growth has been less expansive than in the trend scenario but has shown a more diffused territorial pattern. The winning regions have generally been nonmetropolitan regions of the periphery or located within or in proximity to the pentagon. Progress in accessibility has been more widespread than in the trend scenario. The dynamics of medium-size towns have counterbalanced metropolitan growth. The competitiveness of European metropolitan areas has seen less progress than in the trend scenario. Integration policies have contributed to limiting social and physical segregation in cities, as well as the resulting feeling of insecurity. Gated communities have not emerged, and the originally less favored population groups have been better integrated into the labor markets.

The evolution of rural areas up to 2030 has been more prosperous and balanced than in the trend scenario. Strengthened Structural Funds and rural development policies have accelerated economic diversification in rural areas. The negative impacts of climate change on rural areas in southern Europe have been less damaging because of significant support for adaptation measures. Generally, the natural and cultural heritage of European rural regions was better protected and enhanced than in the trend scenario.

Figure 7.2 reveals a less concentrated but more widespread pattern in respect to the *attraction and polarization potential of metropolitan areas* in 2030. Urban settlements are characterized by greater *polycentricity*, stretching over much larger swathes of the European territory than in the baseline scenario. The number of areas at *risk of marginalization* and of *declining industrial activity* is comparable to that prevailing in the baseline scenario, but their size is reduced and their intensity

**FIGURE 7.2**

## Cohesion-Oriented Scenario: Final Image, 2030

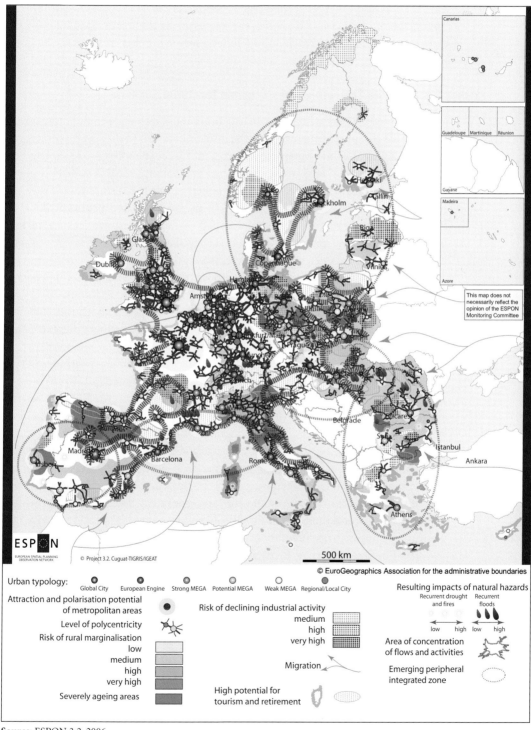

Urban typology:
  Global City    European Engine    Strong MEGA    Potential MEGA    Weak MEGA    Regional/Local City

Attraction and polarisation potential of metropolitan areas

Level of polycentricity

Risk of rural marginalisation
  low
  medium
  high
  very high
  Severely ageing areas

Risk of declining industrial activity
  medium
  high
  very high

Migration

High potential for tourism and retirement

Resulting impacts of natural hazards
  Recurrent drought and fires    Recurrent floods
  low    high    low    high

Area of concentration of flows and activities

Emerging peripheral integrated zone

© EuroGeographics Association for the administrative boundaries

**Source**: ESPON 3.2. 2006.

lower. The areas with *high potential for tourism and retirement*, as well as those with *severe population aging*, remain similar to the baseline scenario, but the *impacts of natural hazards* (drought, fires, and floods) are much lower. Another fundamental difference is the emergence of several *peripheral integrated zones*. The *area of concentration of flows and activities*, the successor of the former pentagon of the early 2000s, has a wider reach and includes a larger number of cities in the inner periphery.

## The Policy System of the Competitiveness-Oriented Territorial Scenario

In the competitiveness-oriented scenario, fundamental changes in policy are motivated by the disappointing results of the implementation of the Lisbon Strategy in the early 2000s. The EU budget is reduced, and EU expenditures are targeted on R&D, education, ICT, and strategic external accessibility. CAP is subject to rapid and radical liberalization. The structural policies budget is also reduced, with the renationalization of a portion of former EU interventions and a concentration on the most competitive areas of less developed regions. Public services are further liberalized and privatized, labor markets are regulated in a more flexible way, and the second and third pillars of EU policies (foreign policy, justice, security, etc.) are strengthened. Widening of the market through further EU enlargements is part of the strategy of increasing competitiveness. The western Balkans join in 2015, with Turkey and the Ukraine following suit in 2020. The Neighborhood Policy is strengthened with the Maghreb countries becoming ever further integrated into the European Economic Area.

Generous pension schemes are abandoned as life expectancy continues to rise. Retirement age is increased. Maintaining a dynamic labor market is uppermost in the policy considerations of both national governments and the EU. The restrictions on the free circulation of workers following the accession of new member countries to the EU are abolished. A significant difference between this scenario and the trend scenario is the opening of external EU borders to (selective) immigration to plug the gap caused by the expanding support ratio, targeting young and/or highly skilled labor from across the world. The policy is strictly regulated, as political and economic immigration are separated. Social frictions provoke strong reactions, and there is a noticeable increase in surveillance and security, creating major business opportunities.

The European Council focuses efforts and European as well as national resources on increasing global competitiveness. Technological development is the cornerstone of the new policies, the objective being to reduce the gap between Europe and other advanced economies and to maintain sufficient distance in technological development from emerging economies such as China, India, and Brazil. Europe is ready to give up large segments of its economic structure with dwindling productivity, provided growth can be achieved in high-tech segments of manufacturing and services with strong knowledge and capital intensity. Transport is also meant to contribute to global competitiveness, and policies are shaped accordingly. Significant EU resources are injected into the Trans-European Transport

Networks (TEN-T) and research and technological development, aiming to counteract progressive oil depletion and the related price increase. In numerous regions, road and motorway investments are higher than in the trend scenario. The energy policy apportions considerable resources to the development of technologies likely to facilitate the supply of energy to metropolitan areas, such as new generations of nuclear power plants, but also coal gasification and liquefaction and hydrogen technologies. A breakthrough occurs in the field of hydrogen technology after 2010, with a large number of applications in transport, heating, and electricity generation for a number of engines and electronic devices. TEN-E policy focuses on metropolitan areas. EU credits for technological development and energy transport infrastructure are allocated to developed, rather than lagging, regions. Environmental policy is subordinated to economic development. Climate change is recognized as a major problem, but measures to adapt to its consequences are principally taken at the global or international level. Preventive measures to limit the territorial impacts of climate change are generally considered too costly and insufficiently profitable in the short term. Those measures taken often have a short-term or issue-based (e.g., anti-flooding) character.

## A Territorial View of the Impacts of Competitiveness-Oriented Policies

By 2030 the median age of the population is lower. Economic growth is more expansive but also more concentrated than in the trend scenario. Regions with metropolitan areas experience strong demographic and economic growth. Large cities of central and eastern Europe also benefit. However, growing immigration in a context of weak integration policies has led to increasing xenophobia, protective attitudes, and social unrest. Gated communities have emerged in and around cities as well as in attractive coastal regions. Suburbanization is significant, not only because of metropolitan population growth, but also because of segregation and insecurity in cities.

Market forces have been important drivers of change, even in rural areas. The evolution of rural areas has been more dichotomous than in the trend scenario, with those located around metropolitan areas or with good agricultural conditions booming, but with an increasing number becoming further marginalized and abandoned, in both eastern and western Europe. Marginal rural areas have been more seriously affected than in the trend scenario, especially those with a heavily aging population and much emigration, low levels of soil fertility, increasing drought, and low accessibility and attractiveness.

Figure 7.3 shows that the *attraction and polarization potential of metropolitan areas* is particularly strong and concentrated in the pentagon. Only a few metropolitan areas outside the pentagon are able to generate significant attraction and polarization through agglomeration effects. The *area of concentration of flows and activities* is much more limited than in the baseline scenario, covering only parts of what was the economic core of Europe at the beginning of the century, although it also reaches out from there along a few major corridors to Vienna and Copenhagen. The *risk of rural marginalization* is much greater than in the baseline

**FIGURE 7.3**

## Competitiveness-Oriented Scenario: Final Image, 2030

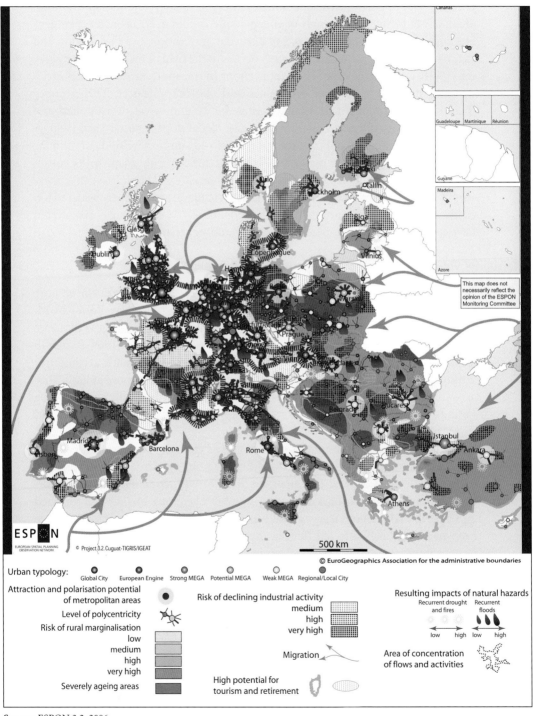

**Source:** ESPON 3.2. 2006.

scenario. The areas at *risk of declining industrial activity* are more extensive, and the intensity of risk is higher. *External migration* flows are particularly intense. The areas with *high potential for tourism and retirement* are similar to the baseline scenario, but the areas with *severe population aging*, generally in remote rural regions, are larger. The *impacts of natural hazards* (drought, fires, and floods) are greater than under baseline assumptions.

## Comparing Scenarios

The main didactic value of scenarios lies in their comparison (see figure 7.4). The trend scenario has shown that basically unchanged policies are not an appropriate response to emerging challenges. Shortcomings relate to the inefficiency of the Lisbon Strategy; the weakness and heterogeneity of family and integration policies; the absence of responses to the fragmentation of the European economy; and the support given to all types of infrastructures, including those with low profitability and those less appropriate with regard to the new energy paradigm. The competitiveness-oriented scenario has generated stronger economic growth and higher competitiveness, with a more substantial emergence of new technologies. It has also produced higher social costs through growing disparities at various scales, which are likely to result in economic and social problems. Economic activities and dynamic population development will be concentrated in central areas. On a meso scale, capital cities will reinforce their polarization. The cohesion-oriented scenario has produced significant added value in terms of territorial cohesion and balance, of demographic revival, of sociocultural integration, of less damage caused by natural hazards, and of fewer negative impacts in rural regions; but its economic and technological performance has been lower than that of the two other scenarios. The pentagon will extend significantly in all directions, and several new areas of economic integration outside the pentagon will emerge. On the meso scale, polarization potentials are distributed among a greater number of urban areas with medium-size cities playing an important role.

## Conclusion: Reshaping Policy for a More Promising Territorial Future

Territorial issues are significant in Europe, and various new challenges are emerging. The scenarios elaborated above demonstrate that classical spatial policies on their own will not succeed in promoting harmonious, competitive, and balanced territories unless they are part of a more comprehensive policy system pursuing the same objectives. A desirable territorial perspective is a real societal choice, to which the policies of a variety of sectors—including education, innovation, transport, and agriculture—have to contribute. It is also clear that, unless backed by efficient national and regional policies, EU policies, even though enunciating overall objectives and providing strategic impulses, cannot by themselves realize a preferred territorial perspective. The purpose of this final section then is to sketch a possible approach to reshaping policies, the proviso being that there are multiple

FIGURE 7.4

## Spatial Structure and Urban Hierarchy

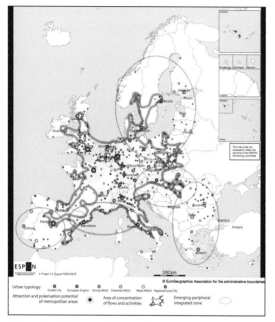

Cohesion-Oriented Scenario

Trend Scenario

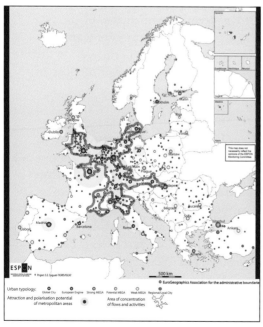

Competitiveness-Oriented Scenario

**Source:** ESPON 3.2. 2006.

conceivable paths of which more than one is scientifically defendable. The intention here is not to provide detailed policies, but rather to propose more general principles along which such policies could be organized.

An initial prerequisite for successful and coherent territorial development in Europe is explicitly taking into account the challenges identified as important for the coming decades. These are, in particular, the territorial impacts of population aging, immigration, sociocultural integration, the various facets of globalization, the new energy paradigm, and climate change. These new challenges are on top of existing challenges and those reinforced by the recent EU enlargements, such as the disparities between European regions in such categories as economic wealth, development opportunities, accessibility, and environmental quality.

In relation to the challenges above, a number of specific priorities and objectives have to be considered. The first is the importance of human resources in relation to population aging, immigration, integration, and productivity. This is likely to become a critical variable for more and more regions and calls for innovative approaches. The objectives should be to reach high levels of productivity, to create sufficient jobs, to ensure that there is a basic correspondence between the labor force and available jobs and thus to ensure the integration of less favored groups both into the labor market and into society, to favor synergies between generations so as to draw more benefits from the knowledge and experience of the aged, and to facilitate the integration of the young. In addition to competitiveness, addressed by the Lisbon Strategy, various other facets of globalization will have to be taken into account, such as the increasing intercontinental competition in services and agricultural products and the need to favor the emergence of more European "majors" or "champions," so as to protect the European economy against increasing external economic control through mergers and acquisitions. The new energy paradigm, apart from being a handicap for the European economy, represents an important opportunity for the development of numerous, especially rural and technology regions. Such opportunities should be systematically exploited and supported by the respective policies concerned, because they are likely to reduce Europe's external energy dependence, generate new regional income sources, and strengthen European leadership in technologies related to the exploitation of renewable energy sources.

European policies should obviously focus on those policy fields where a common EU approach provides significant added value. In relation to the challenges above, this is clearly the case for transnational issues such as climate change, water management, migration (internal and external), energy production and transport, and the strengthening of the European business structure with a view to overcoming the economic fragmentation of the European economy. In many of these fields, some form of EU policy already exists, although not always at the scale and with the targets needed. Such policies are not always free of contradictions, however, either with other policies or with national policies. In all such areas, improvements could certainly be made.

In many respects the new challenges call for a strengthening and adaptation of various EU policies, though that could be achieved only within the context of a reshaped governance system. In the context of applying the subsidiarity principle, the territorial dimension should gain in importance, so that regionally defined objectives and strategies are considered more seriously and by a wide range of EU and national policies with important territorial impacts. For this purpose, tools and procedures such as territorial impact assessment—the topic of chapter 2— should be more systematically applied in defining and applying such policies. A particular challenge here will be to establish a balance between the respect and support for regional strategies defined by the respective regional authorities and the need to counteract increases in regional disparities through territorially differentiated support measures, considering that not all regions have similar potential and development opportunities. The necessary arbitration will require coordination between various relevant policies, and not only at the level of classical "regional policies," in order to ensure coherence by avoiding counterproductive policy impacts and promoting synergies. This is probably the most important innovation to be pursued in the future governance system.

The definition of a new policy system likely to face up to these emerging challenges and promote the realization of the territorial goals chosen inevitably raises the question of the level of resources to be allocated to it. It must first be stated that the most important task in this respect is certainly the reorganization of the present resource allocation system, in order to make it more rational and productive. This may involve changes in resource allocation between the respective policy levels and sectors and, above all, a better coordination of the allocation of resources. One must also consider that the achievement of these territorial goals requires important public investments, and that more resources, in addition to those currently committed, will probably be necessary. These can best be viewed as necessary short- to medium-term investments to reduce long-term social costs that would inevitably accrue from pursuing less ambitious goals and from suboptimal resource allocation.

A further task in reshaping the policy system is the consideration of possible contradictions in spatial development issues, requiring policy choices to be made at appropriate levels and according to a variety of possible territorial contexts. Contradictions obviously exist between the pursuit of global competitiveness, relying on strengthening already advanced regions, and a more balanced territorial development, enabling more or less homogeneous standards of living, including access to services and jobs throughout Europe. Further potential contradictions can be found in the need to reduce the environmental footprint of transport and to promote the accessibility of more peripheral regions, which in turn will increase transport flows. Additional examples of contradictions could easily be found. Solving them will require in-depth territorial analyses and the search for new differentiated answers using *complementary* rather than *exclusive* measures likely to neglect the development of various types of territories.

Finally, reshaping the policy system in the direction of more desirable long-term territorial development should not be taken to imply that by 2030 regional inequalities will have disappeared. Each of the scenarios above has shown that natural evolution and market forces play a considerable and, indeed, often growing role in the processes of territorial change. The aim here, however, is to identify the benefits offered by such developments, while limiting their possible negative impacts. In a rapidly changing context, this requires a substantial reconsideration of the policy system in order to provide appropriate policy.

## References

ESPON 3.2. 2006. *Spatial scenarios and orientations in relation to the ESDP and cohesion policy: Final report.* http://www.espon.eu/mmp/online/website/content/projects/260/716/index_EN .html.

ESPON 3.4.2. 2006. *EU economic policies and location of economic activities: Final report.* http:// www.espon.eu/mmp/online/website/content/projects/260/720/index_EN.html.

Hübner, D. 2007. Cohesion policy: Genuinely modern and still reinventing itself. Closing speech, Fourth Cohesion Forum, Brussels, 28 September 2007. http://ec.europa.eu/commission_barroso/hubner/speeches/pdf/4thcf_closing.pdf.

Territorial Agenda. 2007. *Territorial Agenda of the European Union: Towards a more competitive and sustainable Europe of diverse regions* (Agreed on the occasion of the Informal Ministerial Meeting on Urban Development and Territorial Cohesion in Leipzig on 24/25 May 2007). http://www.bmvbs.de/Anlage/original_1005295/Territorial-Agenda-of-the-European-Union -Agreed-on-25-May-2007-accessible.pdf.

Territorial State. 2007. *The Territorial State and Perspectives of the European Union: Towards a stronger European territorial cohesion in the light of the Lisbon and Gothenburg ambitions* (A background document for the *Territorial Agenda of the European Union*). http://www .bmvbs.de/Anlage/original_1005296/The-Territorial-State-and-Perspectives-of-the -European-Union.pdf.

# CHAPTER 8

# North-South Regionalism: A Challenge for Europe in a Changing World

Pierre Beckouche and Claude Grasland

Internal and external policies are generally considered as independent parts of the political agenda of the European Union. This is especially true if we examine the general lack of a linkage between the activities of the directorate-general responsible for regional policy (DG Regio), which focuses on the reduction of economic and social disparities inside the territory of the EU, and the activities of the directorate-general responsible for the external relations between the EU and the rest of the world (DG Relex). As typical examples, the third cohesion report and the *Territorial State and Perspectives of the European Union* (TSP) are illustrated with many maps that present the heterogeneity of states and regions of Europe in much detail but no maps on the situation of Europe in the world or even on the states located in the immediate neighborhood. The recent *Territorial Agenda* (TA) of the European Union, of course, speaks often of European "cities," "regions," and "territories"—more than 200 times as a whole. Surprisingly, however, whereas everyone knows that globalization has major impacts on Europe and more in particular on its territory, the word "world" appears only two times. Surprisingly, too, whereas the neighborhood policy was launched several years ago, "neighborhood policy" is referred to only once in the TA and not at all in the TSP. The ESPON program (2002–2006) is an exception to this general rule. Indeed, that applied research program supported by DG Regio and by member states' ministers of spatial planning was initially compelled to focus on internal differences between European regions. But the researchers and policy makers involved in the project recognized early that the strengths, weaknesses, opportunities, and threats that European regions and cities facing globalization are exposed to could not be understood without the launch of a specific research project on Europe in the world (ESPON 3.4.1, Grasland and Didelon 2007).

The aim of that contribution is to relate the main political conclusion of this ESPON report and explain the consequences for the future development of regional policy in Europe. Our central assumption is that internal and external policies should not be developed separately but should be strongly interlinked, as they both depend on a global political project that we propose to call Vision of Europe in the World. Based on political and scientific inputs, this global vision of Europe in the world is not clearly formulated at the EU level. Moreover, different visions of the EU's situation in the world are currently circulating that imply different challenges for internal and external policies (figure 8.1).

## Role of the Vision of Europe in the World for Internal and External Policies

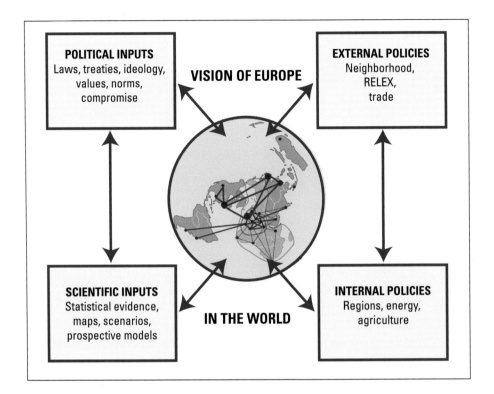

Various dominant representations of the world are currently available: the "continents" view, which describes territories in the traditional—but still topical—shape of continents or, more recently, in "civilization areas" (Huntington 1996); the "center-periphery" view, which stresses the asymmetry of north-south relations and the real, yet decreasing, northern domination; and the "archipelago" view, based on a networking organization of space, which highlights the connections of remote territories. Each of these views partially reflects the reality of the contemporary world. They are not really contradictory: Continental territories may have strong frontiers *and* asymmetrical relations with the developing countries located in their periphery *and* intense exchanges with global nodes of other parts of the world. But these three patterns have to be analytically distinguished, because their territorial impacts are quite different. The goal of this chapter is to show that none of these views provides a sustainable future for the European territory. But it is perhaps possible to combine them in a fourth vision called north-south regionalism, which appears more relevant for the EU, and to draw conclusions for such a regionalism for European planning policies.*

*Each vision is illustrated by selected evidence derived from the ESPON 3.4.1 report.

## The Continent View: Toward a Giant "Swiss Europe"?

The continent view relies on the apparently obvious evidence that the size of the European Union in the world is sufficient for it to retain relative autonomy in the process of globalization and, more generally, to have the possibility of partly closing its borders to ensure internal protection.

### Selected Evidence

The *Territorial Agenda* acknowledges the "accelerating integration of our regions, including cross-border areas, in the global economic competition, at the same time increasing dependencies of state and regions in the world" (2007, par. 7). But in fact the EU continues to be confident about its growth. The first paragraph of the TA declares, "The EU looks with confidence at the progress achieved in economic, social and ecological terms. Together the EU Member States operate a combined economy, which is about *one-third* of the world-wide Gross Domestic Product. It is this economic power as well as a territory covering more than 4 million km$^2$ and a population of 490 million inhabitants in a variety of regions and cities, which characterises the territorial dimension of the EU" (Territorial Agenda 2007, par. 1; emphasis added).

The *Europe in the World* ESPON report (Grasland and Didelon 2007) gives figures on the actual weight of the European territory in the world. We are far from the "confidence" referred to in the *Territorial Agenda*. The size of the EU27 has been compared to big countries (United States, China, Japan, India, Brazil) as well as to other international economic blocks (NAFTA, MERCOSUR+5, ASEAN+3). The EU27 territory represents 3 percent of the world's continental land area, 9 percent of agricultural land, 8 percent of the world's population, 13 percent of its urban population, and a bit more than one-fifth—and not "one-third"—of its GDP (measured of course in purchasing parity). As a whole, it can be said that Europe represents something like 12 percent (i.e., one-eighth) of the world, not more (see table 8.1).

Furthermore, the trend is worrisome. The share of population and GDP of Europe at world scale has been steadily decreasing since the 1950s. Since then, however, and although this structural decline continues, it has always been counterbalanced by the dynamics of EU enlargement (figure 8.2). The question is what will happen once enlargement is over. The answer is very much related to the success of the neighborhood policy, and its success depends on the vision of Europe in the world that will be promoted within the EU.

### Main Political Features

In the continent scheme, priority is given to the EU's internal integration—that is, to the convergence between the new member states and the rest of the EU. As to the rest of the world, the emphasis is on security. The geographical idea is that Europe is a world civilization, is strictly circumscribed and defined, should be internally as homogeneous as possible, and should be highly protected against

**TABLE 8.1**

## Percentage of EU27 in the World

| Area | Surface | Agricultural Land | Population | Urban Population | GDP (PPS) | $CO_2$ Emissions | MEAN |
|---|---|---|---|---|---|---|---|
| NAFTA | 16 | 18 | 7 | 11 | 26 | 28 | 17.6 |
| ASEAN+3[a] | 11 | 14 | 33 | 28 | 25 | 24 | 22.4 |
| MERCOSUR+5 | 13 | 7 | 6 | 10 | 6 | 3 | 7.4 |
| **EU27** | **3** | **9** | **8** | **13** | **23** | **17** | **12.0** |
| Rest of the world | 57 | 52 | 47 | 38 | 22 | 28 | 38.7 |
| **Total** | **100** | **100** | **100** | **100** | **100** | **100** | **100.0** |

**Source**: Grasland and Didelon 2007.

[a] ASEAN plus Japan, China, and South Korea. Australia and New Zealand discussed their participation at the December 2005 Kuala Lumpur Summit.

external threats (e.g., illegal migrations, environmental menace, human trafficking). Borders are of high significance; planning policy is devoted to cohesion. This vision implies a restriction of the European treaties, which stipulate that the condition of accession to the EU is being a "European state." Initially, no unequivocal interpretation of that criterion existed. It could be read equally well in geographical, cultural, or political terms. But with the "continent" vision, the idea of final geographic borders of Europe is clearly at stake. Cooperation with neighbors remains important but only if the neighbors are clearly defined as outside the perimeter of Europe.

This could be one interpretation of the European Neighborhood Policy (ENP) launched in 2004.* Beyond the EU27, a "ring of friends" (Prodi 2002), from Morocco to Russia, is essential to European stability and development, and, with a ring of friends, "everything but institutions should be shared." The goal is to spread "the four freedoms" to the neighborhood: the free flows of goods, services, people, and capital. But since the policy came into force, agreements have been enhanced for capital and investments, goods and services (a free trade zone including agri-

---

*The European Neighborhood Policy consolidates various previous policies and budgets dedicated to the surrounding countries: MEDA for Mediterranean countries ("Barcelona process"), PHARE for eastern countries, TACIS for ex-USSR, etc. The new European and Neighborhood Partnership Instrument (ENPI) concerns (1) nine Mediterranean countries—those of the former Barcelona process, minus Turkey (benefiting from a specific budget), Cyprus, and Malta, but plus Libya; (2) the three Caucasus countries; and (3) the three eastern countries that are located between the EU and Russia (Moldova, Ukraine, and Belarus, though Belarus is still not included for well-known political reasons). The Balkan countries are not included because they have been given an entry perspective. Nor is Russia, because it has a specific strategic agreement with the EU—the general goals of which are nevertheless quite similar to the ENP's: Create a common space for trade, finance, migrations, training, culture, and security.

**FIGURE 8.2**

## Evolution of the EU Share of World Population and GDP (PPS), 1950–2020

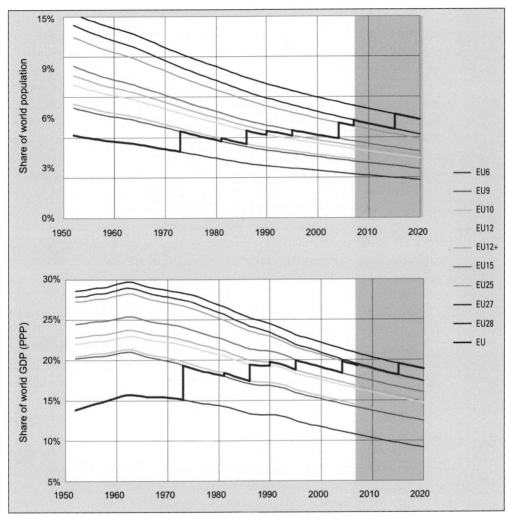

**Source:** Grasland and Didelon 2007.

**Note:** EU28 is a scenario based on the entry of Turkey into the EU.

cultural trade is scheduled for 2010 with the Mediterranean neighbors)—but not for people. Restrictions to entry into the EU's territory remain severe, and asylum has become more difficult to obtain than it used to be. Many see the ENP as a way to avoid the accession of Turkey into the EU, since the neighborhood policy would—in theory—give Turkey several of the advantages of a member state.

The continent view is consistent with a strong European integration as part of the ongoing process of eastern enlargement. Eastern new member states would be, and already are, favored in the industrial relocation of western firms. Since the beginning of the 1990s, many EU foreign direct investments (FDIs) have targeted central and eastern European countries. The fact that their entry into the EU was certain has given them credibility for investors. And the move continues: Between 2002 and 2006, 80 percent of the FDI by western European investors has been in other western European countries (innovative industries, banks, and services) or in eastern new member states (automobile industry and other manufacturing sectors). The so-called European continent is actually becoming one integrated productive system (Hatem 2007). Table 8.2 shows that during recent years, the continent has hosted more than 40 percent of the world FDI inward flows, mostly in western Europe, and more than 30 percent of the jobs created by FDI, mostly in eastern Europe; western European firms have in both cases been the major investors. According to the continent view, this evolution of the European economic geography would intensify with new members and, maybe later on, with Ukraine, Georgia, and other countries of the Caucasus.

As to agriculture and subsidies, the bulk of European funds would be devoted to the adjustment of the new eastern member states' agriculture, in order to rapidly reach a homogenous European agricultural market. As to regional policy, these states would also benefit from the main subsidies because many of their regions are much poorer than the European average. Trans-European Networks would be mostly implemented in eastern Europe, too, for transport, telecommunication, and energy facilities (European Commission 2005). This view is simply the continuation of what has been occurring since the beginning of the 1990s. Since then, the central and eastern European countries have become by far the greatest beneficiaries of EU grants so as to prepare their entry into the EU.

A major geoeconomical feature should be stressed: Central and eastern Europe have been integrated into western Europe's economic and political influence in an incredibly short period of time—less than 15 years. European former members of the Soviet bloc have experienced a surprisingly rapid shift from the COMECON integrated trade system to a highly westernized trade system. Eastward flows have declined to almost zero; flows to the West have boomed. Concerning subsidies and political influence, the European share (Commission + member states) in the total assistance given to the CEE countries has been booming, too. It has been a little less so in the Balkans (where reconstruction is largely supported by the EU) and in the Maghreb countries, and significantly lower in the Near and Middle East, where the share of the United States is impressive. Since the 1990s, Europe's share has declined in North Africa, the Near East, and the Middle East.

## Territorial Impacts

The territorial impact of such a template entails several assets:

- Trans-European Networks would be implemented on a large European scale, which would be favorable to the internal integration of the European territory.
- The German territory would become the genuine center of Europe.
- Central and eastern European member states would benefit from western subsidies and private foreign direct investments and be expected to catch up with the EU's GDP average.

TABLE 8.2

## The Place of Western and Eastern Europe in Foreign Direct Investment

| Inward Foreign Direct Investment (annual average, 2002–2006) | | |
|---|---|---|
| | **Billion $** | **Percent** |
| **EU15** | 361 | 37.9 |
| **10 new member states** | 34 | 3.5 |
| Southeastern Europe and NIS | 47 | 4.9 |
| Africa | 29 | 3.0 |
| Western Asia | 32 | 3.4 |
| Japan | 1 | 0.1 |
| China (incl. Hong Kong) | 105 | 11.0 |
| Other East and Southeast Asia | 59 | 6.1 |
| United States | 133 | 14.0 |
| Latin America | 101 | 10.6 |
| World | 953 | 100.0 |

Source: UNCTAD.

| Jobs Created by Foreign Direct Investment (annual average, 2003–2006) | |
|---|---|
| | **Percent** |
| **Western Europe** | **11.9** |
| **Central and Eastern Europe** | **19.4** |
| Africa | 2.5 |
| Middle East | 1.0 |
| East Asia and Pacific (industrialized countries) | 2.3 |
| East Asia and Pacific (developing countries) | 42.6 |
| North America | 12.0 |
| Latin America | 8.5 |
| World | 100.0 |

Source: OCO Consulting, IBM/PLI 2006, in Hatem 2007.

■ The regional policy focus on these countries—namely, their less developed areas—would foster these territories.

On the other hand, this view would have territorial shortcomings:

■ Focusing on EU border security, and the NIMBY interpretation of the ENP, would have negative impacts on the other peripheral parts of EU space. The southern part of the EU would be misused, especially cities like Sevilla, Barcelona, Marseille, Napoli, Athens, and Valetta.

■ The outcome would be still worse on the eastern frontier. The benefits from European money would mainly benefit great metropolitan areas of eastern

Europe (e.g., Warsaw, Prague, Budapest) but not the peripheral regions. With the closing of the eastern borders, European peripheries could lose their traditional complementarities with regions of Ukraine, Russia, or Belarus.

■ The worsening relationship between the Baltic states and Russia is the reason the borders there have almost become barriers. The EU has financed high-tech devices for electronic surveillance on the border. Russians have chosen to avoid the Baltic states as logistic interfaces with the West. They have rather been developing new port facilities near Saint Petersburg and have implemented a direct submarine route for the new pipeline to Germany and countries of northwest Europe. Such a path could well be extended to the whole eastern side of the EU, which would diminish the dynamism of peripheral territories that would experience "tunnel effects."

■ Due to the rise of salaries, western industries could relocate to other competitive labor markets, most certainly in East Asia—where European FDI goes more and more—which would certainly hamper eastern territories.

■ The size of these eastern markets would not be a sufficient asset per se for western investors. The absolute size of these markets is quite small (100 million people), and the population is rapidly decreasing.

■ The closing of borders would make it difficult for the EU to gain a new labor supply (due to the overall demographic decline of the EU discussed in chapter 4), especially skilled labor (for the Lisbon Strategy cannot be fulfilled if the EU bases its strategy of attracting skilled workers only on distant and uncertain links with Asia or Latin America). A continental European scheme obstructing population exchanges with the eastern and southern neighborhood would therefore hamper the European economy and territory as a whole, and intensify the process of population aging.

■ The continental view is based on a "fear of migration," especially from Muslim and African countries. But contrary to what is often said, the percentage of today's population that comes from Mediterranean neighboring countries and lives in Europe is not large—documented or undocumented. Generally speaking, North America hosts many more Latin Americans than Europe hosts migrants coming from its own neighborhood. Foreigners (of whom 4 percent are undocumented) make up 15 percent of the U.S. population; the share of Mexicans alone is more than 8 percent. By comparison, at most 7 percent of the EU15's population consists of foreigners (of whom less than 1 percent are undocumented); the migrants from the southern Mediterranean are less than 4 percent.

Finally, this dominant vision of Europe as a continent is something like the dream of becoming a giant Switzerland, an island of prosperity protected from the external world by its borders. But the EU is at once too small and too big for that dream to be fulfilled—too small because its real size in the world is insufficient to enhance an autonomous development without connections with other countries;

too big because what is possible for Switzerland, a small state embedded in the prosperous area of the EU, is impossible for a large economy surrounded by developing countries.

## The Center-Periphery View: Toward a Dissymmetrical Euromed Pattern

Europe has center-periphery relations with all its surrounding countries. But this is particularly true with the southern neighbors. The Barcelona process, or "Euromed," launched in 1995, has hitherto shown to be quite dissymmetrical.

### Selected Evidence

The center-periphery vision of the world is based on evidence that the countries of the world that have experienced the fastest economic and demographic growth during the past 50 years are located in a kind of golden ring around the three dominant economic centers of the triad (figure 8.3). The problem for the EU, therefore, is to maneuver its growing periphery into a position of competition with other economic centers of the world, such as Japan and the United States. But this vision is based on an asymmetrical relationship with the neighborhood.

This vision does not claim that the EU represents one-third of the global economy, and it acknowledges that some cooperation with the neighbors is necessary in order to remain a global player. But it is also unrealistic in considering that northern countries could ask the southern ones to open their borders for economic investment but at the same time refuse to open their own borders to immigration (the majority of migrants into the EU are coming from those peripheral countries; see figure 8.4).

### Main Political Features

This center-periphery vision could well be regarded as a subcategory of the continental vision. The difference is that here the ENP would be more dynamic—not for people but at least for economic exchanges. This view is based on the complementarities between low-cost peripheries and high-tech centers, based on the assumption that Europe has a valuable area where it can exert influence that it should take advantage of, and not leave it to U.S. or Asian competitors (as the Chinese happen to do more and more in Africa, including North Africa).

Such a north-south combination could allow Europe to compete with East Asia and North America. Those two regions have achieved a huge relocation of firms and extended a transnational production system based on north-south complementarities. In the American and East Asian cases, there is either little (East Asia) or a lot of (Mexicans to the United States) migration, but in both cases there has been significant foreign direct investment from rich countries into neighboring developing countries. Out of $100 invested abroad by the United States, $18 goes to Latin America; out of $100 invested by Japan, $18 is invested in its develop-

**FIGURE 8.3**

Joint Evolution of the Share of the World Population and GDP (PPS) from 1950–1954 to 1996–2000

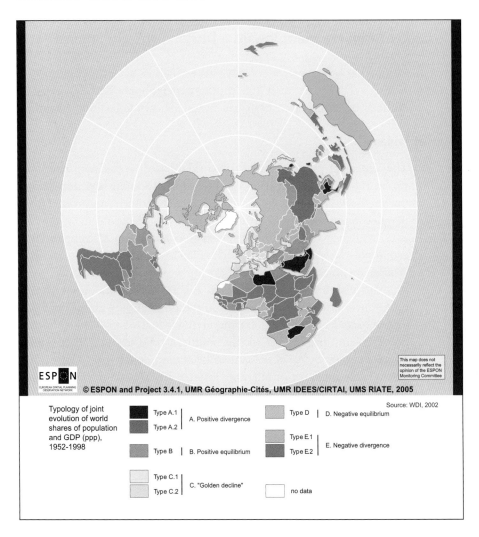

ment or emergent East Asian peripheries. But out of $100 invested abroad by western Europe, only $10 is invested in its peripheries—almost all of it in the central and eastern European countries, less than $2 in the Mediterranean developing countries.

What if a north-south strategy were to be adopted by Europe, according to the center-periphery pattern?

■ Competitive delocalization would increase toward eastern and especially southern neighbors located between the Mediterranean and the Sahara.

**FIGURE 8.4**

## Origin of Migrants in ESPON Territory According to Country of Birth

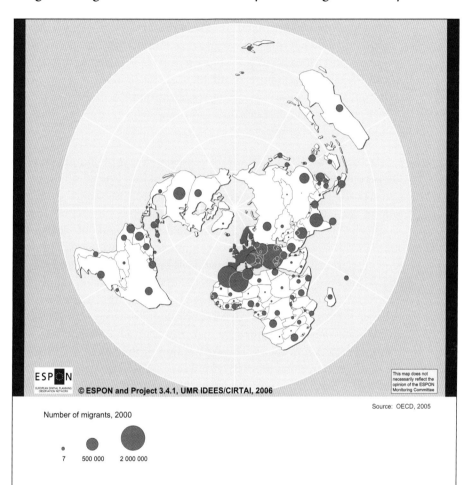

- The unwanted European activities in particular would be relocated to these "friendly" partners. An example of such "three D" activities (dirty, difficult, dangerous) is the construction of power plants and refinery facilities: For environmental reasons, they become difficult to build in Europe; they could be more easily built on the southern shore of the Mediterranean, which urgently needs industrial investment and would thus "benefit" from less attention being paid to environmental concerns there.

- Europe would benefit from secured procurement of oil, gas, and electricity (thanks to the ongoing connection of the electricity grid in the Euro-Mediterranean space). Beyond North Africa and the Middle East, Europe would benefit from secured procurement of African raw materials.

■ This north-south partnership does not amount to more than the optimization by Europe of a low-cost input strategy for raw materials, energy, and manufacturing, as well as the service sectors. Friendly partners could accommodate the growing European demand for cheap call centers, of course, but also for safe tourism, sanitary tourism (a growing number of Europeans go to Tunisia, Turkey, and Morocco to get surgery in first-rank hospitals that only rich people can afford), and attractive affordable areas for retirement. A growing number of European retirees are spending several months a year in southern Mediterranean areas and are easily making round trips to Europe, thanks to cheaper and cheaper air tickets.

In this context, the ENP would be used as a way of compensating for making the peripheral areas secure and bringing them into line with European standards (good health systems in some first-rank hospitals in the capital cities, international schools close to European dwellings, good Internet connections, protection and security). Countries in North Africa would play the role of "gatekeepers" against sub-Saharan countries, with European financial counterparts. This is roughly the kind of relationship that currently prevails in the Euro-Mediterranean partnership and is the reason for the failure of the 2005 Barcelona Summit (for the tenth anniversary of the Barcelona Euromed Agreements), which was supposed to enhance the Mediterranean partnership through the new, ambitious ENP. While all EU states were represented by their heads of government, only two Mediterranean partners sent theirs. The explanation of the failure relates to the inherent limits of the Barcelona process: asymmetry, paternalism, and overall weak attention to the developing peripheries by European leaders. Politically, the initiative and the money come from Europe. Economically, the Mediterranean partner countries are highly dependent upon western European markets and investors, though they are significant partners for neither European exports nor investments. This is reflected in the statistics for the past decade, when EU subsidies reached 300 euro per inhabitant in Greece, 27 euro in the CEE countries, and less than 2 euro in the southern Mediterranean countries.

## Territorial Impacts

Such a pattern would enhance the European economy and would quite deeply change the regional geography due to greater Euro-Mediterranean economic integration, despite being asymmetrical. The 2010 Euro-Mediterranean free trade zone would accelerate the new geography of the value chains in all sectors, with strong impacts in the Mediterranean cities of the EU. The southern peripheral parts of the EU would benefit from this change more than the eastern parts, although in some sectors such as fruits and vegetables, Euro-Mediterranean rural areas would be harmed by the relocation of production to the southern shore. In the short run, European growth would partly catch up with Asian and American growth, although not in the high-tech base that is demanded by the Lisbon Strategy.

Nevertheless, the following are true:

- The relocation of the environmental burden to the southern shore can only be a short-term solution. The ongoing telluric pollution of rivers, for instance, would increase the pollution of the Mediterranean. This would help the EU to fulfill its objective of $CO_2$ reduction according to the Kyoto Protocol, but it would, in fact, be a statistical illusion because it would simply transfer the burden to the other side of the Mediterranean without any progress on the world scale (Grasland 2001).

- The prominent policy of migration control would in the long run impede the rise of the European Mediterranean rim. No change would occur in the European migration mix: The lowest levels of education are observed in the migration toward southwestern Europe—that is, France, Italy, Spain, and Portugal—and the highest levels in the migration to northern Europe (Sweden, Norway, the U.K., Ireland) and to a lesser degree to Germany and Switzerland. In other words, the Mediterranean territories of Europe would not experience any in-depth advantage from this center-periphery deal. The most probable evolution would be the accelerated departure of highly skilled people from Africa, North Africa, and the Middle East to North America, as it has been growing during the last two decades.

- For these Mediterranean neighboring countries, the brain drain would not be stopped, because the center-periphery offers only low- and medium-skilled new jobs to the developing peripheries. Moreover, the social problems of integrating southern immigrants into EU metropolitan areas would become worse. There is no doubt that in such a scenario xenophobia and racism would develop.

- The worst consequences could be obtained if the EU was to try to use North African countries as gatekeepers against poor migrants from sub-Saharan countries, in a context of increasing pressure induced by poverty, climate change, and reduction of water resources. The thousands of people who die trying to enter the Schengen area would be nothing compared to the horror of what could happen in this scenario at the gates of the fortress Europe (Faludi 2006).

## The Archipelago View: Toward Rising Territorial Disparities

The archipelago vision is based on a contrasting body of evidence, as it starts from the assumption that the network relations are more important than purely geographical proximity.

### Selected Evidence

Typically, this vision can be illustrated by the distribution of air connections between world cities, measured in passengers weighted by kilometer (instead of raw numbers of passengers; figure 8.5). With that type of evidence, the strategic vision of the EU does not focus on the immediate neighborhood but rather on the connection with the major American and Asian centers of innovation.

The EU is part of the world metropolitan archipelago and benefits from major nodes in the global city. London, Paris, Frankfurt, and Madrid are well connected to the global network, but they also have special connections: London to North America, Paris to Africa, Frankfurt to Asia, and Madrid to Latin America (figure 8.6). These powerful gateway cities could therefore be considered as major points for the future development of a European economy fully based on research and innovation.

## Main Political Features

The axis of this view is the openness to global networks, free trade and deregulation, low European protection, and decreasing subsidies. In this view, globalization has prevailed over regionalization, the directorates-general responsible for trade and research have prevailed over the one responsible for regional policy. European policies are dedicated to R&D and trade rather than to regional policy or to the Common Agricultural Policy. The only territorial policy promoted by the European Commission would be the Trans-European Networks, but mainly as regards the major spokes of the system.

Here the Lisbon Strategy is at the top of the agenda, and the main commercial targets are the rapidly growing markets of East Asia and, in particular, China. The main European partnership remains with North America, far from any Euro-Mediterranean partnership. The ENP is strictly limited to the implementation of liberal reforms in the partner countries; the Euro-Mediterranean free trade zone becomes a purely free trade area, implying direct competition with North African economies (including agriculture), as well as with any other part of the world.

The geographical pattern is dominated by networks. This is Manuel Castells's "space of flows" rather than "space of places" (Castells 1996; see also Dillard 1967; Kenwood and Lougheed 1989; Pollard 1991). Due to the foremost importance of capital flows, the prominent territory is the global city (see Sassen 1991, 2002; Beaverstock, Smith, and Taylor 2000; Taylor 2005), also called the "megalopolitan metropolitan archipelago" by French geographers (Brunet and Dollfus 1990; Ghorra-Gobin 2006). Of course, authors like Cattan (2004) and Veltz (1996) argue that the network is more important than the nodes themselves: What really matters is not the power of each world city, but rather the degree of interconnectivity that they provide between different parts of the world. Still, the multidirectional connection to world territories is the main feature of this archipelago view.

When it comes to migration, whereas the migration of low-skilled workers follows the center-periphery pattern, that of high-skilled workers is more closely aligned with the archipelago view. In that prospect, migration policy focuses on attracting international, highly skilled people, including those from neighboring countries—which means that the brain drain would increase dramatically. On the European side, in contrast, the strategy would be to reduce the emigration of researchers and young entrepreneurs, persuading them not to leave for North America.

FIGURE 8.5

## Major Air Connections Between Cities of the World in 2000: Global Network

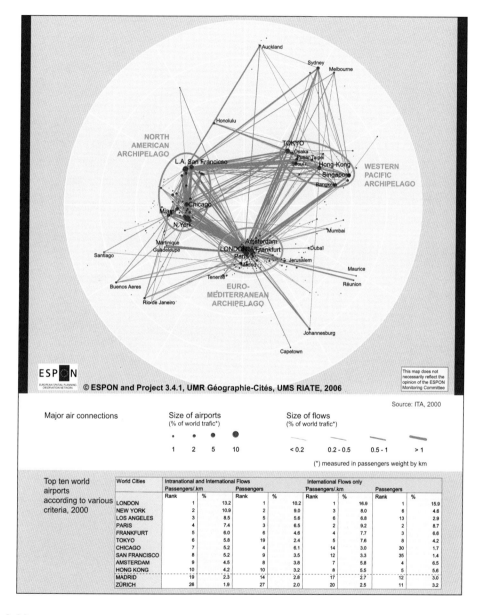

© ESPON and Project 3.4.1, UMR Géographie-Cités, UMS RIATE, 2006

This map does not necessarily reflect the opinion of the ESPON Monitoring Committee

Source: ITA, 2000

Major air connections

Size of airports (% of world trafic*): 1 2 5 10

Size of flows (% of world trafic*): < 0.2 | 0.2 - 0.5 | 0.5 - 1 | > 1

(*) measured in passengers weight by km

Top ten world airports according to various criteria, 2000

| World Cities | Intranational and International Flows | | | | International Flows only | | | |
|---|---|---|---|---|---|---|---|---|
| | Passengers/.km | | Passengers | | Passengers/.km | | Passengers | |
| | Rank | % | Rank | % | Rank | % | Rank | % |
| LONDON | 1 | 13.2 | 1 | 10.2 | 1 | 16.9 | 1 | 15.9 |
| NEW YORK | 2 | 10.9 | 2 | 9.0 | 3 | 8.0 | 6 | 4.6 |
| LOS ANGELES | 3 | 8.5 | 5 | 5.6 | 6 | 6.8 | 13 | 2.9 |
| PARIS | 4 | 7.4 | 3 | 6.5 | 2 | 9.2 | 2 | 8.7 |
| FRANKFURT | 5 | 6.0 | 6 | 4.6 | 4 | 7.7 | 3 | 6.6 |
| TOKYO | 6 | 5.8 | 19 | 2.4 | 5 | 7.6 | 8 | 4.2 |
| CHICAGO | 7 | 5.2 | 4 | 6.1 | 14 | 3.0 | 30 | 1.7 |
| SAN FRANCISCO | 8 | 5.2 | 9 | 3.5 | 12 | 3.3 | 35 | 1.4 |
| AMSTERDAM | 9 | 4.5 | 8 | 3.8 | 7 | 5.8 | 4 | 6.5 |
| HONG KONG | 10 | 4.2 | 10 | 3.2 | 8 | 5.5 | 5 | 5.6 |
| MADRID | 19 | 2.3 | 14 | 2.8 | 17 | 2.7 | 12 | 3.0 |
| ZÜRICH | 26 | 1.9 | 27 | 2.0 | 20 | 2.5 | 11 | 3.2 |

## Territorial Impacts

The archipelago view has many territorial advantages:

■ In this view, most of the major European cities become highly internationalized metropolitan areas. The top of the league is dominated by London and Paris, but many others become major gateway cities, connecting their countries to the rest of the world (e.g., developing long-distance air connections, transnational

FIGURE 8.6

## Major Air Connections Between Cities of the World in 2000: European Gateway Cities

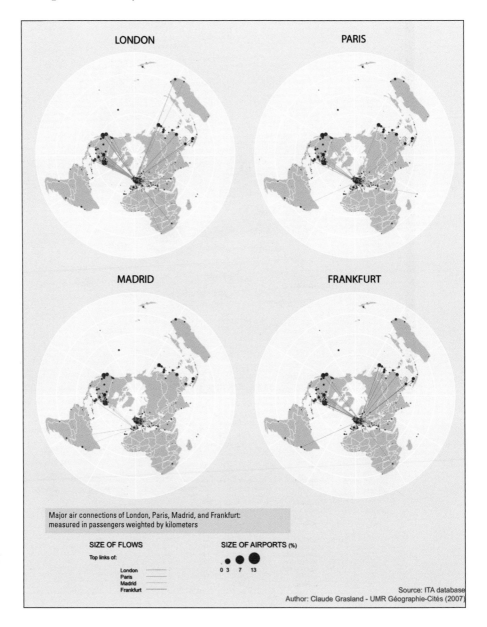

Major air connections of London, Paris, Madrid, and Frankfurt: measured in passengers weighted by kilometers

SIZE OF FLOWS          SIZE OF AIRPORTS (%)

Top links of:

London
Paris
Madrid
Frankfurt

0  3   7   13

Source: ITA database
Author: Claude Grasland - UMR Géographie-Cités (2007)

corporation networks, financial services, and international events such as fairs and congresses).

- The western countries that have many international metropolises (U.K., France, northern Spain, northern Italy, Netherlands, Belgium, western and southern Germany) experience fast economic growth.

- The western large metropolises are more and more integrated into a high-level urban network, which increases their comparative advantage and nourishes increasingly profitable transport links between them.

It also entails specific shortcomings, though:

- The main one is the increase of territorial disparities in Europe: within western Europe, in favor of the large metropolitan regions; in the eastern member states, too, because the emphasis would be put on the capital cities.

- Quite rapidly, the eastern member states would lose their competitive advantage due to the rise of salaries and costs in their capital cities. For example, the *European Cities Monitor* indicated that in 2005, 52 percent of European firms were interested in relocating into cities of the new member states of eastern Europe, but in 2006 only 43 percent were interested. During the same time, relocation increased from 22 percent to 36 percent for China, from 22 percent to 30 percent for India, and from 21 percent to 28 percent for eastern European countries outside the EU (Cushman and Wakefield 2006).

- The degradation of the social, economic, and environmental situations is especially damaging in the neighboring countries. Eastern neighbors might benefit from the rising costs in the CEEC, but the bulk of European business abroad would rather target the remote, large (American) or rapidly growing (East Asian) markets.

- The destabilization would be dramatic in the Mediterranean neighboring countries. The tough 2010 liberalization of trade would have a terrible impact on their trade. The situation in agriculture would be particularly worrisome: Highly protected products such as cereals would disappear in less than a decade, leaving millions of farmers without revenues. The pressure for rural emigration—probably reinforced by climate change—would reach a critical level. No regional policy would ever compensate for such a destabilization.

- Many sectors would be destabilized. In the logistics sector, for example, European firms would gain major positions on the southern shore of the Mediterranean. In a highly liberalized framework, this logistical integration would happen exclusively in favor of the large northern companies, provoking vast job losses on the southern shore.

- The only neighboring winner could well be Russia, since the oil and gas procurement would follow purely commercial considerations. Europe would fail at breaking up a Russia-Algeria cartel in gas, because Europe would offer no valuable alternative strategy to Algeria.

## A Strategic Vision of Europe Embedded in a World Region

As stated previously, each of the three views of Europe in the world addresses a part of the reality. This section tries to arrive at a positive synthesis and proposes a desirable and feasible vision of Europe that includes the territorial assets of the three former views without their main shortcomings. This optimistic vision —invoking a term culled from French, one might rather say *voluntaristic* vision, which implies determined policies, in particular in the territorial field—is based on the idea that Europe and its neighbors represent a single major world region. This means that the ENP is the key policy to complement the Lisbon Strategy and to enhance all European territorial policies. Such a vision is, indeed, embedded in the three dominant views of Europe in the world, but in a sort of politically enhanced position:

- This ambitious vision rejects the center-periphery paternalism and asymmetry and focuses on the north and south being reconnected in an in-depth, regulated relationship.

- It rejects the archipelago's purely liberal aspect and the credo that territorial areas no longer matter but accepts the openness of borders that would serve as hinges rather than barriers, since nodes are crucial for the connection of territories not only at the global scale; it also stresses the mobility of people, as well as of capital, goods, and services.

- It rejects the purely protective aspect of the continent vision, the geographical approach of "natural facts" (continents as geological evidence) or "permanent civilization areas," but accepts the necessity of cohesion—this time enlarged to a new, wide definition of the region—and the need for secure Russian and Arab-Islamic territories, which implies a strong win-win connection between the core and its immediate neighbors (Mediterranean countries, Ukraine, Caucasus countries) and more distant ones (sub-Saharan countries, Central Asia).

### Selected Evidence

The previous visions were based on relatively simple pieces of evidence, generally limited to one dominant criterion from both a statistical and a conceptual point of view. In developing the vision in the ESPON 3.4.1 project, we assumed that reality is more complex. When it comes to the delimitation of a so-called European area of influence in the world, we decided to combine 18 criteria related to four dimensions (accessibility, networks, flows, dissimilarity), as explained in table 8.3. We chose "ESPON29" (i.e., the 27 member states of the EU plus Switzerland and Norway) as reference for the delimitation of the "Europe" that was used in the computation of the so-called European influence area. The results would not have been very different with another initial core (EU15 or EU25).

The resulting map of the European influence area (figure 8.7 and table 8.4) shows the geographical limits of the potential "world region" where the EU could promote integration. The area clearly constitutes one-third of the world, from

Russia to southern Africa, including all Mediterranean countries but excluding some countries of the Persian Gulf and Central Asia, which are rather linked to East Asia or North America for economical and political reasons. That world region is more a potentiality than a reality, however, as many of the criteria are not based on effective flows but on accessibility, networks, and complementarities.

## North-South Regionalism

Businesses receive many incentives to locate in remote dynamic areas, but they also may find it convenient to locate "near shore." The strategic advantages of proximity are all the more important as oil prices and transportation costs rise. As a result, regional trade agreements have multiplied during the last decade, encompassing both north and south. Deblock and Regnault (2006) say that they reconnect north and south, after the large disconnection due to the end of colonialism and the cold war in the second half of the twentieth century. Such a reconnection, by the way, is the reason UNCTAD (UN Conference on Trade and Development) now pleads for regionalism (Mashayekhi and Ito 2005), seen as a positive interface vis-à-vis globalization.

Such a view is a major issue for the southern Mediterranean countries—all the more so as they happen to be in the most favorable demographic situation for economic development, with a good proportion of young adults with relatively high life expectancies and a stable fertility rate, which means neither too many children nor too many old people to look after. That moment in history, in which a country has its maximum proportion of active population, provides a unique opportunity, for both the country itself and the EU.

North-south regions provide four assets. The first one is economic. Firms, whether they are small or transnational, need a regional stable location based on partnership, because they have to deal with the uncertainty and the challenges of globalization. International trade increases faster within a region than with the rest of the world; growing numbers of people live on both sides of the border between two countries. In East Asia, the networks of Chinese traders have been reinforced since the 1990s. In the Mediterranean, migrant workers send more than eight billion euro every year from Europe to the Maghreb country they come from. Every day, two million Mexicans legally cross the border between Mexico and the United States. As Michalet (2004) says, the north-south regions seem to be the winning territories of globalization. This is mainly because they benefit from the complementarities between capital and technology, on one hand, and a large labor force and booming markets, on the other. Martine Azuelos has shown this for America (Azuelos, Cosio-Zavala, and Lacroix 2004), Christian Taillard (2004) for East Asia.

The second asset the north-south regions provide is political: The regional scale has certainly become the best chance for north-south international regulations. The need to reregulate the world economy is an important driving force in response to the excesses of the era of borderless, footloose capitalism. Of course, some rules have been implemented at the global scale, such as those on trade (by

**TABLE 8.3**

## Criteria Used for the Delimitation of EU27 Plus Switzerland and Norway Influence Area in the World

| Code | Definition | Source | Year |
|------|-----------|--------|------|
| **Weight factor** | | | |
| POPTO99 | Population, total (inh.), 1999 (SP, POP, TOTL) | WDI | 1999 |
| **Accessibility criteria** | | | |
| A_GDP | Contribution of ESPON29 to potential GDP PPS 1999 | WDI+CEPII | 1999 |
| A_POP | Contribution of ESPON29 to potential population 1999 | WDI+CEPII | 1999 |
| A_SUP | Contribution of ESPON29 to potential area | WDI+CEPII | 1999 |
| A_BO1 | Existence of a common land border with ESPON29 | CEPII | 2000 |
| A_BO2 | Existence of a common maritime border with ESPON29 | RIATE | 2005 |
| **Networks criteria** | | | |
| N_LA1 | Share with ESPON29 at least one common official or national language or language spoken by at least 20% of the population of the country | CEPII | 2000 |
| N_LA2 | Share with ESPON29 at least one language (mother tongue, lingua franca, or second language) | CEPII | 2000 |
| N_CO1 | Colonizers or colonized by at least one ESPON29 country for a relatively long period of time and with a substantial participation in the governance of the colonized country | CEPII | 2000 |
| N_CO2 | Idem, but with colonial relations still active in 1945 | CEPII | 2000 |
| **Flows criteria** | | | |
| F_EXP | Ratio between observed and expected exports from ESPON29 (under the assumption of random allocation of trade flows according to capacity of imports and exports of world states) | PC-TAS | 1996–2000 |
| F_IMP | Ratio between observed and expected imports to ESPON29 (under the assumption of random allocation of trade flows according to capacity of imports and exports of world states) | PC-TAS | 1996–2000 |
| F_AIR | Ratio between observed and expected air flows with ESPON29 (under the assumption of random allocation of air flows according to total sum of air relations of each state) | OACI | 2000 |
| F_TRA | Intensity of trade flows with ESPON29 measured by the ratio between bilateral trade flows 1996–2000 and GDP PPS 1999 (normalized to 1) | PC-TAS+WDI | 1996–2000 |
| F_AIR2 | Intensity of air flows with ESPON29 measured by the ratio between bilateral air flows 2000 and population 1999 (normalized to 1) | ITA+WDI | 2000 |
| **Dissimilarity criteria** | | | |
| S_LIF | Ratio between HDI life component of ESPON29 and HDI life component of the state | HDR | 2002 |
| S_EDU | Ratio between HDI education component of ESPON29 and HDI education component of the state | HDR | 2002 |
| S_GDP | Ratio between HDI economic component of ESPON29 and HDI economic component of the state | HDR | 2002 |
| S_AGE | Ratio between median age of population of ESPON29 and median age of population of the state | UNPP | 2002 |

**Source:** Grasland and Didelon 2007.

**FIGURE 8.7**

Global Influence of EU Plus Switzerland and Norway

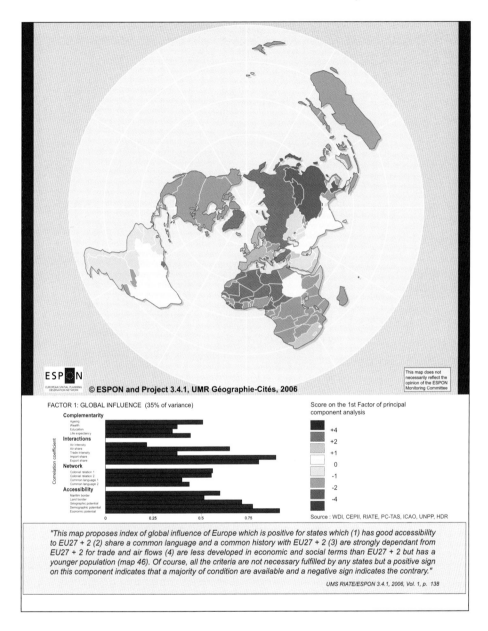

FACTOR 1: GLOBAL INFLUENCE (35% of variance)

Score on the 1st Factor of principal component analysis

+4
+2
+1
0
-1
-2
-4

Source : WDI, CEPII, RIATE, PC-TAS, ICAO, UNPP, HDR

© ESPON and Project 3.4.1, UMR Géographie-Cités, 2006

This map does not necessarily reflect the opinion of the ESPON Monitoring Committee

*"This map proposes index of global influence of Europe which is positive for states which (1) has good accessibility to EU27 + 2 (2) share a common language and a common history with EU27 + 2 (3) are strongly dependant from EU27 + 2 for trade and air flows (4) are less developed in economic and social terms than EU27 + 2 but has a younger population (map 46). Of course, all the criteria are not necessary fulfilled by any states but a positive sign on this component indicates that a majority of condition are available and a negative sign indicates the contrary."*

UMS RIATE/ESPON 3.4.1, 2006, Vol. 1, p. 138

TABLE 8.4

## Maximum and Minimum Values of ESPON29 Influence

| Maximum Influence of ESPON29 | | | Minimum Influence of ESPON29 | | |
|---|---|---|---|---|---|
| Rank | Score | State | Rank | Score | State |
| 1 | 9.36 | Croatia | 1 | −3.19 | Japan |
| 2 | 9.12 | Iceland | 2 | −3.14 | Taiwan |
| 3 | 8.90 | Tunisia | 3 | −3.01 | North Korea |
| 4 | 7.93 | Serbia/Montenegro | 4 | −2.85 | Korea, Rep. of |
| 5 | 7.92 | Albania | 5 | −2.46 | China |
| 6 | 7.46 | Macedonia, TFYR | 6 | −2.31 | Thailand |
| 7 | 7.19 | Morocco | 7 | −2.08 | Bhutan |
| 8 | 7.15 | Turkey | 8 | −2.02 | Mongolia |
| 9 | 7.12 | Algeria | 9 | −1.59 | Myanmar |
| 10 | 7.12 | Greenland | 10 | −1.56 | El Salvador |
| 11 | 7.09 | Libyan Arab Jamahiriya | 11 | −1.51 | Uruguay |
| 12 | 6.38 | Liberia | 12 | −1.51 | Mexico |
| 13 | 6.00 | Bosnia and Herzegovina | 13 | −1.46 | Australia |
| 14 | 5.62 | Sierra Leone | 14 | −1.46 | Philippines |
| 15 | 5.06 | Russian Federation | 15 | −1.44 | Indonesia |

**Source:** Grasland and Didelon 2007.

the WTO). However, the failure of the WTO's Cancún meeting concerning the Doha Round (to make development and free trade compatible) and the Millennium Goals, the failure of the Kyoto Agenda, and the lack of common global legislation on labor or public health show how difficult it is to regulate the wide world. For example, Grasland (2001) argues that the reduction of $CO_2$ is impossible with an international approach (where each state defends its own interest) and suggests the organization of three regional agencies combining developed and developing countries. The regional scale can be seen as more relevant for the introduction of new public policies, due to the complementarities between the national economies concerned; common environmental stakes (pollution of rivers, seas, and air); shared cultural values, or at least an understanding of each other's cultural values; historical links; migratory flows; and any other assets important in creating win-win codevelopment. That is why regional trade agreements have multiplied worldwide in the last 15 years and why existing agreements have been reinvigorated with new environmental and social concerns. As demonstrated by the French economist J. M. Siroën, the debate over the economic benefits of multilateralism and regionalization at the world scale is a false one, because both forms of global integration are, in fact, complementary. What is really important is not the liberalization of trade (which is not an objective in itself) but rather "the question of defining the scale where public goods and services can be produced the most efficiently according to the cost and the preferences of societies for certain specific characteristics which are often associated with geographical territories" (Siroën 2000). The European reader will easily recognize the principle of *subsidiarity*, which is the basis for the political organization of the EU.

The third asset is cultural: It is more relevant to define collective preferences on the regional scale than on a global one. The fourth asset is geopolitical: Regionalization is the best and maybe the only way to impose multilateralism on the United States, because it would have to deal with strong European and Asian regions, which promote a more regulated liberalism than that of NAFTA—even if that North American liberalism is not as "pure" as Europeans often think.

This is why the notion of "region" is a key territorial, economical, and analytical issue. It is of utmost importance to distinguish between the two geographical notions of "Europe." The first notion is the institutional one. Europe means the EU. Its borders are established, not necessarily forever (the western Balkans will enter one day and perhaps Turkey), but at any one time they are precisely defined. The second notion is what we may call the functional Europe. This means the Euro-Mediterranean (Euro-Africa in a wider sense), which is the socioeconomic region in which Europe is embedded. Its geography is unclear; its borders vary according to the index one uses (very large when it comes to trade, less so when it comes to pollution of the sea). But in any case its dimensions are broader than those of the institutional definition of the EU. The geographical difference between the two definitions is the "neighborhood."

Compared to the eastern neighbors, the potential demographic and economic dynamism of the North African and Middle Eastern countries is a major opportunity for Europe, the harvesting of which probably provides the only possible way of maintaining Europe's position as a global actor. But if the ENP were to be the continuation of the asymmetric Barcelona process, if the major part of the financial instrument of the ENP were to go to the eastern neighbors, if European firms keep on targeting eastern Europe and remote developing countries rather than the enormous potential of the Mediterranean markets, and if the Arab countries refrain from speeding up their very necessary reforms, the two shores of the Mediterranean will miss the opportunity of a north-south reconnection.

Almost all the Mediterranean neighbors face high rates of structural unemployment due to their economic structure; their lack of economic reform; the need to modernize their agricultural systems, which will have severe effects on employment; and the persistence of numerous internal and external conflicts. In addition, they face growing competition from other developing countries (e.g., the entrance of China into the WTO, and the dismantling of import quotas in the textile industry). They absolutely need a strong partnership with Europe to tackle the reforms that this situation implies. Plus, various models have the impacts of climate change converging in the Mediterranean: rain precipitation will diminish from −20 percent to –40 percent within 50 years. The southern shore of the Mediterranean will not cope with the dramatic need for water management and soil protection without a very strong European commitment.

This takes us to a political issue, that of the philosophy of regional integration. The European states have a crucial choice to make between (1) remaining a continental integrated area based on homogeneity—that is, gathering comparable countries, with cohesion as the main goal, through a process promoted mainly by states via public policies, what could be called "convergence regionalism"—and (2) building a more ambitious regional entity with the southern and eastern Mediterranean countries, a north-south regionalism that gathers unequal countries, with economic growth as the main goal, through a process promoted by business, as in NAFTA and ASEAN+3. Needless to say, this second pattern of regionalization promises much better economic results than the first one.

## Political Stakes

Security issues and the fear of terrorism have come to preoccupy the Barcelona process, which was initially based on a much wider vision of joint economic, social, ecological, and cultural development on both sides of the Mediterranean. In the short term, and any moral consideration apart, a "bunker-continent" or "center-periphery" strategy could appear realistic for an economically declining and demographically aging Europe. In reality, the construction of an island of prosperity surrounded by oceans of poverty would have tragic consequences:

- Migration has never been stopped by borders when wealth differentials are greater than 1 to 5. In such a scenario, the EU would be obliged to invest more and more in the military control of its southern border. In a context of limited economic growth, that policy option would necessarily imply limiting EU budget allocations to other objectives like social cohesion, sustainable development, and R&D.

- The developing states of the southern shore of the Mediterranean will never agree to simply being gatekeepers for the EU against the poorest societies of sub-Saharan Africa. They could therefore develop partnerships with other parts of the world, like the United States (see its "Broader Middle East" vision) or China, instead of being allied to Europe, and would become competitors in Europe's immediate neighborhood.

- The integration of immigrants from the southern shore of the Mediterranean would be profoundly affected by the limitation on travel and family reunification, multiplying the problems in Europe's inner cities and suburban "ghettos." Conversely, tourism flows and the retirement of European people to southern countries would be affected by the degradation of political relations, producing increasing economic and ecological pressure on the coastal areas of the northern shore of the Mediterranean.

■ The psychological climate of the EU would be affected by the fear and guilt produced by Europe's isolation from the poorest people of Africa. The universal dimension of the European project would be seen as hypocritical. Moreover, the degradation of the international image of Europe could have significant negative political consequences.

## Territorial Stakes and Impacts

A north-south regulated regional vision has an important territorial aspect to it (see Beckouche and Richard 2005):

■ The large European region, that is Europe plus its neighbors, would become a reference in the regulation of agricultural and energy markets. For the latter that means that the—slow and difficult—regulation of the European gas and electricity market should right away *encompass* the southern neighbors, the facilities of which are compatible with those of western Europe (contrary to the facilities of eastern new member states), and some of whom are strategic energy resources providers. For the former (agriculture) that means that Europe and its neighbors should negotiate a regional set of regulations with the WTO—for example, through a regional label for Mediterranean products, maybe even through a regional tariff to protect and promote the modernization of agriculture on the southern shore during a period of transition.

■ The ENP should manage this transition time in order to prepare the liberalization of the free trade zone of 2010 (in fact, probably 2013, because the agreements between the EU and the neighbors entail transition periods). In 2013, the southern Mediterranean countries will have either given up free trade agreements with Europe, so that the Mediterranean will become an actual barrier for a long time to come—meaning that the continent view will have won—or accepted the rough free trade that the ongoing negotiations are promoting, and the archipelago view will have won. In either case, this kind of partnership will be unlikely to avoid the destabilization of the south and therefore of the whole region. Alternatively, a genuine regional regulation will have been implemented in order both to allow an effective transition period for the southern shore and to deepen the partnerships between north and south.

■ A policy of networking the common Euro-Mediterranean regional territory would be implemented: gas and electricity, but also transports and logistics, telecom, a Euromed postal network, a Euromed financial space (already under way, thanks to the European Investment Bank), and a common structure of diplomas in order to promote the mobility of skilled people.

■ Common policies would regulate regional public goods. In particular, several environmental issues have a regional dimension. Those include the pollution of common seas (Black and Mediterranean seas, the pollution of which was one of the main issues of the November 2005 Barcelona Summit); air pollution;

nuclear risks relating to the maintenance of the antiquated power plants in the east; the expectation of new nuclear power plants (Russia is building on the Black Sea coast); and the potential of new plants in the Mediterranean (in Turkey, Egypt, and Algeria after 2010).

- Balanced relocation of the value chain between north and south would enhance the competitive advantage of complementary and neighboring territories, especially if the price of oil remains high and limits the comparative advantage of long-distance trade.

- Mobility of the elites, other workers, and students would be promoted, so that the fourth freedom of the ENP, of the circulation of people, could ultimately be fulfilled, rather than the brain drain continuing. For what the people on the southern shore want is *not* to emigrate to Europe—what they want is to have easy opportunities to go there and come back home as often as necessary.

This broad regional vision would undoubtedly have very positive impacts on demography and the economy overall, as well as specific territorial impacts:

- The main one would, of course, be the dynamism of the peripheral parts of the EU territory eastward (and not only in capital cities) and mostly southward.

- The networking of the Euromed space would give a gateway function to many ports and cities on both shores of the Mediterranean rim. Many partnerships, such as decentralized cooperation between actors of the north and south, would be facilitated, enhancing mobility, the way of life and work astride the two shores.

- The regional integration of the western Balkans and Turkey would be facilitated.

- The role of North Africa as an interface between Europe and sub-Saharan Africa would be fostered. The Maghreb would no longer be a series of buffer states, but a genuine interface.

## Conclusion: Coordinating the Directorates-General

Expanding European policies southward links economic and territorial issues for many reasons:

- Efficient local territories are a genuine factor of production nowadays. Therefore, territorial action is necessary to enhance the economic development of the Euromed countries. By enhancing the local dimension of ENP projects with a strong commitment from local public and private actors, the EU could more easily monitor implementation of projects and make regular evaluations, using a similar method to that used in the context of European regional policy.

- Many social issues in the south cannot be dealt with without taking the local territories into account, be it in rural areas or in informal urban suburbs.

- Promotion of local actors is a key way of democratizing the south. The promotion of local projects is one way of encouraging decentralization in neighboring countries that happen to be poorly developed. Although expectations of immediate changes to the political organization of those countries' local structures are unrealistic, the initiation of such a process could ultimately improve their development and the efficiency of cross-border cooperation programs. Decentralized cooperation and cooperation between NGOs from the two shores of the Mediterranean are currently the best means of building an in-depth north-south regionalism.

■ Last but not least, there is the need for coordinating these various territorial actions, be it at the local or the Mediterranean regional level.

That is why the directorate-general responsible for regional policy should have a prominent role: Its methods for local development have proved efficient; its connection to local actors and especially to European regional councils would facilitate their involvement in the Euromed region; its knowledge of drawing up overall regional strategies is useful because the region needs a comprehensive vision of the Euro-Mediterranean territory—which certainly neither the bilateral action plans nor the ENP's four freedoms provide. The directorate-general should point the way to a "Euro-*Mediterranean* Spatial Development Perspective" like the one it helped bring about a decade ago for European space. The EU has already spent a lot of money to launch studies on depollution in the Mediterranean, Mediterranean migratory movements, Mediterranean agriculture, Mediterranean macroeconomics, and so forth. What is needed now is a comprehensive regional view.

Our geographical analysis shows (1) how important the ENP is for fulfilling the goals of the Lisbon Strategy (we do not believe that the continent view of Europe could be a relevant one); (2) how necessary it is to enhance territorial projects within the ENP to avoid a rough confrontation between the two shores of the Mediterranean (the center-periphery view); (3) how obvious it is that regional territories matter, that a purely hub-and-spokes pattern cannot meet the needs of sustainable development (the archipelago view); and (4) that globalization does not mean the abolition of borders but rather the reemergence of borders to the higher scale of a world region ("The spaceless, borderless world is still a Platonic ideal, a long way from coming into existence," says Krugman [2004]). Therefore, it also shows the relevance of a strong coordination of Euro-Mediterranean territorial policies. Indeed, in the interest of a large European region policy, coordinating the actions and budgets of the directorate-general in charge of the ENP with those of the directorate-general responsible for regional policy should be promoted from the very beginning.

### References

Azuelos, M., M-E. Cosio-Zavala, and J-M. Lacroix, eds. 2004. *Intégration dans les Amériques, dix ans d'Alena.* Paris: Presses Sorbonne Nouvelle.

Beaverstock, J. V., R. H. Smith, and P. J. Taylor. 2000. World city network: A new metageography? *Annals of the Association of American Geographers* 90(1).

Beckouche, P., and Y. Richard. 2005. *Atlas d'une nouvelle Europe. Elargissement, Turquie, voisinages: Le débat.* Paris: Editions Autrement.

Brunet, R., and O. Dollfus. 1990. *Mondes nouveaux.* Vol. 1 of *Géographie universelle.* Paris: Hachette.

Castells, M. 1996. *The rise of the network society.* Vol. 1 of *The information age: Economy, society and culture.* Cambridge, MA; Oxford, U.K.: Blackwell.

Cattan, N. 2004. Le monde au prisme des réseaux aériens [The world through the prism of air transport]. *Territoire et Communications, FLUX,* no. 58: 32–43.

Cushman and Wakefield. 2006. *European Cities Monitor.* Paris: Cushman and Wakefield. Available for downloading from http://www.cushmanwakefield.com.

Deblock, C., and H. Regnault, eds. 2006. *Nord-sud: La reconnexion périphérique.* Montréal: Editions Athéna.

Dillard, D. 1967. *Economic development of the North Atlantic community.* New York: Prentice-Hall.

European Commission. 2005. *RTE-T, axes et projets prioritaires 2005* [TEN-T priority axes and projects 2005]. http://ec.europa.eu/ten/transport/projects/doc/2005_ten_t_fr.pdf.

Faludi, A. 2006. Planning without passport: A project of and for the elites? In *Lineae Terrarum: International Borders Conference,* T. Payan, T. Kruszewski, M. Socorro Tabuenca, F. Llera Pacheco, and N. Harvey, eds., 1–16. El Paso: University of Texas. http://www.research.utep.edu/Default.aspx?tabid=38294.

Ghorra-Gobin, C., ed. 2006. *Dictionnaire des mondialisations.* Paris: Armand Colin.

Grasland, C. 2001. Essai de représentation cartographique des émissions de $CO_2$ dans le monde vers 1985: Problèmes cartographiques et enjeux politiques. *Annales des Mines/Réalités Industrielles* 2:79–87.

Grasland, C., and C. Didelon. 2007. *Europe in the world: Final report.* ESPON 3.4.1, European Commission. http://www.espon.eu/mmp/online/website/content/projects/260/720/index_EN.html.

Hatem, F. 2007. Les grandes tendances des investissements internationaux en Europe: Une analyse à partir des bases de données AFII pour la période 2002–2006. *Les notes bleues de Berçy,* no. 324.

Huntington, S. 1996. *The clash of civilizations and the remaking of world order.* New York: Simon & Schuster.

Kenwood, A. G., and A. L. Lougheed. 1989. *The growth of the international economy, 1820–1980.* London: Unwin & Hyman.

Krugman, P. 2004. The new economic geography: Where are we? Discussion paper presented at the International Symposium on Globalization and Regional Integration from the Viewpoint of Spatial Economics, IDE-JETRO, 26 November 2004.

Mashayekhi, M., and T. Ito, eds. 2005. *Multilateralism and regionalism: The new interface.* Geneva: UNCTAD.

Michalet, C-A. 2004. *Qu'est-ce que la mondialisation?* Paris: La Découverte Poche/Essais.

Pollard, S. 1991. *Peaceful conquest: The industrialization of Europe, 1760–1970.* Hong Kong: Oxford University Press.

Prodi, R. 2002. A wider Europe: A proximity policy as the key to stability. *Peace, security and stability: International dialogue and the role of the EU. Sixth ECSA–World Conference.* Jean Monnet Project, Brussels, 5–6 December 2002. http://ec.europa.eu/external_relations/news/prodi/sp02_619.htm.

Sassen, S. 1991. *The global city: New York, London, Tokyo.* Princeton, NJ: Princeton University Press.

———. 2002. *Global networks, linked cities.* New York: Routledge.

Siroën, J. M. 2000. *La régionalisation de l'économie mondiale.* Paris: La découverte, Repères, no. 288.

Taillard, C., ed. 2004. *Intégrations régionales en Asie orientale.* Paris: Groupe NORAO, Les Indes Savantes.

Taylor, P. J. 2005. New political geographies: Global civil society and global governance through world city networks. *Political Geography* 24:703–730.

Territorial Agenda. 2007. *Territorial Agenda of the European Union: Towards a more competitive and sustainable Europe of diverse regions* (Agreed on the occasion of the Informal Ministerial Meeting on Urban Development and Territorial Cohesion in Leipzig on 24/25 May 2007). http://www.bmvbs.de/Anlage/original_1005295/Territorial-Agenda-of-the-European-Union -Agreed-on-25-May-2007-accessible.pdf.

Veltz, P. 1996. *Mondialisation, villes et territoires: L'économie d'archipel.* Paris: PUF.

# CHAPTER 9

# The Europeanization of Planning

## Kai Böhme and Bas Waterhout

*patial planning* became a new catchphrase in the European planning and policy discourse about 10 to 15 years ago. Somehow the emergence of the term articulated an increasing Europeanization of planning, in the form of the *Territorial Agenda* and in European influence on planning at national, regional, and local levels.

In many cases, spatial planning—although there is no generally agreed upon definition—challenged the understanding of planning as focusing merely on land use planning and on blueprints. Indeed, spatial planning connotes strategy building and is closely intertwined with regional and environmental policies, among others. As such it might be perceived as spatial development policy or territorial governance.

Although planning and, in particular, spatial planning or territorial governance remain vaguely defined, when engaging in comparative European research, one needs to be aware that the term *European spatial planning* covers at least two different concepts, notably planning *for* Europe and planning *in* Europe (Böhme 2002).

Ever since the first official draft of the *European Spatial Development Perspective* (ESDP) was presented in 1997 (CEC 1997b) and the final version in 1999 (CEC 1999), European spatial planning has been mainly connected to the idea of *planning for Europe*—that is, creating strategies and policies for the development of the European territory. This has been followed up by the analytical work of ESPON (European Spatial Planning Observation Network); the policy-oriented work on the *Territorial Agenda*; the document *The Territorial State and Perspectives of the European Union*, resulting from intergovernmental cooperation; and the cohesion reports issued by the European Commission (see Territorial Agenda 2007; Territorial State 2007; CEC 2007).

Spatial planning at the European level requires intergovernmental cooperation between the EU member states, as the EU has no explicit mandate for spatial planning; whereas there is an EU mandate for regional policy and, if the EU Reform (or Lisbon) Treaty is ratified, for territorial cohesion.

European spatial planning also describes the variety and diversity of national spatial planning concepts and systems within Europe—that is, *planning in Europe.* This is of particular interest, as planning for Europe is shaped by existing planning traditions in Europe and relies on the activities of various member states and their regions.

Thus, planning for Europe is conditioned by and at the same time changes the context (or system environment) of planning in Europe. In addition, a wide range of other EU policies, often referred to as *sector policies*, influence planning in Europe. These policies potentially can also contribute to the Europeanization of planning; some authors even suggest that some sector policies might lead to a harmonization of planning in Europe, rather than any form of planning for Europe (cf. Williams 1996; Böhme 2006a). Therefore, the influences of sector policies deserve particular attention when discussing the Europeanization of planning.

Europeanization of planning thus implies (1) the emergence of planning for Europe; (2) the influence of planning for Europe on planning in Europe and on EU policies; and (3) the influence of EU policies and European integration on planning in Europe.

## The Concept of Europeanization

The literature on Europeanization in general allows for a better understanding of the processes involved in the Europeanization of planning. Europeanization as such is the topic of a growing body of literature and has been described as having all the hallmarks of becoming an emergent field of inquiry (Radaelli 2004). Judging by the vast number of publications with "Europeanization" in their titles, Olsen (2002) concludes that it has become a fashionable term and that research into processes of Europeanization forms a growth industry. Yet there is no single meaning of *Europeanization*, as the term is applied in a number of ways to describe a variety of phenomena and processes of change.

Nevertheless, within that variety some common elements can be distinguished. For example, Europeanization is always related to the EU. Also, it is seen as a process rather than a state of affairs (Lenschow 2006). Moreover, it is important to realize that, following Gualini (2003, in Radaelli 2004), Europeanization is not the *explanans* (i.e., the solution or the phenomenon that explains the dependent variables), but the *explanandum* (i.e., the problem that needs to be explained).

Having said that, Olsen (2002) distinguishes between no fewer than five uses of the concept:

1. Changes in external boundaries of the EU

2. Developing institutions at the European level

3. Central penetration of national systems of governance

4. Exporting forms of political organization beyond the European territory

5. A political unification project

Of these, the second and third are of interest to us as they relate to planning for Europe and planning in Europe, respectively.

*Europeanization* in terms of developing institutions at the European level refers to both the strengthening of organizational capacity for collective action and the development of common ideas, in this case in the field of planning *for* Europe. This use of the word was common among students of international relations until the mid-1990s. As Olsen (2002) notes, several theoretical frameworks have been developed to study this phenomenon, which can be interpreted as institution building. In the field of planning it has become pretty common to view the development of the ESDP and its application to the process of constructing a spatial planning discourse as providing leverage for institutional change (Böhme 2002; Jensen and Richardson 2004; Waterhout 2008). In the following section we will briefly discuss the development of this discourse and how it is becoming institutionalized at the EU level as planning for Europe. Below and in the section discussing examples of Europeanization, we will come back to the use of discourse as a means of Europeanizing planning in Europe.

## Ways Leading to the Europeanization of Planning in Europe

In the mid-1990s the debate on Europeanization started to pay increasing attention to the third interpretation of the concept of Europeanization identified by Olsen: the influence of the EU on domestic policies. Today that is the most common use of the concept (Olsen 2002).

The influence of the EU on domestic policies can be exerted through several types of processes. Lenschow (2006) distinguishes between at least three types: top-down (EU → national state), horizontal (state → state), and roundabout (national state → EU → national state). As will become clear, each of these processes, or a combination of them, also affects planning in Europe.

Interpreting Europeanization as a *top-down* process means that the EU is often perceived as the direct or indirect instigator of developments at the national level. That understanding is especially common in literature that describes the impact of EU policies on national policy goals, choices, and instruments. The "top" is considered an independent variable and typically clearly identifiable—for example, a particular EU directive or regulation. Because planners have no influence on the development of EU policies, in the case of planning the EU can indeed be considered an independent variable.

Although this top-down view of Europeanization is often perceived as the EU imposing legislation on the member states, it needs to be emphasized that each member state is responsible for the way it transposes such legislation into domestic legislation. That is why Europeanization will have different effects in different member states.

*Horizontal,* state-to-state (or region-to-region) transfer may take place independently from the EU, but can also be facilitated by the EU providing the arena for interstate or interregional cooperation or competition. In the field of planning what comes to mind is INTERREG, which facilitates cooperation between regions, as a stimulator of this type of Europeanization. As will be elaborated upon below, INTERREG seems especially relevant, as it may lead to forms of organizational learning. However, one can also think of the more abstract notion of European integration being the driving force (Scharpf 2003 in Lenschow 2006). The growing awareness of domestic actors that they form part of something larger than a member state gives them pause to reflect on their position within that wider context. In relation to planning, Williams (1996) has referred to this process as spatial positioning, something we will discuss further below.

As Lenschow indicates, horizontal Europeanization can also be the result of the committee governance model of the EU bringing member state officials together and facilitating the exchange of ideas, which in turn may diffuse into national practices. In the case of planning, one can think of the committees that have either developed or managed the ESDP, the ESPON program, the INTERREG programs, and the *Territorial Agenda* documents. Here officials of the Commission, the member states, and regions from all over Europe meet and exchange ideas and best practices. Together they form a system of network governance in the field of spatial planning, which, as will become clear below, facilitates a process of discursive integration (Böhme 2002). The Commission supports and facilitates such networks through sponsoring and by developing new mechanisms intended to stimulate such horizontal transfers and learning, such as the Open Method of Coordination (Faludi 2004).

The third, roundabout conception proposes to look at processes of Europeanization from a *cyclical*, more dynamic point of view. "Europeanization is considered a discursive context, creating a frame of reference for domestic actors who not merely react to European impulses but anticipate such impulses by either including bottom-up processes changing the European level or by 'using' or 'endogenising' Europe in domestic politics independent of specific pressures from Brussels" (Lenschow 2006, 59). Committee governance, as discussed above, often also plays a role in cyclical processes, relating them closely to what elsewhere has been described as discursive integration of planning (Böhme 2002).

In fact, the cycle "member states–ESDP–ESDP application–EU *Territorial Agenda*" reminds us of such a roundabout process, which in reality, of course, is very complex. Several processes, including ESPON, the development of the *Territorial Agenda*, and INTERREG, as well as domestic planning processes, are becoming mixed together and form the carriers and drivers of a European spatial planning discourse. The concept of discursive integration explains this process by relating network governance (Kohler-Koch 1999) and the emergence of planning communities to the development of discourse (Hajer 1995).

## Catalysts and Outcomes of Europeanization

Radaelli (2004) distinguishes two instances where researchers could search for evidence of Europeanization taking place:

- Where the EU becomes a cognitive and normative frame and provides orientations to the logics of meaning and action
- Where there is a process of change taking place either in response to EU pressure or as a result of using the EU

So conceived, Europeanization ultimately leads to the institutionalization of a

European dimension in domestic policies. This similarity between Europeanization and institutionalization is important in order to understand how processes of
Europeanization are being instigated. Generally, as regards catalysts the authors
writing about institutionalization distinguish between rules, resources, and ideas
(Healey 2006). With regard to planning, too, such catalysts can be found. In short,
they are the following:

- EU regulations
- EU spending policies and INTERREG
- European spatial planning discourse

In the area of rules, obviously EU regulations and directives play the most
important role. As indicated, they are related to Europeanization as a top-down
process. Resources form a second category of catalysts, and among them we can
rank EU regional policy that stimulates economic development in lagging regions;
the Common Agricultural Policy (through income guarantees); and TEN policies
(aiming at creating Trans-European Transport Networks), in particular where
incentives for high-speed rail lines and motorways are concerned. The INTERREG
program, too, belongs to this category.

INTERREG, however, also belongs to the category of catalysts that forms part
of the European spatial planning discourse. Other carriers of this discourse are the
ESDP and the ESPON program. Also, this discourse is likely to be influenced by
the *Territorial Agenda* and *Territorial State and Perspectives of the European Union*,
as discussed in the introduction and in chapter 10.

Up to now the effects and influences of the EU on planning in Europe have
been rather diverse. Current evidence on the Europeanization of planning by,
among others, Janin Rivolin and Faludi (2005) and Giannakourou (2005) concerning southern Europe; by Böhme (2002) concerning the Nordic countries; by
Tewdwr-Jones and Williams (2001), Sykes (2004, 2007), and Dabinett and Richardson (2005) concerning the U.K.; and, in the case of Sykes, also France; as well as by
the ESPON project 2.3.1 on the application of the ESDP in the EU29 (including
Norway and Switzerland) (Nordregio/ESPON 2.3.1 2007), shows that, if anything,
planning in Europe does not converge or harmonize, but rather translates into
various processes and formats. Before discussing that, however, the next section
addresses the creation of the European planning discourse.

## Creating Instruments for Planning for Europe

Taking the emergence of planning for Europe—for example, strategies and policies for the spatial or territorial development of Europe—as an indication of the
Europeanization of planning, one first has to distinguish between initiatives of the
European Commission and intergovernmental initiatives taken by the member
states.

## Intergovernmental Initiatives for Planning for Europe

The ESDP certainly kick-started a lot of spatial planning thinking at the European level. That document, which Rusca (1998) describes as a "strange animal," managed to put territorial and spatial thinking on the European agenda. More about the genesis of the ESDP and the way it prepared the ground for planning for Europe can be found in the many publications by Faludi and others devoted to that specific topic.

In the discussion of the Europeanization of spatial planning, the ESDP may be merely the first and so far main point of reference, and all that followed in its wake can be considered an indication of the increasing Europeanization of planning for Europe.

Böhme and Schön (2006) describe how work on the ESDP successively led to the establishment of the European Spatial Planning Observation Network (ESPON), an analytical program providing comparative territorial evidence at the European level to support policy (see also chapter 1). Accordingly, the use of ESPON material in policy making at European, national, regional, and local levels might be seen as a further step in the Europeanization of planning. Indeed, as will become evident, the provision of new European information can be considered an important step in the Europeanization of planning.

The story continues via the elaboration of an evidence-based document, *The Territorial State and Perspectives of the European Union*, mainly based on ESPON contributions. This resulted in the policy document called the *Territorial Agenda of the European Union* (cf. chapter 10 and the introduction). The *Territorial Agenda*, adopted by the EU ministers responsible for spatial planning and development in May 2007, forms the latest achievement with regard to the Europeanization of planning at the intergovernmental European level.

This document still has to prove itself, but its mere existence suggests that the momentum of European spatial planning has so far been sustained since the start of the ESDP work in 1989. In policy terms those 18 years have meant important steps in the creation of an intergovernmental spatial policy agenda, serving as a frame of reference for other policies, including existing EU policies and planning and sector policies in Europe.

Another intergovernmental contribution to the Europeanization of planning is CEMAT (Conférence Européenne des Ministres Responsables de l'Aménagement du Territoire), which is part of the Council of Europe. CEMAT started its activities in 1970, when it first met in Bonn, and since then has brought together representatives of the now 46 members of the Council of Europe to pursue the common objective of sustainable spatial development of the European continent. CEMAT is relevant as a means of Europeanization because of the general assumption that the Council of Europe paves the way for future EU enlargement.

In the field of spatial planning the way was paved with the development of the policy document *Guiding Principles for Sustainable Spatial Development of the European Continent* (CEMAT 2000). These guiding principles were developed in the wake of the ESDP and are essentially a more concise and coherent version of that document. They have been positively received and have aroused interest in territorial issues in CEMAT countries, in particular those outside the EU15, which considered the principles more "European" than the ESDP. Now that the 2004 and 2007 enlargements of the EU have taken place, the focus of CEMAT moves eastward to third and accession countries.

## Community Initiatives for Planning for Europe

Whereas the intergovernmental setting of the European policy agenda appears natural in a field where the European Community does not have an explicit mandate, the contribution of the European Commission to the Europeanization of planning is hidden.

In addition to the unintentional influences on planning in Europe via the various sector policies, EU regional policy has taken deliberate steps toward the Europeanization of planning for Europe.

First there are the European Commission's cohesion reports coming out every three years, prepared by the Directorate-General for Regional Policy. They set the agenda for regional development and socioeconomic cohesion policy. As such, they do not influence planning directly. However, their tone and approach to related issues are such that they influence the context of planning by way of their influence on European and national regional policies.

In the evolution of the cohesion reports spatial issues and territorial cohesion are increasingly acknowledged. In the 2001 report there have been references to territorial issues; in the 2004 report territorial cohesion has been approached; and the 2007 report increasingly frames regional disparities in territorial terms (although perhaps less than was expected by close followers).

Second, the European Structural Funds, the main instrument of European regional policy, are used to promote territorial thinking in Europe and thus, indirectly, spatial planning. Looking at the three Structural Funds periods, 1994–1999, 2000–2006, and 2007–2013, we can discern a clear shift toward addressing more territorial cohesion issues. Bachtler and Polverari (2007) illustrate the emergence of a more spatial and urban focus in Structural Funds regulations, which can also be seen by looking more deeply into the individual programs and the activities funded by them. So the Structural Funds are another example of EU policies, the lack of a mandate notwithstanding, contributing to the promotion of spatial or territorial thinking at the European level, and thus indirectly contributing to the Europeanization of planning.

Third, as was found in the ESPON 2.3.1/ESDP study, a more autonomous trend seems to emerge within the European Commission, or parts thereof, to increasingly integrate territorial concerns into policies (Nordregio/ESPON 2.3.1 2007). An indication of this trend concerns the Commission's impact assessment procedure (cf. chapter 2). Since 2003, all major legislative and policy-defining proposals contained in the Commission's annual work program have been subject to impact assessment, and around 90 impact assessments have been carried out to date. In terms of territorial or spatial analysis, the new guidelines clearly specify that assessment should consider "the geographical distribution of effects" using various qualitative and quantitative techniques (CEC 2005). However, there is currently no standardized way of assessing the spatial effects of programs or policies within the European Commission.

Other examples that illustrate this trend concern various policies. According to an interviewee from the Directorate-General for Employment, Social Affairs and Equal Opportunities, spatial disparities are becoming "an increasing part of employment policy discourse"; the interviewee cited the specific example of the 2002 Implementation Package of the European Employment Strategy, which refers to "considerable regional disparities [in Ireland] . . . in employment and unemployment rates but also educational levels and earnings [that] risk impeding sustained and balanced development." According to an interviewee in the Directorate-General for the Environment, one example of an area of policy that has become more spatially oriented is the Water Framework Directive (2000), which requires water resources to be managed by river basins, implying a coordinated and sometimes a cross-border approach. Other examples are the 2004 Regulation on Rural Development, the Urban Agenda, and Integrated Coastal Zone Management.

Fourth, the establishment in 1996 of INTERREG IIC as a funding framework for transnational cooperation of regional and local actors in the field of spatial planning can be seen as one of the most direct contributions of the European Commission toward the Europeanization of planning. This supported cooperation between national, regional, and local authorities in at least three different countries. The themes for cooperation were mainly linked to the exchange of experience, the condition of joint studies, or the development of common approaches to spatial development topics. This was later followed by INTERREG IIIB (2000–2006). In the Structural Funds period 2007–2013 it has been integrated in the mainstream policy under Objective 3, "European Territorial Cooperation."

## Planning for Europe: Summing Up

Generally, it seems that initiatives to further institutionalize (or Europeanize, in Olsen's second meaning) forms of planning for Europe mainly lead to establishing reference frameworks for action. The strategic documents and policies may set the agenda or provide partial funding for activities contributing to the Europeanization of planning. Their influence is mainly on lower policy and planning levels— that is, planning in Europe. Although many of these documents argue for more horizontal integration and consideration of the territorial dimension at the European level, until now their influence has remained limited in that regard. Yet, as we have seen, within the European Commission a more autonomous trend seems to be emerging to pay more attention to the territorial aspects of policy.

In conclusion, whereas the Europeanization (or creation) of planning for Europe might be targeted at EU policies, its greatest effects can be found in the member states themselves, as we will see in the following section. So planning for Europe deals mainly with providing the means for the Europeanization of planning in Europe.

## Examples of Europeanization of Planning in Europe

As discussed above, there are many ways and means of Europeanizing planning in Europe. The following will present some examples and considerations that illustrate the diversity of formats as well as the diversity of Europe and its actors, policy settings, and geography.

### Top-Down Europeanization Through EU Sector Policies

As mentioned above, spatial planning and territorial development are not the subject of a specific EU policy. Yet planning and development at national, regional, and local levels is influenced by a wide range of EU policies. This influence is top-down, and it was this observation, among others, that inspired the development of the ESDP.

The degree to which EU policies—for example, in the areas of competition, environment, transportation, or regional policy—influence decisions at lower levels varies greatly. Studies on various aspects of this question show that the influence is rather great, although the studies focus on different ways of influencing and different substantive themes (Robert et al. 2001; chapter 2 in this work; and several ESPON studies). An investigation by the Swedish Association of Local Authorities came to the conclusion that about 90 percent of the decisions made by local councils are in one way or another related to EU directives, regulations, recommendations, policy aims, or funding (cf. Böhme 2006b).

Based on an increasing amount of reporting in the Netherlands, a similar suspicion grew about the actual influence of various EU policies. That led to a study of the EU influence on spatial development in the Netherlands, with the telling title *Unseen Europe* (Ravesteyn and Evers 2004). The study shows how EU policies influence spatial development both directly and indirectly. The influence on actual territorial development certainly implies—albeit sometimes indirectly—an influence on spatial planning. The study also shows, for example, European cohesion policy influencing structural change in rural areas and cities through its various forms of infrastructure cofinancing. Furthermore, it exercises influence through network building and governance processes that are supported by the EU. European transport policy requires national governments to preselect lines for high-speed trains, which affects the location of the lines and the selection of cities and stations where high-speed trains will stop. Through this policy, accessibility for some cities is improved, whereas others will find it difficult to plug into the international high-speed rail system. The European Common Agricultural Policy (CAP) has clear territorial effects, too, for example, through supporting intensive cattle farming in certain areas. European competition regulations and policy affect territorial development—for example, via the liberalization of the energy and aviation markets. Indeed, the liberalization of the air transport sector made the success of low-budget airlines possible. Competition policy, which deals with state aid and procurement, among other things, can even restrict options for public authorities to grant economic support—for example, via the regulation of land prices (cf.

Korthals Altes 2006). European environmental policy intervenes directly in territorial development and spatial planning—for example, via Natura 2000 and the Habitat and Water Framework directives, and through the requirement for strategic environmental assessments (SEA).

What is true for the Netherlands is also true for other parts of Europe. Policies such as those above influence, directly or in more subtle ways, territorial development. Moreover, they influence not only spatial development but also spatial planning policies and the way spatial planning decisions are made at any given administrative level. The exact way and the degree of impact differ greatly throughout the EU, due to the great variety of spatial conditions, governance systems, and the variety of ways member states transpose EU sector policies into national legislation.

The latter may be particularly relevant in some cases. For example, because of "mistakes" at the national level, EU air quality objectives have been integrated into spatial planning in the Netherlands, the effect being that they now severely limit the possibilities for spatial development in areas where air quality does not meet European standards (Priemus 2005). At the national level this led to political intervention and subsequent organizational and procedural change within the national administration (Waterhout 2007).

A similar example can be found in Slovenia, which included about one-third of its total land area in the Natura 2000 network (European Environmental Agency 2005). This is another instance in which, faced with demands from EU sector policies, and depending on local circumstances, planning practice throughout Europe reacts differently, with outcomes that reflect the diversity of Europe.

After analyzing planning responses in France, Germany, the Netherlands, and the U.K. to various EU policies, Buunk (2003) comes to the same conclusion. In the terms outlined at the beginning of this chapter, this means that any Europeanization of planning emanating from Brussels with national, regional, and local practices ("planning in Europe") as the target, even when it appears top-down, will nevertheless have outcomes that are far from uniform.

As regards spatial preconditions, it is interesting to note that a few studies have been carried out under ESPON on the territorial effects of EU sector policies in Europe that provide first comparative insights into what kinds of effects those policies have in what kinds of areas (cf. chapter 2).

Although there is no explicit European planning policy, nor the desire to harmonize planning in Europe, the Europeanization of planning by way of sector policies is ongoing. The examples above show that sector policies influence territorial development (thus changing the substantive issues dealt with) as well as planning regulations and procedures, but that until now there has been no identifiable pattern to suggest that that leads to the harmonization of planning systems. Perhaps here we may refer to Williams (1996), who suggests that, if harmonization of planning systems occurs, it will be the effect of single-market policies attempting to remove significant nontariff barriers due to differences between planning systems.

## Organizational Learning Through Transnational Cooperation

As mentioned above, the transnational cooperation scheme under the INTERREG Community Initiative has been set up in the wake of the ESDP. As a result, the main priorities of the programs under INTERREG are quite coherent; the three main aims formulated in the ESDP are (1) development of a balanced and poly-centric urban system and a new urban-rural relationship; (2) securing parity of access to infrastructure and knowledge; and (3) sustainable development, prudent management, and protection of nature and cultural heritage.

An analysis of the transnational cooperation programs between 2000 and 2006, INTERREG IIIB, shows to what degree funding has been allocated to the aims of the ESDP (cf. table 9.1). In some areas, programming priorities reflect the ESDP policy aims directly (e.g., Atlantic Area, CADSES, and the North Sea Region), whereas in other areas programming priorities show fewer similarities with the ESDP (e.g., Baltic Sea, Indian Ocean area, and Northern Periphery). As table 9.1 shows, an analysis of the allocation of financial resources reveals that funding is generally skewed toward priorities of sustainable development, prudent management, and protection of nature and cultural heritage. Funding related to a balanced and polycentric urban system and new urban-rural relationship is limited.

Another ESPON study (BBR/ESPON 2.4.2 2006) has gone even further into detail and shows the locations of actors that use the available funding in relation to various ESDP policy aims. For example, figure 9.1 shows the intensity of interregional cooperation under INTERREG IIIB on polycentric development. An outcome is that cooperation is relatively denser in areas that are traditionally monocentric, which may indicate that the ESDP discourse has rung a bell there. Similar maps have been drawn for the two other policy aims of the ESDP.

The provision of funding for transnational cooperation related to ESDP policy aims and related projects shows how INTERREG operates as a transmitter of those aims to territorial development and spatial planning at the regional or local level.

Indeed, INTERREG is an interesting instrument in that regard, as it brings together policy aims deriving from European and transnational policy debates and regionally and locally felt needs (see Waterhout and Stead 2007). Thus, INTERREG functions as a top-down stimulus for bottom-up processes.

Within this setup transnational cooperation funding under INTERREG contributes to the Europeanization of planning—through funding concrete projects, on one hand, and through bringing actors together in projects, on the other hand, which facilitates organizational learning (Böhme 2005).

As regards concrete actions, there are numerous reports (i.e., INTERREG mid-term and final evaluations) that illustrate the degree to which INTERREG projects contribute to achieving ESDP policy aims as well as shaping spatial planning at local and regional levels and developing and promoting new planning tools and methodologies (cf. Pedrazzini 2005).

By way of illustration, Zaucha and Szydarowski (2005) discuss the contribution of INTERREG to spatial planning and development in Poland. The contribu-

**TABLE 9.1**

## Funding According to ESDP Priorities and INTERREG IIIB Cooperation Area

| Cooperation Area | ERDF Contribution, 2000–2006 (M€) | Polycentric Spatial Development | New Urban-Rural Relationship | Parity of Access to Infrastructure and Knowledge | Wise Management of the Cultural and Natural Heritage | Spatial Integration | Other (including program administration) |
|---|---|---|---|---|---|---|---|
| Alpine Space | 60.6 | 7.6% | 7.6% | 32.1% | 35.6% | 11.3% | 5.9% |
| Archimed | 79.5 | 3.3% | 6.4% | 19.7% | 44.8% | 9.3% | 16.5% |
| Atlantic Area | 118.7 | 17.8% | 5.9% | 28.2% | 30.1% | | 18.0% |
| Azores, Madeira, Canaries (MAC) | 136.0 | 3.9% | 7.4% | 34.3% | 18.0% | 8.2% | 28.2% |
| Baltic Sea | 100.2 | 28.2% | 8.7% | 19.5% | 15.6% | 22.7% | 5.4% |
| Caribbean Space | 12.0 | <5.4% | <5.4% | >35.8% | 31.7% | | >21.7% |
| Central and Danubian Space (CADSES) | 153.7 | 12.8% | 5.5% | 18.3% | 40.2% | 13.9% | 9.4% |
| Indian Ocean/Réunion | 5.0 | 26.0% | 13.0% | | 24.0% | | 37.0% |
| Northern Periphery | 21.2 | | 8.9% | 22.5% | 24.1% | | 43.9% |
| North Sea | 129.3 | 9.0% | 8.7% | 16.7% | 42.1% | 14.1% | 9.5% |
| Northwest Europe | 328.6 | 19.1% | 4.8% | 26.1% | 29.7% | 9.4% | 10.9% |
| Southwest Europe (SUDOE) | 66.0 | 7.0% | 10.0% | 28.9% | 27.0% | | 27.1% |
| Western Mediterranean | 103.6 | 15.2% | 4.8% | 21.6% | 39.5% | 11.9% | 7.0% |
| **Total** | **1314.4** | **>13.5%** | **6.5%** | **>24.4%** | **31.6%** | **10.8%** | **>13.2%** |

Source: Nordregio/ESPON 2.3.1 2007; Waterhout and Stead 2007.

tion occurred partly by way of performing analytical work that could be used by local and regional authorities and partly through projects contributing more generally to the further development of the spatial planning discipline and practice:

Spatial planning, in order to respond to the new reality of European integration, has to abandon its traditional land use management approach associated with the concept of zoning—and try to assume a role of an agent synchronizing various human activities affecting the space. Therefore through its principle of sustainable development spatial planning methodologies ought to be applied to mitigate unharmonized goals of

**FIGURE 9.1**

# Intensity of Cooperation on Polycentric Development Under INTERREG

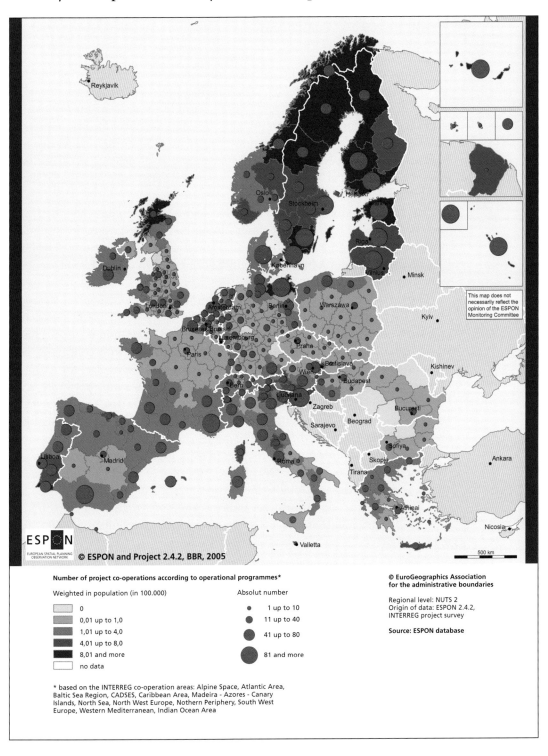

**Number of project co-operations according to operational programmes***

Weighted in population (in 100.000)      Absolut number

- 0
- 0,01 up to 1,0
- 1,01 up to 4,0
- 4,01 up to 8,0
- 8,01 and more
- no data

- 1 up to 10
- 11 up to 40
- 41 up to 80
- 81 and more

© ESPON and Project 2.4.2, BBR, 2005

© EuroGeographics Association
for the administrative boundaries

Regional level: NUTS 2
Origin of data: ESPON 2.4.2,
INTERREG project survey

**Source: ESPON database**

* based on the INTERREG co-operation areas: Alpine Space, Atlantic Area,
Baltic Sea Region, CADSES, Caribbean Area, Madeira - Azores - Canary
Islands, North Sea, North West Europe, Nothern Periphery, South West
Europe, Western Mediterranean, Indian Ocean Area

sector policies, business activities and consumer needs, the latter expressed e.g. in commuting. This assignment is not easy due to lack of proper tools for such a cross-sector and cross-institutional dialogue. Some INTERREG IIIB projects have contributed to overcoming this limitation. (Zaucha and Szydarowski 2005, 735)

Similar experiences can be reported from many other countries, although it has to be acknowledged that there are also critical voices regarding the meaning-fulness of INTERREG (Dühr and Nadin 2007). Nevertheless, the conclusion of Jančič (2005) for Slovenia can probably be considered valid for large parts of the EU: "Experience from cooperation enables us to use more knowledge and experience in coping with development issues and challenges" (748). This illus-trates the usefulness of INTERREG as a means for horizontal processes of Euro-peanization.

The crucial question, however, is to what degree the experiences and the results gained and the contact networks built during INTERREG projects will remain influential once the projects are completed. The organizational learning in INTER-REG projects provides some hints about the degree to which INTERREG cooper-ation contributes to some more long-lasting changes.

Organizational learning addresses the question of how learning that has taken place at the transnational and national or regional levels of INTERREG projects is translated from the participants in the project to their home organizations (Hachmann 2008). That involves sharing new knowledge with colleagues, but, more important, it involves the continuous use of that knowledge, for example, through the change of routines. A study of organizational learning in Nordic-Scot-tish INTERREG IIC projects (Böhme 2005) suggests that the transfer of knowledge between the different arenas and organizations is often considered challenging or even impossible. However, the study also quotes some examples in which organiza-tional learning has contributed to changes in planning routines and practices.

The above illustrates that INTERREG has great potential to contribute to social capital building and, thus, to the Europeanization of planning. However, the way that happens will mostly be indirect and, not unlike Europeanization processes in general (Radaelli 2004; Tewdwr-Jones and Williams 2001), may remain hidden even from the participants themselves.

### Discursive Integration of Planning at the National Level

Europeanization of planning via the application of the ESDP, and more generally the European planning discourse, in the various member states has been a topic of debate for some years, and various studies have investigated it for single countries and groups of countries. There have also been at least two attempts to review the ESDP application at the European level.

As part of the intergovernmental cooperation during the ESDP process, the Belgian delegation conducted a survey—unpublished—on the application of the ESDP in the EU member states; also, within the ESPON program a study looked at the ESDP application in 29 European countries.

Those studies show that the spatial planning philosophy put forward in the ESDP does not go very well with the sector approach that can be found in most countries at the national level and, thus, with the national understanding of planning in general. Whereas the ESDP argues for an integrated way of planning, combining land use planning, regional economic development, and environmental and cultural management, those individual aspects are often the subject of separate sector policies. As the ESDP is a nonbinding, or soft, policy document, its impact on formal national planning systems remains limited at best.

Leaving aside the formal framework of planning, the question arises to what degree national and ESDP policy objectives are coherent. As the objectives of planning in and planning for Europe develop in closely related discourses (Böhme 2002), it is not always possible to trace the exact causal links (see also Nordregio/ESPON 2.3.1 2007). Therefore, the main focus is on the coherence or conformity between the policies.

The ESPON study (Nordregio/ESPON 2.3.1 2007) concludes on this issue that the three main ESDP policy guidelines are generally present in national planning discourses, but often without specific reference to the ESDP. To some extent, then, the ESDP has made sure that national planning now more fully addresses European issues.

Overall, there are only minor variations between national policies and single ESDP policy aims. For all 29 countries combined the degree of conformity for the three policy guidelines is between 88 percent and 95 percent. This means that aims similar to those found in the ESDP are discernible in the national policies of almost all countries.

The study also checked to what degree the different types of planning traditions and perspectives on planning in Europe play a role in differences between countries (cf. Newman and Thornley 1996; CEC 1997a; Janin Rivolin and Faludi 2005). As figure 9.2 illustrates, for all three policy guidelines, unsurprisingly, the level of conformity is larger for the EU15 countries than for the 12 new member states. This probably does reflect the genesis of the ESDP and the influence of the participating member states.

Within the old member states, there are also some variations. The conformity between national policies and the ESDP is more clearly pronounced in the northwest (Austria, Belgium, France, Germany, Luxembourg, Netherlands), Nordic (Denmark, Finland, Sweden), and British (Ireland, U.K.) planning families, while the Mediterranean countries (Greece, Italy, Portugal, Spain) recognize the policy principles of the ESDP to a lesser degree (cf. Giannakourou 2005).

Based on national expert views, it is to some degree possible to also assess the background for the conformity of European and national policy aims. Table 9.2 shows that the planning discourse was the main entrance point for the ESDP into national planning. In Austria, Belgium (Wallonia and Brussels), Denmark, Ireland, Portugal, and Slovenia the planning discourse shows clear evidence of changes in the spatial representation—for instance, in images and maps showing the country's position in Europe.

Further developments depend on the enthusiasm of key people and the degree

**FIGURE 9.2**

## Application of ESDP Policy Guidelines in Groups of European Countries

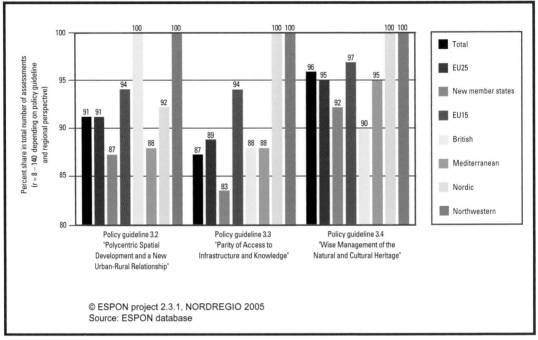

© ESPON project 2.3.1, NORDREGIO 2005
Source: ESPON database

**Source:** Nordregio/ESPON 2.3.1 2007, 123.

of matching between national and European policy development. One could expect to see an explicit use of the ESDP, therefore, if that served the purpose of the main national interest within spatial development; otherwise, it would be less likely. Belgium (Flanders), the Czech Republic, France, Ireland, Lithuania, Luxembourg, and Spain all report that influence on the planning discourse came first and the planning policies followed (Nordregio/ESPON 2.3.1 2007). That largely follows the idea of discursive European integration.

The degree of ESDP inspiration leading to institutional changes within such national processes generally depends on coincidences in timing—if a change was going to take place anyway, arguments emanating from the European professional debate could be used, for as long as they provided support for the particular form of reorganization in question. In some countries, however, institutional changes seem to have emerged before the ESDP could influence the situation. In Hungary and Latvia, new planning institutions were set up as a precondition for institutional reforms. In Italy, the reform of the constitution led to the strengthening of the regional level through the inclusion of European ideas as a backdrop to it—even if the ESDP as such cannot claim to have had a major influence on that process. In the Netherlands, the International Affairs Unit was set up within the Directorate-General of Spatial Policies in response to developments in the increasingly international discussion in this field. These are some of the examples found.

In summary, the ESDP has influenced domestic planning discourses and to some extent also formal planning systems. However, it has to be noted that none of

TABLE 9.2

## Fields Where the Ideas of the ESDP Application Were First Used

| First Field of Application | Country | Total |
|---|---|---|
| Changes in planning discourses | Austria, Belgium, Czech Republic, Denmark, France, Greece, Ireland, Lithuania, Luxembourg, Malta, Slovenia, Spain, Sweden | 13 |
| Institutional changes | Finland, Germany, Hungary, Italy, Latvia, Netherlands, Portugal | 7 |
| Changes in planning policies | Bulgaria, U.K. | 2 |
| Changes in planning practices | Romania | 1 |
| No change | Cyprus, Estonia, Norway, Poland, Slovak Republic, Switzerland | 6 |

**Source**: Nordregio/ESPON 2.3.1 2007, 128.

this happened only because of the ESDP. Indeed, there is no country in which the ESDP alone has led to changes, since ESDP policy aims reflect the zeitgeist and are to some degree already coherent with those policy aims existing in most of the planning systems in Europe. That is not so, however, in the EU member states that joined after the adoption of the ESDP, where the level of conformance is still recognized as mainly implicit (and the CEMAT guiding principles are a more likely source). Also, in countries that were main drivers of the ESDP process and exported their national planning views, actors seem less impressed by the ESDP, considering that its messages were anything but new to them. This illustrates the interplay between planning for Europe and planning in Europe, as discussed above.

## Regional and Local Levels

Examples of the Europeanization of planning less directly related to a certain instrument concern responses of regions to the more abstract notion of European integration as such. Here the driving forces are not primarily specific policies or initiatives, developed either by planners or by certain policy sectors, but rather the overall institutional environment of the EU. In particular, the establishment of the European Union in 1992 raised the awareness of domestic actors that they are part of something larger than their national context. Although there are early examples (National Spatial Planning Agency 2000), since the mid-1990s we see this awareness increasingly reflected in national and regional planning policies and practices.

If one were to compare current national and regional planning documents with those of even 10 or 15 years ago, probably the most glaring difference, apart from arguably a more strategic and economic orientation, would be a section in the current documents about how the region fits into the EU and often a new set of maps, if indeed there are maps at all, on which the territory is shown in its spatial context rather than bordering on terra incognita. Williams (1996) has referred to this as spatial positioning.

Current planning documents increasingly pay attention to a region's position at the EU or, often more appropriate, transnational or cross-border scale. This is done, for example, by specifying relations with bordering regions and countries, indicating complementarities and possible means of cooperation and mutual strengthening, and by highlighting competitive advantages and disadvantages. If maps are used, such findings are often displayed by means of arrows and other cartographic language that suggest relations and flows of people and goods between certain places (Zonneveld 2005a, 2007; Dühr 2007).

ESPON results have given another boost to attempts at spatial positioning at the national level. Currently, primarily based on ESPON material, the Dutch ministry responsible for spatial planning conducts a project on positioning the Netherlands in Europe, which aims at forming a better understanding of transnational spatial relations and Dutch strengths and weaknesses. Similar projects are being, or have been, carried out in Germany, Ireland, Flanders, and Austria, the latter of which carefully scrutinized the 25,000 or more pages that ESPON has delivered up to this date.

This Europeanization of planning expresses itself in an increasing number of cross-border and transnational cooperation initiatives between regions. Although such initiatives are currently often sponsored by INTERREG, many of them existed well before INTERREG and the ESDP. At the Dutch-German border there has been cooperation in the field of spatial planning for well over 50 years (National Spatial Planning Agency 2000), and similar examples, though perhaps shorter in duration, can be found all over western Europe (think for example of the cooperation in the so-called Saar-Lor-Lux region, between Basel and Freiburg, around the Baltic Sea, and in the Alpine area).

An extensive research project on cross-border planning around the Flemish-Dutch border indicates, first, that there is a wealth of overlapping cooperation networks, and, second, that most of them have come about without being influenced by the ESDP (which often was considered too abstract) and without support from INTERREG. On the contrary, the requirements of INTERREG and the administrative burden of its program were considered counterproductive by most cooperation networks, which operate better in a flexible environment around concrete issues (De Vries 2004, 2006).

Early examples at the transnational level are CRONWE; the Benelux (National Spatial Planning Agency 2000; Zonneveld 2005a); and Vision and Strategies Around the Baltic Sea 2010 (VASAB), which was founded in 1992 (Zonneveld 2005b). Whereas CRONWE and the Benelux cooperation have been superseded by INTERREG and the ESDP, VASAB has been able to use INTERREG IIC/IIIB support to its advantage, though at the same time it steers its own course as set out by the Nordic Council of Ministers promoting cooperation from the bottom up.

The Europeanization of planning via processes of spatial positioning and cross-border and transnational cooperation can be understood as examples of what Eriksen (2005) calls "reflexive integration." Reflexive integration basically amounts to domestic actors appreciating the relevance of and incorporating EU elements in their own business. As we have seen, this path to the Europeanization of planning should not be considered as simply a form of domestic response to EU policies or the spatial planning discourse, but rather as a response to general processes of upscaling due to European integration, EU enlargement, and, more generally, globalization.

## Conclusion: Toward a Typology of Europeanization in Planning

Europeanization in planning has many dimensions, including the levels of planning subject to Europeanization (cf. planning for and in Europe), the processes of Europeanization (cf. top-down, horizontal, cyclic), and the means and effects of Europeanization.

We have tried to cast light on a number of these aspects in order to illustrate how manifold the facets of Europeanization are. Figure 9.3 provides a simple scheme that brings together some of the main elements discussed in this article.

The discussion has also shown that the process of Europeanization does not stand on its own and that in practice outcomes of policy processes are a mix of domestic and EU concerns. For the researcher the challenge is to filter out how the outcomes of these complex processes can be related to the European dimensions. Often the EU influence is only rarely visible. One sees merely the emergence of

**FIGURE 9.3**

**Processes and Influences Underlying the Europeanization of Planning**

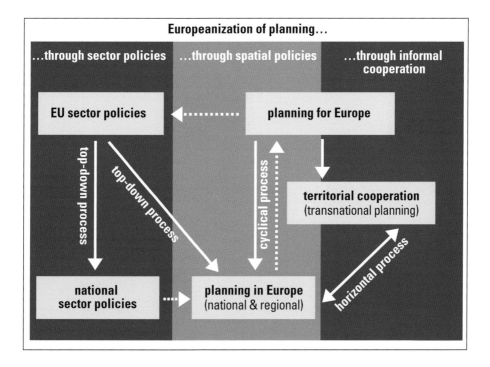

European policy documents and the conformity between planning discourses and systems.

Based on the above discussion, this chapter ends with an attempt to develop a typology of Europeanization in planning, distinguishing—as far as possible—a number of means and effects (see table 9.3). Both face the difficulty that they will hardly ever be comprehensive enough to fully reflect the European diversity, as illustrated in the examples. Furthermore, such a typology can certainly also be differentiated according to geographical levels, something that we have done to some extent in the text, but not in the table.

Table 9.3 shows that there are three different catalysts of the Europeanization of planning, each of which has various types of effects. We leave it to the reader to take the table forward and fill it in with examples of Europeanization.

All in all, the discussion in this chapter shows that there is no one-size-fits-all approach to the Europeanization of spatial planning; however, a few conclusions can be drawn:

- Europeanization is by and large a bottom-up process and should be understood as change in policies and systems due to domestic responses to EU initiatives.

- Europeanization of planning has multiple facets, the most important of which are EU sector policies (regulations and spending policies) and the European spatial planning discourse as taken forward by the *Territorial Agenda, The Terri-*

**TABLE 9.3**
## Toward a Typology of Europeanization in Planning

| Means ↓ / Effects → | Long-Term Influence | | Short-Term Influence | |
|---|---|---|---|---|
| **Effects →**<br><br>**Means ↓** | *Change of self perception and position in Europe* | *Change of laws, "daily" practice, procedures, coopera-tion patterns (organizational learning)* | *Change in the use of terminology, tempo-rary application of new terms and concepts* | *Implementation of single concrete action that would not hap-pen or would happen differently without EU influence* |
| *Implementation of directives and regulations* | Possibly environ-mental directives in the long run | EU regulations in various sector fields, Structural Funds regulations | Formal terminology put down in regulations | Application of EU directives in general |
| *Use of EU funding as incentive* | ESDP application in INTERREG | Structural Funds, organizational learning through INTERREG, LEADER | INTERREG, Structural Funds | Where EU provides cofunding, infra-structure projects, INTERREG |
| *Influenced by a (hegemonic) discourse at the European level* | ESDP application, ESPON use | ESDP application at national level in rare cases | ESDP application, ESPON | |

*torial State and Perspectives of the European Union*, the ESDP, ESPON, and INTERREG (territorial cooperation), among others.

- Europeanization of planning leads to more confluence between planning and planning systems in Europe, but not to uniformity, as the outcomes of Europeanization processes reflect the heterogeneity of Europe in terms of governance and government structures, as well as its spatial diversity.

- Europe is and will remain diverse, but Europeanization processes make sure that its diversity will be closely connected to and can be used as a strength in European development and planning. The ongoing Europeanization of planning in Europe may, in turn, lead to an increased sense of urgency to further develop planning for Europe.

- Discourses and market forces are the strongest elements keeping Europe together and consequently exert the strongest influence on the Europeanization of planning.

## References

Bachtler, J., and L. Polverari. 2007. Delivering territorial cohesion: European cohesion policy and the European model of society. In *Territorial cohesion and the European model of society*, A. Faludi, ed., 105–128. Cambridge, MA: Lincoln Institute of Land Policy.

BBR/ESPON 2.4.2. 2006. *Integrated analysis of transnational and national territories based on ESPON results: Draft final report of ESPON project 2.4.2.* http://www.espon.eu/mmp/online/website/content/projects/243/388/index_EN.html.

Böhme, K. 2002. *Nordic echoes of European spatial planning.* Stockholm: Nordregio.

———. 2005. The ability to learn in transnational projects. *Informationen zur Raumentwicklung* 11/12:691–700.

———. 2006a. Discursive European integration: The case of Nordic spatial planning. In *Rethinking European spatial policy as a hologram*, L. Doria, V. Fedeli, and C. Tedesco, eds., 215–234. Aldershot, U.K.: Ashgate.

———. 2006b. Visst påverkar EU fysisk planering i Sverige. In *Planering med nya förutsättningar*, G. Blücher and G. Graninger, eds., 39–56. Linköping, Sweden: Linköping University Interdisciplinary Studies Program.

Böhme, K., and P. Schön. 2006. From Leipzig to Leipzig: Territorial research delivers evidence for the new *Territorial Agenda of the European Union*. In *Evidence-based planning*, A. Faludi, ed. Special issue, *disP* 165, 42(2):61–70.

Buunk, W. W. 2003. *Discovering the locus of European integration.* Delft, Netherlands: Eburon.

CEC (Commission of the European Communities). 1997a. *The EU compendium of spatial planning systems and policies.* Regional Development Studies 28. Luxembourg: Office for Official Publications of the European Communities.

———. 1997b. *European Spatial Development Perspective: First official draft (presented at the informal meeting of ministers responsible for spatial planning of the member states of the European Union, Noordwijk, 9 and 10 June 1997).* Luxembourg: Office for Official Publications of the European Communities.

———. 1999. *European Spatial Development Perspective: Towards balanced and sustainable development of the territory of the EU.* Luxembourg: Office for Official Publications of the European Communities.

———. 2005. *Impact assessment guidelines.* SEC (2005) 791. Luxembourg: Office for Official Publications of the European Communities.

———. 2007. *Growing regions, growing Europe.* Fourth report on economic and social cohesion, provisional version. Luxembourg: Office for Official Publications of the European Communities.

CEMAT (Conférence Européenne des Ministres Responsables de l'Aménagement du Territoire). 2000. *Guiding principles for sustainable spatial development of the European continent.* Strasbourg: Council of Europe.

Dabinett, G., and T. Richardson. 2005. The Europeanization of spatial strategy: Shaping regions and spatial justice through governmental ideas. *International Planning Studies* 10(3): 201–218.

Dühr, S. 2007. *The visual language of spatial planning.* Abingdon, Oxon, U.K.: Routledge.

Dühr, S., and V. Nadin. 2007. Learning from transnational cooperation on spatial planning: The case of INTERREG IIIB in North-west Europe. *Planning Practice and Research* 22(3): 373–394.

European Environmental Agency. 2005. *The European environment: State and outlook 2005.* State of Environment Report No. 1. Copenhagen: European Environmental Agency.

Eriksen, E. O. 2005. Reflexive integration in Europe. In *Making the European policy: Reflexive integration in the EU*, E. O. Eriksen, ed., 9–29. Abingdon, Oxon, U.K.: Routledge.

Faludi, A. 2004. The open method of co-ordination and "post-regulatory" territorial cohesion policy. *European Planning Studies* 12(7):1019–1033.

Giannakourou, G. 2005. Transforming spatial planning policy in Mediterranean countries: Europeanization and domestic change. *European Planning Studies* 13(2): 319–331.

Hachmann, V. 2008. Promoting learning in transnational networks. *disP*, forthcoming.

Hajer, M. A. 1995. *The politics of environmental discourse: Ecological modernization and the policy process.* New York: Oxford University Press.

Healey, P. 2006. Transforming governance: Challenges of institutional adaptation and a new politics of space. *European Planning Studies* 14(3): 299–320.

Jančič, M. 2005. INTERREG IIIB in Slovenia. *Informationen zur Raumentwicklung* 11/12: 741–748.

Janin Rivolin, U., and A. Faludi. 2005. The hidden face of European spatial planning: Innovations in governance. *European Planning Studies* 13(2): 195–215.

Jensen, O. B., and T. Richardson. 2004. *Making European space: Mobility, power and territorial identity.* London: Routledge.

Kohler-Koch, B. 1999. The evolution and transformation of European governance. In *The transformation of governance in the European Union*, B. Kohler-Koch and R. Eising, eds., 14–35. London: Routledge.

Korthals Altes, W. K. 2006. The single European market and land development. *Planning Theory and Practice* 7(3): 247–266.

Lenschow, A. 2006. Europeanisation of public policy. In *European Union: Power and policy making*, J. Richardson, ed., 3rd ed., 55–71. Abingdon, Oxon, U.K.: Routledge.

National Spatial Planning Agency. 2000. *Spatial perspectives in Europe: Spatial reconnaissance 1999.* The Hague: Ministry of Housing, Spatial Planning and the Environment.

Newman, P., and A. Thornley. 1996. *Urban planning in Europe: International competition, national systems, and planning projects.* London: Routledge.

Nordregio/ESPON 2.3.1. 2007. *Application and effects of the ESDP in member states: Final report of ESPON project 2.3.1.* http://www.espon.eu/mmp/online/website/content/projects/243/366/index_EN.html.

Olsen, J. P. 2002. The many faces of Europeanization. *Journal of Common Market Studies* 40(5): 921–952.

Pedrazzini, L. 2005. Applying the ESDP through INTERREG IIIB: A southern perspective. *European Planning Studies* 13(2): 297–317.

Priemus, H. 2005. Fijnstof: Splijtzwam tussen milieu en bouwen? *Rooilijn* 38(10): 507–511.

Radaelli, C. M. 2004. Europeanisation: Solution or problem? *European Integration Online Papers (EioP)* 8(16): 1–23. http://eiop.or.at/eiop/index.php/eiop.

Ravesteyn, N. van, and D. Evers. 2004. *Unseen Europe: A survey of EU politics and its impacts on spatial development in the Netherlands.* The Hague: Netherlands Institute for Spatial Research.

Robert, J., T. Stumm, J. M. de Vet, G. J. Reincke, M. Hollanders, and M. A. Figueiredo. 2001. *Spatial impacts of community policies and the costs of non-coordination.* Brussels: European Commission, Directorate-General for Regional Policy.

Rusca, R. 1998. The development of a European spatial planning policy. In *The progress of European spatial planning,* C. Bengs and K. Böhme, eds., 503–520. Stockholm: Nordregio.

Sykes, O. 2004. Diversity and context dependency in European spatial planning: Investigating the application of the *European Spatial Development Perspective.* PhD thesis, University of Liverpool.

———. 2007. Examining the relationship between transnational and national planning: French and British spatial planning and the *European Spatial Development Perspective.* In *Spatial planning systems of Britain and France: A comparative analysis,* P. Booth, M. Breuillard, C. Fraser, and D. Paris, eds., 99–118. London: Routledge.

Territorial Agenda. 2007. *Territorial Agenda of the European Union: Towards a more competitive and sustainable Europe of diverse regions* (Agreed on the occasion of the Informal Ministerial Meeting on Urban Development and Territorial Cohesion in Leipzig on 24/25 May 2007). http://www.bmvbs.de/Anlage/original_1005295/Territorial-Agenda-of-the-European-Union-Agreed-on-25-May-2007-barrier-free.pdf.

Territorial State. 2007. *The Territorial State and Perspectives of the European Union: Towards a stronger European territorial cohesion in the light of the Lisbon and Gothenburg ambitions* (A background document for the *Territorial Agenda of the European Union*). http://www.bmvbs.de/Anlage/original_1005296/The-Territorial-State-and-Perspectives-of-the-European-Union.pdf.

Tewdwr-Jones, M., and R. H. Williams. 2001. *The European dimension of British planning.* London: Routledge.

Vries, J. de. 2004. Borders never die, but they might fade away: Cross-border capacity building for territorial governance in the Rhine-Scheldt Delta. In *Environmental and infrastructure planning,* G. Linden and H. Voogd, eds., 111–138. Groningen, Netherlands: GEO Press.

———. 2006. Grensoverschrijdend samenwerken in de Rijn-Schelde Delta: Over fragmentatie en beperkte Europese invloed. In *Grenzeloze Ruimte: Gebiedsgerichte ontwikkelingsplanologie in regionaal perspectief,* L. Janssen-Jansen and B. Waterhout, eds., 157–172. The Hague: SDU Uitgevers.

Waterhout, B. 2007. Episodes of Europeanization of Dutch national spatial planning. *Planning Practice and Research* 22(3):309–327.

———. 2008. *The institutionalisation of European spatial planning.* Amsterdam: IOS Press.

Waterhout, B., and D. Stead. 2007. Mixed messages: How the ESDP's messages have been applied in INTERREG IIIB programmes, priorities and projects. *Planning, Practice and Research* 22(3): 395–415.

Williams, R. H. 1996. *European Union spatial policy and planning.* London: Paul Chapman.

Zaucha, J., and W. Szydarowski. 2005. Transnational cooperation and its contribution to spatial development and EU enlargement: The case of INTERREG IIIB in northern Poland. *Informationen zur Raumentwicklung* 11/12:731–740.

Zonneveld, W. 2005a. Expansive spatial planning: The new European transnational spatial visions. *European Planning Studies* 13(1): 137–155.

———. 2005b. Multiple visioning: New ways of constructing transnational spatial visions. *Environment and Planning C* 23(1): 41–62.

———. 2007. Unraveling Europe's spatial structure through spatial visioning. In *Territorial cohesion and the European model of society*, A. Faludi, ed., 191–208. Cambridge, MA: Lincoln Institute of Land Policy.

# CHAPTER 10

# The Making of the *Territorial Agenda of the European Union*: Policy, Polity, and Politics

Thiemo W. Eser and Peter Schmeitz

This chapter describes the rationale and logic of the making of the *Territorial Agenda of the European Union* (TA) and the evidence document on which the TA is based, *The Territorial State and Perspectives of the European Union* (TSP). It does so, beyond the description of the process (Faludi 2007), from different points of view that are traditionally used in the political sciences: the thematic perspective of policy, the institutional perspective of polity, and the purely strategic perspective of politics. One can tell three different stories from those three perspectives (see, e.g., Kohler-Koch 1996; Bauer 2001; Dyson and Goetz 2003; Rittberger and Zangl 2006; Eser 2007) concerning the making of the TSP and TA.

In principle, the TSP (Territorial State 2007) and the TA (Territorial Agenda 2007) are complementary documents, which for pragmatic reasons are separated. The TSP is the longer evidence and discussion document, and the TA is the shorter political document endorsed by ministers. It is widely accepted that longer policy documents are not likely to reach a broad readership, particularly in a field where policy makers use neither carrots nor sticks, but rely on a convincing presentation and argument to make their case. That is one of the reasons the documents are separated.

The elaboration of the *European Spatial Development Perspective* (ESDP) made it clear that it is impossible for the European Union (EU) ministers for spatial development to come to a common understanding and decide on a document that includes maps that go beyond describing the geography and population of Europe. Even a classification of the height of mountains can become a political issue, considering the range of such heights in the Netherlands and Austria, just to name a rather innocent example. There is a simple and understandable reason for this: No common European understanding exists of how to select and read certain facts on maps in such a way that ministers would not risk being criticized at home. This is in particular the case where the maps are not imposed and signed for "from above," as, for example, in the case of the cohesion reports of the European Commission (with its explicit mandate under the EU Treaty).

However, particularly since "evidence-based" has become one of the buzz words for territorial policy making, it is clear that territorial observations have to

The chapter is based on the opinion of the authors and does not represent an official view.

be conveyed somehow. The European Spatial Planning Observation Network (ESPON) offers a wealth of information that provides a refined and complex picture of European territorial development and avoids biased and simplistic political statements. Consequently, the meaning of a single map or statement becomes embedded in a broader framework. The TSP restricts itself to reporting on the evidence and is therefore not considered a political document. It includes many maps, mostly prepared by ESPON; whereas, after the ESDP experience, the inclusion of maps in the TA was never seriously considered.

Most suitable for an introduction to the whole policy process around the TA and the TSP seems to be the *policy* question concerning the thematic orientation section of this chapter, as the authors are (still) convinced that the rationale of content and themes is the most important factor for the policy process. However, the rationale of *polity* describing the policy process from the point of view of institutional dynamics and that of the *politics* involved, relating as it does to the rationale of the tactics employed by the actors participating in the process, is challenging the thematic content as the driving factor and key to the understanding of the whole process. The conclusions offer some further perspectives. It should be noted that since 2004 the ministers responsible for spatial development have met as ministers responsible for territorial cohesion, due to the changing thematic focus (Faludi 2006); at the informal ministerial meeting in Leipzig the titles were combined to make them "ministers for spatial development/territorial cohesion."

## Policy: Focusing on Thematic Orientations

The thematic context is vital for understanding the thematic orientations of TA and TSP and should be dealt with first.

### Introducing the Thematic Context

Currently, the EU policy process is organized in a sectoral way and does not take the territorial dimension into account in any structured way. That lack of territorial coordination at the EU level was the driving force behind the preparation of the ESDP, which focused on developing a territorial perspective of the EU. In thematic terms the ESDP broadened the scope of EU regional policy, which until then had focused only on economic and social cohesion. At the EU level, as well as in many member states, regional policy was and still is mostly *economic* policy, supporting economic and social cohesion. The ESDP, resulting from a longer process (Williams 1999; Eser and Konstadakopulos 2000; Faludi and Waterhout 2002; Davoudi 2005; see also the introduction by Faludi), was adopted in 1999. It considered the contribution of EU sector policies, such as those on transport and research and development, to cohesion. It developed a more integrated view of a sustainable and balanced territorial development.

After its finalization, the ESDP was supposed to be applied in regional and sector policies, at both EU and national levels. However, it was unable to play a significant role in thematically coordinating policies with regard to their horizontal and vertical interactions and to geographical integration as intended (CEC 1999). It became a clear reference for the formulation of INTERREG IIIB programs for transnational territorial cooperation. Moreover, it inspired some regions and member states without planning traditions to develop a spatial planning policy for their territory. In fact, the necessity of sector policy coordination is evident, and it was broadly recognized in 1999, at both EU and national levels. The problem was that the ESDP had not become the convincing stimulus to do it (Faludi 2007).

While the ESDP was in the process of being applied and elaborated, the Lisbon (CEC 2005) and Gothenburg (CEC 2001a) Strategies were set up as the new key political drivers for the development of the EU. However, it soon became clear that the twin strategies were not getting the necessary response in EU and national policies. At the end of 2003, it became evident that the Lisbon Strategy was not taken up by the political actors particularly at the national level, and consequently the strategy did not have any impact. In the beginning of 2005 the Lisbon Strategy was reviewed and relaunched due to increased economic problems in many EU member states. It moved to the fore in comparison to the Gothenburg Strategy: Jobs and growth became the mantra for the EU (CEC 2005; see also the introduction to this volume).

Having learned from their experience with the ESDP, territorial policy makers from the Netherlands, who were preparing their EU presidency, felt they had to directly contribute to the Lisbon Strategy, the most important political agenda of the EU. This was particularly necessary, as the Lisbon Strategy is organized strictly by sectors. Its main shortcoming is that all the sectoral measures, such as competition and innovation policy, could cumulate and result in increasing concentration in the economic core of the EU (the so-called pentagon area between London, Paris, Milan, Munich, and Hamburg) and, therefore, require complementary territorial considerations (Luxembourg scoping document 2005). In fact, the European Commission's Directorate-General for Regional Policy had to struggle until the end of the review of the Lisbon Strategy to obtain recognition for the Structural Funds and cohesion policy as instruments in the Lisbon framework. Thus, operationalization of the ESDP with regard to the latest and most important policy developments could strengthen the strategy in a thematic way.

That idea was supported by the debate on the focus of the programming of the 2007–2013 Structural Funds. The Structural Funds were supposed to become one of the key instruments of the Lisbon Agenda. Territorial policy makers were of the conviction that a strong territorial dimension of the Structural Funds could contribute to and should enrich regional policy, as well as other sector policies that should contribute to the Lisbon process.

In addition, territorial policy makers could now benefit from the results of the ESPON 2006 program. ESPON was established in 2002 after the adoption of the ESDP because of the lack of empirical evidence to describe the key territorial structures and trends in the EU, and to make political proposals in concrete cases (Böhme and Schön 2006; Davoudi 2006; Faludi and Waterhout 2006; Gestel and Faludi 2005). In 2004, five years after the adoption of the ESDP and the establishment of ESPON, it looked as if sufficient empirical evidence and results were available to start creating a new evidence-based document that would operationalize the ESDP and position it in the light of the Lisbon Strategy; that is what eventually became the TSP.

In November 2004 the horizontal and thematic gaps regarding a coordinated approach in the Lisbon Strategy and its key instrument, the Structural Funds, and the new evidence base delivered by ESPON gave the EU Ministers for Territorial Cohesion in Rotterdam the confidence to start a new phase in their cooperation by contributing to the key EU political agenda. Already at their next meeting in Luxembourg, in May 2005, they adopted a scoping document for the TSP, describing the contours of a knowledge base and concrete thematic proposals for policy development in the field of territorially relevant sectoral policies (Territorial State 2007). At the informal ministerial meeting in Leipzig, ministers and the European institutions participating in the process agreed on the final version of the thematic orientations of the TA, which provides the basis for further concrete actions.

### The Making of TSP and TA and the Identification of Thematic Orientations

In the thematic context, the TSP follows a strict line of making prominent references to Lisbon. In the first part, it considers the objective of territorial cohesion in light of the Lisbon aims. It concludes that the key challenge for strengthening cohesion is enhancing the territorial capital and potential of all EU regions and promoting territorial integration, for example, by promoting trans-European synergies and clusters of competitive and innovative activities. In that light, the TSP elaborates the concept of territorial cohesion as follows (Territorial State 2007):

- By focusing regional and national territorial development policies on better exploiting regional potential and territorial capital—Europe's territorial and cultural diversity
- By better positioning of regions in Europe, both by strengthening their profiles and by trans-European cooperation aimed at facilitating their connectivity and territorial integration
- By promoting the coherence of EU policies with a territorial impact, both horizontally and vertically, so that they support sustainable development at national and regional levels

So, if territorial cohesion is the policy objective, territorial development policies are the policy tools. In that light, the challenge of territorial cohesion covers more than EU cohesion policy in the narrow sense. It adds an integrated and long-term approach to the process of exploiting territorial potentials in the EU—an approach that has to be addressed at, and across, different policy levels (regional, national, cross-border, transnational, and EU) and across sectors (agriculture, transport, environment, regional-economic development, competition, etc.). In this sense, trends and policies are judged to be contributing to the strengthening of territorial cohesion if they assist with the better exploitation of inherent regional potential—comparative territorial advantages. Relevant key territorial indicators are currently being discussed at the expert level, a topic elaborated upon by Böhme and Eser in chapter 2.

In the second part, under the headline "Territorial State," before describing the contours of the EU's territorial structure, the TSP elaborates further on the cross-sectoral issue by considering the huge diversity of territorial potentials in Europe by themes:

- Growth and innovation
- Transport and energy
- Risk management
- Environment, nature, and culture

These issues are clearly linked to the Lisbon and Gothenburg Strategy and its most important EU instrument, EU cohesion policy. Following the thematic assessment, a general picture of the EU territorial structure is described in three parts:

- Demographic imbalances
- Urban regions and major cities
- Rural diversity

In addition, the recent discussion on climate change has led to its upgrade to not only an environmental but also a cross-sectoral issue, which surely has strong territorial impacts, as discussed by Schmidt-Thomé and Greiving in chapter 6.

Third, following the assessment of the "territorial state," the TSP describes territorial perspectives for the future: how to achieve a more competitive Europe of diverse regions. The document discusses and proposes six priorities for strengthening the structure of the EU territory on the basis of the Luxembourg scoping document (Territorial State 2007).

The TA builds on the TSP as its political mirror document. This separation between analysis and politics creates the opportunity for the TA to become more political and more concrete in making its proposals than the ESDP. The TA, first of all, describes the key territorial challenges for the EU in the coming years, based on the analyses of the TSP. On that basis it identifies the priorities for EU territorial development and the key actions to be undertaken, for example, in strengthening the coherence of EU policies with a territorial impact.

The TA did not take over the priorities in exactly the form of the TSP and the prior scoping document. The discussion process between Luxembourg and Leipzig during the U.K., Austrian, and Finnish presidencies led to some readjustments in the orientation of the priorities. Under the impression of the recent development, particularly in weak and handicapped regions, the first adjustment concerned the strengthening of the social-territorial dimension. Furthermore, under the influence of the finally obvious climate change in the winter and spring of 2006–2007, the environmental and energy dimension was enforced. In Leipzig the following six territorial priorities were agreed upon on the ground of strengthening regional identities and making better use of territorial diversity (Territorial Agenda 2007):

1. Aim to strengthen polycentric development and innovation through networking of city-regions and cities

2. Need for new forms of partnership and territorial governance between rural and urban areas

3. Promotion of regional clusters of competition and innovation in Europe

4. Support for the strengthening and extension of Trans-European Networks

5. Promotion of trans-European risk management, including the impacts of climate change

6. Requirement of strengthening ecological structures and cultural resources as an added value for development

The TA, as a document of eight pages, concentrates much less on an elaborate description of thematic issues than the TSP of around 90 pages does. As a political document that sets the frame for policy action, it just sketches the main fields of action and devotes a relatively larger part to the implementation issues of how, when, and where action is needed.

In thematic and content terms, the TA, indeed, fills an important gap in the policy spectrum of the EU and complements the sectoral orientation of most EU policies. This is true despite criticisms from different sides asking for more overall consistency, more economy, more social elements, and more attention to the environment, as it has to be taken into account that the document represents the accord between 27 countries and their EU institutions. The question, however, is how the policy "performs" in a given institutional setting.

## Polity: Focusing on Institutional Development

As described above, TA and TSP are driven by content. However, they can also be seen as an element in the institutional setup. The wider institutional context is critical for understanding the exact positioning of TA and TSP in the policy process.

### The Wider Context

The EU does not have a very strong mandate for territorial development, as regional policy is mainly geared toward achieving economic and social cohesion. Therefore, the European Commission cannot develop a policy addressing territorial development at the EU level in the same way as it develops policy addressing economic and social cohesion. The way for the Commission to cover territorial aspects is by exploiting for that purpose the scope of the policies for which it has a full mandate. The way the Commission interprets scope surely influences how the member states oppose such an interpretation. During the elaboration of the ESDP, the Commission explored its margins in supporting the intergovernmental process through financing the Committee on Spatial Development (CSD) along with a range of studies. However, after the adoption of the ESDP, the Commission realized the limited influence of the new document and felt that the lack of response to the ESDP could lead to the criticism of using EU funds for purposes outside the scope of the EU treaties. Therefore, the Commission, in principle in favor of the thematic orientation of the ESDP, tried to improve the link between its efforts in territorial development and its Structural Funds policy by establishing the Working Group on Spatial and Urban Development (SUD), a subcommittee of the management committee of the Structural Funds, the Committee for the Development and Conversion of Regions (CDCR). As these structures need to be reestablished for each Structural Funds period, SUD continues as the Working Group for Territorial Cohesion and Urban Matters (TCUM) of the Coordination Committee of the Funds (COCOF) for the period 2007–2013.

Although this looked like the ideal solution, covering all requirements, it had two effects that were not perceived positively by member states. Because the national representatives on the CDCR were entitled to choose their country's representation in SUD, SUD in the beginning consisted more of representatives from ministries responsible for managing the Structural Funds than of those dealing with territorial development. This meant that its thematic influence was limited. Gradually, however, the situation changed as ministries responsible for managing the Structural Funds accepted that SUD had a clear, content-oriented agenda focused on urban and territorial development.

The second negative effect was that the debate on issues of territorial development had to be limited to the 2000–2006 Structural Funds programming period, as the SUD committee's legal basis is in the 2000–2006 Structural Funds regulations. In order to keep a broad and strategic focus in the EU debate, the incoming Dutch presidency initiated a high-level intergovernmental process. In cooperation with the Dutch and the acting Danish presidency the French DATAR (Délégation à l'Aménagement du Territoire et à l'Action Régionale or Delegation for Territorial Planning and Regional Action) hosted a first high-level conference in Paris in May 2004.

In real terms this meant at that time that the territorial dimension was dealt with in two parallel and complementary processes: (1) the work of the SUD, focusing on the Structural Funds and chaired by the Commission (but later cochaired by the EU presidency of the day), giving the Commission a strong influence on the agenda; and (2) intergovernmental cooperation, most certainly including full cooperation with the Commission, but under the guidance of the EU presidency and with a broader scope—the territorial dimension of all EU and national policies.

Meanwhile, the Commission had tried to improve the situation by supporting incorporation of territorial cohesion as a new objective at the same level as economic and social cohesion in the draft EU Constitutional Treaty prepared by the European Convention. This idea was actually first mentioned by the French in a letter to Michel Barnier, Commissioner for Regional Policy until March 2004 (Faludi 2006). It would help define a clear status for territorial development in the canon of EU policy by offering an explicit legal base and therefore avoiding the necessity of deducing activities from other articles of the treaty (see the next section).

The Commission succeeded in its lobby, with the support of the member states, and territorial cohesion became an objective alongside economic and social cohesion in the constitution adopted by the European Council of heads of state and government. At the ministerial meeting in Luxembourg in 2005, it was proposed that the Commission should formulate a white paper on territorial cohesion on the basis of the relevant articles in the Constitutional Treaty. However, this strengthening of the thematic responsibility of the Commission was later put into question when ratification of the new treaty was stalled.

The fact that the Constitutional Treaty included a clause on territorial cohesion supported the conviction of the EU territorial cohesion ministers in Rotterdam and Luxembourg that the time was ripe to address the territorial impacts of all EU policies, both regional and sectoral. This gave the TSP particular importance and increased the impetus toward its further elaboration. With a view toward strengthening the coordinating role of the informal TSP document, it was decided in Luxembourg to hold a dialogue with the stakeholders and to endorse a scoping document defining the basic line of thinking for the TSP.

Supported by the renewed cooperation between the member states, the Commission acknowledged the importance of the territorial dimension in the *Community Strategic Guidelines* for the 2007–2013 EU cohesion policy, to be implemented via the National Strategic Reference Framework and the subsequent operational programs under the Structural Funds (Council of the European Union 2006; Official Journal of the European Union 2006; Polverari et al. 2006; Bachtler et al. 2007). A debate under the U.K. presidency among the EU25 at the working level of administrators on the elaboration of the TSP led to the conclusion that the TSP would be too descriptive and not political enough to be endorsed at the political level under the German EU presidency in May 2007. Therefore, it was decided to split the elaboration into a political document, the TA, and a descriptive one, the TSP.

Because of the stalled ratification of the constitution, the Commission lacked its expected mandate and could no longer openly lead the discussion on territorial cohesion. In institutional terms, the rationale for the TSP and TA was turned on its head: Because the constitution could not be taken as a reference, a strong and convincing evidence base would be needed to keep the discussion on territorial development and cohesion alive. It follows that making a success of the TSP and the TA became even more important, until a new treaty would open a more solid window of opportunity.

The situation changed again at the EU summit in June 2007 when the German EU presidency succeeded in unlocking the discussion on the constitution and guiding the heads of state toward a mandate for the preparation of a new, slimmer EU Treaty instead of the Constitutional Treaty. The mandate took over the formulation of territorial cohesion as an objective of the EU in the final version of the EU Reform (Lisbon) Treaty adopted by the heads of state in October 2007 under the Portuguese presidency and now subject to ratification by the member states.

## The Importance of the TSP and the TA for Institution Building

The Rotterdam process was started on the assumption that territorial cohesion would receive a strong position in the EU Constitutional Treaty in the form of a shared competence. The renewed EU territorial cooperation of ministers responsible for spatial development started under the Dutch presidency in November 2004 would focus on the period until the adoption of the new constitution. The current EU Treaty offers an implicit legal basis for territorial activities at EU level via Articles 2 (balanced and sustainable development of the EU), 16 (providing services of general interest for enhancing territorial cohesion), and 158 (strengthening economic and social cohesion). These articles offered a basis for the TA and the TSP, which provides at least some legal and political legitimacy, more than is the case with just another intergovernmental undertaking. In this respect the TA has to be seen as a territorial translation of the specific articles of the EU Treaty mentioned above.

In the framework described, the ministers based the TA on four principles agreed upon in Rotterdam (*Presidency Conclusions*) and reiterated in Luxembourg:

- Integration: The aim of the TA is not the creation of a separate and top-down EU territorial policy but improving integration of the territorial dimension into EU policies.
- Subsidiarity: Territorial development policies are the responsibility of the member states, but the EU does have a role in strengthening territorial cohesion and coherence.
- Development orientation: The Rotterdam agenda facilitates the Lisbon ambitions for sustainable economic growth.
- No new rules, procedures, or bureaucracy: Better use will be made of existing opportunities and possibilities that the EU policy process offers for integrating the territorial dimension.

In basing the TA on those principles, the EU ministers for territorial cohesion clearly defined their role in the framework of the EU. They defined for themselves the role of putting territorial challenges on the broader EU agenda and stimulating debate on these issues. The Council and the European parliament are responsible for EU decision making, but the ministers can influence EU decision making by triggering debate both in the EU member states and at the EU level.

Moreover, since the 2004 enlargement, the EU ministers for territorial cohesion are in most member states responsible for managing or coordinating all Structural Funds programs, or at least the two specifically territorial instruments of the EU. Both the ESPON and the INTERREG programs for transnational territorial cooperation have not only delivered operational results for the use of policy makers, but have also given the EU ministers responsible for territorial cohesion a stronger position in the EU framework, as both are formal EU instruments.

However, as long as there is no strong legal basis for territorial cohesion, there is no formal obligation or incentive to take the territorial impact of policies into account in the EU policy process. Effective management of the territorial impact seems possible only with strong political leadership and broad political ownership at the EU level. The TSP and the TA, therefore, aim at forming a strong network of stakeholders that can build on a sound base of territorial knowledge, information, and expertise, with effective links to the EU policy process. Legally, there are good opportunities for addressing the territorial impact (for a detailed discussion see chapter 2), especially in the preparatory phase, which in legal and political terms is the most open. A key challenge is the sectoral organization of the EU policy process. The Commission and the member states are not prepared to include any notion of territorial impact assessment (TIA) in the TA, as discussions of that issue have been controversial. There were dominant objections due to mixed experiences with the strategic environmental impact assessment (see chapter 2). However, the *Presidency Conclusions* mention that the Commission should report in 2010 on the possibility of embedding impact assessment in the existing institutions and procedures (German EU Council Presidency 2007, point 8).

In order to strengthen ownership of the issue, several spatial development ministers and senior officials in the EU member states have committed themselves to a dialogue with key territorial cohesion stakeholders, like EU institutions; national, regional, and local representatives; nongovernmental organizations; and private actors involved in territorially relevant policies. Sharing information and achieving more clarity and insight about the territorial impact of EU policies is a key priority in such a dialogue. So far, the dialogue has been a very informal and flexible process, focused mainly on creating a common understanding. Ministers are of the conviction that information and dialogue are key elements in coordinating sector policies without creating a new sector (Luxembourg conclusions). The stakeholder dialogue was launched in Amsterdam on 28 June 2006 by the ministers responsible for territorial cohesion of the Netherlands, Luxembourg, and Germany, who were organizing ministerial meetings, along with high-level representatives of EU institutions and stakeholders at the EU level. That dialogue was followed by a series of about 15 presentations of members of the coming presidencies group at different meetings of EU-level stakeholder groups. In addition, supported by the efforts of both the Commission and the member states, it was possible to replace the SUD with the TCUM committee in the beginning of 2007; and, in fact, the parallel process mentioned above between the member states and the TCUM was better coordinated by the Commission.

The TA highlights a range of actions on when, where, and how to be active, based on a philosophy of information and dialogue (Territorial Agenda 2007). Accordingly, nearly one-third of the document is devoted to implementation at the EU level and the level of member states, setting out a strategy of information and dialogue in relation to the thematic priorities that have been identified. Thus, a learning process is apparent in comparison with the ESDP process, which fell short in recognizing the importance of active communication in relation to important EU files and at high-level events. There was also a critical demand for stronger measures. However, it has to be taken into account that the TA represents an agreement between 25 member states plus two accession countries and the EU institutions, whereas in some countries territorial development is deemed a task of lower importance or the responsibility of regional and local authorities. Here, too, the quasi-nonhierarchical setting of the whole policy process has to be considered. In any case, the proof of the TA's robustness is left to the incoming presidency of Portugal, which committed itself to organize an action program—a fact that once again points to the importance of process in this policy field. In July 2007 the Portuguese presidency launched the Network of Territorial Cohesion Related Contact Points (NTCCP) of all member states agreed upon under point 39 of the TA. The NTCCP already proved to be the backbone for the coordination of the First Action Programme (2007; FAP), announced under point 42 for implementation of the TA and agreed upon at the ministerial meeting at the end of November 2007 in Ponte Delgada in the Azores. The FAP presented a coherent framework for action; a first set of activities initiated by member states and EU institutions were presented and will be complemented in a further ongoing process. It is certainly too early to judge the success of the FAP at this stage. Most actions are related to increasing knowledge and posting the territorial dimension in different sectoral and regional contexts.

Finally, the Commission, supported by the tailwind of the TA, seemed ready to embark again on a "report on territorial cohesion" in the year 2008, interestingly mentioned in the German *Presidency Conclusions* (German EU Council Presidency 2007, point 11) and not in the TA; that effort could be the continuation of one begun in 2004 as an "Interim Territorial Cohesion Report" (CEC 2004) and not followed up after ratification. However, backed by the EU Reform (Lisbon) Treaty, in the Azores the Commission clarified its intent to prepare a green paper on territorial cohesion by summer 2008. This is a fundamental turning point in the process. The Commission is climbing in the driver's seat of territorial cohesion, but first informing itself by a questionnaire to the member states on the TCUM committee on how territorial cohesion is understood at the national level.

## Politics: Focusing on the Actors' Tactics

The story of the TSP and TA and strategic politics could be told in a different way. The context of politics focuses on the question of how actors try to maximize their influence in the narrow sense—that is, within a given institutional environment— using the described thematic concerns about territorial cohesion as a tool for the primary extension of their sphere of influence instead of focusing on the real progress on territorial cohesion (Downs 1967; Buchanan and Tullock 1965; Benz 2003).

### The Context

We could start with the point that the ministers for territorial cohesion have a weak statutory mandate with regard to recognition of their policies at the EU level and thus lack influence. Also, in a number of countries planning is traditionally not a strong priority or is mainly the task of regional and local authorities, with regional and national guidance usually restricted to soft instruments and without financial incentives.

In general, the aim of any ministry or minister can be described as gaining influence. The impacts of sector policies on territorial development offer a good reason for territorial policy makers to call for influence in sector policy. It is evident that the current distribution of powers does not allow for any stronger influence on EU and national sector policies by either the Commission's Directorate-General for Regional Policy (DG Regio; only a weak mandate under the treaties) or the national ministers for territorial development (in their member state or at the EU level).

As the entity responsible for achieving the objectives of the Structural Funds, the DG Regio may have a clear interest in gaining influence over national policy making with regard to regional development and the coordination of national and EU sector policies, in order to achieve its own objectives. The same is true for national planning ministers pursuing their responsibility for promoting balanced and sustainable territorial development in their own countries. Structural Funds offer the DG Regio tools for exerting direct influence, however; the EU ministers for territorial cohesion lack that direct influence. A unified position at the intergovernmental level is their only real tool. The DG Regio and the EU territorial cohesion ministers can both profit from cooperation, as together they may gain influence over national regional policy and EU sector policy.

However, such a coalition would be a two-sided sword, as the Commission would be exposed to the criticism of going beyond its statutory mandate. The DG Regio might be suspected of collaborating with a team of ministers who, under a narrow interpretation, do not have any such mandate at the EU level, apart from being able to initiate intergovernmental cooperation in any field of their choice, as long as it is tolerated by their heads of state and national foreign offices. In practice, this means that support for the EU territorial cohesion ministers from the DG Regio could be considered fragile, depending on the general political climate in the College of Commissioners and on its relation with the national ministries responsible for managing the Structural Funds.

By way of example, as indicated, the positive attitude of the DG Regio toward the preparation of the ESDP changed after the final result was presented, because the document proved to be too weak to influence sector policies at the EU level or to guide the Structural Funds programs. According to some administrators and politicians, it was too "distribution oriented," "very sustainable," "not sharp enough," and not a hard policy document; it represented a consensus document to which nobody could say no, but suspicion remained about the evidence and reasoning behind it, as well as its financial consequences. The follow-up of the ESDP in the form of the Tampere Programme was rather weak. It became obvious that the DG Regio's coalition partners, the EU ministers for spatial development, were lacking influence and commitment in the form of steady involvement. The directorate-general withdrew its support for the CSD in 2000 and tried instead to deal with territorial development in the comitology of the Structural Funds.

In 2004, recognizing the strength of the results of the ESPON program, the member states, by the initiative of the Netherlands, made another attempt to get back into the game by addressing the territorial dimension of the Lisbon Strategy and the question of territorial cohesion. At first, the DG Regio was not enthusiastic. It was still under the influence of the negative experiences of the past. The efforts by the presidencies only got a positive response from the Commission when it had become clear that they were supportive of the directorate-general in its intention of formulating a more strategic approach to regional policy. Moreover, the directorate-general was searching for a coalition partner for implementation of the community objective of territorial cohesion within its future regional policy.

It is clear that both strategies pursued by DG Regio, the strategic approach in the Structural Funds and the Community objective in the EU Constitutional Treaty, would broaden the mandate of the EU. Therefore, the suspicion could arise that such collaboration would be temporary, only until the EU Constitutional Treaty was ratified. After all, support from the EU territorial cohesion ministers would then be unnecessary to defend territorial development activities at the EU level. One could only speculate about whether the coalition might break up once the treaty was settled. After ratification of the EU Constitutional Treaty was stalled, however, the power balance changed again, because from then onward DG Regio needed the territorial cohesion ministers to keep the focus on the EU political agenda.

What is the role of the EU territorial cohesion ministers? What is their advantage in cooperating with the DG Regio, considering that they incur the risk of losing the intergovernmental territorial dossier at the EU level to the Commission once a reformed Treaty is in force? Their common efforts would surely be rewarded by the fact that a DG Regio with an EU mandate for territorial development would have good reasons to invite not only ministers for regional economic policy, but also territorial cohesion ministers to participate in the development and implementation of the EU Structural Funds programs.

In real terms, this situation would slightly strengthen the mandates of the EU territorial cohesion ministers, at both national and EU levels. It would also increase the power of the DG Regio against the national level, however, simply because in negotiations about cohesion policy it would allow the Commission to form a coalition with either the spatial or the economic ministers responsible for the Structural Funds, in particular in cases where the national-level ministers would be in disagreement. Also, in the case of national unanimity, consent between all member states is still necessary. In the end the probable winner in this power game would be the Commission; the territorial policy makers would be partial winners, while the regional economic policy makers and the national level would lose relatively, as the probability and possibility of sustaining a national policy against the Commission would be reduced.

## TSP and TA as Instruments in the Power Game

The TSP and TA are important tools for the EU ministers for territorial cohesion in signaling their willingness to participate in cohesion policy, because in many member states they face multiple problems in doing so. The EU informal ministerial meeting on territorial cohesion and regional policy in Luxembourg in May 2005 was of crucial importance for the ministers for territorial cohesion to get broader support and more formal recognition of their activties in the framework of the EU. By linking themselves to the Lisbon Strategy, the ministers also claimed their role in areas of key concern for the heads of state and government (the European Council), an important step, as spatial development is not the main focus of the heads of state. More and more, it is accepted that EU policies have a territorial dimension and that the EU ministers for territorial cohesion have a certain role at the EU level in analyzing that dimension and raising awareness of it. Of course, the Commission, too, has a strong interest in bringing the two groups of ministers—territorial cohesion and regional policy—closer together in view of making its post-2006 regional policy more strategic and territorially oriented. Policy makers of both groups met again under the Austrian presidency, in June 2006, to analyze how much the territorial dimension had been taken into account in the development of the national strategic reference frameworks for the 2007–2013 EU regional policy (see also the introduction to this volume). Again, the Commission recognized the interest and was present at the political level. However, the DG Regio's criticism that the territorial and urban ministries or departments did not play a strong enough role at home vis-à-vis the ministries in charge of the Structural Funds (if, indeed, that was another ministry) was only too evident.

A new instrument for the EU ministers for territorial cohesion to obtain support and recognition in the EU is the stakeholder dialogue mentioned previously. The Commission appeared to receive the stakeholder dialogue with mixed feelings. On one hand, it recognized its importance for increasing the acceptance of possible activities at the EU level in the field of territorial development. On the other hand, following its experience with the ESDP, the lack of operational and political focus within the group of spatial policy makers could have an adverse effect. So far, the stakeholder dialogue proved that stakeholders accepted the political focus in the TA and operational content in the TSP, viewing those documents as works in progress in a relatively new EU policy field. Of course, if ESPON cannot fulfill the high level of expectations from cities, regions, member states, the Commission, and other stakeholders in the coming years, that might change.

One of the key points of discussion between the Commission and the member states in drafting the TA for Leipzig was the preparation of some kind of paper on the territorial dimension of cohesion by the Commission. The question was not only the role and status of such a paper (a DG Regio working paper, a Commission communication, or even a white paper), but also and more fundamentally whether the Commission should prepare such a paper at all before a new Constitutional Treaty defines an EU mandate for territorial cohesion policy. Such a paper would ease the work of the ministers, as the difficult process of finding agreement on a clear description of the concept of territorial cohesion would then be left to the Commission. Any clear definition is politically a dangerous enterprise at that time, as it would be a reference to not only where to go but also where not to go, and thus could run into opposition. It is striking that not even economic and social cohesion are officially defined as concepts. Real meaning is defined only in a particular policy context. Any definition could cause disagreement even between member states and lead to more centrifugal than centripetal tendencies. After all, ministers know that the carrying capacity of a mainly intergovernmental TA is doomed to be weak. On the other hand, there was a risk that the Commission would not take enough account of the common efforts by the ministers to define territorial cohesion in the framework of the TA.

Nevertheless, such a paper would strengthen the Commission's position considerably as it would once again give the impression that the ministers were not capable of keeping the ball in the air on their own after the German presidency. The Commission has already published a communication on the urban dimension of EU policies, so legal arguments against a comparable paper on the territorial dimension did not necessarily cut wood. On the other hand, the directorates-general responsible for policy sectors within the Commission might have seen such a paper as an attempt by the DG Regio to get a grip on their policies. The problem of the DG Regio is political: Is it strong enough to engage in internal struggles within the Commission? In the light of the EU Reform (Lisbon) Treaty, DG Regio now has sufficient backing to launch the discussion inside the Commission by preparing a green paper.

The same goes for TIAs, discussed in chapter 2. ESPON will soon be able to elaborate inputs for a TIA concerning new Commission proposals. The DG Regio, as the host directorate-general for territorial development, could try to place TIA elements into the existing formal and obligatory (integrated) impact assessment procedure for all Commission proposals. The ministers could use the TIA to instigate debates in their governments, so the TIA could be a bonus for both the DG Regio and the ministers responsible for territorial cohesion. Now the DG Regio and EU institutions have agreed to discuss the coordination of urban and territorial impacts within the existing institutions and procedures such as impact assessments (German EU Council Presidency 2007, point 8). The outcome of this process between the ministers and the DG Regio on one hand and the DG Regio and the sector directorates-general within the Commission on the other is still open. The EU Reform (Lisbon) Treaty appears on the horizon of 2009, and the real power of the FAP developed under the Portuguese presidency still has to unfold.

## Conclusions and Perspectives

The analysis of the three stories from three different points of view is certainly incomplete unless we try to assess them together. An integrated view allows the development of further perspectives in this policy field.

## Power Game Between Thematic Intentions and Institutional Constraints

The TA and the TSP have been analyzed from the three perspectives of policy, polity, and politics, which together offered good insights into the key challenges of developing an EU territorial cohesion policy and showed that a rational argument can be made in favor of territorial policy from the thematic point of view. There are, indeed, evidence and good arguments supporting the view that territorial cohesion is not a platform for spatial redistribution but an important concept that highlights the territorial dimension of sustainable economic, social, and environmental development.

However, the problem of institutional backing is apparent. Because of the uncertain perspective of the EU Constitutional Treaty at that time, the role of the two documents that form the backbone for territorial cohesion in the coming years is important. The challenges complicate the process of territorial cooperation at the EU level. As long as the institutional perspective is blurred and territorial cohesion is not a statutory EU objective, whether the issues addressed in the TA and TSP are grounded in policy still depends on the political climate. Indeed, this is a situation where politics and the balance of power gain in importance. It is interesting that at this particular time the European parliament and the Committee of the Regions are both playing a less prominent role. Via its influence on the orientation of the Structural Funds, the Commission has the most powerful tools, but it needs to form coalitions, as its position is vulnerable—and that is where the TSP and particularly the TA come into play again as a firm expression of support from the member states. In the end, the Commission's green paper and the institutional development based on the EU Reform (Lisbon) Treaty is decisive for concrete political action toward achievement of the territorial cohesion objective. We would like to contribute to this discussion.

## Community Strategic Guidelines on Cohesion and Beyond

The TA is certainly on the move, boosted at a time of European skepticism by the Dutch and Luxembourg presidencies of 2004–2005 and taken on by the German presidency of 2007. The key to the TA is integration—integration of the territorial dimension into EU cohesion and sector policies and integration of the impact of those policies on the spatial policies of regions, towns, and cities in the member states. That will lead not only to shifts in the focus of EU policies, but also and inevitably to shifts in governance. The TA will have to be applied on different fronts in different ways by different stakeholders: in the Lisbon Strategy, in the sustainable development strategy, in structural policies, in sector polices, in area-specific policies.

The *Community Strategic Guidelines* for cohesion policy in 2007–2013 include a chapter on the territorial dimension of cohesion, which forms the basis for addressing the territorial dimension within the National Strategic Reference Frameworks and the operational programs for the 2007–2013 EU cohesion policy (Bachtler et al. 2007). A seminar in Baden of the Austrian EU presidency and interventions by the Commission at different occasions showed that the *Community*

*Strategic Guidelines* have been elaborated in very different ways by the member states. Nevertheless, it seems that some countries have a clear impetus for integrating the territorial dimension into the 2007–2013 Structural Funds programs.

The next important EU document to address the territorial dimension was the fourth cohesion report, published in May 2007 (CEC 2007). That report is setting the scene for the future of EU cohesion policy after 2013. The key challenge here is how the territorial dimension is to be operationalized. There is an attempt in the report to build a bridge to a more strategic and integrated EU structural policy that can focus on strengthening the EU territorial structure and helping cities and regions to better exploit their unique territorial potential. However, the report rests very much on the Lisbon approach.

The Directorate-General of the Environment also seems willing to address the territorial dimension more clearly within its policy development, as, for example, the strategy on the urban environment shows. What will be interesting is the development of the Common Agricultural Policy. The relevant directorate-general is considering ways to formulate a more integrated rural development policy, now that it has become clear that income support and market protection for farmers will lose their importance after 2013. Until now, the TA and TSP have focused mainly on the urban dimension of EU territorial development.

## Territorial Governance: Toward Stronger Policy Integration?

At Rotterdam the decision was made to integrate the *Territorial Agenda* into other policies and not to choose the path of a separate role and comitology. There are two aspects to this integration issue:

- Total integration of what is called spatial policy and regional economic policy

- Acceptance by the "territorially relevant" sectors of the need to address the potential territorial impact of their own policy changes

In many EU member states we see a tendency toward the integration of regional economic development and spatial development. Ireland and the Netherlands are good examples. France and many new member states, too, keep spatial development and regional policy in the same ministry. Globalization demands more competitiveness and therefore a more economic approach to strategic spatial development, but it also demands integration of the environmental and sustainability components, which are regaining their previous levels of political priority. The total integration of both areas of policy is often held back only by the continued separation of responsible ministries. However, a number of EU member states, such as Austria and France and some new member states, do have integrated regional development and spatial planning under one ministry, if not one minister, at the national level. There it seems that the complementarity of economic, social, and territorial cohesion already represents a kind of common sense.

In the fields of both spatial development and regional policy, regions are increasingly becoming the key players in territorial development policies, while the national level is focusing on a strategic role as a linchpin between the EU and the regions. That role might include coordinating and managing strategic frameworks for national and EU cooperation, the potential impact of EU policies on national territorial developments, and EU Structural Funds programs. At the EU level we see a trend toward integrated and strategic EU policy making and the creation of framework policies instead of legislation. Witness the *Strategic Guidelines* and the National Strategic Reference Frameworks, which would probably never have been introduced without the work of the ESDP process. EU spatial monitoring—for example, via the ESPON program—can also play an important role in that respect.

This is why the ministers responsible for territorial cohesion agreed and reiterated in Rotterdam, Luxembourg, Leipzig, and the Azores to focus on the integration of the territorial dimension in EU policies instead of creating a separate EU territorial development framework. Delivering the evidence base for integrating the territorial dimension in EU policies, rather than creating EU spatial visions, is the new policy. Still, that leaves unanswered the question of what the role of the ministers for territorial cohesion will be in strengthening territorial cohesion after the ratification of the EU Reform (Lisbon) Treaty.

The new cohesion policy is crucial. Will there be a sufficient evidence base to influence the programs for 2007–2013? The interdepartmental competition for power will have to be addressed in those countries where there are separate ministries.

The territorial impact issue has confronted the sectors with the need to look seriously at the impact of their own EU policies on the spatial organization of national territories. It has exposed the degree to which sectors have operated in relative isolation, focusing on their own policy objectives instead of on broader, more integrated goals such as sustainability, competitiveness, and territorial harmonization. The crucial question for the future is to what extent the sectors will allow the "territorial" administrations to influence their policies. The key is their acceptance of the territorial evidence and the involvement of their colleagues for spatial development on "their" turf.

The position of territorial cohesion ministers in national cabinets will be an important factor in determining to what extent integration succeeds or if the present degree of separation continues or even widens.

## The Longer-Term Perspective

Present-day EU policies are based very much on the implementation of measures backed by specific budgets and clear, legally based competences. The EU does it entirely or does not do it at all—it is not easy to find the "middle" way. That approach is not favorable for developing the *Territorial Agenda*, and whether that approach continues or will be adapted is crucial for the future of that agenda. Shared competence is a sign of things to come, and it could be a suitable instrument for implementation of the TA. A shared competence merely signifies that the Commission has the right of initiative, while the member states represented on the

Council are the decision makers and the European parliament has to agree. In other words, areas of shared competence are the areas where the full vigor of the EU legislative process is brought into play, including a strong say by the Commission over the implementation of legislation, such as in the case of regional policy under Structural Funds regulations.

A common approach between the EU and the member states without granting a mandate to the EU is the Open Method of Coordination (OMC; Gore 2004; Faludi 2004), which is sometimes mentioned as the ideal method for EU territorial development cooperation. The Lisbon European Council in March 2000 established the OMC, and it was, in principle, confirmed in the relaunch in Luxembourg in 2005. It is a form of coordination of national policies by which the member states, at their own initiative or the initiative of the Commission, define collectively, paying due respect to national and regional diversities, objectives, and indicators in a specific area. The member states are then allowed, on the basis of national reports, to improve their knowledge; to develop exchanges of information, views, expertise, and practices; and to promote further agreed objectives and innovative approaches that could lead to guidelines or recommendations. The method is applied in different ways to different areas, with an ad hoc procedure worked out each time. That is why sometimes "Open Method of Coordination" in the plural is used.

The question is whether such an approach would be effective or even desirable for EU territorial development cooperation, which is still in the phase of strengthening common understanding and elaborating the evidence base (what are the key indicators?). Moreover, most international territorial issues are transnational instead of European. Using the OMC for dealing with the territorial impact of EU policies would simply be ineffective and undesirable, as it would add new (shadow) structures and procedures to the already complicated EU policy process.

Once the EU Reform (Lisbon) Treaty is to enter into force, the Community method of legislation (with the right of initiative for the Commission) will become the practice. That will present an opportunity for the Commission to play an initiating role on strategic territorial development issues, but not without the complete and active involvement of the member states. The advantage would be that EU policies would then have to take account of their territorial dimension in a more structural and thorough way.

Conservative forces within and outside the European institutions criticize OMC and try to brand it as ineffective and unworkable, underlining its negative connotations. The Luxembourg Spring European Council of March 2005 actually recognized that the OMC was not effective in achieving the Lisbon aims in the way it was so far constructed. It decided on a new start for the Lisbon Strategy with a stronger focus, a more active role for the Commission, national Lisbon Action Plans, and an annual reporting mechanism. As mentioned previously, there will (also) be a need for more intergovernmental cooperation, but invoking the OMC under that name will not be advisable. In any constitutional or treaty context, elements of OMC would likely respond to the key principles of territorial development cooperation, which consider that the territory is diverse and solutions have to be found that take that diversity and subsidiarity of actors into account: information and dialogue.

## References

Bachtler, J., M. Ferry, C. Méndez, and I. McMaster. 2007. The 2007–2013 operational programmes: A preliminary assessment. *IQ-NET Thematic Papers* (European Policies Research Centre, University of Strathclyde, Glasgow), 19(2).

Bauer, M. W. 2001. *A creeping transformation? The European Commission and the management of EU Structural Funds in Germany, 2001.* Dordrecht: Kluwer.

Benz, A. 2003. Mehrebenenverflechtung in der Europäischen Union. In *Europäische Integration*, M. Jachtenfuchs and B. Kohler-Koch, eds., 317–351. Opladen: Leske und Budrich.

Böhme, K., and P. Schön. 2006. From Leipzig to Leipzig: Territorial research delivers evidence for the new *Territorial Agenda of the European Union.* In *Evidence-based planning*, A. Faludi, ed. Special issue, *disP* 165, 42(2): 61–70.

Buchanan, J. M., and G. Tullock. 1965. *The calculus of consent.* Ann Arbor: University of Michigan Press.

CEC (Commission of the European Communities). 1999. *European Spatial Development Perspective: Towards balanced and sustainable development of the territory of the EU.* Luxembourg: Office for Official Publications of the European Communities.

———. 2001a. *European governance: A white paper.* Luxembourg: Office for Official Publications of the European Communities.

———. 2001b. *A sustainable Europe for a better world: A European Union strategy for sustainable development.* Luxembourg: Office for Official Publications of the European Communities.

———. 2004. *Interim territorial cohesion report (Preliminary results of ESPON and EU Commission studies).* Luxembourg: Office for Official Publications of the European Communities. http://ec.europa.eu/regional_policy/sources/docoffic/official/reports/coheter/coheter1_en.pdf.

———. 2005. *Working together for growth and jobs: A new start for the Lisbon Strategy.* Luxembourg: Office for Official Publications of the European Communities.

———. 2007. *Growing regions, growing Europe.* Fourth report on economic and social cohesion. http://ec.europa.eu/regional_policy/sources/docoffic/official/reports/cohesion4/index_en .htm.

Council of the European Union. 2006. *Council decision on community strategic guidelines on cohesion.* Interinstitutional file 2006/0131, 18 August. http://register.consilium.europa.eu /pdf/en/06/st11/st11807.en06.pdf.

Davoudi, S. 2005. Understanding territorial cohesion. In *Planning Practice and Research* 20(4): 433–441.

———. 2006. Evidence-based planning: Rhetoric and reality. In *Evidence-based planning*, A. Faludi, ed. Special issue, *disP* 165, 42(2): 14–24.

Downs, A. 1967. *Inside bureaucracy.* Boston: Little, Brown.

Dyson, K., and K. H. Goetz, eds. 2003. *Germany, Europe and the politics of constraint.* New York: Oxford University Press.

Eser, T. W. 2007. An evaluation framework for multilevel government. In *Sustainable development in Europe: Concepts, evaluation and application*, U. Schubert and E. Störmer, eds., 63–81. Cheltenham, U.K.: Edward Elgar Press.

Eser, T. W., and D. Konstadakopulos. 2000. Power shifts in the European Union? The case of spatial planning. *European Planning Studies* 8(6): 783–798.

Faludi, A. 2004. The open method of co-ordination and post-regulatory territorial cohesion policy. *European Planning Studies* 12(7): 1019–1033.

———. 2006. From European spatial development to territorial cohesion policy. *Regional Studies* 40(6): 667–678.

———, ed. 2007. *Territorial cohesion and the European model of society*, Cambridge, MA: Lincoln Institute of Land Policy.

Faludi, A., and B. Waterhout. 2002. *The making of the European spatial development perspective: No masterplan* (RTPI Library Series). London: Routledge.

———. 2006. Introducing evidence-based planning. In *Evidence-based planning*, A. Faludi, ed. Special issue, *disP* 165, 42(2), 3–13.

———. 2007. Making sense of the "Territorial Agenda of the European Union." *European Journal of Spatial Development* (November), no. 25. http://www.nordregio.se/EJSD/refereed25.pdf.

First Action Programme. 2007. (Agreed on the occasion of the Informal Ministerial Meeting on Territorial Cohesion and Regional Policy on the Azores on 23/24 November 2007). http://www.dgotdu.pt/rimotr/documentos.htm.

German EU Council Presidency. 2007. *Conclusions of the German EU Council presidency on the informal ministerial meeting on urban dvelopment and territorial cohesion.* http://www.bmvbs .de/Anlage/original_1005297/Conclusions-of-the-German-EU-Council-Presidency-on-the -Informal-Ministerial-Meeting-accessible.pdf.

Gestel, T. van, and A. Faludi. 2005. Towards a European territorial cohesion assessment network: A bright future for ESPON? In *Territorial cohesion: An unidentified political objective*, A. Faludi, ed. Special issue, *Town Planning Review* 76(1): 69–80.

Gore, T. 2004. The open method of coordination and policy mainstreaming: The European employment strategy and regional conversion programmes in the UK. *European Planning Studies* 12(1): 123–141.

Kohler-Koch, B. 1996. Catching up with change: The transformation of governance in the European Union. *Journal of European Public Policy* 3(3): 359–380.

Luxembourg scoping document. 2005. *Scoping document and summary of political messages for an assessment of the Territorial State and Perspectives of the European Union: Towards a stronger European territorial cohesion in the light of the Lisbon and Gothenburg ambitions.* http://www.sharedspaces.nl/docs/internationaal/Scoping.pdf.

Official Journal of the European Union. 2006. *Council Regulation (EC) No. 1083/2006 of 11 July 2006 laying down general provisions on the European Regional Development Fund, the European Social Fund and the Cohesion Fund and repealing Regulation (EC) No. 1260/1999.* http://ec.europa.eu/regional_policy/sources/docoffic/official/regulation/pdf/2007/feder/ce _1080(2006)_en.pdf.

Polverari, L., I. McMaster, F. Gross, J. Bachtler, M. Ferry, and D. Yuill. 2006. Strategic planning for Structural Funds in 2007–2013: A review of strategies and porgrammes. *IQ-NET Thematic Papers* (European Policies Research Centre, University of Strathclyde, Glasgow), 18(2).

Rittberger, V., and B. Zangl. 2006. *International organization: Polity, politics and policies.* Basingstoke, U.K.: Palgrave Macmillan.

Territorial Agenda. 2007. *Territorial Agenda of the European Union: Towards a more competitive Europe of diverse regions* (Agreed on the occasion of the Informal Ministerial Meeting on Urban Development and Territorial Cohesion in Leipzig on 24/25 May 2007). http://www .bmvbs.de/Anlage/original_1005295/Territorial-Agenda-of-the-European-Union-Agreed -on-25-May-2007-accessible.pdf.

Territorial State. 2007. *The Territorial State and Perspectives of the European Union: Towards a stronger European territorial cohesion in the light of the Lisbon and Gothenburg ambitions* (A

background document for the *Territorial Agenda of the European Union*). http://www
.bmvbs.de/Anlage/original_1005296/The-Territorial-State-and-Perspectives-of-the-European
-Union.pdf.

Williams, R. H. 1999. Constructing the *European Spatial Development Perspective*: Consensus
without a competence. *Regional Studies* 33(8): 793–797.

## Editor

**Andreas Faludi**
Professor
OTB Research Institute for Housing,
Urban and Mobility Studies
Delft University of Technology
The Netherlands

## Authors

**Diogo de Abreu**
Associate Professor
Geography Department
University of Lisbon, Portugal

**Janne Antikainen**
Head of Programmes
Ministry of Employment and the Economy
Department for Regional Development
Programme Group
Helsinki, Finland

**Pierre Bekouche**
Professor of Regional and Economic
Geography
University Paris 1 Pantheon-Sorbonne
Paris, France

**Kai Böhme**
Director
Spatial Foresight GmbH
Heisdorf, Luxembourg;
Visiting Research Fellow
University of Sheffield, United Kingdom,
and Blekinge Institute of Technology
Karlskrona, Sweden

**Armando Carbonell**
Senior Fellow
Lincoln Institute of Land Policy
Cambridge, Massachusetts, USA

**Thiemo W. Eser**
Responsible for European Affairs
Ministry of the Interior and for Spatial
Development
Directorate for Spatial Development
Luxembourg City, Luxembourg

**Claude Grasland**
Professor of Human Geography and
Spatial Analysis
University Paris 7 Denis Diderot
Paris, France

**Stefan Greiving**
Head of the Research Unit
Institute of Spatial Planning (IRPUD)
Faculty of Spatial Planning
University of Dortmund, Germany;
Director
Plan and Risk Consult
Dortmund, Germany

**Verena Hachmann**
Researcher
School of the Built Environment
Heriot-Watt University
Edinburgh, Scotland

**Cliff Hague**
Author and Teacher
Planning and Development
Edinburgh, Scotland

**Moritz Lennert**
Researcher
Institute of Environmental Management
and Spatial Planning
Free University of Brussels (ULB), Belgium

**Jacques Robert**
Director
TERSYN (Agence Européenne Territoires
et Synergies)
Strasbourg, France

**Peter Schmeitz**
Policy and Cluster Coordinator
Ministry of Agriculture, Nature and
Food Quality
The Hague, The Netherlands

**Philipp Schmidt-Thomé**
Senior Scientist
Geological Survey of Finland (GTK)
Espoo, Finland

**Klaus Spiekermann**
Partner
Spiekermann & Wegener (S&W) Urban
and Regional Research
Dortmund, Germany

**Bas Waterhout**
Research Fellow
OTB Research Institute for Housing,
Urban and Mobility Studies
Delft University of Technology
The Netherlands

**Michael Wegener**
Partner
Spiekermann & Wegener (S&W) Urban
and Regional Research
Dortmund, Germany

The Lincoln Institute of Land Policy is a private operating foundation whose mission is to improve the quality of public debate and decisions in the areas of land policy and land-related taxation in the United States and around the world. The Institute's goals are to integrate theory and practice to better shape land policy and to provide a nonpartisan forum for discussion of the multidisciplinary forces that influence public policy. This focus on land derives from the Institute's founding objective—to address the links between land policy and social and economic progress—that was identified and analyzed by political economist and author Henry George.

The work of the Institute is organized in four departments: Valuation and Taxation, Planning and Urban Form, Economic and Community Development, and International Studies. We seek to inform decision making through education, research, demonstration projects, and the dissemination of information through publications, our Web site, and other media. Our programs bring together scholars, practitioners, public officials, policy advisers, and involved citizens in a collegial learning environment. The Institute does not take a particular point of view, but rather serves as a catalyst to facilitate analysis and discussion of land use and taxation issues—to make a difference today and to help policy makers plan for tomorrow.

The Lincoln Institute of Land Policy is an equal opportunity institution.

## LINCOLN INSTITUTE
### OF LAND POLICY

113 Brattle Street
Cambridge, MA 02138-3400 USA

Phone: 1-617-661-3016 x127 or 1-800-LAND-USE (800-526-3873)
Fax: 1-617-661-7235 or 1-800-LAND-944 (800-526-3944)
E-mail: help@lincolninst.edu
Web: www.lincolninst.edu